Financing the American Dream

✳

Financing the American Dream

A CULTURAL HISTORY OF CONSUMER CREDIT

*

LENDOL CALDER

PRINCETON UNIVERSITY PRESS

PRINCETON, NEW JERSEY

Library of Congress Cataloging-in-Publication Data

Calder, Lendol Glen.
Financing the American dream : a cultural history of
consumer credit / Lendol Calder.
p. cm.
Revision of author's thesis (doctoral)—University
of Chicago, 1993.
Includes bibliographical references and index.
ISBN 0-691-05827-X (cloth : alk. paper)
1. Consumer credit—United States—History.
2. Consumption (Economics)—United States—History.
3. Consumers—United States—History   I. Title.
HG3756.U54C35   1999
332.7'0973—dc21   98-34875

FOR KATHY

WITH LOVE AND THANKS

✳

I have no doubt that some of you who read this book . . .
are trying to get out of debt, a very ancient swamp.
—Henry David Thoreau, *Walden*

* Contents *

Acknowledgments   xiii

INTRODUCTION
Credit, Consumer Culture, and the American Dream   3

The Culture of Consumption   6
Consumer Credit: A Dark Continent   9
The Most Remarkable Phenomena in Modern History   16
The Myth of Lost Economic Virtue   23
The Credit Revolution and Consumer Culture   26
The Myth of Easy Payments   28

PART ONE:
GETTING TRUSTED: DEBT AND CREDIT BEFORE
CONSUMER CREDIT   35

CHAPTER 1
Beautiful Credit! The Foundation of Modern Society   37

A Mountain Load of Debt   38
I Buy Everything on Credit   41
Pawnbrokers: Bankers for the Poor   42
Small-Loan Lenders: Sharks and Leeches   49
Peddlers and Borax Houses   55
A Poverty of Which No Man Heareth   58
On the Book and on Time   59
Friends and Family   60
A Most Interesting Problem in Practical Finance   64
Trends in the Gilded Age Credit System   69

CHAPTER 2
Debt in the Victorian Money Management Ethic   74
The Economical Century   75
Mastering the Meaning of Money   80
The Victorian Way to Wealth   87
The Ethics of Debt   91
I Have Ever Been Opposed to Borrowing Money   104

PART TWO:
GETTING THE GOODS: THE MAKING OF A
CREDIT REVOLUTION — 109

CHAPTER 3
Small-Loan Lending and the Rise of the Personal
Finance Company — 111

Usury and Illegal Lending — 112
Arthur Ham and the Fight for Legal Lending — 124
From Loan Sharks to Industrial Lenders — 135
Counselors to the Consumer — 147

CHAPTER 4
Hard Payments: The Rise of Installment Selling — 156

Aladdin's Lamp: The Origins of Installment Credit — 157
Growth and Stigmatization, 1880–1915 — 166
Growth and Legitimization, 1915–1930 — 183
Automobiles on Time Payments — 184
Financing Other Consumer Durables — 199
He Makes Only $3,000 a Year, but Is Worth $112,290! — 202
Regulated Abundance — 206

PART THREE:
GETTING CREDIT: THE LEGITIMIZATION OF
CONSUMER DEBT — 209

CHAPTER 5
From Consumptive Credit to Consumer Credit — 211

The Latest Ally of the Devil — 212
New Anxieties about Debt — 217
Beware of the Slimy Coils of the Installment Evil — 221
The Root of All Fears — 230
A Cloud of Unrespectability — 234
Defenders Come Forward — 235
E.R.A. Seligman and a New Language of Credit — 237
"A Vindication for Installment Paying" — 249
Wise Borrowing and Foolish Borrowing — 254
We Do Lend for Production — 257

CHAPTER 6
Consumer Credit in the Great Depression   262

  1929: Now We Test Installment Selling   262
  Passing the Test   265
  Consumer Constipation   271
  Now You Can Owe Macy's!—and the Government
    and the Banks, Too   274
  Roads Not Taken   287

Epilogue   291

Notes   305

Index   365

✳ *Acknowledgments* ✳

I OWE A great deal to several groups of people for help in writing this book. It began nine years ago as a dissertation, so first I want to thank my advisor, Neil Harris of the University of Chicago, for his unfailing support from the very beginning of the project. He supplied me with an abundance of advice and encouragement and, best of all, seemed to know when I needed one or the other. The other members of my committee, Arthur Mann and Leora Auslander, gave close readings to all my drafts of chapters and provided foundational advice. Arthur did not live to see the completed manuscript, but he left his imprint on the work in his good-natured refusal to let me talk nonsense when I was forming my arguments. Leora helped me think more deeply about the theoretical implications of consumer culture.

In the early going, the Chicago Eutychus Society gave me helpful criticism, while several members of that group, Fred Beuttler and Mike Kugler especially, helped me stay the course during some difficult personal moments. During that time my parents Leslie and Arvella Calder came to my aid and saved me from having to do some unwanted personal research into the subject of debt; the love and support they have given me over these years is impossible to calculate.

Since leaving graduate school, many of the ideas in this book were refined and improved while teaching them to undergraduate students, an experience that confirms for me the fruitful compatibility of writing and teaching. I want to thank all the members of my "History of Consumer Culture in America" courses and seminars at the University of Washington, Colby-Sawyer College, and Augustana College, particularly Julie Clifton, Shannon Smith, Jacqueline Swain, and David Morgan. Troy Swanson, my research assistant at Augustana College, did yeoman work in helping me gather research materials for revisions made to the dissertation.

The University of Chicago Social History Workshop and the University of Washington History Research Group offered generous advice and comments on drafts of several chapters. Beth Barton Schweiger gave of her time to read and comment on a chapter; I only regret I did not ask her to read the entire manuscript. I owe a special debt of thanks to two people who did. Otis Pease and William Childs pointed me in some new directions, corrected errors, and encouraged me to think others might want to read what I had written. Their careful attention to the manuscript, right down to checking the notes, set a high standard I can only repay by emulating their example when asked to do the same for others.

Several librarians and archivists came to my aid in especially helpful ways, including Frank Conway at the University of Chicago's Regenstein Library; the librarians at the Library of Congress who let me browse through their considerable collection of materials on nineteenth-century money management; the staff of the Rockefeller Archive Center, where the Russell Sage Foundation files are located; staff at the Ford Motor Company archives, who expertly guided me to just what I needed to see in their vast collections; Daniel Wren, curator of the Harry Bass Collection in Business History at the University of Oklahoma, where some of E.R.A. Seligman's papers are kept; and Barbara Doyle-Wilch, director of the Augustana College Library, who brought me helpful articles without my even asking.

I am especially grateful to those who were generous with the various kinds of moral and material support without which no book could be written, including Ann Brown, Denis and Margie Haack, Connie Jennings, Tom Mayer, Peter Rooney, Jack and Nancy Swearengen, Tara Rice, Jane Tiedge, and Jeff and Jill Webb.

My editor at Princeton University Press, Brigitta van Rheinberg, made me the envy of all my colleagues. From the moment we first corresponded she never let me doubt the worth of the book. She was quick with advice, firm in moving me along, flexible when I could not make deadlines, and lavish with encouragement. Indeed, everyone I came into contact with at Princeton University Press impressed me with their professionalism and friendly support. In particular, I thank Brian MacDonald for his expert copy editing.

My greatest debts of all are to my wife, Kathy, to whom this book is dedicated. Her considerable gifts as a writer are manifest on nearly every page. On top of her own busy schedule she read at least two drafts of each chapter and helped me to see what was clear and what was not, what really made sense and what was still wishful thinking. Beyond editing, it would be impossible to list all that she sacrificed to see this book finished. In spite of all the hardships placed on her this past year, and many were of my making as I ignored everything to work on this book, she lived up to the tribute that has special meaning for native Texans like her—"splendid behavior." She gave me her all. Her love is boundless.

Finally, I want to thank my children, Abigail and Andrew. They frequently interrupted my writing to invite me to tea parties and to "play rough." Because of these intermissions, their contribution to my happiness while writing was incalculable.

Financing the American Dream

*

✳ *Introduction* ✳

CREDIT, CONSUMER CULTURE, AND

THE AMERICAN DREAM

T HE AMERICAN dream is a puzzle, both for those who study it and for those who pursue it.

"What would you say is the 'American Dream'?" writes a man to "Ask Marilyn," a syndicated newspaper column featuring riddles, brainteasers, and philosophical conundrums. Who better to ask than the author of "Ask Marilyn"? Listed in the *Guinness Book of World Records* Hall of Fame for "Highest IQ," Marilyn vos Savant slices Gordian knots for a living. "Today's American Dream," she replies, "includes a house in the suburbs with a backyard for the kids to play in, a patio for barbecues, a shady street, bright and obedient children, camping trips, fishing, two family cars, seeing the kids taking part in school and church plays, and online access to the world."[1] A good answer—this is the American dream as most people know it. But it is not the end of the puzzle. In fact, it is just the beginning.

I think of an illustration of the American dream that appeared forty years ago on the cover of the *Saturday Evening Post*. In the picture, a young man and woman sit close together against a tree on a warm summer night. They gaze dreamily at the heavens, where they see images in the night sky: not centaurs and winged horses, not Orion and the Pleiades, but objects more familiar and perhaps more fabulous. They see a split-level ranch house and a swimming pool. They see a son playing ball and a daughter playing the piano. They see a sports car and a family station wagon, a hi-fi stereo set and a television, rugged power tools and helpful home appliances—all the twinkling constellations of the American dream. In the inky sky above them they see an American-made zodiac, and the horoscope to be found there is not for them alone but for all the *Post*'s readers: "Soon the Good Life will be yours, along with all the good things of your dreams."[2]

It would be hard to say whether the picture is satire or honest sentiment.[3] But the ambiguity is perfect. It mirrors the paradoxical nature of the American dream itself.

The puzzle begins with attempts to define it. The term seems to have originated with historian James Truslow Adams, who wrote in 1931 of "that dream of a land in which life should be better and richer and fuller for every man, according to his ability or achievement." Adams, an idealist of the first rank, insisted the American dream was more than "motor cars and high wages merely." But the fact he had to say this was an indication that even then, in the darkest days of the Great Depression, most Americans defined "better and richer and fuller" primarily in terms of a material plenty.[4] So from the beginning the American dream has had a double nature. On the one hand it alludes to noble ends such as "freedom," "self-fulfillment," and "a better life." On the other hand it commonly refers to a particular means to these ends—a house, a yard, a couple of cars—the things sociologist David Riesman termed "the standard package" of consumer goods and leisure opportunities.[5] The package is so standardized that the *Post*'s picture of it in 1959 is duplicated almost item-by-item forty years later in vos Savant's description, with the addition of a personal computer. The American dream then is both a set of "free" ideals whose worth cannot be measured in market terms, and a wish list of goods with expensive price tags. And here is where the puzzle deepens, at least for me. It is not unusual in human history for means to become confused with ends, and even to replace them. But in the case of the American dream, how strange that the means have always been rather more expensive than the ends.

In the picture on the cover of the *Saturday Evening Post*, the goods on display in the heavens cost tens of thousands of dollars more than any young couple of 1959 could be expected to have. Yet the lovers show no awareness of this fact. On the contrary, they gaze at the sky with patient expectancy, as if they believe the goods are "in their stars" and that someday the whole sky will be theirs. In their confident faces we can see another paradox of the American dream, a paradox inscribed so deeply in the everydayness of contemporary life it easily goes unremarked: the American dream is both fabulously expensive *and* generally affordable, and this well beyond the ranks of the affluent. How is this possible? How have Americans managed it, to finance the American dream?

The answer is familiar from my own life. Years ago when I was just out of college, dreaming of a good life and without a lot of money, I found the answer in a department store. There my wife and I performed what we recognized at the time to be a rite of passage into American adulthood: we applied for our first credit card. The signing of a few papers allowed us to bring home a suite of furniture costing twice as much money as we could have scraped from our bank account. It was our introduction to consumer credit; also our first experience with debt.

Consumer credit, as economists define it, is "short- and intermediate-term credit extended to individuals through regular business channels, usually to finance the purchase of consumer goods and services or to refinance debts incurred for such purposes."[6] So it is. But consumer credit as most first-time users think about it is explained more lyrically in lines from the musical *Miss Saigon*: "What's that I smell in the air? / The American Dream. / All yours for ten percent down, / The American Dream."[7]

It takes more than a credit card to secure the American dream. Patience and luck and keeping one's nose to the grindstone figure in, too. But since the 1920s the most crucial element in the pursuit of the good life has been access to consumer credit. Consumer credit finances American dreams; by means of it, money is loaned out to car buyers and home furnishers, travelers and vacationers, diners and shoppers, hospital patients and public utilities customers—nowadays to almost anyone for virtually any purpose. Today the idea behind giving credit to consumers seems natural enough, but not so long ago it was an open question whether households deserved the same access to credit as business enterprises. How consumer credit came to be invented and legitimized, how it came to finance American dreams, is the subject of this book.

The Culture of Consumption

The history of the financing of American dreams unfolded as part and parcel of a larger development in American history, a transformation of American culture that consumer credit had no small role in assisting.

"The act of buying something is at the root of our world," wrote the poet Randall Jarrell.[8] In recent years this assertion has proved to be a fertile field for historical research. It is now generally recognized that just as it would be ridiculous to write a history of a medieval European town without attention to its cathedral, so twentieth-century America cannot be understood apart from its department stores and shopping malls. Sites for employment and commerce, but also entertainment, recreation, education, and leisure, shopping centers are, in the words of one historian, the "common denominator of our national life," the symbols of a social and cultural order in which Americans live and move and have their being. Historians sometimes call this way of life the "culture of consumption."[9]

Because consumer credit played a large role in determining the nature of consumer culture and sustaining it over time, it is important to define what I mean by culture and consumption. As I use the concept, "culture" refers to the knowledge, language, values, customs, assumptions, and material objects that are passed from person to person and from one generation to the next, for the purpose of instructing people in how they should live. It may help to think of culture as the "software" of human groups, the codes and rules of behavior that enable people in a society to operate on at least a minimum degree of order, efficiency, and well-being. I am particularly interested in the core ministry of cultural traditions, the way they address the existential questions that confront all of us as we navigate our way through life: Who am I? What is worth doing? How am I to live, and what is the best way to cope with the hardships I must suffer?[10] Cultures, including consumer culture, exist to answer such questions.

Ironically, "consumption" is a term rarely heard among consumers. To economists it means the use of goods and services in the satisfaction of human wants. But scholars studying the history of consumption have enlarged their understanding of the concept to include all the ways human beings interact with goods beyond the point of their physical manufacture. In this broader sense, consumption encompasses not merely the using of goods but also the dreaming, shopping, buying, personalizing, and disposing of commodities as well. Following the work of the French theorist Jean Baudrillard, historians have emphasized that consumption is not primarily the satisfying of material needs, but rather is largely an idealized practice that takes place in people's heads.[11] It is primarily mental and emotional, so that commodity goods become building blocks in the construction of a personal identity, or are used as symbols of communication with other human beings, or as therapeutic remedies for the problems that ail us. Understood this way, the thrill of driving a car very fast is a type of consumption, as is the mixing and matching of garments to achieve a personal style. Consumption is the reading of advertisements in a newspaper. It is the shopping for goods at a mall. It is the hesitation in an automobile showroom, and the moment of sale at the supermarket. It is the feeling of discontent after a new suit has been worn several times. It is also and finally the pile of forgotten shoes in a closet, the recycling of aluminum cans and newspapers, and the swelling of landfills.

Putting these terms together then, the "culture of consumption" is a particular way of living that attempts to make sense of the nexus of selling, buying, using, and disposing of commodities in which most people today conduct their affairs. It defines the "good life" not primarily in terms of satisfying work, or economic independence, or devotion to God, or commitment to the group, or any other ideal honored by people past and present, but rather is dedicated to the proposition that "good living" means having lots of goods—goods bought in the market and made by unknown hands, more goods this year than last year, the "things," as one of its advertisers once promised, "that make life worth living!" Like all cultures, this one, too, has its priests and authorities, the people William Leach has called "the brokers" of desire—retailers, advertisers, economists, bankers, business boosters, and the like.[12] They provide the indoctrination, lead in the celebrations, and set forth the ideal images of what human beings should be like. In the culture of consumption, the ideal man or woman is the consumer. The ideal consumer is someone who believes the meaning of life is to be found in consumption, so that it is in consumption he or she feels most fully alive and human, as opposed to at work, in prayer, on a mountain, or through acts of service. Thus, the consumer, as Randall Jarrell described him, is "someone who, when he comes to Weimar, knows how to buy a Weimaraner."[13]

Historians disagree about when the culture of consumption first became meaningful for large groups of people.[14] But whether this happened at the turn of the twentieth century or in the eighteenth century or even for some groups as far back as the sixteenth century, wherever the culture of consumption first appeared it was restrained by older, established cultures. In the United States these restraints were moderated by the early twentieth century when consumer culture surpassed republicanism, Victorian producerism, and Protestant Christianity as the foremost cultural authority for American society. Its momentum was fueled by a dynamic form of capitalism whose influence overwhelmed that of church, family, and state, the nonmarket social institutions Adam Smith had counted on to be antidotes to the market's veneration of desire. By the 1950s, the culture brought forth by capitalism had become a power plant within capitalism, supplying it with a surprising and, to some, confounding vitality. Today, the culture of consumption is largely responsible for legitimizing capitalism in the eyes of the world.

Despite the power of consumer culture, older ways of seeing and living have not been totally abandoned, and on its own terms the culture of consumption is profoundly misunderstood if it is regarded as being only about pleasure seeking and living for today. Warren Susman, a pioneer in the study of consumer culture, struck the right chord when he observed: "One of the fundamental conflicts of Twentieth Century America is between two cultures—an older culture, often loosely labeled Puritan-republican, producer-capitalist culture, and a newly emerging culture of abundance."[15] Unlike many later scholars who presumed the unalloyed triumph of an essentially hedonistic culture of consumption, Susman left open the possibility that the victory of a culture of abundance over older cultures of scarcity might not have been a total victory, that the paling cultures and some of their restraints might have left a mark on the ascending way of life. It is the contention of this book that the history of consumer credit illustrates precisely this phenomenon.

CONSUMER CREDIT: A DARK CONTINENT

I first became aware of the tremendous importance of consumer credit in building a culture of consumption a decade ago when I could not get some numbers to fit on a page.

I had come to the library to find out how much personal debt was on the books for every year since records had first been collected. Deep in the library stacks I found the government statistics I wanted. Lugging a dozen or so large volumes to a table, I took out a sheet of paper and began making a graph.

On a horizontal axis I marked off the years since 1928, the year the Federal Reserve began collecting data on consumer debt. On a vertical axis I marked off debt levels in millions of dollars. Opening up a volume of statistics, I came across the first of several surprises: in the 1920s, consumer debt was already measured in *billions* of dollars. Crossing out "millions" on my vertical axis and writing in "billions," I plotted my first point: 1928, $6.5 billion. After that I plotted a point for 1929 ($7.7 billion), and a point for 1930 ($6.9 billion), and so on, working my way steadily through the next thirty years.[16]

Work on the graph went smoothly until I reached 1958. That year consumer debt totaled $45 billion, and suddenly the trend line soared off the top of my graph. To cope with the steeply ascending curve of debt, I taped an additional sheet of paper to the top of my original page, and continued plotting. But when consumer debt reached $94.8 billion in 1965, once again the trend line shot off the top of the page—and this time it had taken only six years to burst the bounds of my chart! Unsure how to proceed, I scanned the remaining statistics from 1966 to the late 1980s, and with a little figuring determined it would take *sixteen* more pages of paper to complete my graph on its original scale. The figures for 1988 showed the amount of consumer debt at $666 billion, which meant the average American household owed roughly $7,400 for consumer purchases.[17] Here were "billions and billions" of dollars of debt, numbers on the sort of scale that made Carl Sagan famous. Full of questions, I folded up my unfinished graph and headed off to find out what historians had written about America's apparent debt wish.

I presumed they had written quite a lot, because the 1980s had seen an enormous production of scholarly work on the history of American consumption. But to my great surprise I found very little: a chapter by Daniel Boorstin, a scholarly article by Helena Flam, a popular history of the personal finance business by Irving Michelman, and a pile of journalistic reporting written in the exposé mode.[18] It was all very interesting, but the studies I found were too short, too narrow, too old, or too present-oriented to answer fully the questions I was beginning to ask. When did consumer credit first appear, and why then? What types of credit preceded it, competed with it, and were in time eclipsed by it? Who created consumer credit, and what were their intentions? Who were the first consumers to obtain access to credit and use it extensively? How did consumer credit conflict with older ways of thinking about debt and money management? How did it succeed in a seemingly unfriendly environment, a public culture steeped in the Bible ("Owe no man anything") and Shakespeare ("Neither a borrower nor a lender be") and republican common sense ("He who goes a-borrowing goes a-sorrowing")? In short, how did consumer credit become morally permissible so that consumers could both borrow money and feel good about it?

In the decade I have been studying consumer credit, the situation has improved with the publication in 1989 of Martha Olney's *Buy Now, Pay Later*, a pioneering work of economic history examining credit and advertising in the 1920s.[19] But much remains to be done if historians are to follow up on the insights of Randall Jarrell, who, casting about for just the right metaphor to express how important credit was in American life in the early 1960s, finally found one on the ceiling of the Sistine Chapel. "If anyone wishes to paint the genesis of things in our society," wrote the poet, "he will paint a picture of God holding out to Adam a check-book or credit card or Charge-A-Plate."[20]

Poets are not the only ones who have recognized how immensely important debt and credit have been in the financing of American dreams. Seventy years ago, in their famous "Middletown" study of Muncie, Indiana, Robert and Helen Lynd gave special attention to the local credit economy because they believed the credit networks being formed in the 1920s bore more responsibility for stimulating consumption and conformity than anything else, even national advertising.[21] Agreeing with the Lynds, David Riesman went so far as to describe middle-income Americans as "the debtor class." In his celebrated book, *The Affluent Society*, Riesman's colleague at Harvard, John Kenneth Galbraith, pointed to the rising tide of consumer red ink in the 1950s and wondered, "Can the bill collector be the central figure in the good society?"[22]

Some years later, as if to answer Galbraith's question, Daniel Boorstin allowed "it was hardly an exaggeration to say that the American standard of living was bought on the installment plan." One of the first historians to move the consumption experience to the center of American history, Boorstin was also first to survey the history of consumer credit. In *The Americans: The Democratic Experience*, Boorstin argued that credit buying blurs and dilutes the concept of ownership, thereby contributing to "the thinner life of things" in the modern world. Equally intriguing (and equally difficult to demonstrate), Boorstin maintained that consumer credit helped bring into existence "consumption communities," which, in his optimistic view, were new, democratic communities binding Americans together less by place, creed, or work than by what they dreamed about, bought, and consumed.[23] This notion of a national "fellowship of consumers" was itself a thinner version of a sociological concept introduced in the 1970s—"consumer society." As

11

Daniel Bell and others described it, the edifice of consumer society rests squarely upon the pillars of three social inventions: mass production, mass marketing, and mass finance, or consumer credit. More recently, George Ritzer, a sociologist specializing in the social worlds of consumption, has gone so far as to picture consumer credit as the "linchpin" holding consumer society together.[24]

No single "linchpin" explains the vitality of modern consumer societies. Nevertheless, the economic and cultural importance of consumer credit is hard to overestimate. Hailed by some as the key to American prosperity, vilified by others as the cause of cultural decline, consumer credit is widely noticed and commented on.

How strange then that while advertising, retailing, and consumer goods such as the automobile have their dozens of historical monographs, consumer credit has almost none at all.[25] Why this is so is worth exploring, not least because the difficulties inherent in researching this topic help explain some of the features and limitations of this book.

To begin with, consumer credit is obviously an economic topic, and it must be admitted that economic history is not everyone's cup of tea. Most historians lack the quantitative skills and theoretical preparation a study of economic topics would seem to require. Surely this has checked many from examining the history of credit; it almost deterred me. Fortunately, publication of Martha Olney's *Buy Now, Pay Later* removed the necessity for investigating questions that require knowledge of formal economic models and sophisticated statistical techniques.

This book, then, is not concerned with the effect of consumer credit on the business cycle, or proving, as Olney has done, that consumer credit shaped the nature of American consumption patterns. I am not interested in determining the exact amounts of money lent over a given time period, or addressing the question of whether consumer credit has helped or hindered the growth of certain industries. In fact I am little interested in any of the questions whose chief usefulness lies in making possible the rational planning required to orchestrate an orderly, progressive growth for the national economy. Instead, as is apparent from the questions mentioned earlier, I come to this topic wanting to know more about the cultural significance of consumer credit—particularly what it can tell us about the nature of American consumer culture.

Another reason credit has been the neglected stepchild of consumer culture is that it appears to lack the interesting features of other oft-studied institutions and practices. The business of mass finance is not like the business of advertising, retailing, or industrial design; for one thing, it produces few material artifacts that can be "read" as texts. Small wonder, then, that those wishing to study the culture of consumption have focused their attention on Madison Avenue, fountainhead of the most popular art forms of the twentieth century, and on the retail environments of consumer culture—its grand downtown department stores, its humble roadside eateries, its sprawling suburban shopping malls—and on the commodities themselves: Coca-Cola and Crisco, automobiles and pianos, home furnishings and so on. Each of these potential subjects possesses a lineage of design changes that makes their histories fascinating for scholars, collectors, and general readers alike. In contrast with all this, the material culture of consumer credit seems utterly mundane. On the surface there is little to look at but contracts and receipts, tables and graphs, tiny ads for "money to loan," and second-floor loan offices cluttered with secondhand furniture. Compared with the history of goods, the history of how goods were paid for appears tedious in the extreme.

Lacking an eye-popping material product, the consumer credit industry also seems to lack interesting leadership, at least at first glance. The consumer credit system was not built through the vision and energy of a Henry Ford, a Raymond Loevy, an Earnest Elmo Calkins, or a John Wanamaker. It was built up mostly by shopkeepers, credit managers, reformed loan sharks, and unsung reformers, people who shared the values, as well as the anonymity, of the middle class. The absence of notable personages, not to mention the documentary evidence they tend to produce, is another reason credit has gone unstudied.

But if the test of a subject's historical importance is the amount of controversy it generated, then consumer credit is one of the most significant subjects in the history of the American twentieth century. Not at all the dry, narrow economic topic it appears to be, the history of consumer credit demonstrates the truth of what Johann Heuzinga, the Dutch cultural historian, once wrote, that "every historical fact opens immediately onto eternity."[26] The tables and graphs charting the rise of consumer credit lead to a wide plain of interesting episodes, topics, and people. Because so little of this territory has been mapped, I found it necessary to combine in this book the perspectives of several kinds of history, from the institutional history of the consumer credit industry to the social history of consumers to the cultural history of debt. If readers expect a book on consumer credit to be a work of pure economic history, I must warn them I found it to be a topic for which no one historical approach would do.

By far the greatest impediment to writing a history of American household finance is one that, at the end of the day, is impossible to overcome completely, and that is the serious dearth of evidence on the subject. It is a vexing problem. To be sure, the credit industry has left a paper trail to follow, found in trade journals, annual reports, public relations pamphlets, and occasional releases of statistical information. But the trail is faint indeed, since most of the credit industry's records are either lost or unavailable. One would expect this to be true for nineteenth-century pawnbrokers and loan sharks, who had little interest in making their records public. But it is no less true for the twentieth-century giants of the personal finance business, none of which were willing to make their archives, if they have them, available to me.

From the borrowers' side, the difficulties in finding evidence are even more severe. Money is an intensely private matter. Private debts are not the sort of thing people like to discuss in public, and often not in private either, not even to themselves in diaries and journals. Today, in an age of public confessions, when a letter writer to an advice columnist can write: "I am a twenty-three-year-old liberated woman who has been on the pill for two years. It's getting pretty expensive and I think my boyfriend should share half the cost, but I don't know him well enough to discuss money with him,"[27] one gets an idea of the problems involved in trying to learn how people two and three generations ago lived with debt, and what they thought about it. Thus, throughout my research, this book threatened to run aground on the same shoals encountered by Robert Porter, superintendent of the 1890 federal census, when he contemplated taking a survey of the nation's private debts. After preliminary investigations, Porter feared that "the people regarded their debt . . . as a part of their private affairs, and that they would resent any inquiries in regard to it." Disappointed, the superintendent gave up on his original plans.[28] Many were the times I shared Porter's frustration. It is the nature of the subject that consumer debt lends itself to easy opinions and facile claims, not to historical research.

To deal with the scantiness of evidence, I adopted a national approach, which enabled me to cast my nets widely so as to bring in as much documentation as possible. There were other reasons for a national study, too. A broad approach directs attention to what I take to be the most culturally significant aspect of the creation of a consumer credit system: the way in which it focused public debate on the morality of consumption as a way of life. Moreover, with so little written about consumer credit, it seemed necessary to try first for an aerial reconnaissance of sorts, useful for surveying answers to the most basic questions about how this key element in the culture of consumption came to be created. Of course, seizing the advantages of a national approach means having to put up with its disadvantages. Generalizations may not apply to specific cases; regional variations may remain undiscovered; my concentration on national public culture runs the risk of discounting the beliefs, practices, and experiences of those whose lives were not represented there. It is hard to see the details when flying a reconnaissance mission. This book is one of the first to take household financial management seriously as a historical subject. It should not be the last.

As with the mining of precious metals, the lack of a "mother lode" of easily available evidence led me to probe and sift through a number of disparate sources. What I have written in this book about the rise of consumer credit, the fight for its moral legitimacy, and the ways people thought about new money management principles comes from research examining government records and reports, social surveys and budget studies, trade journals for the credit and banking industries, articles and advertisements in mass-circulation magazines, the Library of Congress's rich collection of financial advice literature of the nineteenth and early twentieth centuries, "realist" novels and short stories that gave primary attention to money matters, corporate and business archives, and, probably more helpful than anything else, the voluminous social science literature on the "credit revolution" published between 1905 and 1940.

This book aims to tell the story of how consumer credit was invented and how it helped to make the culture of consumption what it is today. Sixty years ago, one of consumer credit's first historians, Evans Clark, described his subject as a "dark continent."[29] So it remains today. When I set out to explore the peaks and valleys of consumer credit, all I had to guide me were a set of common presumptions about the history of debt and what that history means. I did not get very far before it became necessary to toss out most of them.

The Most Remarkable Phenomena in Modern History

In the beginning, I thought I would be writing more or less a history of the credit card as yet another chapter in the long story of capitalism's impatience with traditional values. Was not the history of consumer credit the history of credit cards? Were not credit cards to blame for the decline of thrift? Was not the rise of "little easy payments" the story of how hedonism came to be bought and sold on the installment plan? No, I discovered, to all three suppositions. The history of consumer credit turned out to be full of surprises.

When was consumer credit invented? The credit era is often said to have begun in the 1950s, and not without reason.[30] As I saw in

my attempt at graph making, consumer credit swelled tremendously between 1945 and 1958, dwarfing earlier expansions.
Moreover, the 1950s witnessed the introduction of credit cards,
the most prominent symbol of consumer credit today, if not consumer culture itself.

But consumer credit is older than the credit card, and the postwar expansion of household credit was only possible because the
legal, institutional, and moral foundations of consumer credit had
already been set in place. Credit for consumer goods is the oldest
of all forms of credit, with a history stretching back to antiquity.
But the modern system of credit for consumption has its roots in
the two decades after 1915. In this period are found the most crucial chapters in the story of how consumer credit came to finance
American dreams.

Modern consumer credit was built on two institutional foundations. The first was a particular *method* of credit—the installment
plan. In the installment method of finance, money is lent or a good
is sold on the condition that the borrower or purchaser repays the
loan with fixed payments to be made at regular times over a speci-
fied period. Installment credit contrasts markedly with other types
of debts. With demand obligations, debts must be repaid when the
creditor "calls" the loan. With book credit, loans are repayable at
the convenience of the debtor. With single-payment loans, debts
run for a stated period and then the borrower faces the daunting
obligation of repaying in a single lump sum. None of these methods were as suited to the culture of consumption as the installment
method of financing. The installment plan was to consumer credit
what the moving assembly line was to the automobile industry.
Without it, today's trillion dollar consumer credit industry would
be inconceivable.

The other institutional foundation for consumer credit was an
array of particular *sources* of credit. Those extending the largest
amounts of credit in 1940 were retailers, commercial banks, personal finance companies, and sales finance companies. Like the installment plan, each of these creditors has a history extending well
back into the nineteenth century. But it was in the two decades
following 1915 that new types of retailers, small-loan lenders, and

"industrial" and commercial bankers adopted new strategies to pursue aggressively the profits to be made in consumer lending markets. Their innovations in lending practices, particularly their adoption of the installment plan, led to enormous changes in the ways people borrowed money.

What were these changes? American household finance was remade after 1915, and numbers tell part of the story. The statistical record of lending and borrowing in the early twentieth century is fragmentary and much of it based on interpolations, making it difficult to offer precise statements about the rising level of consumer debt. But all the numbers point in the same direction—up—at rates steeper than ever before. The best available figures are still those of Raymond Goldsmith. For every year after 1896, Goldsmith found that personal debt increased at rates well ahead of the rate of population growth. But from 1920 to 1929, the volume of consumer debt soared upward 131 percent, from $3.3 billion to $7.6 billion outstanding. The Depression interrupted this rising curve, but by 1937 consumer debt reached its pre-Depression levels and continued rising upward, until it was halted by credit controls during World War II.[31]

This large increase in the volume of credit extended in the 1920s suggests that there were more borrowers than before, or that people were borrowing in larger amounts, or both. To throw light on this question, Martha Olney has used Goldsmith's data to calculate the increase of debt per household from 1900 to 1939. She found that before World War I, households increased their debt burden about four dollars per year. But in the 1920s, the increases averaged fourteen dollars per year. Looking at debt as a percentage of the income that could be used to pay it off, a more telling statistic than simple increases in the amount of debt, Olney found that between 1900 and 1920 debt hovered between 4 and 6 percent of income. But in the 1920s the ratio doubled, rising to almost 10 percent. The most impressive evidence produced by Olney's econometric analysis concerns "real debt"—that is, total debt that is deflated by an index of prices of major durable goods. Between 1900 and 1916 real debt actually declined somewhat. But from

1920 to 1929, real debt per household almost doubled, rising (in 1982 dollars) from \$388 to \$739. As Olney points out, the burden of debt on indebted households was in many cases much higher than that indicated by aggregate figures, because some households remained debt-free in the 1920s. But clearly many people in the 1920s became consumer debtors for the first time, or added significantly to their debt load.[32]

The driving force behind this huge expansion of debt was, literally, the driver. By 1926 two of every three cars sold in the nation were bought on credit.[33] Credit financing made the automobile the quintessential commodity of the American consumer culture. Credit plans also figured prominently in the selling of radios, refrigerators, vacuum cleaners, fine jewelry, and other expensive consumer durable goods.

Who was lending all this money? In the Gilded Age credit system, household lending and borrowing was generally conducted on the subterranean levels of society. Credit was usually a matter between private individuals. If it was necessary to go outside the circle of family and friends for a loan, the likely options were retailers, pawnbrokers, and illegal moneylenders, or "loan sharks." Because this kind of credit operated mostly in secret, it was easy for later generations to forget it existed.

But in the early twentieth century a new structure of household finance emerged. Erected by enterprising businessmen, progressive reformers, and illegal lenders seeking a legitimate business, the new system included installment sales finance companies (such as the General Motors Finance Company), retail installment lenders (particularly department stores), licensed consumer finance companies (such as the Beneficial Loan Company), and a number of other lenders, such as "industrial" banks, remedial loan societies, credit unions, and personal loan departments of commercial banks. These new institutions brought capital, bureaucracy, and rationalized procedures to the very old business of consumption credit. They contributed to a system of credit Janet Ford aptly describes as "continuous, regular, organized, a series of increasingly impersonal, often visible bureaucratic transactions between individuals and institutions."[34] This system grew up so quickly in the 1920s that Evans Clark, one of the first to study it, compared it to "a skyscraper that rises from a hole in the ground to fifty stories of towering efficiency between spring and autumn."[35]

In the age of ballyhoo, the new lenders brought the blaze of publicity to what had been formerly a hidden, private matter. Painfully aware of the stigma attached to their forerunners in the consumer lending business—pawnbrokers and loan sharks—the innovators of the credit revolution used advertising and "educational" public relations campaigns to bring lending and borrowing out of the urban shadows. In the process, they made household credit one of the most heavily promoted consumer services of the 1920s. By the end of the decade, phrases such as "Buy Now, Pay Later!" and "Take Advantage of Our Easy Payment Plan!" were standard phrases in the vocabulary of American consumership.

As consumer debt in the American household increased beyond people's experience and memory, attitudes about consumption debt began to change, and not just from shame to acceptance but, particularly among social scientists, away from the idea that debt was a moral issue to begin with. "Credit for consumers," observed Paul Douglass, an editor for the proceedings of one of the many academic conferences held on the subject in the 1930s, "has . . . expanded beyond the stage where it can be condemned or justified. Its existence is an almost universal reality."[36]

A picture of what happened to credit between 1915 and 1940 can now be glimpsed in its outlines. A large number of new credit institutions used new methods of lending to advance higher amounts of money to more and more people in order to finance new types of consumption. In the process, the meaning of "consumptive" debt changed considerably. Less and less a marker of improvidence and poverty, it became in time a badge of middle-class respectability.

The rise of consumer credit inspired passionate debate among those who watched it grow, some with fascination, many with dismay. "Not in years has any business subject stirred up so much controversy," observed a reporter in 1926.[37] So much controversy,

Redrawn from *The Saturday Evening Post*. By permission. © Curtis Pub. Co.

" I just paid the doctor another ten dollars on his bill."
" Oh goody, two more payments and the baby's ours."

Figure 1. The rise of modern consumer credit inspired abundant commentary in the 1920s. This cartoon, which appeared in *World's Work*, 26 January 1926, accompanied an article on the new popularity of "Living and Dying on Installments."

in fact, that between 1915 and 1930 over fifteen hundred articles on consumer credit appeared in national magazines and scholarly journals.[38] Hollywood brought the perils and pitfalls of consumer debt to the screen, examining the rise of the "debt way of life" in such films as Harry Garson's *Charge It* (1921) and Lloyd Ingraham's *Keeping Up with Lizzie* (1921), an adaptation of Irving Bacheller's best-selling novel about modern thriftlessness. Scholars, too, witnessed the transformations in personal money management and made attempts to size up what was going on. "The

American family's plunge into debt for commodities during the last few years," wrote Harvard economist Franklin W. Ryan in 1930, "constitutes one of the most remarkable phenomena in modern history."[39]

The biggest question for observers then—as for historians now—was what did it all mean? While the changes in the credit system ran their course in the 1920s and 1930s, careful assessments about what was going on were crowded out by an efflorescence of quick-draw analysis and superficial criticism of "easy credit." In a variation on Gresham's law, bad talk drove out the good. The result was a standard interpretation of the rise of consumer credit, an interpretation that persists today and is widespread among both scholars and the public.

In a nutshell, this point of view interprets the rise of consumer credit as a significant departure from a thrifty past when, as Franklin W. Ryan remembered it, "most people 'never got into debt and always lived within their means.'"[40] The inconceivably large expansion of credit since the 1920s makes it easy to believe in a golden age of thrift before the rise of consumer credit, an age whose pocketbook prudence has been abandoned by a contemporary generation demanding instant gratification. "In the good old days," one writer begins her history of consumer credit, "economic life for the average person was conducted on a cash-and-carry basis." But now, as another continues the story, "babyboomers routinely [go] into debt for restaurant meals or new shoes."[41] This simple narrative of decline is often used to summarize the domestic economic history of the United States in the twentieth century.[42] But if ever there was a historical belief drawn up, in Carl Becker's famous phrase, "without fear and without research," this is a choice example.

The view just described is such a common and influential belief—indeed, it was the view I carried with me when I began my research for this book—I have given it a name: the myth of lost economic virtue. Because the myth of lost economic virtue continues to influence the way most people think about the rise of consumer credit, a summary of its history may be of interest to readers and help clear the way for a different analysis.

THE MYTH OF LOST ECONOMIC VIRTUE

The myth of lost economic virtue actually predates the rise of consumer credit. Early traces appear in Mark Twain's first novel, *The Gilded Age* (1873), written with the help of his friend Charles Dudley Warner. Subtitled *A Tale of Today*, the book contrasted the financial conservatism of the antebellum generation with the speculative fever of those living after the Civil War. One of the former is Silas Hawkins. Though not immune to grandiose schemes, Hawkins "always had a horror of debt" and generally did his best to pay as he went along. Not so with his friend, the comically ambitious Colonel Beriah Sellers. Sellers, one of Twain's most memorable characters, is a man who knows how to live on "Beautiful credit! The foundation of modern society." No stranger to the merchants in his town, he is known to them by "his old customary formula, 'Charge it,'" the earliest known literary record of this expression.[43] In *The Gilded Age*, Twain satirized the lustful acquisitiveness and greedy speculation of the postbellum era, clearly implying that once it was not always so, that earlier Americans knew better how to live within their means. The book registered the beginning of a belief that American money morals were deteriorating.

After 1900 this belief was heard more and more often, until in the 1920s it became a part of "what everyone knows." "We are living in an age of credit," wrote George Horace Lorimer of the *Saturday Evening Post* in 1924, "or perhaps a more accurate delineation would be an age of debt. The firmly rooted aversion to debt in any form which prevailed a generation ago has almost completely evaporated."[44] Lorimer either had a very bad memory or was overgeneralizing from his own family history, but he was hardly alone in misremembering the way things used to be. In the 1920s, nostalgia for a lost golden age was widespread as Americans looked to sentimentalized reconstructions of the past to provide a baseline for measuring the extent of the rapid, overwhelming changes taking place about them. A tendency developed to view the past in romantic terms, remembering it as an untroubled pastoral era, a time when the moral lines were more clearly drawn and more faithfully followed. "In other and simpler days," recalled an editorialist in the *New York Times* in 1923, "debt was a thing dreaded as the worst of ogres."[45] This was the myth of lost economic virtue, a piece of nostalgia entirely in harmony with the times.[46]

Remembering the past this way, many viewed the development of a consumer credit system as a "credit revolution," something entirely new and without precedent. In the estimation of M. R. Neifeld, one of the new credit industry's stoutest apologists, consumer credit was "a revolution second in importance only to the great shift from handicraft to machinery."[47] Critics agreed it was revolutionary, but were less sanguine about the results, believing that installment borrowing and buying signaled a "breakdown" in the moral nature of economic decision making. "Consumer credits," wrote the historian Preston William Slosson in 1930, put thrift "at a discount in all classes."[48]

If this was true, it was no small development in the history of the United States. Thrift had long been deemed a core value of American citizenship, as well as a mainspring for national prosperity. This helps explain why credit was one of the most vilified institutions of the new culture of consumption. Before consumer credit, it was possible to believe the average person was insulated from the temptations of affluence. "No nation was ever hurt by luxury," maintained Samuel Johnson, "for it can reach but to a very few."[49] For a century and more after Johnson, a dearth of disposable income functioned as a moat preventing most Americans from entering Vanity Fair. But consumer credit bridged the moat. When the millions stormed over, it seemed obvious to many that a moral revolution was in progress. More than with advertising and mass merchandising, critics saw that consumer credit not only tempted people to sin, it provided the means for sinning as well.

The notion that Puritan thrift had been abandoned lived on after the 1920s. But eventually a correction was made in the dating. For Mark Twain, the baseline for measuring the nation's departure from thrift had been the antebellum years. In the 1920s, the baseline was relocated to be the late nineteenth century—Twain's era of "beautiful credit"! In the 1950s, the baseline was moved yet again. The generation that grew up during the Great Depression now remembered the golden age of thrift as the penny-pinching years of the 1930s. Penny-pinching there was, but it was forgotten that the 1930s also witnessed the final years of a credit revolution that drove consumer debt levels to new highs.

Since World War II the myth of lost economic virtue has only grown stronger. "Thrift now *is* un-American," claimed journalist William H. Whyte in 1956, unaware that others had said the same thing thirty years before.[50] Scholars critical of the indebted way of life have often blamed the prodigality of the people on the requirements of the capitalist system. "People have changed their view of debt," wrote John Kenneth Galbraith in *The Affluent Society* (1958). "Thus there has been an inexplicable but very real retreat from the Puritan canon that required an individual to save first and enjoy later." But it was not really so inexplicable. "The Puritan ethos was not abandoned," Galbraith maintained. "It was merely overwhelmed by the massive power of modern merchandising." Galbraith worried that if the trend toward more debt continued, the effects would be "considerable and disagreeable."[51]

Since Galbraith wrote *The Affluent Society*, the number of households in the United States has doubled, while consumer debt has increased 26-fold.[52] Rising indebtedness on such a scale makes it easy to believe in the myth of lost economic virtue, and not just for senior citizens reminiscing about the good old days. The myth is well entrenched among scholars, too. Christopher Lasch blamed modern advertising for obliterating "the horror of indebtedness," while David Tucker, in *The Decline of Thrift in America*, argues that "installment buying required a moral revolution against the Puritan ethic."[53] Few have made more out of the myth than Daniel Bell. In *The Cultural Contradictions of Capitalism*, Bell asserts that "the greatest single engine in the destruction of the Protestant ethic was the invention of the installment plan, or instant credit." This is the myth of lost economic virtue in a pure and concise form. Presumptions of a national decline from the heights of thrift continue to offer a powerful interpretive narrative for understanding the economic and cultural history of debt in the twentieth century.[54]

In the beginning of my research, I also subscribed fully to the two key notions that make up the myth: first, that before consumer credit people "rarely went into debt and always lived within their means"; and second, that consumer credit destabilized traditional moral values by making it easier for people to live lives devoted to instant gratification and consumer hedonism. But the more I learned about the history of consumer credit and its effects on personal money management, the harder it became to accept the myth's central presumptions.

Other interpretations of the credit revolution are possible. They begin by facing certain facts. To begin with, it is simply not true that the invention of consumer credit was the invention of the indebted American. Debt, in fact, was a "heavy burthen" for the Pilgrims, a chronic headache for colonial planters (including George Washington and Thomas Jefferson), and a common hardship for nineteenth-century farmers and workers.[55] A river of red ink runs through American history. Occasionally it has overflowed its banks to effect alterations in the political landscape, generating famous events like the Nonimportation Resolutions, Shays's Rebellion, the Workingmen's Movement of the 1830s, and the formation in the 1890s of the Populist Party. At other times indebtedness has been a wide and covert river, concealed in the grocer's book and the pawnshop ledger, in the butcher's tab and the memory of friends, its current no less great for being hidden from view in people's private affairs. From colonial days through the 1890s, who did not know that life in the United States required financing, which meant debt?

The Credit Revolution and Consumer Culture

The myth of lost economic virtue is not baseless, but it hides too much. Making the rise of consumer credit seem more revolutionary than it was, it leaves historians in a quandary to explain how a consumer credit industry in the 1920s was built so quickly and adopted so enthusiastically. Due to an overproduction of "revolutions" in historical scholarship, claims for newly discovered "revolutions" deserve a healthy skepticism, the same given by nineteenth-century merchants to out-of-town bank notes. Nevertheless, the main argument of this book is that consumer credit was revolutionary—but I contend it was revolutionary in *both* senses of the word.

In common speech "revolution" refers to a radical change of some sort, as in the French Revolution, the industrial revolution, and the sexual revolution. So when Loren Baritz claims that automobile installment financing was as "revolutionary as the assembly line," he means installment selling introduced fundamental alterations into American patterns of money management.[56] This is certainly true. But it is not the whole truth.

Like the word "revolution," the history of consumer credit has another side. In the scientific community, "revolution" has a meaning fairly opposite from common speech. Astronomers and physicists speak of "revolutions" as rotational motions, as in the orbits of stars and planets around other celestial bodies. It was this kind of astronomical movement that provided the analogy for the Glorious Revolution of 1688, the first political event to be so designated. When Parliament replaced James II with his daughter Mary and her husband, William of Orange, the new state of affairs was thought to be a *revolving* of English society back to an earlier political state, less a plunge into uncharted political waters than a turning back to old and familiar harbors.

In just this sense consumer credit was revolutionary, too. When twentieth-century American consumers took to indebtedness as a way life, they followed in the tracks of seventeenth-century colonists, eighteenth-century planters, and nineteenth-century farmers and small businessmen. It is often forgotten, but from Plymouth Rock to the present, American dreams have usually required a lien on the future.

This truth is entirely missing from the myth of lost economic virtue. Consequently, the history of consumer credit, when it is told at all, is usually presented as a story of discontinuity and rupture, as a repudiation of the way money was managed in the past. This book demurs. I have found the continuities to be equally striking.

THE MYTH OF EASY PAYMENTS

If one of the continuities is that debt was a primary strategy of household finance long before consumer credit, another is the non-disappearance of economic discipline in the face of an "easy credit" environment supposedly hostile to "traditional" values from previous ages of scarcity. In the culture of consumption, prudence, saving, and industry survive, and their persistence demonstrates in what sense consumer culture is about much more than hedonism. The currents of consumer culture do not all flow in the same direction. They may stream generally toward the gratification of desire and away from Puritan "in-the-world" asceticism, but the current is not all one way. There are backcurrents and riptides. If it were not so, consumer culture could not endure. Consumption as a way of being in the world has developed restraints of its own, mechanisms of control that enable it to function as an integrating force for society. One of the most effective of these mechanisms is consumer credit.

Most people responding to the allure of "little easy payments" have found that the indebted way of life forces enough external disciplines on them that the culture of consumption is preserved from its own reckless imperatives. Installment financing saddles borrowers with a strict schedule of payments. To satisfy their obligations, modern consumers are forced to commit themselves to regimens of disciplined financial management. In this way, consumer credit has limited the hedonistic impulse within consumerism, while preserving the relevance of traditional values such as "budgeting," "saving," "hard work," and even "thrift." Thus, consumer credit has done for personal money management what Frederick W. Taylor's scientific management theories did for work routines in the factory. It has imposed strict, exogenous disciplines

28

of money management on consumers, in the interest of improving their efficiency in the "work" of being a consumer. Because "easy payments" turned out to be not so easy—work and discipline were required to pay them—consumer credit made it easy for Americans to think of consumption as "work," which greatly eased the passage from a society oriented around production to a society dedicated to consumption. By preserving the relevance of many nineteenth-century producer culture values, it made the culture of consumption less a playground for hedonists than an extension of Max Weber's "iron cage" of disciplined rationality.[57]

As Philip Rieff has argued, cultural orders consist of both controls and releases. Controls are moral demands used to interdict antisocial behavior; releases are carefully regulated permissions to bend and break the moral demands, so that individuals can bear the pressure of having to put communal purposes first. Rieff believes the era of traditional Christian controls has come to an end—"Religious man was born to be saved; psychological man is born to be pleased"—and that Western societies stand on the edge of a brave new culture that, for the moment at least, is composed almost entirely of releases. But Rieff has little doubt that "therapeutic" consumer culture will in time produce its own effective controls. It must, because no viable culture can preach only releases from the economic, social, and moral disciplines necessary for the survival and flourishing of society.[58]

Building on Rieff's provocative analysis, Jackson Lears has turned away from the view, which he helped to create, that sees the rise of consumer culture as a simple, linear shift from a society oriented around self-denying production to a society oriented around self-indulgent consumption. On the contrary, Lears now believes that consumer culture is "less a riot of hedonism than a new way of ordering the existing balance of tensions between control and release." Lears arrived at this view while studying the history of modern corporate advertising, an important social authority whose messages are commonly thought to emphasize fun, lust, sensuality, and materialism—in other words, hedonistic releases from traditional moral codes. But Lears finds themes of materialistic hedonism have been less predominant in corporate advertising than other messages of restraint, messages that amount to a "rhetoric of control" advising people to manage their desires in the interest of "personal efficiency"—robust physical health, psychic well-being, productive relationships with others, and the like.[59] This is an intriguing argument, full of promise for new ways of thinking about the culture of consumption. But the pendulum of interpretation should not be allowed to swing so far that we underestimate the hedonism that abounds in consumer culture, or overestimate the actual influence of advertising's "rhetoric of control."

The history of consumer credit provides a more concrete case for understanding the culture of consumption as a balance of tensions between permissions and restraints. Until recently the permissions have received all the emphasis, which is certainly understandable—they are more obvious. In the case of consumer credit, scholars such as Daniel Bell, Christopher Lasch, David Tucker, and others have correctly perceived the first and most obvious way consumer installment credit shaped the development of a culture of consumption: it enabled the American public to purchase expensive durable goods that, without credit, most of them could not or would not have bought. Consumer lenders accomplished what advertisers were powerless to do, which was to provide people with the means to turn expensive consumer dreams into instant realities. Credit, in short, made consumers of the millions.

But to stop here is to take a seriously truncated view of consumer credit. It is possible to make too much of catchphrases such as "buy now, pay later" and "little easy payments," pointing to them as evidence that consumer credit is an engine of consumeristic hedonism and instant gratification. Jeremiads against installment buying focus exclusively on a single moment in time—the moment of purchase when desire is satisfied—and ignore the months and years following the day an installment contract is signed.

Thus, it is possible to overlook a second and less obvious contribution consumer credit makes to the culture of consumption. Once consumers step onto the treadmill of regular monthly payments, it becomes clear that consumer credit is about much more than instant gratification. It is also about discipline, hard work, and the channeling of one's productivity toward durable consumer goods. The nature of installment credit ensures that if there is hedonism in consumer culture, it is a disciplined hedonism, and if there are hedonists in consumer culture, they are less likely to be found lounging on island beaches than keeping their noses to the grindstone at one or more places of employment. Thus, I regard consumer credit as an instrument of both cupidity and control. And by "control," I mean not a rhetoric of control as Lears sees in advertisements, but an actual enforcement of economic imperatives in the lives of consumer debtors.

The general argument of this book agrees with an observation made by the literary critic C. S. Lewis. Humanity, argued Lewis, does not pass through history as a train passes through stations: "Being alive, it has the privilege of always moving yet never leaving anything behind. Whatever we have been, in some sort we are still."[60] Indebted Americans of the 1990s are different from American debtors of the 1790s and 1890s, but not completely different. The rise of consumer credit cannot be accounted for until it is recognized as a continuation of a long-standing American willingness to get ahead by getting into debt. Moreover, consumer credit carried into consumer culture financial values and practices from an older age of scarcity: discipline, hard work, budgeting, and saving. This happened because even in an age of abundance, money itself always seems to be in short supply. Despite the efforts of advertisers, retailers, and all the other brokers of consumerism to make people into hedonistic consumers, values and practices attuned to scarcity and production persist. It is my contention that they persist not despite consumer credit, but because of it.

The book is divided into three parts. Part One sets the stage by showing how the modern system of consumer credit grew from a previously existing credit system used by millions of Americans in the nineteenth and early twentieth centuries. Credit in this period was not static, but for my purposes the years before 1915 are best seen as a prelude to what was to come. Contrary to popular belief, debts appeared often on the balance sheets of Victorian families. Moreover, debt was not something the Victorian money management ethic taught people to "fear," as is so often claimed. On the contrary, the antidebt maxims of Poor Richard were hardly the Victorians' last word on the subject of credit. Nineteenth-century financial advice books actually encouraged some forms of indebtedness, including, in certain situations, debt for consumer goods.

This helps explain why, in the twenty years following World War I, working- and middle-class Americans adopted consumer credit so readily. Part Two examines the meteoric rise of two new sources of credit in the 1910s and 1920s: legalized small-loan lending and installment selling. Though they followed different trajectories of development, both present a story of unintended consequences. The builders of the small-loan industry were firm believers in the Victorian ideology of producerism, and hardly intended their lending to create a market for "consumptive" credit. Yet, in time, that is exactly what these credit pioneers accomplished. Conversely, the creators of the installment plan from the beginning sang the praises of unbridled consumerism. Yet their form of credit, with its rigid schemes of repayment, actually had the effect of reviving traditional principles and practices of Victorian money management, breathing new life into old values such as budgeting, saving, and the importance of choosing "productive" investments.

Nonetheless, critics of the new system of credit abounded. Part Three tells the story of how in the 1920s and 1930s "consumptive" credit came under heavy attack, first for debauching the nation's morals, then later, during the Depression, for ruining the nation's economy. It examines how the fledgling consumer credit industry responded to concerns about the propriety of consumer borrowing, and how it finally succeeded in winning public acceptance. By 1940, on the eve of a war that would bring severe credit restrictions, the legal, moral, and economic foundations of consumer credit were securely in place. Consumer credit had survived its critical shakedown period, and credit-based consumerism, marked by constant tensions between instant gratification and sobering monthly payments, between the blandishments of the salesman and the constraints of the bill collector, had become a characteristic feature of the American way of life.

The conclusions I reached while writing this book surprised me. In the beginning I very much wanted to buy into the myth of lost economic virtue and blame consumer credit for the hedonism and loss of self-discipline so evident in contemporary society. But my fundamental motivation in writing this book was neither to praise nor condemn the culture we live in, but simply to follow the evidence where it led in a search for better understanding. As it happens, my own view of consumer culture is rather skeptical. I certainly believe there have been worse ways of living and being in the world, but in my view consumer culture is a pleasant, and therefore all the more deceptive, detour from where true joys are to be found. To conclude that consumer credit helps prolong the viability of this culture by providing it with mechanisms of control to counterbalance its releases is to me no great cause for celebration. On the contrary, as one who lives in a consumer culture it leaves me doubly wary. If my analysis means anything, it means modern consumers run the risk of being both deceived by consumerism and dragged along by consumer credit. To say there have been worse ways of living is not to say this is a good way to live.

PART ONE

GETTING TRUSTED: DEBT AND CREDIT
BEFORE CONSUMER CREDIT

*

CHAPTER 1

Beautiful Credit!
The Foundation of Modern Society

Consumer credit is an invention of the early twentieth century, but borrowing and lending are not. Before there were loan offices and credit unions, before there were charge cards and "easy payment plans," what did people do when they needed things or simply wanted things but lacked money to pay for them?

It is a mistake to think they always saved up for the things they wanted, or did without. We remember nineteenth-century Americans as living in a golden age of thrift, savings, and economic self-discipline. But humorists of the time knew better. Charles Farrar Browne, otherwise known as Artemus Ward, drew hearty guffaws and knowing winks when he mock-lectured his audiences, "Let us all be happy, and live within our means, even if we have to borrer money to do it with."[1] This was advice late nineteenth-century Americans took very seriously. It was "the golden age of mutual trust, of unlimited reliance on human promises," wrote Mark Twain. Looking for an anecdote to express the essential character of what he termed "the Gilded Age," Twain found one in a "familiar" newspaper story about a speculator overheard to boast on the street, "I wasn't worth a cent two years ago, and now I owe two millions of dollars." This was business debt, of course, but the point and meaning of the story also touched the "thousands of families in America" obtaining "prosperity and luxury" the same way: with "Beautiful credit! The foundation of modern society."[2]

It is true that thrift, frugality, and the delay of gratification were important cultural ideals in eighteenth- and nineteenth-century America; later, it will be necessary to examine such ideals closely. But exaggerated ideas about the thriftiness of nineteenth-century Americans and their alleged hatred of debt make it difficult to explain how consumer credit, when it did appear, caught on so quickly and spread so fast. For now, it is worth remembering that in the Victorian era saving, frugality, and self-denial were ideals practiced by some, popular with many, but only in retrospect credited to all.

Long before the credit revolution of the 1920s, credit for consumption played an important role in American household economies. It is generally recognized that nineteenth-century producers—farmers, say, or shopkeepers, or entrepreneurs—floated on a vast sea of credit. Credit made it possible to buy land, conduct business, put in a crop, and start new enterprises. But nineteenth-century consumers depended on credit, too—credit obtained from a subterranean network of formal and informal lending sources. Appreciating this fact will help us understand better how consumer credit came to be invented and why it took some of the forms that it did.

It will be the simple task of this chapter to examine the available figures reporting the indebtedness of late nineteenth-century Americans and, looking beyond them, to reconstruct from other sources the essential features of the Gilded Age credit system serving the consumption needs of individuals and households. Late nineteenth-century households sought financial assistance from five major credit sources: pawnbrokers, illegal small-loan lenders, retailers, friends and family, and mortgage lenders. Which households relied on which sources of credit depended a great deal on the borrower's economic standing and social class; the system conformed to patterns of gender, race, and ethnicity as well. This was the *ancien regime* whose inadequacies led to a credit revolution.

A MOUNTAIN LOAD OF DEBT

Just how much personal debt was on the books in the late nineteenth century? It is hard to know. The audiences who laughed at the quips of Artemus Ward are not available for questioning; even if they were, they would not answer queries about such a private matter as their debts. The "beautiful credit" of Mark Twain's day was intensely personal, extremely private, and therefore, at least for historians, frustratingly off-the-record. Modern lenders keep good records, but their predecessors did not. In this respect the credit system of the Gilded Age was not so different from that of the seventeenth century, a system R. H. Tawney described as "spasmodic, irregular, unorganized, a series of individual, and sometimes surreptitious, transactions between neighbors."[3] So it remained over two centuries later.

But that borrowing and lending were prevalent practices in late nineteenth-century America is clear enough based on contemporary estimates of the private indebtedness of the American people. Perhaps the first to make such an estimate was the celebrated orator and statesman Edward Everett. Seeking to explain the cause of the panic of 1857, Everett blamed it on "a mountain load of debt" taken on by the entire country—individuals and communities, businesses and governments. Putting aside business debt, Everett estimated the nation's total household indebtedness in 1858 to be $1.5 billion, or $300 per household. The figure was conjectural, based solely on Everett's observation and experience, but it is relevant that Everett observed everywhere around him a "natural proclivity to anticipate income, to buy on credit, to live a little beyond our means." He at least was confident his estimate was not far off the mark.[4]

Estimates compiled thirty years later by the United States Census Bureau confirm that long before credit cards many Americans bought the good life, or at least a life, on credit. The 1890 census survey of personal debt was a response to demands made by people in the 1880s who wanted to know how badly the nation's private citizens were "over head and ears" in debt. In an address to the National Board of Trade, J. A. Price gave as his opinion that private indebtedness amounted to around $6 billion in 1888. But farmers' and workers' associations, joined by Single Taxers, Greenbackers, Christian Socialists, and other dissenters, alleged the amount was much higher, perhaps as high as $25 or $30 billion.[5] With little hard information available, guesses became assertions, and assertions passed as statements of accepted fact. Data from a handful of states were not enough to answer the question at hand: could Americans produce enough wealth to pay back the principal on their debts, or even the interest? For this purpose Congress directed the Eleventh Decennial Census to "collect the statistics of, and relating to, the recorded indebtedness of private corporations and individuals."[6]

For our purposes, it would have been fortunate if the census had been able to comply with its charge. But the undertaking was simply too large, too intrusive, and too unprecedented. The problem lay in finding a suitable method. One way to determine the total private debt of the nation would have been to print questions about indebtedness in a schedule, hand it to enumerators, and send them house to house. But would people answer truthfully questions about their financial affairs? Robert Porter, the census superintendent, "feared that the people regarded their debt . . . as a part of their private affairs, and that they would resent any inquiries in regard to it." The image was not a pleasant one: unarmed census workers thrown out of the homes of angry debtors resentful of governmental prying into their personal affairs. Porter concluded that any attempt to ask the people about their debts would cause collateral damage to the rest of the survey, enough to wreck the entire 1890 census. For this reason, census officials decided to calculate the private debt of the nation on the basis of public records. But even this undertaking proved to be too ambitious. In the end, due to matters of expense and practicability, the only debts assayed were private real estate mortgages.[7]

This in itself was a large achievement. But the census did not entirely sidestep the charge laid upon it by Congress. Mixing hard figures on mortgages with round numbers and educated guesses as to other types of consumption debt, Robert Porter's census staff estimated the *minimum* private debt of the people of the United States in 1890 to be $11 trillion.[8]

The 1890 census figure would apportion to each household in the United States about $880 of debt. The amount is striking when it is considered that the average annual wage of nonfarm workers that year was $475.[9] Of course, many were not in this deep and some owed no money at all, while others owed more. But census officials admitted that their figures almost certainly underreported the true amount of household debt. After all, they could hardly estimate the *unrecorded* debts of the people, the debts owed to pawnbrokers, loan sharks, retailers, and friends and family members. Still, taking the figure as it stands, the census estimate confirms what has often been forgotten. Large numbers of late nineteenth-century households were familiar—perhaps, from their perspective, all too familiar—with debt. And even before the consumer credit revolution, wealth, as a journalist put it in 1876, was "shouting itself hoarse in the effort to get itself loaned."[10]

Estimates of total private debt say nothing about who went into debt, for what purposes, or with the aid of what creditors. But with the help of other sources, it is possible to reconstruct the outlines of the credit system preceding consumer credit. In the late nineteenth century, where a person went to secure a loan or to get credit depended to a great extent on the social identity of the borrower: whether one was male or female, white or black, Italian or native-born American, Jewish or Catholic, a resident of New York City or San Francisco. But at the highest level of generalization the major boundary in the social organization of credit was social class. There was overlap, of course, but poor and working-class households tended to rely on certain types of lenders for certain types of credit for certain types of needs. With middle-class households it was a different story.

I Buy Everything on Credit

"I buy everything on credit until I get no more, then I go to another store and do the same there," a German American housewife wrote to the *New Yorker Volks-Zeitung* in December 1882, when the German American newspaper, the second largest German American daily in New York City, asked its working-class readers to comment on the costs and expenditures of their family budgets. From the discussion that followed, it became clear that most working-class families in the 1880s with three to four children and a wage earner making up to thirteen dollars a week were barely scraping by, and many were in debt.[11] The stories of those who wrote to the *Volks-Zeitung* were not untypical for late nineteenth-century workers' households. Households with low and irregular incomes regularly used credit to manage the exigencies of poverty.

In the Gilded Age, families at the large base of the working-class pyramid struggled daily to make ends meet, and stood desperately in need of credit assistance. Budget studies conducted in the early years of the new century show that at least half of working-class families in large cities waged a constant, teetering effort to match income with expenses, while a little over a quarter experienced deficits at some point in a year.[12] Nor was this a problem limited to workers in large cities. In Buffalo, New York, the president of the carpenters union reported in 1897 that "in 72 cases out of 100 our members are not able to earn enough to pay for actual necessaries of life."[13] In Lynn, Massachusetts, Alan Dawley has found that "most [i.e., four out of five] self-supporting factory workers lived at the knife-edge of poverty in constant fear that an increase in their needs would make the blanket too small to cover essentials."[14] On a national scale, workers' average wages rose modestly yet steadily from the Civil War to World War I, but Peter Shergold's extensive research has shown that the fruits of economic growth were mostly out of reach for those outside the highly paid ranks of the highly skilled. Thus, what Melvyn Dubofsky has said holds true, "Poverty remained a fact of life for most working-class families and a condition of existence for many."[15] The slightest disturbance in the balance between income and expenses, whether brought on by illness, unemployment, injury, or simply the desire to help a relative in need, sent families looking for money. In these situations, children could be put out to work, meals could be cut back, boarders could be taken in, and charity solicited, but sometimes borrowing money was the only way to pay the bills.

Pawnbrokers: Bankers for the Poor

When working-class wage earners in large cities needed money, one important source of credit they could turn to was "my uncle," the pawnbroker. Much of what we would like to know about pawnbrokers cannot be known; American pawnbrokers, unlike their English brothers in trade, left almost no records in which they speak for themselves.[16] But fortunately the middle class's fascination with urban poverty in the late nineteenth century ("Could this happen also to *me?*") made pawnbroking a favorite topic of journalists and writers, who wrote detailed descriptions of pawnshops for newspapers and the mass-circulation magazines. Their investigative reports are of much help in recreating the world of the pawnshop, which was a familiar feature in almost all working-class districts and played a vital role in the lives of urban working-class families. "The city can no more dispense with the pawnbroker," claimed one reform-minded journalist, "than it can with the baker or the milkman."[17]

The testimony of laboring people themselves confirms this. Maria Ganz, a Jewish immigrant from Galicia who grew up on New York's Lower East Side during the turn of the century, remembered the critical role of the pawnshop in her neighborhood's life. Her family lived next to a widow, a Mrs. Zulinsky, who one day found that her entire life's savings of six hundred dollars had been stolen from her mattress. Charity could not support three children, so Mrs. Zulinsky was forced to become, in the slang of the day, "a furniture dealer." Her table, her two beds, all her chairs, and "even the marble clock surmounted by a bronze horseman armed with a spear" were hauled down to the pawnshop and "put up the spout." When night fell, Mrs. Zulinsky's family was "sitting on boxes and sleeping on the floor," but the immediate emergency had been bridged.[18]

Incidents like this suggest the important role pawnbroking played in the life of working-class families. A wide variety of people found their way into pawnshops, including salesmen and travelers with emergency needs for cash, and petty shopkeepers in need of a quick loan to pay off creditors. But the pawnbroker's principal patrons were the families of industrial wage earners. In Robert Chapin's 1909 budget study of 318 families in New York City, 23 families admitted they had articles in pawn. But this hardly represented the actual number, as Louise More, director of a similar study two years before, found the shame of pawning made it likely that the practice was "more common than [her respondents] would admit." She observed that pawning was "typical of every workingman's neighborhood."[19] In the Bowery of New York one journalist estimated that almost the entire population held at least one pawn ticket at all times, and most had a dozen or more during the slack winter months.[20] In Pittsburgh, Peter Shergold has estimated that in 1898 pawnbrokers made one loan for every 11.6 city dwellers.[21]

Located in low-rent areas like New York's Bowery district, pawnbrokers conducted their business under the familiar sign of the three golden balls.[22] Large pawnshops in some cases looked almost like banks, with impressive facades and clean, uncluttered interiors. But most were small and dingy. The front entrance opened into a dim hallway or directly into the room where business was transacted (some had side entrances for customers who did not want to enter from the public street). Across one end of the room ran a long, narrow counter. One end of the counter was partitioned by narrow stalls capable of holding one person each. These allowed shy customers a measure of privacy. Behind the counter a case of pigeonholes rose from floor to ceiling, for temporary storage of parcels wrapped and ticketed. Clerks made appraisals—on clothing, one-fifth to one-third of the value; on valuable items, two-thirds of what it would get at auction—and wrote up tickets from behind the counter. After the transaction was completed, clerks placed the pawn into a dumbwaiter that transported it "up the spout" to storage rooms located above the shop.

If we take everything written by Victorian journalists at face value, the shelves of the pawnbroker's shop were filled mostly with pawned wedding rings, family Bibles, and the baptismal gowns of dead infants. But in fact the most common pawns were items of clothing—shawls, bonnets, undergarments, dresses, suits, shoes—and jewelry. Specialization in one or the other types of pawns occurred early and by late in the century was common. Other items commonly pawned were bedding, musical instruments, clocks, silver cutlery, guns, household furniture, flatirons, dishpans, and pictures. Then there were the unusual pawns: coffins, false teeth, wooden legs, anvils, anchors, and eventually, even automobiles.[23]

Figure 2. The Star Loan Bank, South State Street, Chicago, as seen in a detail from a 1905 photograph. The three golden balls advertise this is a pawnbroker's establishment. (Chicago Historical Society, ICHi-04780)

The first American pawnshops appeared in the early decades of the nineteenth century. Before 1800 merchants occasionally lent money on pledges of personal property, but pawnbroking as a business was not possible until industrial cities brought together large numbers of wage earners who needed credit and had little

Figure 3. A lender's-eye view from *Harper's Weekly*, 10 March 1894.
In one stall a fashionably dressed young woman offers a jewel; in another,
an injured worker clutches a clock; in the middle stall, a working-class
housewife, the most typical of a pawnbroker's customers,
brings in some clothes "to hock."

opportunity to get it. In New York City pawnbrokers were legally
recognized in the 1803 city charter, and first regulated by city ordi-
nances in 1812. Six years later the mayor licensed ten pawnbrokers; by 1897, 134 licensed pawnbrokers operated in New
York City. In the same year there were 92 in Philadelphia, 86 in
Boston, 11 in Pittsburgh, 68 in Chicago, 7 in New Orleans, 22 in
Omaha, and 243 in San Francisco, where the absence of state
usury laws encouraged a flourishing business catering to the city's
large numbers of migratory workers and seamen. In 1911, when
pawnbroking neared the height of its business, 2,000 pawnshops
did business in 300 cities, in the hands of 400 owners.[24]

Pawnbrokers were known as the "poor man's banker," but this
was a misnomer. The typical pawner was female. Pawnshop investigators observed that three-quarters of the patrons in a shop were

ESTABLISHED 1870.

AMERICAN
PAWN-BROKERS

FORT DEARBORN BLDG., 184 CLARK ST.,
Private Entrance Through Corridor Fort Dearborn Building.

HARRIS & CO., Props. Fifth Rational Loan Office.
Liberal Advances made on Diamonds, Watches and Precious Stones at the lowest possible rates.

Pawnbrokers.

Andrews Henrietta Mrs. 322 State
Barnett Lena, 2542 State
Bauman Loan Co. 159 and 173 Clark
Bock H. & Co. 82 N. Wells
Bomash Louis, 432 State
Bomash Morris, 307 Clark
Bomash Samuel, 261 Clark
Curtis Harry, 492 State
Cassriel Alexander, 194 W. Madison
Cohn Michael, 276 Clark
Delamater S. & Co. 154 Clark
Donnelly Tom V. & Co. 118 Dearborn
Ferderber William & Co. 275 Clark
Franks Collateral Loan Bank, 122 Madison and 163 Clark
Frisch Adolph, 161 S. Halsted
Gelder Isaac, 1716 State
Grace Stephen, 176 S. Halsted
Greenburg Abraham, 316 S. Halsted
Greenberg Simon, 192 Vanburen
Grossman Harry, 227 S. Halsted
Grossman Isaac L. 241 S. Halsted
Harris & Co. 184 Clark
Hernrich Jeannette L. Mrs. 125 S. Halsted
Hernrich Morris, 111 S. Halsted
Hirtenstein Jacob, 212 S. Halsted
Isaacs Hyman, 265 Clark
Jersky E. D. 353 Clark and 496 State
Kuhn Fannie Mrs. 198 Clark
Lowy Henry, 201 W. Madison
Marks Leo S. 2002 State
Marks Rosa Mrs. 206 W. Madison
Marks S. & Son, 104 W. Madison
McGuite Mary Mrs. 16 N. Halsted
Michael Alfred, 810 Milwaukee av.
Michael James, 258 W. Madison
Moe Charles A. Co. 82 Adams
Mulvaney Simon P. 306 S. Halsted
Nemkovsky Jacob, 189 State
Newman Abraham, 1702 State
Newman Naftuly, 1894 State
Nierman Peter, 263 Clark
Richter Simon, 2120 State
Robinson Jacob, 353 Clark
Schoen Emanuel, 44 S. Halsted
Schwartz Morris, 177 S. Halsted
Silverman Myer, 325 Clark

SLATTS & POE,
167 Clark

Spingold E. & Co. 317 and 327 Clark
Steinberg Louis, 251 Clark
Stern David, 292 W. Madison
Sixth & Co. 237 S. Halsted
Unger Herman, 271 Clark
Unger Nathan, 444 State
Weber Bros. 131 Clark
Weber Louis, 341 Clark
Weiss Moses, 3412 State
Wolf F. & Son, 319 S. Halsted
Wolf Herman, 189 S. Halsted

*Pea Meal, Peas and Pea Grits.
(Patent Roasted.)

MORTON W. O.
MILLING CO. 47 W. Lake. tel. Main 4978

*Peanut Roasters.
(Manufacturer of.)

EVANS WILLIAM J.
127-9 Harrison

*Pencils.
(Advertising.)

WESTERN PENCIL CO.
412, 269 Dearborn

*Pens.
(Manufacturers.)

CROWN PEN CO.
6th floor, 78 State

*Pension Attorneys.

STEVENS MILO B. & CO.
4, 163 Randolph

---

*Perforated Metals.

FRASER & CHALMERS,
S. Washtenaw av. ne. cor. 12th

HARRINGTON & KING
PERFORATING CO. The, 224 N. Union

*Perforated Sheet Metals.

AITCHISON ROBERT
PERFORATED METAL CO. 510, 269 Dearborn

*Perfumery.

Baldwin B. D. Co. 6 Market
Buford Chemical Co. 26, 94 Washington
Catlin George, 118 Lake
Consolidated Perfume Co. 560, 100 Lake
Eastman Perfume Co. 199 Randolph
Ladd & Coffin, 3, 52 State
LaFleur Perfume Co. 376 S. Hermitage av.
Lueders George & Co. 118 Lake
Regent Perfume Co. 521, 56, 5th av.
Smith Justus J. 305, 100 Lake
Woodworth C. B. Sons Co. 6439 Ellis av.
Zehring & Co. 146, 5th av.

*Perfumery.
(Manufacturers and Wholesale Dealers.)

BALDWIN B. D. CO.
6 and 8 Market

*Pharmaceutical and Chemical Machinery and Apparatus.

THE WM. FRECK CO.
116 to 120 S. Clinton

Philatelists and Numismatists.

Doherty Archie L. 106 Dearborn

EDMUNDS R. E.
518, 7 Blue Island av.
Masoth F. N. & Co. 651, 204 Dearborn
Michael Fred, stamp collections bought, 258 W. Madison
Owen & Co. 412, 171 Lasalle
Pierce John A. 7, 191 Clark
Stevens & Co. 15, 69 Dearborn
Wilcox Charles S. 910, 138 Washington
Wolseiffer Philip M. 75 State and 12, 201 Clark

Phonographs.

Columbia Phonograph Co. (Gen'l) 211 State
Douglass Charles H. 50 Pine
Hamilton Edward J. 6547 S. Halsted
National Gramophone Co. 161 State

TALKING MACHINE CO.
THE, 107 Madison
United States Talking Machine Co. 509, 358 Dearborn

*Photo Brooches and Buttons.
(Patentees.)

PIN-LOCK BUTTON CO.
174 S. Clinton

*Photo Buttons.

PHOTO JEWELRY MFG.
CO. 408, 195 to 199 State

*Photo Buttons.
(Campaign and Society.)

Geraghty Manufacturing Co.
SUITE 17 to 20, 177 LA SALLE ST.
Manufacturers of
Photograph Buttons, Medallions, Campaign, Society and Advertising Buttons and Badges
of all descriptions. Mounting and Cutting of Photographs a Specialty. Buttons, Parts and Holders for the trade only. Send for Price List.

---

*Photo Buttons.
(Manufacturers.)

CRANLEY PHOTO BUTTON MFG. CO. 3331 State
(Originators.)

LAPHAM PHOTO-
BUTTON CO. 146 State

*Photo Colorist.

BUTLER FRANK E.
815, 21 E. Quincy

*Photo Engravers.

Geo. H. Benedict & Co.
MONROE & CLARK STS.

CHICAGO PHOTO ENGRAVING CO.
79-81 FIFTH AVE

FRANKLIN
ENGRAVING AND ELECTROTYPING CO.
341-351 DEARBORN STREET.

NATIONAL PHOTO
ENGRAVING CO. 93, 5th av.

A. ZEESE & CO.
500-306 DEARBORN ST.
PHOTO-PROCESS ENGRAVERS

*Photo Engravers' and Printers' Proof Presses.

SHNIEDEWEND PAUL &
CO. 195, 197 and 199 S. Canal

*Photo Engravers' and Zinc Etchers' Supplies.

FUCHS & LANG MNFG. CO.
THE, 328 Dearborn

*Photo Engraving.

CHICAGO ELECTRO-
TYPE & STEREOTYPE CO. 149 Plymouth ct.

*Photo Gravure.

CHICAGO PHOTO-
GRAVURE CO. 8th floor 358 Dearborn
See adv.

SYNNBERG PHOTO-
GRAVURE & PRINTING CO. THE, 1240 to 1265 Caxton bldg

women and children.[25] Why were most of the pawnbroker's customers women? In working-class families it was usually the wife's responsibility to see that paychecks lasted to the next payday. Strategies for stretching an income included homework, boarding, scavenging, and even petty thievery, but many housewives found they could supplement their meager allowances by pawning household items for cash, with or without their husbands' knowledge. If hocking a suit of clothes or a piece of jewelry was the best available strategy for getting through a difficult midweek, it was nevertheless a costly strategy. But as Louise More's settlement survey discovered, once in debt to a pawner it was hard to give up the practice.[26]

And pawning, for many, was a regular practice. A large portion of the pawnbroker's business came from regular weekly customers who counted on the pawnbroker's loan as an integral part of the family budget. These customers made Mondays and Saturday nights at the pawnshop the busiest times of the week. A common practice was to put a suit in "to soak" on Monday, redeem it Saturday, wear it Sunday, and then pawn it again on Monday. The rhythm of pawning intensified during the winter because of seasonal layoffs and higher expenses. In addition to clothing, workmen's tools were often left with the pawnbroker during periods of unemployment, inspiring yet another of the pawnbroker's many nicknames: the "mechanics depot." In this way, pawnshops functioned as a "storage and loan" for working-class families.[27]

Pawning offered advantages over other remedies for distress. Compared with charity, it was more convenient, and did not require the humiliation of an interview. Unlike straight cash lending, no elaborate contract was needed. In addition, the pawnshop provided quick money on unused collateral. Waiting for charity or a cash loan extended the borrower's distress, and help might not come until after the need had passed.

But, of course, there was a large disadvantage. While "usury" was considered to be any rate of interest above 6 percent per year, interest on pawn loans could reach as high as 300 percent, or even higher, on the smallest loans.[28] The high rate was explained less by the pawnbroker's greed than by the nature of small lending. Most pawn loans were small, around five dollars or less. Yet lending one dollar required the same time and labor as lending a hundred dollars. At 250 pawns per day, pawnbrokers had to charge higher rates on small loans in order to receive a return that would make them profitable.[29] Legal interest rates were laid down by a patchwork quilt of state and municipal laws regulating pawnbroking. New York City, for example, fixed a sliding rate of interest that allowed a high of 3 percent per month on loans under one hundred dollars, and 2 percent per month on larger loans. But extra charges for insurance and "hanging up" clothing could make the actual rate much higher.[30]

In the second half of the nineteenth century, concern over high rates prompted the establishment of charitable pawnshops, but they played a small role in the credit system. Inspired by the French *monts-de-piété*, philanthropic pawnshops in the United States were private and semipublic businesses that aimed to lend money at low rates, with secure storage, honest dealings, and in dignified settings that philanthropists hoped would save the "self-respect" of female pawners. Rates ranged from 1.5 percent per month at the Pawner's Bank of Boston, established in 1859 and the oldest of the charity pawnshops, to an even lower rate of 1 percent offered by the Provident Loan Society of New York, the largest and best organized of this type of lender. But lending at low rates could only be profitable if philanthropic pawnbrokers lent higher amounts on items of higher value. In fact, charitable pawnshops made loans averaging five times the amount loaned by regular pawnbrokers. By century's end, the principal effect of philanthropic pawning was to encourage a dual pawnbroking system. High-grade pawnshops catered mostly to skilled workers, offering loans on jewelry and other small, high-value items. Low-grade pawnshops continued to lend very small amounts on clothing and items of personal value.[31]

SMALL-LOAN LENDERS: SHARKS AND LEECHES

Pawnbrokers were important lenders in the working-class credit system of the nineteenth century, but they were not the only cash lenders, or the largest. One investigator in New York City estimated that two-thirds of the city's total lending came from small-loan agencies.[32] These businesses were operated by men of capital who loaned small amounts of money—in the range of ten to forty dollars—for short periods of time, at rates often well above the statutory limits. For security, small-loan companies accepted either chattel mortgages or assignments of the borrower's wages, sometimes specializing in one or the other. Some loan companies were chain outlets, such as those belonging to D. H. Tolman, who owned offices in sixty-three cities. Of whatever type, small-loan outfits sustained a voluminous business in any American city with over twenty-five thousand people.[33]

Small-loan companies lacked the picturesque exoticism of the pawnbroker's shop. If the pawnbroker's windows were crowded with a material record of human heartbreak and misery for all the world to see, small-loan lenders usually operated under a cloud of illegality and conducted their business out of sight of the public eye.[34] Business was conducted in inconspicuous rooms often located on second floors at the top of a dark flight of stairs. Furnishings were sparse, both to save capital and, when officers of the law came calling, to make flight easier. In states where the need for credit was greatest, the small-loan business was made effectively illegal by general usury laws setting the legal interest rate at 6 percent per annum. As reformers later argued, it was impossible to make small loans at 6 percent and run a profitable business. Small lenders stayed in business only because usury laws were sporadically enforced and because a number of subterfuges allowed them to hide behind a tissue of legality. A lender might require borrowers to purchase a worthless oil painting in order to compensate for a loan of "6 percent." Even more ingenious, D. H. Tolman, whose chain of lenders relied on wage assignments for security, claimed that his offices were not money lenders at all but "salary buyers" who were no more subject to usury laws than any other traders in commodity futures.[35]

Contemporary critics alleged that small lenders charged absurdly high rates of interest, even as high as 1,000 percent. Legal testimony shows that this was true in some cases, but simple an-

Figure 5. A Chicago tobacco shop, circa 1900. But note the signs in the archway
advertising "Chattel Loans" and directing borrowers up the flight of stairs to
an office for the A. E. Greenwood and Company, small-loan brokers.
Small-loan offices were abundant in late nineteenth-century cities,
but borrowers—and the law—had to look hard for them.
(Chicago Historical Society, ICHi 21766)

nual interest rates more generally ranged from 20 to 300 percent.[36]
As would be expected, the smaller the loan, the higher the rate. But
as with pawnbrokers, the high rates could be explained by the nature of the market economy in which small lenders operated. Because smaller loans carried higher risks and lower profits, in order
to stay in business lenders were forced to charge rates well in excess
of the standard banking rate of 6 percent. Even so, the rates were
clearly illegal and clearly inequitable when compared to the 6 percent rate given commercial businessmen. This earned small lenders
the opprobrium of being "sharks, leeches, and remorseless extortioners."[37]

In spite of public scorn, illegal lenders played a major role in
helping working-class families make ends meet. A conservative

51

estimate numbers the small-loan offices in New York City in 1907 at 70; Pittsburgh had 37; and Chicago, where the first professional small lenders appeared in 1870, had 139 loan offices in 1916.[38] In New York City, Clarence Wassam's careful investigations in 1907 discovered that loan sharks received weekly payments from 90 percent of the employees of the largest transportation company. A similar study by Arthur Ham led him to set the number of workers in the nation who owed money to loan sharks at one in five. This seems like a high number, but data for Pittsburgh compiled by Peter Shergold show that Ham may have underestimated. As Shergold has concluded, "One fact is indisputable—small loans were a big business."[39]

Loan sharks catered to a class of borrowers that overlapped the high end of the pawnbroker's clientele. The nature of the small lender's security made it imperative that borrowers have a steady income or own some item of high value, like a piano or suite of furniture. Loan office records made public by Progressive reformers clearly show that workers with marginal incomes were not the loan shark's principal borrowers. Borrowers came in an impressive variety, but they tended to be government employees (including firemen and policemen), low-level white-collar workers, and skilled tradesmen and foremen. Thus, loan offices served the credit needs of moderate-income workers who struggled to keep up with their middle-class ambitions.[40]

Unlike most pawnbrokers, whose shop windows were their only advertisement, loan sharks used a variety of aggressive methods to solicit customers. They relied heavily on newspaper advertisements in the major dailies, whose classified sections were filled with loan agency ads emphasizing secrecy, convenience, and respectability. Some ads were modest:

> EMPLOYEES who need money, appreciate absolute privacy,
> prompt action, address Box 284, Madison Square.

Others grabbed attention with promises of "Holiday Money," "Vacation Money," or just "Money!" And other advertisements worked very hard to lure customers:

CAN'T STOP THE RUN ON HERON AND CO.
The line is getting longer every minute, but we still continue
to hand out money.

NO SCARCITY OF READY CASH HERE.
Come and get all you need on your name; we procure the money
for you without mortgage or endorsers. The only requirement
that you are working and holding a steady position. No one need
ever know. You can pay us in small, easy payments that soon get
you out of debt.

OUR RATES THE CHEAPEST. OUR TERMS THE EASIEST.
Our office private.

HERE IS THE PLACE
99 NASSAU ST., ROOM 715.[41]

Business was also drummed up with circulars delivered through the mail. With promises of "happiness and sunlight," mass mailings were sent just before holidays and vacation periods, or mailed to persons known to have past-due accounts with other lenders. Prospective borrowers were also pulled in by solicitors. Solicitors often were customers of the loan office working on commission in order to repay their own debts. Loan offices also secured the part-time services of foremen, timekeepers, barbers, and other persons who were likely to know people who needed money.[42]

A visit to the loan office was a very different procedure than shopping a pawn.[43] To begin with, most loan office agents were women. Owners found that female agents could be hired more cheaply and, in the event of tough talk, were less likely to be assaulted. Agents asked prospective borrowers to complete an application with perhaps fifty questions relating to past and present employment, their current financial situation, and credit references. Signatures were also required on other complicated-looking documents, including a promissory note for the amount being borrowed, a mortgage of chattels or an assignment of wages, a form giving power of attorney to impound the security, and a statement of present indebtedness. Since illegal interest was being charged, such documents had no real legal standing. But loan sharks banked on the ignorance and gullibility of borrowers and hoped the impressive documents would reduce the number of "skips."

While the applicant waited at home, a credit investigation verified the information on the forms. This could take one or two days. Even the smallest loans on chattel mortgages required that references be checked. Loans were quickly approved for those who worked for companies that forbade wage assignments, because threatening a man with his job was the ultimate collection tactic. Without this threat, loan offices usually required the additional security of two or three endorsers.

After the loan was approved and money handed over to the borrower, the problem of collections began. Payments were scheduled for every payday, so most loans required weekly payments. For an average loan of twenty-five dollars, payments were scheduled for thirteen weeks. If the borrower met his obligations on time he received a receipt at the final payment and all the documents were destroyed. But delinquent accounts prompted a chain of progressive enforcements. Lenders differed in their patience, but the general pattern of collection began with contacting the delinquent borrower first through letters, then telephone calls, then personal visits. For the latter, small lenders relied on the professional services of the "bawlerout," a female employee who was assigned the job of trapping the delinquent borrower before co-workers and family in order to browbeat him publicly for being a sorry deadbeat.[44] If harassment proved unsuccessful, lenders had two options: execute a judgment for the delinquent's mortgaged property or wages (not usually a real option given the illegality of the loan), or arrange for the debt to be repaid with another loan, usually from another loan company.

With all of the risks and paperwork involved in getting money from a loan office, how is it that loan sharks conducted a larger volume of business than pawnbrokers? Advertising and aggressive solicitation had something to do with it. In addition, loan sharks typically offered more credit than pawnbrokers. This in turn was made possible by the loan shark's primary advantage: the method of his lending. The small, weekly payments made possible the larger loans because they provided an enforced discipline that made repayment easier, even while concealing the levy of a high rate of interest. Finally, a loan on chattel mortgage or wage assignment, unlike a pawn, did not require anything to be sacrificed up front. This must have been an important consideration for many.

PEDDLERS AND BORAX HOUSES

Loansharking was closely connected to a third leg of the credit system: retail lending. Small loans, in fact, often refinanced the debts of people who had fallen behind on their retail installment payments. Thus, the rising number of loan sharks in the late nineteenth century went hand in hand with the rising importance of installment credit, which became a common method of capitalizing the poor and low-income family's home.[45]

As will be related in Chapter 4, when installment selling first appeared in the early 1800s, it was conservatively managed and extended as a privilege to people of means. But during the 1880s and 1890s installment buying became a fixture in the financial management of working-class households. The practice seems to have become popular first among immigrant families who needed goods but could little afford to pay cash for them. Into this situation stepped the "custom" peddler, who made the immigrant family's need his own opportunity. Selling door to door on installment terms, peddlers acted as "pullers-in," middlemen hired by large retail stores to pull immigrant customers into the American world of department store shopping.

The peddling trade worked in the following manner. An immigrant wanting to break into the retail trade, but lacking previous trade or professional experience, would arrange with a store or a wholesaler for credit. A line of credit would then be used to finance a stock of items known to be in high demand in the immigrant's own neighborhood, including furniture, housewares, sewing machines, clothing, jewelry, and assorted ornamental wares. Now the immigrant was in business. He peddled his goods within a network of customers that over the years, if everything went well, would be built up into the hundreds and even thousands. Contacts were not hard to make because many immigrants found American consumer culture a little bewildering. Problems of language and shopping etiquette could make a trip to the stores an embarrassing, not to mention expensive, business. For this reason, many immigrant women welcomed a peddler who could teach them the ropes of American-style consumption, even taking them to the right stores and showing them exactly what they needed to buy. When they were not working as consumer counselors, peddlers sold their own goods on an extremely lenient installment basis. Maria Ganz recalled that the peddler who sold her mother a sewing machine called on her family for twenty-five cents a week for eighteen years until the debt was fully paid off. In the meantime he had become a trusted family friend.[46]

The successful example of installment peddlers encouraged some retail stores to switch from cash selling and/or thirty-day credit terms to installment plan merchandising. Competition forced others to follow suit, and in the 1880s a new kind of business was created: the "borax" store. "Borax" referred to cheap, shoddy, overpriced goods sold to low- and moderate-income customers on installments through high-pressure sales tactics. It is not clear how the name for this kind of store originated. It is likely that "borax" is a corruption of the Yiddish word for credit (borgs). Whether this is true or not, English-speaking customers were quick to compare goods of this type to borax because both "cleaned a person out." For this reason, borax retailers seriously compromised the respectability of installment buying among middle-class shoppers, who accounted for only a small volume of total installment merchandising.[47]

The borax installment business was primarily concentrated in the furniture and clothing trades. Customers desiring to pay on installments were investigated as to their employment and character and, if found satisfactory, goods were sold to them on weekly payment terms that varied widely. In Boston, a retail trade investigation of 1899 found that half of the city's furniture dealers sold primarily on installments. These were of the class selling medium- and low-grade goods to working-class families, and they sold on

Figure 6. Bell's Easy Payment Store, South State Street, Chicago. "We Trust the People" was the motto of this turn-of-the-century borax house specializing in men's clothing. Bell's motto contrasted with the policy of the store next door, whose sign proclaimed Lloyd's Dry Goods a "cash dealer."
(Chicago Historical Society, CRC-95B)

average 75 percent of their goods on installments. In the clothing trade, one large store reported that it had thirty-five thousand customers, of which 95 percent bought on the installment plan. These patterns seem to have been typical for most major cities.[48]

Credit on installments made sense in a number of ways. From the dealer's point of view, competition made it essential that every possible means be used to widen the market of prospective buyers. In addition, some retailers discovered what became the driving principle of modern consumer credit: that high interest rates concealed under "easy" weekly terms meant there was money to be made in credit sales. From the consumer's perspective, buying out of future income solved the vexing problem of how to buy goods when low wages made saving money a difficult proposition. Moreover, installment credit made it possible to "buy up," that is, to purchase goods more expensive and durable than could be bought with cash alone.

But, of course, "buying up" was not a motivation limited to families on the lower steps of the social ladder.

A POVERTY OF WHICH NO MAN HEARETH

If the large and increasing volume of debt in the Gilded Age owed something to working-class poverty, middle-class prosperity also had something to do with it. Poor and working-class families with small incomes typically borrowed money under the pressure of economic emergencies in order to prevent their low standard of living from declining further. Middle-class households, by contrast, typically borrowed money to improve their standard of living. For them, credit satisfied "needs" that were more social and psychic.

By the late nineteenth century, much of what it meant to be "middle class" lay in a style of living that required ownership of a home and an array of commodities to adorn the home.[49] But homes and household goods did not come cheaply. Consequently, many families with bourgeois aspirations resorted to purchasing the symbols of middle-class life out of future earnings. Middle-class Victorians have been lionized as patient patrons of the savings bank, and many were. But contemporaries sometimes expressed a different view. "There is a poverty of which no man heareth," observed investigators of the standard of living in Boston in 1870, whose study of middle-class homes resulted in a report on what they called "the poverty of the middle class." The middle-class worker had a higher income than the low-paid unskilled worker, but, as the investigators pointed out, "the wage of the one, though double, it may be, of that of the other, is consumed in his necessary cost of living."[50] The net result of higher incomes and higher expenses was that middle-class people required access to credit just as much as lower-class families.

This point can be illustrated with the case of a young, newly married couple in St. Paul, Minnesota, whose surviving letters reveal how they capitalized their home. In the early months of 1895, Walter and Lillie Post decided they had had enough of bare walls and uncovered floors in their rented house. Post, a railroad clerk, did not like being in debt, and Lillie liked it even less. But "getting trusted" was the only way the couple could afford to furnish their house. One hundred fifty dollars bought them two rooms of furniture, carpets, and a stove, on terms of one hundred dollars down and the balance in sixty days.[51] The credit experience of the Posts was not uncommon. "Has not the middle class its poverty?" asked labor leader Ira Steward in 1873. "Very few among them are saving money. Many of them are in debt; and all they can earn for years, is, in many cases, mortgaged to pay such debt."[52]

On the Book and on Time

The case of the Posts illustrates that retail credit was not a strategy of financial management limited to the poor and the working class. In fact, it played a large role in the lives of many "thrifty" middle-class Victorians.

In the early days of the Republic, when money was hard to come by due to a shortage of specie, buying goods on "book credit"— which got its name from the log book in which credit purchases were recorded—for thirty days or a crop season was almost the universal practice among American households. After the Civil War, book credit declined in relation to the total volume of retail sales, though outstanding volume still increased. Because the long deflation of prices in the late nineteenth century made collections harder to manage, retailers in agricultural areas pressed for more frequent settlements. In the cities, a number of grocers, druggists, and shoe stores converted to a cash-only business. Still, even though open-book credit terms were reined in after 1875, the "grocer book" and the "butcher book" continued to be common family institutions. "Buying on tic" remained, after home mortgage credit, the largest single source of credit in the credit system.[53]

If book credit from some merchants dried up, retail installment credit more than compensated. A high-grade installment trade helped an increasing number of families to buy the goods that defined a middle-class life: furniture sets, pianos, encyclopedias, books. Furniture dealers sold sets averaging seventy-five to one hundred dollars on terms, generally, of 10 percent down and payments for up to eighteen months. The installment plan, or buying "on time" as it was known then, was introduced to many families by sewing machine salesmen after 1851. Terms for a thirty-dollar machine were one dollar down and fifty cents a week, which meant that the debt would often run for more than a year. Noting the success of the sewing machine agents, other retailers of big ticket items adopted the installment plan. Pianos and organs costing five hundred to one thousand dollars typically were sold on a one-third down payment and arrangements for the debt to be paid off in two to three years. After 1870, itinerant book agents roamed the country selling sets of books—such as the eighth and ninth editions of the *Encyclopedia Britannica*, Bible commentaries, and Shakespeare—door to door on installments. Other items sold on installments were stoves, kitchenware, musical instruments, and jewelry. Mortgage statistics from midwestern states show that installment buying was steadily becoming a more important tool of financial management in the late nineteenth century. A critic of the installment plan complained in 1890 that the new rule for family finance seemed to be "spend before you make, in anticipation of your making."[54]

Installment contracts took the form of a lease or chattel mortgage. This gave retailers the option of repossession in the event of delinquency. Defaults were not uncommon, but they remained well within acceptable levels, probably because middle-class installment buyers were treated with more leniency than borax store customers.[55]

FRIENDS AND FAMILY

Working-class wage earners were not the only ones to have problems meeting payments on store account credit. Walter Post, the railroad clerk from St. Paul, planned to pay his debts with unbudgeted income from his weekly pay, but good intentions were not enough. By year's end in 1895, the Posts owed money not only to the furniture store, but also to the doctor, the dentist, the tailor, the hardware store, and the sewing machine agent. "I wish I could get hold of about $25 for four or five months time, so I could get my stove paid for," Post wrote home to his parents. His father did not take the hint. But Walter found his brother and a local friend to be more sympathetic. He tapped them both for twenty-five dollars and paid off the stove. When it came time to pay his brother back, Post asked for and received an extension on the loan. But later in the year his brother desperately needed the money back. Post put him off for months, suggesting that his brother borrow from someone else, but eventually he gave in to his brother's pleas and made a payment of twenty dollars. "I am as anxious to settle with you and get it off my mind as you are to get it," Post wrote his brother. "If you are at your wit's end I don't know what you would call it in my case, for I have to do some awful close figuring to make ends meet and then they don't meet." It is not known if Post ever fully satisfied the loan; a few months later he lost his job with the railroad and he and Lillie left St. Paul.[56]

When Walter Post and other Americans of the late nineteenth century needed a loan, one option available to them was to court the financial reserves of friends and family. Not surprisingly, lending of this type is impossible to quantify. But a few tentative generalizations can be made. We know friendly lending existed, that it was under fire, and that its importance in the credit system was probably declining.

Through the early nineteenth century, friendly lending provided almost the only source of cash funds for small borrowers. Banks were few and institutional lenders nonexistent. Agricultural and commercial loans could be obtained from agents fronting British, and, eventually, eastern capital, but cash money for personal use was more readily obtained through local networks of highly personalized credit relations. T. H. Breen has examined such relations among Virginia's tidewater planters in the Revolutionary War period. Breen describes how a "culture of debt" made borrowing and lending much more than mere economic transactions. Loans were used to cement friendships, build trust, and extend patronage. A complex "etiquette of debt" governed who got credit and how much, whether interest would be charged, whether loans would be extended and for how long, and whether a court record or a simple handshake was enough to seal a loan. Among the Tidewater planters, as elsewhere, lending and borrowing constituted major patterns in the warp and woof of community life.[57]

The "culture of debt" described by Breen was gradually dissolved in the nineteenth century by more democratic social relations and more impersonal economic relations. But literary evidence at midcentury suggests that friendly lending continued to be common. William Taylor Adams's popular "Oliver Optic" tales are filled with examples of loans between friends and family members.[58] Moreover, in the financial advice literature of the period, family and friends are assumed to be the major source for personal credit. Thus, for example, when Freeman Hunt of *Hunt's Merchant's Magazine* wanted to explain the nation's complicated mercantile credit system, he wrote an imaginary dialogue between a cotton merchant and his young daughter, where the merchant wants to know why his daughter is anxious for him to sell some cotton:

PA: "Well?"

LITTLE DAUGHTER: "Then you could pay ma that gold twenty dollar piece you borrowed of her, you know papa."

PA: "And what then, minx?"

LITTLE DAUGHTER: "Then mamma could pay Aunt Sara that ten dollars she owes her."

PA: "Ay, indeed! And what then?"

LITTLE DAUGHTER: "And Aunt Sara would pay sister Jane that dollar she promised to give her on New Year's, but didn't, 'cos she didn't have no cotton, I mean money, pa."

PA: "Well, and what else?" (Pa lays down the paper and looks at her curiously, with a half smile.)

LITTLE DAUGHTER: "Cousin Jane would pay brother John his fifty cents back, and he said when he got it he would give me the half dime he owes me, and two dimes to buy marbles, and this is what I want the rivers to rise for, and the big boats to run! And I owe nurse the other dime, and must pay my debts."

Hunt chose this story as "the best delineation of the credit system" because he wished to humanize the mysteries of the impersonal market. But his homely vignette assumes that people would identify with a family where each member is a banker for the other members.[59]

Advice literature like Hunt's says something about the prevalence of friendly lending in the middle class, but what about low-income families? They also borrowed and lent among each other, but there is reason to believe that friendly lending existed on a much larger scale among middle-class households. Obviously, industrial laborers had less savings to draw on for loans to one another. To make up for this problem, immigrant communities often organized mutual benefit societies as sources for credit.[60] Moreover, industrial workers do not seem to have modeled their charity after business loans, with written "contracts" and expected terms, a practice so common among middle-class lenders it led a scandalized William Dean Howells to allege that anyone who did not "take and give usury" with his brother felt secretly "defrauded." Rather, loans were made as gifts, with vague expectations that generosity would some day be returned.[61] In addition, friendly lending among some immigrant groups was positively discouraged. Sociologist Robert Park reported that Italians refused to lend to one another, keeping their savings a secret and using the services of the *giornale di Sicilia* ("local gossips") to shun people who might be asking for a loan. In the Italian community studied by Park, immigrants preferred to borrow from pawnbrokers than from their neighbors.[62]

By the late nineteenth century, it seems likely that family and neighborly lending was declining relative to other credit sources. That it remained common is apparent from Victorian financial advice books, which continued to find it necessary to recommend against the practice. Friendly lending was an "insidiously dangerous indulgence" counseled H. L. Reade in *Money and How to Make It*. Friendship, he and others advised, was best preserved when requests for loans were refused.[63] But if small loans between neighbors had once served to seal the bonds of friendship, their declining importance in the Gilded Age credit system had less to do with the prudent advice of Victorian financial counselors than with other factors. Demand lessened as many borrowers no doubt preferred the business-like impersonality of institutional credit to the embarrassment of asking friends for money. Moreover, urbanization and increasing mobility were disrupting the settled, intimate relationships that made the eighteenth-century culture of debt possible.

A Most Interesting Problem in Practical Finance

In a report for the Massachusetts Bureau of Labor Statistics in 1870, an economist working for the bureau observed that the middle-class home "calls for the satisfaction of a thousand wants."[64] This is the reason why retail and friendly credit appeared so often on middle-class balance sheets: often the only way for a couple to fill a house with carpets, furniture, cooking equipment, and a piano was by buying on credit. But what required the most credit was the house itself. "About everyone that lives in what he calls his own house, is in debt!" observed a Massachusetts shoe leather cutter in 1870.[65] In fact, in the late nineteenth century, home mortgages accounted for the largest single portion of household debt.

In *Acres of Diamonds*, Russell Conwell's panegyric to the American way of wealth and the most widely heard lecture of the late nineteenth century, the founder of Temple University maintained that "a man is not really a true man until he owns his own home."[66] Conwell borrowed these words from Walt Whitman, who in turn was simply expressing the sentiment of millions of Americans whose greatest dream was to live in a "home, sweet, home" of their own. But living in a home was one thing, and purchasing it another. Buying a home presented, in the words of a journalist studying the problem in 1876, "a most interesting problem in practical finance." "The paying for it, the winning it," he observed, "is the most interesting part of the whole story."[67]

In the late nineteenth century, the recommended strategy for buying a home was to save money first and then build the house. Thus, in Oliver Optic's "The Savings Bank; Or How to Buy a House," a young wife says to her husband, "If you only had the habit of saving, you would be able to build a house in a few years."[68] Because saving was a ritual requiring the sacrifice of needless expenditures, proponents of domesticity intended the home to be a moral force for good even before a family could move in to its nurturing environment.

So much for the ideal. Savings banks prospered, but theirs was not the financial strategy that put up most of the homes built in the Gilded Age. In the last third of the nineteenth century, houses for low- and moderate-income families ranged in price from $1,000 to $4,500. Thus, in order to buy a modest home of $1,500, a family earning $1,000 a year—about the average salary of white-collar clerical workers—would have to save one-tenth of its income per year for fifteen years. Most did not want to wait that long.

Sam Bass Warner has described how home mortgages worked in the suburbs of Boston in the late nineteenth century.[69] There, he found "a great uniformity of behavior" in the strategies used to finance a home. Prospective home builders, inexperienced with high finance and making the step of a lifetime with hard-earned savings, tended to follow the pattern set by others. In the case of a typical house and lot costing $3,000, the first step to home ownership was to accumulate a savings of $1,500, or roughly half the price of the desired home. Having settled on a lot, the builder then paid $500 cash for the property and put down $1,000 for materials and labor to build the house. The remaining $1,500 was raised with two mortgages. The first mortgage was obtained from a savings bank or, more likely, from one of thousands of private small investors working through downtown mortgage dealers. The first mortgage raised $1,200 (40 percent of the sales price) at 5–6 percent interest and had legal priority over all other debts. When the building neared completion, a second mortgage for $300

(10 percent of the sales price) at 6–8 percent was obtained from a real-estate professional. Thus, when the builder moved into his home, he owed $1,500, and the real work of financing was ahead of him. Using the device of the "straight" mortgage, builders were required to pay interest payments semiannually for the next three to eight years, and the payment of the principal in a lump sum at the end of the term.

Warner found a uniformity of method within Boston, but elsewhere methods for financing a house varied from place to place, neighborhood to neighborhood, and even from mortgagor to mortgagor. A turn-of-the-century investigation of the small housing market in Greater New York City reported that houses were being sold with either one or two straight mortgages and on a variety of installment contracts. One forward-looking plan even offered twenty-year mortgages.[70]

Diversity was also emphasized in eighty-six testimonials published in the *Ladies Home Journal* in 1903. These home builders put up their houses with funds borrowed from relatives, from public and private building and loan associations, from previous owners, from individuals loaning their savings at interest, and from a variety of banks. Methods of financing could get complex. One strategy had the borrower obtaining building supplies and hardware on credit, borrowing twice from a loan office to pay half the money owed on supplies, and securing a mortgage for the rest from a building and loan association—four loans of three different types to build one house! Most down payments were substantial by present standards; one-half or more of the purchase price. But many were less, and some only 10 percent. Rates ranged from 4 to 10 percent, and length of term from a few months to ten years. Nationwide, the typical arrangement for home financing was a mortgage for 69 percent of the sales price, obtained from individual savers with money to lend, savings banks, or building and loan associations, at 5–6 percent interest, for five years. But this should not be allowed to obscure the creative diversity in the sources, methods, and terms of home financing.[71]

In terms of methods, the most important home mortgage lender of the Gilded Age was the building and loan association. Building and loans were cooperative societies designed to make homes affordable for families of modest means. First organized in Philadelphia in 1831, building and loans spread rapidly until there were 5,838 operating in 1893, holding mortgages of half a billion dollars. This made them the third largest home mortgage lender, after private individuals and savings banks.[72] But with their unique method of repayment they made a primary contribution to the history of household credit.

Operating as banks without vaults and, in many cases, without offices and salaried officials, building and loan associations allowed prospective home buyers to invest their savings in the shares of an association. Ultimately, the individual would borrow against those shares in order to finance a house at a low rate of interest. But the method was complicated. Generally, borrowers were required to subscribe for an amount of stock equal to the loan they wished to borrow. Along with a membership fee and premium paid for the loan (determined by auction), the borrower paid monthly interest on the loan at 6 percent and monthly installment payments on the shares. When the shares were paid up, the loan was effectively liquidated. Thus, a typical plan worked in the following manner. A man wanting to borrow $1,400 for a house would buy ten shares in a local association, at one dollar each. As a member of the association, he would be allowed to bid for the privilege of receiving a loan for $2,000, which typically could be obtained at a 30 percent premium. Making the bid, he received an actual loan of $1,400 to pay his contractor to put up the house. For security, the house and the borrower's shares were mortgaged to the association. Repayment of the loan occurred gradually as the new homeowner continued to pay monthly dues on his ten shares and interest on the loan to the association. In eight or nine years the debt was declared paid and the mortgage released. As a pioneer and early historian of the building and loan industry later admitted, "the contract was crude and very few people understood it." But the end result was easily understood: unlike with the straight mortgage, in this scheme of credit interest *and* principal were paid off in monthly payments. Thus, the building and loan method essentially provided for an amortized home mortgage. Amortization, where both principal and interest are paid off together in fixed, monthly payments for the term of the loan, was elsewhere practiced by a few individual lenders, but it did not become popular until the 1920s.[73]

Since amortization made loans much safer for both borrower and lender, it is hard to explain why other mortgage lenders continued to use the method of the single-maturity note. Inertia and ease of administration probably had something to do with it. But it is easy to see why building and loan associations were necessary in the first place. The largest institutional sources of money in 1900 were the nation's twelve thousand commercial banks, but they were not lending money for homes, or for any other "consumptive" purpose. The "soundness" theory of banking discouraged commercial bankers from loaning on anything other than short-term thirty- and sixty-day notes that could be called in quickly. Since real-estate mortgages locked up money for a long period of time, commercial banks declined to assume the risks and the administrative problems of home mortgage lending, while, until 1916, national banks were prevented by law from making real-estate mortgage loans.[74]

At the turn of the century, home ownership in the United States ranged from a low of 11 percent in New York City to a high of 58 percent in Toledo, Ohio (interestingly, the highest rates were among settled immigrants).[75] Most of these homes were bought with mortgages. Stephan Thernstrom's study of workers in Newburyport, Massachusetts, found that about half of the property owners financed their homes with a mortgage. In the *Ladies Home Journal* "How We Saved for Our Home" report of 1903, three out of four homeowners reported they shortened their timetable for moving into a house of their own by using a mortgage to build the house. Census figures show that on 1 January 1890, mortgages were taken out on 29 percent of the homes in the United States, with an average debt of $1,139 per home.[76]

Except for the wealthiest families, mortgage buying compelled homeowners to practice strategies of economy over a long period of time. Letters sent to the 1903 *Ladies Home Journal* survey on house financing often spoke of the joys of home ownership, but also of the "close calculation" and the "struggle, toil, and labor" needed to pay off such large debts. Mortgagees often reported that debt for the home required them to pay cash for everything else, to cut out nonessential consumption, and to adopt strict budgeting procedures. "It was all a question of management," a man from Virginia wrote, explaining how he and his family paid off their loan:

> Bless me, how we did economize. . . . The lifetime of a garment extended far beyond the allotted span for such things. We walked, disdaining street cars. It was good exercise and saved the nickels which were needed to pay interest on our mortgage. We bought the high-priced articles less often; the lower-priced more frequently. I was my own bootblack and barber. Indeed we might almost call our house the house of small economies, for it certainly was only by saving in small matters that we were able to secure it.[77]

The financial discipline imposed by purposeful indebtedness left its mark on people. "So deeply was the habit of saving rooted within us," reported a homeowner from Missouri who had recently retired the mortgage on his house, "we have continued to save, to some extent, and now . . . have bought and paid for several other houses."[78] In this way did millions of Americans who never crossed the threshold of a pawnshop or borax store, or who always paid cash when they went to the store, discovered that credit could be used to convert distant dreams into a present reality. In the process they also learned that debt was a hard master.

Trends in the Gilded Age Credit System

This snapshot view of credit in the Gilded Age risks conveying the impression that credit before consumer credit was static before the winds of change began blowing in the 1910s. Two late nineteenth-century developments are worth noting.

The first was a trend toward increased cash buying of nondurable and even some durable goods among households with enough income to provide a modicum of economic security. The cash ideal was, of course, a cherished principle in the Victorian money management ethic. "Purchasing with ready money," advised William Cobbett in 1831, "really gives you more money to purchase with."[79] Since some retailers offered discounts for cash purchases, cash buying could effect considerable savings. At the same time, the psychology of cash purchasing was said to limit frivolous purchases. "A 'running account' with the grocer, the baker, the tailor, the dressmaker, presents a strong temptation," counseled a financial advice book in the 1870s. "Cash for all such things," the writer went on to say, "should be the invariable rule."[80]

For most of the money-starved nineteenth century, the cash ideal was hard to live up to so long as cash itself was hard to come by. But in the 1880s and 1890s, some middle-class households who wanted to were able to finance their lives on nearly a cash basis. This was made possible by rising disposable income. Clarence Long's painstaking analysis of wage surveys shows that real wages of workers increased 50 percent from 1860 to 1890. Most of this increase occurred after 1880 when rising wages joined with falling prices to boost disposable income. Unfortunately, it is not possible to say whether incomes of white-collar workers mirrored or led this trend; at any rate, it seems doubtful that they lagged behind. Either way, the rise in income made it increasingly possible for some households to pay cash for goods.[81]

More specific evidence for an increase in cash buying can be found in the trade journals and account books of retailers. Since at least the 1820s merchants tried in vain to convince customers to buy goods for cash. Discounts of 10 to 30 percent for cash-paying customers were not unusual. This strategy was usually employed when the merchant's own credit was suffering as a result of overly lenient credit terms for customers. But cash-buying campaigns typically met with almost no success. Through midcentury, account books in the Middle West show a business of only one-fourth to one-third for cash, and these cash entries included bartered transactions. According to Lewis Atherton, historian of the merchants of the Middle West, attempts to convince customers to pay in cash "worked only in theory." When "everyone wanted to buy on time because wealth was just around the corner," merchants found it impossible to escape the credit system.[82]

In the depression years of the 1870s, retail merchants tried even harder to convert to the cash system. The *American Grocer*, a Chicago publication, devoted much print in the 1870s to promoting the idea of "cash and carry." One editorial concluded:

> The value of a snug cash business has never had a better opportunity to commend itself to merchants than during the past two months. The men who have gone on serenely and quietly in business, unmoved by the storm around them, are those whose day books show few charges and whose tall balances may be presented on a few lines. They are the men who are able to walk into the biggest house in this city with a roll of bank bills in their pockets, ask for bottom prices, and if they don't get them, walk out again.[83]

About this time, a certain Currier and Ives lithograph found its way onto the walls of many retailers to announce their tougher stance on extending credit. The print featured a dead hound dog named "Trust" beneath a lettering of "deadbeats" whose bodies were arranged to spell out the message: "Poor Trust Is Dead / Bad Pay Killed Him."[84]

The cash and carry idea, made urgent in the hard times of the 1870s, began to achieve modest results in the more prosperous 1880s. A report commissioned by the American Economic Association in 1887 found that there was still "a strong tendency to avoid credits in buying and selling," and that the more "experienced" dealers were "settling down to a cash basis."[85] This was certainly true of several of the giants in department store and mail-order retailing. In the late nineteenth century, A. T. Stewart's, Macy's, Sears and Roebuck, J. C. Penney's, and Montgomery Ward's were well known for their cash-only policies, which the companies claimed saved their customers 25–50 percent of what credit-granting stores charged for the same goods. Sears in particular used its catalog to preach against "the evil of the credit system" and in favor of cash on the barrelhead.[86]

But there were other voices, other messages. In 1904, the popular Lit Brothers department store in Philadelphia asked its charge customers to recommend the names of "*Not More Than Three* of your acquaintances, to whom we shall be pleased to extend the privilege of an account with us." Campaigns for new charge accounts were made possible by administrative reforms implemented by most department stores in the 1880s and 1890s, which included the centralization of credit operations. As more stores courted the patronage of charge account buyers, clerks were confronted with more and more customers showing up at the counters and expecting charge privileges. To help with identification and to speed up transactions, around the turn of the century merchants began issuing small, metal identification plates to valued charge customers. By the 1920s these "charge plates"—forerunners of the modern credit card—were common in stores throughout the country. Meanwhile, competition from borax installment retailers forced concessions among the cash-only department stores. In 1903, Wanamaker's of Philadelphia relaxed its cash-only policies and began selling pianos on installment terms. A decade later, middle-class customers in New York City could walk into several of their favorite department stores and buy pianos, phonographs, sewing machines, and kitchen cabinets on monthly payment plans. On the basis of such developments, William Leach and Susan Strasser, authors of two of the most comprehensive and provocative histories of modern retailing, have argued that by the end of the Gilded Age department stores were well on their way to developing modern systems of charge account buying.[87]

In spite of increased buying for cash in some areas of the country on the part of some consumers, credit hardly disappeared. "There are hosts of people today who have money in hand and are letting their grocers, butchers, milkman, and others who supply the necessities of life go unpaid," Lyman Abbott chided from the editor's chair of the *Outlook* in 1907. This champion of progressive causes referred not to poor workers but to "people who can still spend money on the theater, the opera, concerts, and other forms of entertainment"—middle- and upper-middle-class people, in other words.[88] " 'Charge It,' " a retail credit man wrote a few years later, "is the slogan of the great American consumer."[89] His comment points to a second trend in the Gilded Age credit system: though cash buying became the practice for some, on the whole credit for consumption continued to expand.

When the U.S. census in 1890 estimated the minimum private debt of the nation's households to be $11 billion, superintendent of the census Robert Porter allowed that debt was often "an indication of prosperity." Still, Porter hastened to add that he hoped publication of the statistics on real-estate mortgage debt would "bring the people to their sober senses." Declaring that the 1890 census closed the door on an epoch of "debt-creating mania," Porter confidently announced the dawn of a new era of "retrenchment and debt-paying."[90]

This prediction went unfulfilled. Figures compiled by Raymond Goldsmith show that from 1896 to 1916, short-term household indebtedness increased at rates as high as 15 percent a year and averaging 9.3 percent per annum.[91] Part of this expansion was due to population growth and part to inflation. But the principal part of the increase reflects a growing need and desire for credit. Rising demand put a strain on the existing credit system and made conditions favorable for new sources of supply, offering new forms of credit, with new enticements—in short, for the credit revolution.

But if Porter's hopes were out of step with what was going on all around him, his manner of speaking about debt was not. In fact, his ambivalence toward credit and the vocabulary he drew on to express his feelings about debt were widely shared. Like Porter, many Americans spoke of debt as if it were a symptom of dementia. But also like Porter, many viewed credit as a sign of prosperity, if not the golden key to greater wealth. This seems contradictory to late twentieth-century readers. But in Porter's day the apparent inconsistency was resolved by a way of thinking about debt that helped make the credit revolution possible even as it became a casualty of it. For this reason, how Americans could celebrate credit while denouncing debt is a matter worth pursuing.

Debt in the Victorian
Money Management Ethic

Dᴇʙᴛ ɪꜱ an economic concept. It is also a moral state. To Americans of the nineteenth and early twentieth centuries, the moral nature of debt—involving matters of trust, fidelity to promises, and the balancing of desires with prudence—loomed at least as large as the economics of borrowed money. For this reason, before exploring the rise of installment buying and borrowing, it will be helpful to first map out the moral topography of money, credit, and debt in the years preceding the credit revolution. The results are surprising and explain a lot. Contrary to stereotypes, nineteenth-century Americans did not "fear" debt. Rather, some debts were considered justifiable, others not.

Victorian attitudes about debt were part of a larger constellation of attitudes about credit and money in general. In their lifetimes, Americans of the Victorian era watched society become increasingly monetarized. The effects of this important process on the household have gone largely unstudied, but one result was the production of a popular way of thinking about money, habits of thought and reaction that made sense of the intricacies of household finance. The value of money, the proprieties of personal finance, the meaning of debt—in the Victorian era these themes acquired greater significance than ever before.

This was true especially for people who aspired to be "middle-class" Americans. At the core of what it meant to be middle class was a money management ethic that located personal character in matters of the budget and pocketbook. Because this ethic was culturally ascendant in the period 1830–1920, I call it the Victorian money management ethic.[1] Its flexible boundaries organized the limits, and opened up possibilities, for how consumer credit would be conceived and legitimized.

THE ECONOMICAL CENTURY

In the United States, common idioms for talking and thinking about debt and credit emerged in response to one of the most important developments of nineteenth-century history: the spread of the modern money economy. Between the inflationary early 1830s and the creation of the Federal Reserve System in 1913 (which authorized the currency notes Americans now use for exchange), American society became fully monetarized. The "tinkling of dollars" in American life often drew comment from foreign travelers, many of whom agreed with the French visitor Michael Chevalier who wrote in 1839 that Americans seemed to be "devoured by a passion for money."[2] But it was not that Americans were uniquely avaricious; on the contrary, they were simply the first people in history to deal with the spread of a money economy into every aspect of daily life, bringing with it money that was different in quantity and quality from that of previous eras. This process demanded means of coping that even now are not yet fully understood.[3]

To see how this happened, consider the nature and extent of money in 1800, when nineteen out of twenty Americans lived on farms, and economic exchange operated as it had for centuries. Weeks and even months went by without money passing through a person's hands. Money was scarce because in the colonial period gold and silver had drained out of the domestic economy to satisfy an unfavorable balance of trade with England. This forced merchant colonists to use exotic substitutes like tobacco and furs, and led to the first American experiments with paper money.[4] The money supply improved after independence, but not all that much, especially for people outside the towns. "In my time," wrote an Indiana pioneer of the 1820s, "rarely indeed, could two cash dollars be seen circulating together."[5] The economist H. C. Carey described economic conditions before the Civil War as being so "clogged" from lack of money that "almost everybody was in debt, and almost everyone unable to obtain the money required for meeting his engagements."[6]

Credit, in fact, substituted for money everywhere. Ledger books show that merchants and professionals conducted a very large business on credit. Debts were paid irregularly, and sometimes not at all. A cabinetmaker in Philadelphia who logged both cash and credit sales recorded that between 1775 and 1811, 92 percent of his business was done on a credit basis, and this was in a city that was a center of commercial activity.[7] Elsewhere credit was even more ubiquitous, creating what Robert Wiebe has described as a "giant web" of credit lacing East and West together with paper promises from the 1820s to the 1850s. With banks scarce and money scarcer, an autonomous inland economy was built up on the basis of highly personalized credit transactions. Credit with payment in kind continued to substitute for money through the end of the century, and in the South, through the lien system, up to World War I.[8]

In addition to credit, barter often substituted for money. Etienne Clavier and Brissot de Warville, visiting the United States in 1787, were so impressed by the way barter obviated the need for coins that they thought—erroneously, as it turned out—they were witnessing the modus operandi of future republican economies.[9] After the Revolution, enough specie accumulated in centers of dense population to put the large cities on a complete money basis. But most Americans lived outside of cities in agricultural communities that approached self-sufficiency. For them, Albert Gallatin reported in 1831 that "barter continues also to be a principal mode of exchange in the country."[10] Baynard Rush Hall described how it worked in the "New Purchase" of Indiana:

> For goods, storekeepers received the vast bulk of their pay in produce, which was converted into cash at Louisville, Cincinnati, or more frequently, New Orleans. The great house of Glenville and Carlton paid for all things in—leather. Hence, occasionally when a woodchopper must have shoes and yet had no produce, but offered to pay in "chopping," we, not needing that article, and being indebted to several neighbors who did, used to send the man and his axe as the circulating medium in demand among our creditors, to chop out the bills against us.[11]

From the Jacksonian period through the Gilded Age, eggs, butter, and exchanges of labor gradually gave way to various forms of paper money as the principal medium of exchange, but the rate of replacement was uneven and unsteady. George Weston observed in 1882 that the transformation from barter to a money economy was "still going on in some localities"; as late as 1940, an American sociologist could speak of the "recent plunge" of American families from semisubsistence agriculture and barter into the cash economy system.[12]

In a plenitude of forms, in a slow and uneven way, money in the nineteenth century gradually moved alongside barter, self-sufficiency, and personalized credit to become the principal medium of exchange. The engine for this development was the wage economy of industrial capitalism, which pushed money into the pockets of people who previously had not depended on it for their livelihood. The rising importance of money in everyday life was reflected by the money supply, which increased from $28 million in 1800 to $2.4 billion in 1900. Most of this money did not wind up in the pockets of farmers and workers; nevertheless, by the end of this period, Americans dealt with money much more frequently than their grandparents did at the beginning of the century.[13]

As more people handled more money, the subject of money management became increasingly important. This happened not only because the quantity of money in circulation was changing, but also because money was changing qualitatively, forcing people to reconsider the essential nature of money. In a process that was neither linear nor neatly accomplished nor always well received, various forms of paper money replaced specie in the nineteenth century as the primary form of everyday money. This was something new in the history of economic life.[14]

Before the nineteenth century, "money" to most people meant "coin," a valuable metal worth something in itself. But the middle third of the nineteenth century witnessed the introduction on a large scale of forms of money that lacked intrinsic value, such as private bank notes, government-sponsored fiat money, and bank checks. Paper money made the nature of money more mysterious; to some initiates, that pieces of paper could be "money" seemed as sensible as if paper could be legally certified as milk fit to nourish small children. Money, once something that could be melted down and weighed, was transformed to a higher level of abstraction. Once "real" enough that it could be bitten and tasted, money became a hidden reality only represented by a bank note or certificate of deposit. Abstraction made for confusion. Inexplicable expansions and contractions of the money supply led the New York *Evening Post* in 1836 to label money "the invisible hand"; there seemed to be no accounting for its capricious movements. The political economist H. C. Carey reported in 1840 that money was "so much mystified . . . [it] is generally deemed incomprehensible, and the consequence is that few persons attempt to understand it."[15]

Paper money may have seemed "invisible" in its inner workings, but not in its physicality, which was visible enough. Before the Civil War, most paper money was issued by private banks. By 1850 so many types of bank notes circulated that only an expert with the aid of a catalog could set values on out-of-town notes. Even bankers found the money supply perplexing. An Indiana banker named Calvin Fletcher, whom we will get to know better later, complained in his diary of how "much difficulty & trouble" it was to effect exchanges between various out-of-state bank notes and U.S. Treasury notes. He wished that paper currency could be abolished.[16]

When bank money was short, local money was devised to remedy the inconvenience of barter. Local money—warehouse receipts, company orders on local merchants, lottery tickets, private tokens ("shinplasters"), merchant's due bills, private bank notes—sometimes formed the exclusive medium of exchange in a locale, without sanction of the law. Confusion and bad money reigned. For this reason, most people moved back and forth between the barter, credit, and money economies, participating in the latter only when they had reliable paper money or coins.[17] After 1863 and the creation of a system of nationally chartered banks, paper money stabilized because it was de facto guaranteed by the national government. But there remained in circulation a kaleidoscopic variety of monetary forms. Between 1861 and 1890, five different types of specie circulated, and eleven different types of paper currency, including greenbacks and yellowbacks, silver certificates and private paper money. The *North American Review* voiced a common complaint when it observed, "The Rebellion has left us with . . . an excessively complicated currency."[18]

The baffling nature of money in nineteenth-century America helps to explain why people then as never before and never since made such great efforts to master the meaning of money. But there is more to the explanation. The paradox of an expanding money economy is that even while money increases quantitatively, from the point of view of wage earners money always seems scarce. Thus, another reason Victorian Americans talked a lot about money and credit was because they lived in a world increasingly dominated by the abstraction of money but short—for some, very short—on its concrete supply.

But the American passion for money was stimulated most of all by the symbolic uses of money in American society. Money was imperialistic; it could not be limited to economic life, but, as Alexis de Tocqueville observed, expanded its reach until it was found "at the bottom of everything" in America. Money of course has never been merely a medium of exchange, but Tocqueville correctly perceived that in a democratic society without fixed social ranks— and, it could be added, in an advanced money economy where impersonal exchange was replacing personal ties—the uses of money multiplied prolifically.[19] William Makepeace Thayer, a popular expositor of the Victorian money ethic, made the point explicit: "Money is bread; money is raiment; money is shelter." More than that, "money is education, refinement, books, pictures, music; money is the society of the learned and accomplished."[20] Instantly convertible for any good or service, money in the late nineteenth century became a prime symbol of wealth.

Money was also American society's equivalent of the law of gravity: it held everything together in relations of value. Money in the United States brought some people together and separated others. It replaced rank as a key determinant of social position. It was a means to social mobility. In this way the economic instrument of money took on important cultural and social significances. Italian immigrants late in the century saw this clearly. Americans, they said, lived "la dolci dollari," the sweet money life.[21]

The expansion of the money economy gave a special character to the nineteenth century, one that led Harvard philosopher Charles Sanders Peirce to wonder if future historians might not label it "The Economical Century."[22] Every age has its economic activity, but in this period money became an essential pivot point for everyone, not just for merchants and traders. As money pushed itself to the center of life, as money management became a crucial responsibility for every household, the variety, instability, and mystery of money demanded explanation and controls.

MASTERING THE MEANING OF MONEY

In Western philosophy, money has been a rich subject for esoteric theorizing. Aristotle, Aquinas, Smith, Walras, Marx, Simmel—all gave their attention to the subject. But common men and women have also struggled to understand the meaning of money. They have formulated what Thomas Crump has called "popular theories" of money, ways of talking about money that make sense of monetary forms and offer a measure of confidence that money can be fruitfully controlled.[23] In Victorian America, the popular attempt to master the meaning of money was a project that advanced on several fronts.

It surfaced in American political culture as the "money question." This was a running debate through the nineteenth century over banking, public debt, specie payment, and coinage; a public argument, in short, over the true nature of money. Hardly the dry economic subject it appears to be now, the money question aroused passions similar in intensity to those found in medieval tracts on demonology, with the same end in view of exorcising the personal devils responsible for the economic problems of the day.[24] Opinion leaders and group elites thought it imperative that every American come to a right understanding of money. "The average voter will tell you," lamented a Populist editor from Kansas in 1892, "that the money question is a great one and altogether too deep for him; that he does not understand it and doubts his ability to fully comprehend it."[25]

This context explains the huge success of William Harvey's Populist primer on money, *Coin's Financial School* (1894). Blending economic theory with fictional narrative, "Coin" Harvey described how a precocious young boy shattered the intellectual illusions of the proponents of gold in a debate in Chicago. The book became a national phenomenon and sold perhaps a million copies. "It is being read by almost everybody," a Mississippi Congressman wrote to a highly placed friend in Washington, D.C.[26] The appeal of Harvey's book lay in its subject, the nature of money, and in its down-to-earth explanations of how money worked (though readers today would probably find the book difficult going, a sign of our contemporary economic illiteracy). Plain "common sense" was welcomed on a subject that defied understanding.

Money played an equally large role in the century's literary productions. In fact, money was something of an obsession with nineteenth-century novelists.[27] A question raised by the main character in William Dean Howell's *The Quality of Mercy* (1892) serves as a motif for an entire generation: "[Northwick] asked himself a queer question, what was money? The idea of it seemed to go to pieces, as a printed word does when you look steadily at it, and to have no meaning. It affected him as droll, fantastic, like a piece of childish make-believe."[28] Earlier, when Samuel Warren's *Ten Thousand a Year* sold unexpectedly well in the United States, Edgar Allan Poe explained its popularity "for the mass" as due to "the pecuniary nature of its theme. . . . It is an affair of pounds, shillings, and pence."[29] "There's no doubt but money is to the fore now," sighed the aristocratic Bromfield Corey in Howells's *The Rise of Silas Lapham*. "It is the romance, the poetry of our age. It's the thing that chiefly strikes the imagination."[30]

Given the passion Americans displayed for money, it is a little surprising that the United States did not come forth with an equal to Smith, Ricardo, and Mill, or a philosopher-sociologist of money on a par with Karl Marx or Georg Simmel. The paradox can partly be explained by the less developed state of American intellectual society. But it also points to the powerful influence of a particular way of thinking about money in Victorian America, a way of thinking that produced popular, rather than esoteric, theories of money. As an attempt by common people to master the meaning of money, popular economic theorizing borrowed from esoteric economic philosophy, but skirted its abstractions. It was most commonly expressed in the form of a money management ethic, a flexible, practical language for talking about money that laid out the proprieties of personal finance. It would not be too much to say that the Victorian money management ethic was less theorized than moralized.

The moralization of money fit comfortably with the well-known Victorian mental habit of viewing the world as a universe of moral laws. This habit had much to do with the central tendency of nineteenth-century American Evangelical Protestantism, its impulse to identify religion with morality. Attempting to build a Christian America, Evangelicals broadened the appeal of their message by collapsing the supernatural into the natural. In the process, belief was reduced to morality, and science made into a moral mission.[31] Thus, when children were taught that ants stored up food and bees collected honey, schoolbooks left it unclear whether the ants operated from biological instinct or out of a highly developed sense of moral responsibility. In Victorian schooling, there was nothing wrong with thinking they had both.

If ants were moral agents, money, too, was charged with moral currents. "The subject of economy mixes itself with morals," wrote Emerson, putting in a nutshell the Victorian outlook on personal finance.[32] Unlike classical economics, the moral approach to money and credit recognized that economic "instruments" possessed powerful symbolic qualities. "Money is not a mere material entity," Washington Gladden was fond of saying in his lecture on "Tainted Money." "It always stands for something."[33] Money signified power or impotence, independence or slavery, success or failure, happiness or misery. As the means for leveraging human wants and aspirations into reality, money and credit raised the question of ends. It was hardly an accident, observed John Mackenzie in his popular *A Manual of Ethics* (1897), that "Economics, like Ethics, is concerned with *goods*. . . . Hence, a certain knowledge of Ethics is presupposed in the intelligent study of Economics."[34] How much knowledge? The president of the University of Rochester indicated how much: "The whole range of economic science is but an application of the Ten Commandments," he wrote. Summing up the central thrust of popular thinking about money, he avowed, "Commerce . . . cannot exist without the controlling presence of moral obligation in the minds of those who carry it on."[35]

Bypassing the abstractions of social philosophy, the moral approach favored "plain practical talk," commonsense notions that were, if not easy to practice, at least simple to understand.[36] P. T. Barnum counted on this habit of thought when he angled for a laugh in his popular lecture "The Art of Money-Getting." Barnum told the story of a philosophical pauper who was kicked out of a cheap boardinghouse because he could not pay his bill. Yet rolled up in the laggard's pocket was a complicated scheme for paying off the national debt of England, without the aid of a penny. "Do your part of the work," Barnum concluded, "or you cannot succeed."[37]

In the Christian tradition, money was often characterized as a great temptation to evil, or even as the physical manifestation of an evil spiritual power, the demon known as Mammon. Mammon, the object of fear and loathing through many centuries of Christian thought, was finally declawed by Victorian moralists. They confidently assumed that the power of money could be mastered if individuals would cage Mammon by rigorously adhering to the moral laws of money management. Philip Lindsley, a Presbyterian educator in the West writing on the money question in the 1830s, asked his readers, "What can the people do for themselves, independently of the government?" His answer: they could practice the virtues of industry, economy, sobriety, honesty, order, regularity, punctuality, and system.[38] Plainspoken personal morality became the yardstick Americans used to take the measure of money. On this basis, the complex abstraction of money was processed into manageable concepts familiar to everyone, simple ethical terms that everyone could practice.

By the mid-Victorian period, a common way of talking about money had been created by American political, literary, and religious elites. Their moralistic idioms for thinking about finance were disseminated through a popular literature of financial advice. This literature appeared in a variety of forms, including sermons, pamphlets, textbooks on political economy, giftbooks for young men and women, didactic short stories, financial advice books, and guides to domestic economy. Late in the century, access to national audiences became possible when financial advice columns became regular departments of the mass-circulation magazines.[39]

The most popular single text was Benjamin Franklin's "The Way to Wealth." By 1928, this collection of Poor Richard's economic aphorisms had been printed in over one thousand editions.[40] Joseph Medill, editor of the Chicago *Tribune* in the 1890s, recalled that, as a boy, his father's advice usually began, "My son, remember what 'Poor Richard' says. . . ."[41] Franklin had been known to eighteenth-century Americans as "Dr. Franklin," the scientist, inventor, statesman, and patriot. Later generations did not forget his scientific discoveries and political service, but *Poor Richard's Almanac* fixed his image for the nineteenth-century public as a folksy counselor and household friend. Dr. Franklin may have "snatched the lightning from the sky, and the scepter from tyrants," but Poor Richard took the measure of money and made it intelligible. Eloquent testimony to this achievement was given by a Mrs. Cummings on Washington Street, Boston, who hung a banner over her door for the 1856 Franklin Statue Dedication Parade. To her, Franklin was "The Great Practical Economist."[42]

Texts like "The Way to Wealth" indicate the norms by which Victorian Americans tried to master the problem of money. Living by making and spending a money income required mental and moral abilities of a kind not inculcated by older systems of exchange, and far harder to acquire than we realize. It required new cultural disciplines that compelled people to become more calculating, more provident, and more intent on self-control, that is, to acquire what came to be called the "economic virtues." As a modern money economy spread throughout the United States, as the jingle of coin and the rustle of paper became familiar to more and

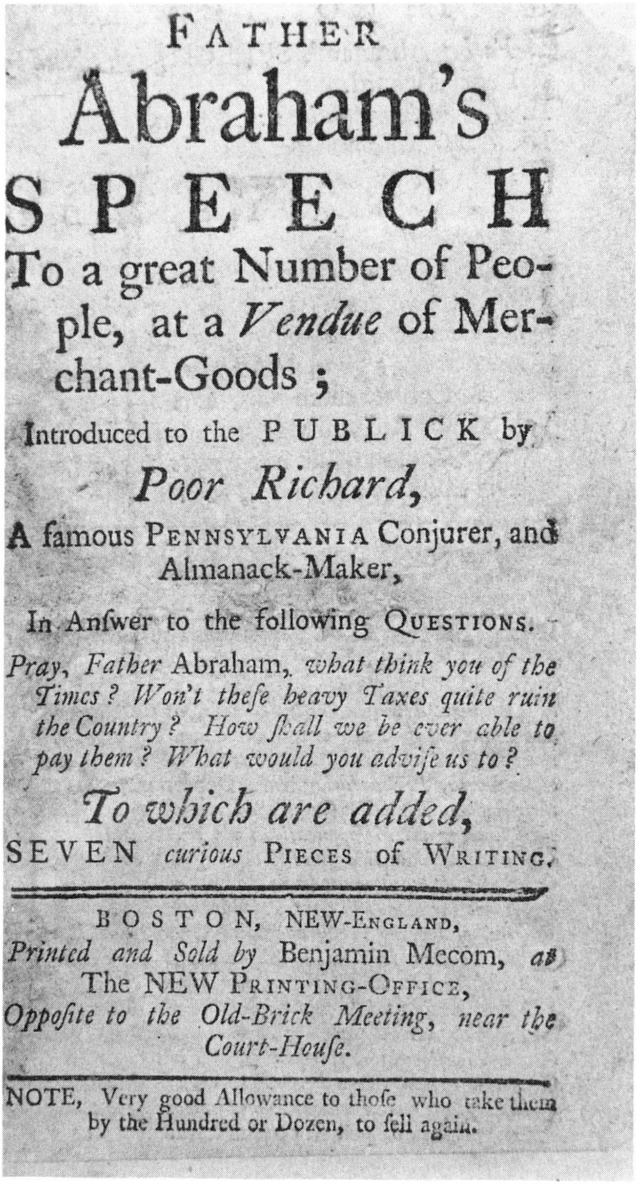

FATHER
Abraham's
S P E E C H

To a great Number of Peo-
ple, at a *Vendue* of Mer-
chant-Goods ;

Introduced to the P U B L I C K by

Poor Richard,

A famous PENNSYLVANIA Conjurer, and
Almanack-Maker,

In Anfwer to the following QUESTIONS.

*Pray, Father Abraham, what think you of the
Times ? Won't thefe heavy Taxes quite ruin
the Country ? How fhall we be ever able to
pay them ? What would you advife us to ?*

To which are added,

SEVEN *curious* PIECES of WRITING.

B O S T O N, NEW-ENGLAND,
Printed and Sold by Benjamin Mecom, *at*
The NEW PRINTING-OFFICE,
Oppofite to the Old-Brick Meeting, near the
Court-Houfe.

NOTE, Very good Allowance to thofe who take them
by the Hundred or Dozen, to fell again.

Figure 7. First edition of "The Way to Wealth," 1758.
Well into the twentieth century, the most quoted financial advisor
in America was Benjamin Franklin's Father Abraham, whose
economical maxims were collected in this celebrated pamphlet.

more people, notions about debt and credit became embedded in an authoritative money management ethic.

The reach and power of the ethic at this time was truly remarkable. Dissenting perspectives on money, if they existed, were muted. Of course, in a country as diverse as the United States, such a claim deserves skepticism. But aside from remnants of the antebellum southern aristocracy, who had their own peculiar "culture of debt," there is no evidence to suggest that minority social groups in the mid- to late nineteenth century subscribed to alternative popular theories of money that diverged seriously from the Victorian ethic sketched here. Indeed, something of the reverse seems to have been true. Nineteenth-century social critics often observed that the thriftiest, most economical people in America were not the white, Anglo-Saxon natives but the recently arrived immigrants. Thus, union organizers in the polyglot cities complained that workers gave more heed to the principles espoused by savings banks and building and loan associations than to alternative programs for organizing economic life. As for women, women's rights advocates, especially when lobbying for Married Women's Property Acts, argued that women were better able to handle money than the general lot of improvident husbands.[43]

The Victorian money management ethic became ascendant in American culture not because it took wage earners from rags to riches, or middle-class clerks from Main Street to easy street, but because its doctrines served the perceived interests of both the powerful and the powerless. To employers, its conservative platitudes were useful for the making of a hardworking, tractable labor force. To employees, its practical prescriptions seemed to work well enough—better, at least, than imaginable alternatives. It better explained how money worked than older, communal understandings of money and credit, which made little sense in an increasingly impersonal economy. In an era of primitive social welfare systems, its emphasis on taking care for the future and on financial discipline offered the best hope for gradual economic advancement. In the deflationary late nineteenth century, its financial conservatism made economic sense. Certainly, the ethic offered little to those who had no chance of living up to it, whether because of unemployment, low wages, racial oppression, or the financial mismanagement of a domineering spouse. But for most people entering the strange new world of the advanced money economy, the moral strictures of the Victorian ethic seemed like a reasonable guide to personal improvement.

THE VICTORIAN WAY TO WEALTH

Americans in the Victorian era made sense out of money with a cluster of related principles that constituted an ethic of money management. This is not to say that the ethic was universally practiced. At the end of Father Abraham's harangue on "The Way to Wealth," Franklin's Poor Richard observed that "the People heard it, and approved the Doctrine, and immediately practiced the contrary."[44] But the Victorian money management ethic defined the boundaries of proper behavior regarding the use of money, the proper way people should think, behave, and relate to money.

Like all ethical systems, the "practical economy" of the money management ethic revolved around a notion of "the good." In Victorian America, the Good was that which elevated personal character. "Character" referred to a cluster of virtues that defined how personal identity was to be constructed and presented. In *The Young Man's Counsellor* (1854), the reverend Daniel Wise summarized these virtues. "To be successful in life," advised Wise, "a young man requires certain elements of character. . . . He must possess INTEGRITY . . . INTELLIGENCE . . . INDUSTRY . . . ECONOMY and FRUGALITY . . . ENERGY . . . and TACT."[45]

What is most striking about this list, and of the Victorian notion of character in general, is its instrumental quality. Character, in short, was presented as a means to economic gain. Moralists were not apologetic about this. "Character," advised the reverend J. M. Austin in *Voice to Youth* (1839), "makes a man rich." In particular, close links were often made between character and credit. Benjamin Franklin, Henry Ward Beecher, and Orison Swett Marden, authors of the three best-selling guides on financial advice in the nineteenth century, all taught the lesson that "character is the poor man's capital." Character earned the confidence of the community, and confidence established credit.[46] Late in the century character became more of an end in itself, an internalized mental attitude of initiative, self-reliance, and usefulness. But the original association of character with credit never faded away completely.[47]

The link between character and credit is one more sign of the symbolic power of money in the nineteenth century. Money was not just used more; it meant more. Victorians responded not by condemning money as an economic institution—consensus held that money and civilization went hand in hand—but by declaring their faith that individuals could rise to the challenge of mastering the money economy. Character was the key, and money the supreme test. A much quoted maxim of Henry Taylor made the point: "If we take account of all the virtues with which dollars are mixed up—honesty, justice, generosity, charity, frugality, freethought, self-sacrifice—and of their correlative vices, it is a knowledge which goes near to cover the length and breadth of humanity, and a right measure in getting, saving, spending, giving, taking, lending, buying and bequeathing, would almost argue a perfect man."[48] On the evidence of passages like this, Ruth Miller Elson has noted that throughout the nineteenth century the virtues most frequently praised in the individual were the economic ones. This may be an overstatement (what about earnestness, sympathy, patriotism?), but certainly the economic virtues symbolized the hardest-fought victories of character.[49] As a writer in the *Eclectic Magazine* put it in 1886, "Our right or wrong use of money is the utmost test of character, as well as the root of happiness or misery, throughout our whole lives."[50]

The Victorian money ethic held out an optimistic promise that was both practical and spiritual: money, as a tool and as a tempter, could be mastered by sheer human will. "The man should always be the master," wrote Andrew Carnegie. "He should keep money in the position of a useful servant. He must never let it master and make a miser out of him."[51] Money was the flashpoint of desire, which in the Victorian ethos was always on the verge of raging out of control. Thus, money could be mastered if the self could be controlled. And the self could be controlled if but four principles were followed.

"Economy" or "frugality" headed the list. "By the term economy," explained B. R. Cowen in *Our Beacon Light* (1888), "I wish to be understood as that which avoids all waste and extravagance."[52] Of these virtues, Catherine Beecher held that "very little can be taught respecting [them] in books."[53] But that did not stop her or others from trying. "Parents should teach their children that it is sinful to waste anything," admonished Franklin Wilson in a textbook on personal finance.[54] On the frontier, frugality may have been a practical necessity, but evangelical revivalism elevated it to a higher plane. In fact, frugality became a requisite of the moral life: "I would most earnestly beseech my young reader to make up his mind, cost what it may, —that he will be truly and strictly economical. . . . It is not merely foolish to spend all you can get, but it is positively wrong. It is positively a sin to waste property."[55] Frugality was important because it was a badge of well-regulated desires and a contented heart. It demonstrated that the self was under control.

But as Poor Richard said, one could be "penny wise and pound foolish," or "save at the spigot and waste at the bung-hole." In other words, there was no point to burning candle ends if the money saved went for ribbons and gewgaws. Thrift, then, denoted another essential principle of the money management code. In traditional peasant societies, thrift and frugality were indistinguishable habits that aimed at accumulating a living sufficiency—and no more. But capitalism brought a new, more ambitious version of thrift. Capitalist thrift encouraged industrious saving in order to build wealth. "If you would be wealthy," said Franklin, "think of Saving as well as Getting."[56]

Thrift, or saving, had consequences for the community as well. In classical political economy, personal savings was the key to capital formation and national wealth. Savers were lauded as public benefactors. But the popular ethic of money management made savings a means to character as much as a means to national prosperity. "The saving of money usually means the saving of a man," counseled Orison Marden.[57] James J. Hill's advice may serve for all who supported the cult of savings: "If you want to know whether you are going to be a success or a failure in life, you can easily find out. The test is simple and infallible. Are you able to save money? If not, drop out."[58] Stern language like this drew a link between thrift and self-denial, a virtue that took on major proportions in the character building of the era. Denying the will to pleasure was itself an "intrinsic pleasure," said Catherine Beecher. She urged that children practice self-denial "by abstaining from certain luxuries, and saving their earnings."[59]

But, of course, saving money never just happened; therefore, the money ethic urged planning as a high priority. Lydia Child recommended budgets to housewives as early as 1829; Emerson, too, lectured the country on behalf of "system in the economies."[60] But it was later in the century that budgeting became a standard principle in the money ethic. "Planning" and "system" for home accounts reflected the currents of rationalization sweeping through late nineteenth-century life in business, government, and the new professions, but there was more to it than that. Budgeting also pointed out one of the many new uses of money. "An expense-book accurately and conscientiously kept" became a way for people "to know themselves" as they saw in black-and-white where their dollars went.[61] "My expenditure is me," Emerson had said.[62] He meant to justify his belief in systematic financial management, not provide the credo for a developing consumer culture.

Frugality, thrift, and planning—the first three principles in the Victorian money management ethic—made up a notional capital that has survived into our time, though the standards for defining them have changed. But even in the nineteenth century the meaning of these concepts was not written in stone. As society accommodated itself to the market life of industrial capitalism, the strictest financial formulas were loosened. Economy, for example, was a serious necessity in frontier areas, but in more settled conditions the concept seemed picayune, even mean. This explains why education in the ways of economy generally started with apologies. Lydia Child dedicated *The American Frugal Housewife* "to those who are not ashamed of economy," noting that economy was generally despised as a "low virtue tending to make people ungenerous and selfish." She advocated a creativity in economy that would make it "the poor man's revenue."[63] Child was unsuccessful in rehabilitating the concept, but others kept trying. Barnum scorned those who "misapprehended" economy, thinking that it consisted in "saving cheese-pairings and candle ends, in cutting off two pence from the laundress' bill and doing all sorts of little, mean, dirty things." Barnum defined economy in a way that better fit the conditions of a "people of plenty." While earlier maxims recommended that expenses be less than income, Barnum took the emphasis off scarcity and self-denial by reversing the maxim, insisting that "true economy" consisted in "always making the income exceed the outgo."[64] In similar fashion the boundaries of the other money ethic principles were also pushed out. By century's end, "*true* economy," "*true* thrift" and "*realistic* budgets" were recommended as improvements over definitions of virtue that assumed a world of scarcity.[65]

THE ETHICS OF DEBT

The money management ethic was most liberalized with regard to its fourth principle, which found expression in positive and negative forms. The positive statement was "live within your means." No principle of personal finance was more often repeated in the literature of Victorian financial advice. As Lydia Child laid down the rule, "A person should never aim to live one cent beyond the income of which he is certain. If you have two dollars a day, let nothing but sickness induce you to spend more than nine shillings; if you have one dollar a day, do not spend but seventy-five cents; if you have half a dollar a day, be satisfied to spend forty cents." Child justified the principle with the usual Victorian appeals to natural and moral law. Spending beyond one's means in order to purchase public esteem was always counterproductive in the long run, and it was morally wrong because it robbed the community of precious capital.[66]

Negatively stated, the keystone of the Victorian money management ethic took the form of a simple warning: avoid debt. Lending and borrowing were often singled out for special attention in money management guides. Indeed, to the extent that didactic literature can be said to have a "plot," the climax in Victorian guides to personal finance often involved hair-raising anecdotes about the fall of spendthrift debtors, with a denouement explaining how to avoid their fate. The title of a fictional money tale by Maria Edgeworth summarized the matter: "Out of Debt Out of Danger."[67]

Credit management received so much attention that the entire money ethic was sometimes boiled down to simple, cautionary admonitions on debt. Thus, when a 1915 poll asked people to describe their early training in money management, one respondent replied: "My financial training at home was not very extensive. . . . I was taught, however, to be strictly honest and was never permitted to go into debt."[68]

Certainly, financial advice givers could be very strict in opposing debt. Quoting Charles Spurgeon, the best-known English preacher of the day, Orison Marden averred that "the trinity of evil" was "debt, dirt, and the devil."[69] Metaphors linking debt to disease and demons abounded. Perhaps because of their familiarity with the latter, Evangelical ministers bested all others at castigating debt. "Debt is an inexhaustible fountain of dishonesty," maintained Henry Ward Beecher. "It has opened in the heart every fountain of iniquity; it has besoiled the conscience, it has tarnished the honor, it has made the man a deliberate student of knavery, a systematic practitioner of fraud; it has dragged him through all the sewers of petty passions, —anger, hate, revenge, malicious folly, or malignant shame."[70] If ministers were concerned with the impact of indebtedness on personal morality, others objected to debt because it inflated prices. And there were still other reasons to oppose it. William Cobbett pointed out a third danger in his widely read *Advice to Young Men* (1831). Credit buying, he observed, mystified the "proper value" of money, making it too easy to buy things when no money visibly and immediately changed hands. Citing the favorite proof text of Protestant ministers on the subject of debt, Cobbett recommended the precept of St. Paul: "Owe no man any thing."[71]

But the range of meaning attributed to borrowing money was wider than such attacks on debt would imply. Borrowed money was, after all, credit, which in nineteenth-century America was a valued necessity. Credit got young men started in life. Credit staked the pioneer with a homestead, enabled immigrants to obtain a business, allowed businessmen to enlarge their plans, and for the poor family obtained medical care. Thus, in a story for children, Jacob Abbott described mortgage credit as "one of the most convenient and useful customs of society." "Credit to a man," declared business journalist Freeman Hunt, "is what cream is to a nice cup of coffee." More extravagant praise came from Whig pamphleteer Calvin Colton, who claimed that "the creative, prolific principle of credit" was "the spring" of American enterprise, "the nurse" of national prosperity, and "the cause" of the Union's greatness. According to Colton, credit was a barometer of public morality, "the exact measure of the soundness of the social state." Indeed, in Victorian America credit was an emblem for the unity and coherence of society as a whole. In the language of the day, people did not "borrow money"; rather, they "got trusted."[72]

Credit was character, credit was trust, credit was good. But debt, the necessary analogue to credit, was an entirely different matter. According to Victorian moralists, debt was "a calamity," "an oppressive and degrading incubus," "an inexhaustible fountain of dishonesty." It afflicted borrowers "with the subdued and sorrow-stricken countenance of a beggar," observed the honorable John Whipple of Rhode Island; the reverend Daniel Wise claimed that "debt destroys more than the cholera." P. T. Barnum's advice to youth was that "there is scarcely anything that drags a person down like debt. . . . Debt robs a man of his self-respect, and makes him almost despise himself."[73]

As with credit, the social and personal consequences of private debt were thought to be considerable. "The existing recklessness of running into debt," contended Samuel Smiles, "saps the public morals, and spreads misery throughout the middle and upper classes of society. The tone of morality has sunk, and it will be long before it is fairly recovered again."[74] The hard line on debt viewed indebtedness to be the terminus of a way of living that ignored the ethics of money. But more importantly, the high profile of debt in the money ethic stemmed from a grave implication posed by indebtedness. If the ethic assumed a notion of the Good, which was character, it also assumed a notion of the Bad, which was weakness, slavery, and the loss of self-control. If credit was a reward for character and therefore an emblem of the Good, debt symbolized what one writer termed "the middle class hell," a state of moral and literal bankruptcy brought on by the inability to face down desire.[75] It signaled to the community that the individual had lost the struggle to master Mammon.

The notion of self-control lay at the back of the money ethic and its caution against debt. This is most evident in the two intellectual sources from which the ethic drew its powerful social authority, Protestant asceticism and republican common sense. The authority of these traditions in American moral education is indicated in William Dean Howells's sketch of Silas Lapham, "a fine type of the successful American," whose parents "taught their children the simple virtues of the Old Testament and Poor Richard's Almanac."[76] It is instructive to look at two representatives of Protestant asceticism and secular republicanism: Cotton Mather and one of his pupils, Benjamin Franklin. They had much to say about how debt undermined self-control.

In his sermons, Cotton Mather continued a tradition of English Protestant preaching on economic topics that began at the end of the sixteenth century when scores of preachers, Anglican and Puritan, began edifying London merchants on sobriety, diligence, and thrift. On the subject of borrowing money, Mather avowed it was "a great Point of religion with me to keep out of debt," and he explained his convictions in a sermon preached in Boston in 1716.[77] Disturbed that so many Christians were running into debt in ways "nothing short of criminal," he chose for his text Romans 13:8: "Owe no man anything, but to love one another." Mather put a colorful gloss on the text: "Come into [debt] with the pace of a Tortoise, and get out of it, with the flight of an Eagle." This was no small teaching, urged Mather, but "a considerable Point of Christianity."[78]

How so? Mather held that debt overwhelmed the Christian's self-control by the sheer force of multiplied temptations. Borrowed money led debtors into dishonesty in order to put off creditors. Debt tempted people to take advantage of neighbors' generosity, placing friends in financial straits to rescue the debtor from his own folly. Borrowing tempted people to contract debts with no clear plan for repaying, a sin Mather likened to "picking the pockets of your God." Worst of all, Mather emphasized that debt was a "Temptation" to rebel against the will of God. "For the sake of their carnal appetites" people borrowed money to run up "Flags of Pride," thus revealing that they were not satisfied with the condition in life God had assigned them. "It should be a principle with a Good Man," said Mather, " 'I may not have, what I cannot have.' " Going into debt, then, indicated that the Christian had succumbed to covetous desires. Mather allowed that necessity and convenience required some forms of credit in matters of trade. But even in these cases, the debtor ought always to feel debt as "the pain of a broken bone unto him."

This message of extreme caution was repeated in Protestant sermons and tracts through the nineteenth century, and continues to be heard in some fundamentalist circles right up to the present day. But the rationales changed as the money economy enlarged its compass. As the supply of capital increased, it became harder to maintain that debt imposed a financial burden on lenders. Moreover, the commandment against covetousness was muted by the new doctrine that material desires advanced civilization. However, Protestant moralists continued to sound Mather's central theme, which was that debt signaled a defeat in the war against "appetites and passions," "wasteful expenditures," and the "present gratification." "The key to success in any department of life," declared the minister who wrote *Our Business Boys* (1844), "is self-denial."[79]

If individuals did not limit themselves, the door was opened for someone else to limit their liberties. The debtor's loss of personal independence was emphasized by republicanism, another powerful tradition in nineteenth-century life. Its archetypal spokesman was Benjamin Franklin.[80]

Franklin's aphorisms shared a common style with Mather's, but the content was distinctly different. Franklin made a few bows in Mather's direction, agreeing that debt undermined honesty ("The second vice is Lying, the first is running into Debt"; "Lying rides upon debt's back") and eroded virtue ("'Tis hard for an empty Bag to stand upright").[81] But Franklin laid greater emphasis on an evil unmentioned in Mather's sermons on debt: the loss of personal independence. "He who goes a borrowing goes a sorrowing," said Father Abraham, because "the Borrower is a Slave to the Lender." Franklin traced debt to "Fond Pride of Dress." But in Franklin's secular morality, pride was not a rebellion against God but the road to social embarrassments: "Pride breakfasted with Plenty, dined with Poverty, and supped with Infamy." Franklin's republicanism lauded the independent producer, but borrowed money wrecked the ideal because debt forced one to "give to another Power over your Liberty." This is how Poor Richard drove the point home: "Your Creditor has Authority at his Pleasure to deprive you of your Liberty, by confining you in Gaol for Life, or to sell you for a Servant, if you should not be able to pay him!" This was not purely figurative talk in a period when bankrupts could be arrested for debt and confined to town. "Maintain your Independency," concluded Franklin, "Be frugal and free."

On the matter of debt, Protestant and republican moralism were different streams of thought running in the same channel. Thus, financial advisers usually called on both traditions for support. John Todd's *The Young Man* justified the Pauline injunction "owe no man anything" with a secular interpretation of debt drawn from republican sources: "The independence of manhood can never be obtained so long as any man can look you in the face and say you owe him."[82] Christian asceticism and republican individualism differed on the harms of debt, but both conceptualized it as a problem of self-control. Debt "blunts the finer sensibilities," declared I. H. Mayer in *Domestic Economy* (1893), "and makes a man a slave. Avoid it!"[83]

But the Victorian ethic's hard line against borrowing was not its last word on the subject. Years later, when the creation of a consumer credit industry inspired the popular myth that strict standards of thrift were crumbling, the antidebt pronouncements of the Victorian code would be incorrectly remembered as the whole of it. But this oversimplified the Victorian approach to debt. Else what is to be made of popular nineteenth-century epigrams such as "one never becomes rich until he is in debt," or the oft-quoted witticism of Artemus Ward: "Let us all live within our means, even if we have to borrer money to do it with"? To what extent was Mark Twain exaggerating when he reported that a man was overheard to say, "I wasn't worth a cent two years ago, and now I owe two millions of dollars"? Why did P. T. Barnum tell audiences the story of an old Quaker who said to his son, "John, never get trusted, but if thee gets trusted for anything, let it be for 'manure,' because that will help thee pay it back again"? Why would General Benjamin Franklin Butler, when asked to summarize his financial advice for young men, say "Buy improved real estate, partly for cash, and partly for small notes"? How could Henry Ward Beecher, author of the most blistering denunciations of debt, also go on record as saying that "if a young man will only get in debt for some land, and then get married, these two things will keep him straight, or nothing will"?[84]

The fact is that Victorian money management ethic proscribed debt, and then winked at some forms of it. "Bible honesty," advised a minister to young men starting out in life, "is never to contract a debt, without the probable means of meeting it when due."[85] The qualification is significant. Like the epigrams that justified debt, it represents the thin end of a wedge in the Victorian prohibition of debt, a wedge that opened up space in the ethic for permission of certain types of borrowing.

As Philip Rieff has argued, all ethical systems of meaning employ a dialectic of complementary constraints and exemptions. Cultures build community and make sense of behavior by first organizing moral demands on people and then sanctioning appropriate releases from those demands. The moral demands make society a friendlier, more trustworthy place, while the approved releases give people relief from the strain of conforming to communal purposes.[86]

This dynamic of constraints and releases reveals itself plainly in the writings of Victorian financial advisers. While generally taking a dim view of debt, they also were ready, and sometimes eager, to make concessions to the opportunities of an advanced money economy. Dimly recognized was the fact that changing economic and monetary systems took the force out of Benjamin Franklin's hard line on debt. Even Cotton Mather recognized that debt could not be absolutely prohibited.[87] Already in the seventeenth century, the new economic and social relations of capitalism made credit, in some situations at least, seem like a sound idea.

Admonitions aside, the Victorian money ethic plainly allowed certain types of borrowing in certain circumstances. The key criterion for determining the propriety of borrowing money depended on how the debt affected the borrower's self-control. Making debt a matter of self-control opened the possibility that debt would be perfectly legitimate when it threatened neither sanctification nor financial independence. With the abolishment of imprisonment for debt, with the leniency shown in many states to debtors, with increasing wealth and social support systems in the late nineteenth century, the window of what could be considered legitimate borrowing opened increasingly wider. Thus, as with the other terms of the money ethic, the boundaries of the debt concept widened to allow for an imprimatur on certain kinds of indebtedness.

Out of the interplay between caution and opportunity, Victorian Americans subscribed to a loose but identifiable taxonomy of debt that distinguished proper and improper indebtedness, "getting trusted" from being "in debt." The crucial categories were "productive" and "consumptive" credit.

These two categories were taken from the esoteric theory of classical economics. Smith, Ricardo, and Mill ignored credit for the purpose of consumption. But central to their general theories was a distinction between productive uses of capital and unproductive, or consumptive, expenditure. Speaking of two kinds of loans, Adam Smith wrote:

> The borrower may use [a loan] either as capital, or as a stock reserved for immediate consumption. If he uses it as capital, he em-

ploys it in the maintenance of productive laborers, who reproduce the value with a profit. He can, in this case, both restore the capital and pay the interest without alienating or encroaching upon any other source of revenue. If he uses it as a stock reserved for immediate consumption, he acts the part of a prodigal, and dissipates in the maintenance of the idle, what was destined for the support of the industrious.

Smith doubted that the latter type of loan could ever become popular. He reckoned that credit for immediate consumption was so contrary to people's self-interest and innate thriftiness that there was no need to speak further on the subject.[88]

But what Smith left ill-defined the popular theory of money management explored much more fully. Financial advisers very carefully distinguished between productive and consumptive credit. Speaking to lenders, W. Cunningham, in *The Use and Abuse of Money* (1891), advised, "If a man burdens his estate not in order to enable him to make permanent improvements, but in order to maintain an extravagant expenditure, he is at least acting foolishly, and it is wrong to help him to make a fool of himself."[89] Productive credit put borrowed money to work in such a way that the debt repaid itself in full and turned a profit, too. If a man had good character, and an opportunity arose requiring a loan but offering reasonable hopes for self-liquidation, then "go ahead" was the attitude:

> To borrow for genuinely productive purpose, for a purpose that will bring you in more than enough to pay off your debt, principle and interest, is a profitable enterprise. It shows business sagacity and courage, and is not a thing to be ashamed of. But it cannot be too much emphasized that the would-be borrower must calculate very carefully and be sure that it is a productive enterprise before he goes into debt.[90]

Indeed, it is doubtful whether Victorian Americans considered productive debt to be debt at all. The conservative *Banker's Magazine* was explicit on this point, avowing that indebtedness "For the creation of a valuable property . . . cannot be truly considered an indebtedness, inasmuch as the capital borrowed is still in existence, and has been the means of a new creation."[91]

This kind of "productive" credit underlay the geographical expansion and entrepreneurial business activity of the United States. In 1895 George Holmes of the Census Bureau estimated that at least 90 percent of the country's private debt went to acquire capital goods or durable property. "There is a great difference," Holmes noted, "between the significance of a debt incurred to acquire the ownership of capital or the more durable property to be used productively . . . and that of a debt incurred for the purpose of property soon to be consumed unproductively."[92] Allan Bogue has estimated that of those farmers who settled in midwestern states, about half made use of "productive" credit to purchase the land or to make improvements.[93] Popular acceptance of the notion of productive credit is indicated by the many nineteenth-century paeans to "public credit," sometimes represented as a goddess.[94] It was productive credit that Calvin Colton praised when he wrote in 1840 that "credit has been the spring of our enterprise, the nurse of our prosperity, the cause of our greatness."[95]

Productive credit was defined by a short list of "legitimate and healthy purposes."[96] First was borrowing for the purpose of starting a business. This was one of "the necessaries of life" said the *Christian Union*. It quoted approvingly one man's story:

> When I started out in life, my father's advice was, "Never borrow. Always save all you can and never run into debt, and you will die well-off." Now, all the success that has come to me has been the result of disregarding my father's injunction. I have borrowed of everyone who would loan money to me, and have used it to advantage in various enterprises. That is the way I have pushed ahead. Had I never run into debt, I should still be a man on a salary.[97]

Loans to purchase land also qualified as productive debt. When Robert Porter, the 1890 census superintendent, contemplated the large level of private debt uncovered by his staff, he consoled himself with the finding that "the prime motive in the private debt has been better fences, better barns, better homes, and more land for the farmer."[98]

100

Going into debt for business ventures or land could involve taking risks based on expectations of rising and falling market values. If the motive was quick profit, this form of indebtedness was termed "speculation." Speculation was not considered to be productive credit; it was sternly frowned upon as a form of gambling, especially by those who did not have the opportunity personally to engage in it. Speculation violated the criteria for productive credit of social usefulness and individual self-control. Because speculation was thought to smooth price fluctuations resulting from variations in the supply of basic commodities, speculation in goods with a fixed supply—like land and shares—was generally ruled out as serving no social purpose. Speculation by uninformed outsiders and those with insufficient capital was considered to be even more illegitimate because it was both a social nuisance and threatened the independence of the borrower with financial ruin.[99]

The concept of productive credit established that "no man has a right to be a borrower who has not the most positive assurance of his ability to pay."[100] In other words, borrowing money was acceptable and safe only when used to purchase things that increased in value or had productive uses. By this criterion, Americans in the late nineteenth-century middle class found increasing scope for borrowing money, whether for houses or for new types of durable goods. In most people's minds, loans obtained for building or buying a house qualified as productive debt. "The installment mortgage . . . is a great incentive to saving, and a very popular method of borrowing money," the *Ladies Home Journal* advised readers in 1898. By putting money in an investment that would increase in value, home mortgages guaranteed that the debt could be paid off. In addition, it diverted money that might have been spent on luxuries to a more productive purpose.[101] This kind of thinking gradually put other items on the list of productive uses for debt, everything from reapers to sewing machines to pianos. H. L. Reade's financial advice book described the sewing machine as "a business necessity," the piano as "a source of delight and perhaps (if needful) of revenue," and the mower something that would "pay for itself." This indicates the manner of thinking when it came to defining productive debts.[102]

101

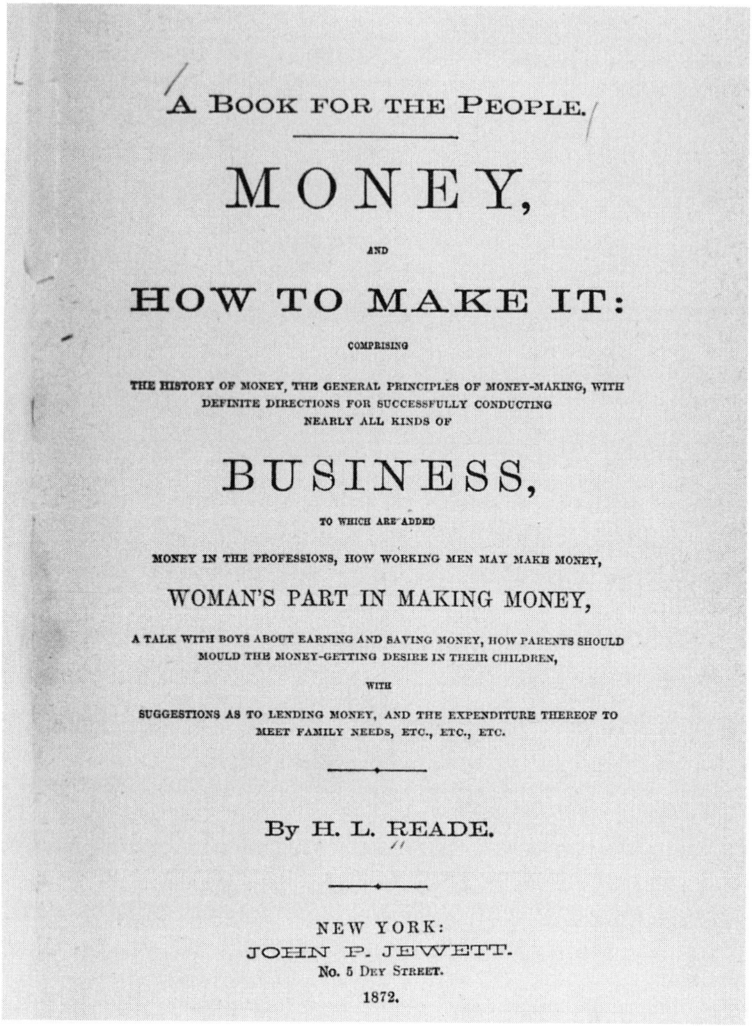

A BOOK FOR THE PEOPLE.

MONEY,

AND

HOW TO MAKE IT:

COMPRISING

THE HISTORY OF MONEY, THE GENERAL PRINCIPLES OF MONEY-MAKING, WITH
DEFINITE DIRECTIONS FOR SUCCESSFULLY CONDUCTING
NEARLY ALL KINDS OF

BUSINESS,

TO WHICH ARE ADDED

MONEY IN THE PROFESSIONS, HOW WORKING MEN MAY MAKE MONEY,

WOMAN'S PART IN MAKING MONEY,

A TALK WITH BOYS ABOUT EARNING AND SAVING MONEY, HOW PARENTS SHOULD
MOULD THE MONEY-GETTING DESIRE IN THEIR CHILDREN,

WITH

SUGGESTIONS AS TO LENDING MONEY, AND THE EXPENDITURE THEREOF TO
MEET FAMILY NEEDS, ETC., ETC., ETC.

By H. L. READE.

NEW YORK:
JOHN P. JEWETT.
No. 5 DEY STREET.
1872.

Figure 8. Title page to H. L. Reade's *Money, and How to Make It*, 1872.
Financial advice books of the late nineteenth century often encouraged
"productive debts," which this book defined as loans used to purchase
houses, reapers, sewing machines, pianos, and other such things that might
grow in value or be profitable for the household.

The mirror image of productive credit was "consumptive debt." "Borrowing money is a strictly business transaction," said *Harper's Weekly*, "to which no reproach should attach, unless the borrower be a spendthrift, and merely raising funds for some reprehensible end."[103] The list of "reprehensible ends" was much larger than the list of proper uses for debt. It included every object that consumed money without yielding a net addition to the balance sheet. Food, clothing, flimsy house furnishings, entertainments, and anything else that put a lien on future earnings was forbidden. Credit for consumables was "bad business"; there was "no excuse for going in debt for the ordinary necessaries of life."[104]

In the everyday language of the Gilded Age, "consumption" did not yet have the connotation it would obtain later in the twentieth century, that is, the using up of goods and services. Rather, consumption signified the wasting disease of tuberculosis. This loathsome association accounts for the stock portrayals of consumptive debtors in the money ethic literature: shivering youths who pawned overcoats to pay gambling debts; sallow New York dandies with showy chains on their vest; drink-sodden men and women pawning furniture for a glass of whiskey. Borrowing money for "gratifications of the moment" was the only kind of debt strictly forbidden by the money ethic.

But even here there were exceptions to be made. One was for those "honest debtors" who through no fault of their own found themselves in financial straits.[105] As will be seen later, the plight of unemployed workers stimulated reform efforts to provide them with the dignified credit they needed to get back on their feet. The other exception applied to reliable people who, for reasons of convenience, kept a "tab" running for groceries and other basic supplies. "Debts of convenience" were considered acceptable if accounts were settled on a regular basis.[106] Money moralists warned that "book credit" had its dangers. It could tempt people to buy things they didn't need. Barnum contrasted it with productive credit: "Debt for what you eat and drink and wear is to be avoided. Some families have a foolish habit of getting credit at 'the stores' and thus frequently purchase many things which might have been dispensed with."[107] But particularly in rural communities, where ready money was scarce, book credit was an acceptable way to pay for goods.

I Have Ever Been Opposed to
Borrowing Money

Some people followed the money management ethic to the letter, others disregarded it entirely. Most operated between these extremes.

A diary kept by an early settler of Indiana offers revealing testimony as to how one man used the money ethic to work out the tensions he felt between economic propriety and financial opportunity. Calvin Fletcher was born in Vermont but moved to Indianapolis in 1826 and lived there until his death in 1867. Married with eleven children, Fletcher arrived in Indiana with little to his name, but in the course of his life combined careers in farming, law, public service, banking, and real estate to end his days comfortably in Indianapolis. Money and personal finances were of constant concern to him, as amply demonstrated by his diary, which he kept faithfully from 1817 until his death.[108]

"I have ever been opposed to borrowing money," Fletcher wrote in January, 1835.[109] The statement comes near to summing up the whole of Fletcher's version of the money management ethic. He had rarely borrowed money before 1835, but then opportunity came knocking. His time in the State House made it clear to him what a pending $12 million internal improvements bill meant for those who owned land in the right places. Persuaded by a friend that it was "good business," Fletcher in 1835 and 1836 cosigned for loans totaling $19,000 and invested in land, a hotel in Indianapolis, and a new bridge at Logansport. In his diary Fletcher recorded his reluctance to borrow, but each expression of reluctance is followed by another opportunity, another loan.[110]

Disaster struck in the Panic of 1837, a crisis which left a lasting mark on Fletcher and his ideas about money management. Already before the bank failures sharply restricted credit, Fletcher confessed that his debts made him feel "hyppocondrical."[111] When the loans were called in he had no choice but to sell off what he could and hope for the best. He consoled himself with the thought that bankruptcy, if it came, would not affect his family's life too much: "We have no carriage no Turkey carpet . . . ," he wrote gloomily.[112] While most of Fletcher's friends and neighbors went broke, he somehow scraped through the crisis. But the unpaid debts from his speculative ventures lingered to trouble him. In following years, every New Year's Day became a time for resolving to get out from under the crushing load of debt. "So long as I remain in debt I shall feel that I am the slave of my creditors," wrote Fletcher in 1839. The following New Year's Day a similar lesson was noted: "The happy & prosperous man . . . never embarks on speculations beyond an investment he is able to advance at once."[113] Finally, on January 2, 1843, Fletcher settled the last payment on his loans. He wrote in his account book that the debt had caused him "more disgrace and mortification during the same period than the acquisition of the largest fortune could compensate—May my children or the reader learn wisdom—be contented with humble stations, small gains & a clear conscience, for no man can feel he is right & have an approving conscience who has bought things he could do without—thereby becoming the slave to those he owes."[114] Earlier, when a friend tried to enlist him in another speculative venture, Fletcher hotly retorted with the advice that experience had taught him: risky indebtedness was "contrary to good morals good economy & all experience of prudent men."[115]

But Fletcher did not consider all debts to be improper. In fact, he continued to take out various loans until his final years. Some loans were a matter of convenience, while others were a matter of necessity during times of scarce money. In any event, Fletcher reasoned with himself, these loans could be covered by his other assets if he died and his estate had to be settled suddenly. Thus, Fletcher borrowed money to build a house. He bought groceries, dry goods, and hardware on account from local merchants, settling his bills at the end of the year. He bought a piano with installment payments.[116] Unlike the speculative debts, these debts did not seem to bother Fletcher. He did not report that they put his affairs "in confusion." They did not place him in the position of being a "slave." He was not troubled about losing "controle" of his life. Fletcher was also convinced in his own mind that these debts were not incurred for "fashions of the world which lead to extravegance [*sic*]."[117] With Fletcher, there was a distinct difference between being "in" debt and getting trusted for money.

Making these kinds of distinctions was important to Fletcher. But not so with his oldest son. A family rift broke out when Calvin Fletcher Jr. failed to follow his father in subjecting indebtedness to the test of "scruple, reason or good purpose." Earlier, when Fletcher was struggling to pay off his bank loans, he had recorded: "I hope this matter may be considered by my sons—never run into debt."[118] But he was to be disappointed. When Calvin Jr. reached adulthood, he urged on his father several plans for setting up a farm of his own on borrowed money. When his father refused, Calvin Jr. went behind his back to arrange the loans. Fletcher's diary records his frustration—"He runs into debt & wastes or has done so without scruple"; "He seems crazy to get into debt"—and the subsequent admission: "I have been disappointed in him. He would be a slave to debt—delighted to make contracts unadvisedly. Had he stuck by me & obeyed my orders bot [sic] nothing only what he was able to pay for, he would this day been one of the most useful men living, a comfort to me."[19] In February 1861, father and son separated their financial concerns and went their own ways. "His views of credit & economy differed from mine," explained Fletcher. "I have viewed debt the greatest tyrant that ever afflicted individuals or states."[120]

The diary of Calvin Fletcher demonstrates how the tenets of the Victorian money management ethic were tested, developed, and used over the course of one man's life. It reveals how Fletcher used the terms of the ethic to formulate justifications for the way he lived in the tension between economic opportunities and the purer formulations of middle-class morality. For example, Fletcher used the concept of productive credit to justify borrowing money for his original real-estate investments. When it turned out that the loans threatened his financial solvency, he repudiated his decision to borrow money, recognizing belatedly that the speculative loans jeopardized his family's ability to control their own lives. But never did Fletcher repudiate debt itself. In his mind some debts were more proper than others.

For Calvin Fletcher and Victorian Americans, debt did not intrinsically signify immorality or impropriety. If it was generally something to avoid, there were times when obtaining a loan was a necessary first step to becoming wealthier, a goal highly recommended by the money ethic. Put another way, the symbolic boundaries of debt were elastic, and Americans took advantage of the give. Fletcher quoted Franklin ("the debtor is slow to the creditor") and the Bible ("owe no man"), but he also admitted "it is an Americanism of modern times to contradict [both these?] declarations."[121]

For some Americans, the Victorian money management ethic retained its authority well into the twentieth century. But for most it was abandoned when, against the backdrop of modern economic life, its inadequacies and contradictions became all too apparent. Productive and consumptive debts were more easily distinguished in 1860 than they could be in 1930, when a flood of mass-produced durable goods defied easy categorization in those terms. In the larger matter of self-control, the ethic actually worked against itself. The ethic gave high priority to delay of gratification as a kind of spiritual exercise for building the muscles of character. But postponing satisfactions can have unintended and opposite effects. It can actually increase desire; it can create what Colin Campbell has called a "permanent desiring mode," a state of daydreaming from which specific desires continually spring.[122]

After 1900, the money management ethic also fell increasingly out of phase with economic realities. A spurt of inflation between 1897 and 1914 disoriented those who believed that savings was the key to wealth. But perhaps the greatest threat to the money ethic came from the money economy itself. Paper money, after all, is a form of debt. It represents a promise by an issuing bank to redeem fiat money with real money. In this sense, the introduction of paper money into everyday life anticipated the arrival of a complex economy operating on the basis of sophisticated credit transactions. Like it or not, Victorian Americans were already being introduced to what their children in the 1920s would call the "debt way of life." Long before the invention of consumer credit, Americans were already learning that sometimes borrowing money was the only way to live within their means.

PART TWO

GETTING THE GOODS:

THE MAKING OF A CREDIT REVOLUTION

*

Small-Loan Lending and the
Rise of the Personal Finance Company

IN 1930, the National Forensic League topic for high school debaters was "Resolved: That installment buying of personal property as now practiced in the United States is both socially and economically desirable."[1] That high schoolers across the nation were debating the advantages and disadvantages of "consumptive" credit was but one sign of a transformation taking place in household financial management, changes that debaters on both sides of the resolution termed a "credit revolution." It was a revolution involving many kinds of lenders, but retailers and small-loan lenders led the way. Both helped to make installment lending for consumption, so firmly discouraged in the Victorian era, part of the modern American way of life. But the story of the small-loan lenders and the personal finance industry they created reveals how easy it is to overstate the intentionality behind change. Small-loan lenders played an important role in making credit for consumption part of the American dream. But such was not their intention.

The lenders and reformers who organized the licensed small-loan industry did not view themselves as advance agents for debt-based mass consumerism. On the contrary, through the mid-1920s small-loan lenders conscientiously resisted modern consumerism, at least what they could see of it. The business of personal finance was conceived as an exercise in philanthropy and social welfare, as a way of liberating workers from the clutches of poverty and the loan shark. In order to combat the odium attached to their business, small-loan lenders characterized themselves as upholders of the American dream. Not the consumerist dream of easy living on an increasingly high standard, but an older dream, one which pictured America as a country where wage laborers who worked hard and saved their money could rise up in the world and become independent producers. Small-loan lenders hoped that with an advance of "capital" and a little financial advice, some workers, at least, would be enabled to take charge of their lives and become "capitalists" themselves.

If the founders of the personal finance industry had known the consequences of their actions, if they had known that they were helping to lay the financial foundation for a culture of consumption, they might have stopped lending and moved into some other line of social work. In fact, when lenders realized what was happening, that is what a few of them did. The others continued to hope that their business directed borrowers onto the straight and narrow path of Victorian thrift, self-discipline, and productive independence. In this hope small-loan lenders were not being entirely selfless; the thrifty borrower made payments, the prodigal borrower did not.

But what they intended never materialized. Instead of building a society of independent, thrifty, and hardworking small businessmen, personal finance companies helped to build a debt-driven consumer culture. The lost vision of the early years of the personal finance industry makes it easier to understand how consumption credit got a foothold in a society that claimed to scorn debt for nonproductive purposes.

USURY AND ILLEGAL LENDING

The origins of commercial small-loan lending lie in the middle of the nineteenth century, when moneylenders first began lending small sums of money on nonpawn security. By 1875 this kind of lending was widespread, well organized, and almost entirely illegal. Usury laws made it so.

The curious persistence of usury laws in nineteenth-century America was not a senseless anachronism. Quite in line with Victorian thinking about debt, the de jure prohibition of high-rate lending amounted to a de facto discouragement of small-loan, or "consumptive," borrowing.

Nineteenth-century usury laws were among the last vestiges of the moral economies of the ancient and medieval eras. For much the greater part of human history, a hostility to interest was expressed in almost all ethical systems of the world. For example, Mosaic law deemed "usury" an unbrotherly exploitation of a fellow Israelite's misfortune, and banned all interest on loans.[2] The Greek philosophers also objected to interest. Aristotle, observing that gold, unlike wheat, cannot reproduce itself, maintained that the sterility of money forces the conclusion that any return on money is a deceit, a fraud against nature as well as humanity.[3] In the fifth century A.D., the church dictated its first canon law prohibiting all forms of interest on loans. Later, usury was declared to be a mortal sin, and unrepentant usurers were denied Christian burial. The case against interest in Scripture and Aristotle was sharpened to a fine edge by the medieval scholastics, whose extended reflection on the subject of usury has been described as "the midwife of modern economics."[4] But while the scholastics found occasional warrant for interest charges where lenders would clearly have used the money themselves if they had not lent it, such cases were circumscribed as the exceptions that proved the rule. According to the church, money was barren, and interest illegitimate.

In agrarian economies not attuned to growth, where borrowers were poor and suffering acute distress, it made sense to regard interest charges as the pirating of the powerless. But after the thirteenth century, growing financial markets emptied the persuasiveness of arguments for the sterility of money. Thus John Calvin, looking around him at bustling Geneva in 1545, found himself forced to admit that "it cannot be said that money does not engender money." It was clear to Calvin that the new wine of market society was bursting the wineskins of the old moral economy. Lending and borrowing were different than before. Most lending now financed business ventures. There was very little borrowing by individuals for the purpose of immediate consumption, because propertyless borrowers could not bid successfully against businessmen who wanted money for productive enterprises. In light of this fact, Calvin concluded that usury should not be wholly forbidden "except it be repugnant both to justice and to charity."[5]

Even before the Reformation, similar concessions were made by church and states across Europe, which for a long time had turned a blind eye to the various dodges and evasions that made usury laws a dead letter. In 1515, the Lateran Council even went so far as to approve a small charge of interest on loans to the poor. Four hundred years later the reasoning behind the council's decision would be seized on by founders of the small-loan industry in the United States, who also wanted to demonstrate that the good work of lending to the poor could not be done under restrictive usury laws. Permission to levy interest on loans to the poor allowed Italian municipalities to establish *monts-de-piété* ("charitable corporations"), which were pawnbroking agencies run under municipal authority. The methods of these successful agencies were widely copied across Europe. But significantly for the United States, no system of *monts-de-piété* was established in England, whose social and legal system laid the foundation for small-loan lending across the Atlantic. Rather, in 1545, King Henry VIII broke from Roman legislation on usury to set his own course toward economic modernization. In that year, he declared that interest on all loans would be permitted at rates not to exceed 10 percent a year. This decree was weakened in 1833 and 1837 to exempt from the usury laws all promissory notes and bills of exchange. Finally, in 1854, after years of prodding from the advocates of laissez-faire, Parliament repealed the usury laws altogether.[6]

Thus, from the mid-thirteenth to the mid-nineteenth century, the idea of usury was the most contested issue between advocates of a moral economy and supporters of the capitalist spirit. Referring to this long-running debate and the victory of the capitalist spirit, Fernand Braudel states that by "the latter half of the eighteenth century, the quarrel was over."[7] Yet the concept of a moral economy continued to cast a long legal shadow in the United States, where usury laws restricted the availability of small, "consumptive" loans.

Usury laws remained in force in the United States long after they disappeared from European statute books.[8] By 1881, almost thirty years after the English stopped regulating interest, only fourteen of the forty-seven American states had followed suit. But even in these states the issue was not dead; many would reinstate usury regulations. The states constantly experimented with various rates, exemptions, and definitions of usury, making it hard to generalize about the law regarding usury.[9] But most states set two rates: a "legal rate," which gave courts a standard for determining a fair rate of return in cases where business contracts stipulated no rate, and a "maximum contract rate," which set the highest rate which could be enforced at law. Six percent a year was commonly recognized as a fair legal rate; only Louisiana set the maximum rate lower (5 percent), while several states allowed rates as high as 12 percent. For most of the nineteenth century, usury laws made no distinction between moneylending to businesses for profit-making purposes, and small-loan lending to individuals and families for household consumption purposes. Was this because people failed to recognize that small loans required a higher rate than 6 percent or even 12 percent to be made profitably? Or was this recognized only too well?

The fact of the matter was that a single maximum rate discriminated heavily against small-loan lending and borrowing. The economics of small-loan lending required that moneylenders charge comparatively high rates of interest for their loans. There were—and still are—several reasons for this. Unlike commercial bankers, most lenders of small sums did not have access to cheap capital in the form of funds from depositors; they either lent their own money or borrowed capital funds from someone else. Consequently, their loans were necessarily more expensive than bank loans. Another reason the rates were higher than bank rates was that small-loan lenders were engaged in a riskier business. Small loans to consumers were generally made for longer periods of time, on less certain security, for purposes not likely to turn a profit and thereby repay the loan. Finally, higher rates on loans helped small-loan lenders offset their office costs, which were relatively higher per loan than that of lenders dealing in large sums. Since a loan of fifty dollars required the same credit investigation and office expense as a loan of five thousand, it becomes easy to see why the lender specializing in small loans charged a higher rate of interest in order to recover the cost of making the loan.

The basic economic principles of small-loan lending had been set forth by William Blackstone and Jeremy Bentham, among others, in the eighteenth century. "Without some profit allowed by law," wrote Blackstone, "there will be but few lenders, and those principally bad men who will break the law and make a profit, and then will endeavor to indemnify themselves from the danger of the penalty by making the profit exorbitant."[10] In the United States, this is exactly what happened.

Usury laws were easily circumvented. Not only was there pressure to break the law in order to make small loans, but also to make certain business loans, such as long-term agricultural mortgages, which in periods of restricted money required more than 6 percent interest. "Note-shaving" lenders discounted a note at the legal rate, then tacked on various charges in the form of fees, premiums, and commissions, in order to shave down the stated interest rate to the legal maximum. The extra charges were paid in cash so that no record remained to prove that the loan was usurious.[11] In a petition to the Massachusetts legislature in 1834, 202 businessmen of Boston demonstrated their familiarity with Blackstone and Bentham when they claimed that note-shaving practices "produce a fearful disregard of the laws, and . . . tend to throw pecuniary negotiations into the hands of unprincipled and dangerous men."[12] This was all the more true where the pressure to lend at high rates was the strongest. The shadow of illegality fell deepest on those who lent and borrowed in small amounts.

After midcentury the market for small loans increased steadily. This was due to a paradox of industrial employment: while on the one hand it denied workers a steady income, on the other hand the wages it paid workers during times of employment lifted many to a higher standard of living. Both conditions were necessary for small-loan lending to develop. Factory workers found their income frequently interrupted by illness, injury, strikes, lockouts, seasonal unemployment, layoffs, and plant closings. Even when times were good, workers were no less subject to errors in judgment that caused people of all classes to mismanage their funds. Now that their lives were fully monetarized, urban workers found that a sudden loss of income or spending all their money brought quick and painful consequences. If they could fall back on a garden, it was not large; if they could call on community support, it was more moral than financial. But because workers (particularly skilled workers) were seeing their wages slowly rise when they were employed, because they were increasingly able to buy more durable and semidurable goods, their status as credit risks during periods of unemployment became increasingly acceptable. This point was not lost on moneylenders.

Consequently, the second half of the nineteenth century witnessed the development of a secretive, underground trade in small loans for workers. According to Louis Robinson and Rolf Nugent, authors of an early history of the small-loan business, in Chicago loans were made on household furniture as early as 1850.[13] Robinson and Nugent interviewed a retired lawyer who had provided legal counsel to some of Chicago's first generation of illegal small-loan lenders. Charles R. Napier recalled that when he came to Chicago in 1882 the most common form of security for a small loan was a wage attachment.[14] Chattel mortgages on household goods and claims on future wages became the two most common types of security for small lenders.

To document the spread of small-loan lending, Robinson and Nugent surveyed the classified advertisements of newspapers around the country after the Civil War, looking for ads placed by lenders. Their research discovered that advertisements for chattel mortgage loans began appearing in Chicago in 1869, in Boston in 1873, in Milwaukee in 1875, in Minneapolis in 1878, and in New York in 1885. The appearance of wage assignment lenders could not be dated so easily, because this type of lender did not advertise in the newspaper as much as those who lent on chattel mortgages. Instead, wage assignment lenders used handbills to concentrate their efforts among certain employee groups, such as city workers, whose incomes were easy to ascertain and relatively immune to interruption. Nevertheless, Robinson and Nugent collected enough evidence to suggest that, by 1885, workers in the principal cities of the United States could call upon both types of loan agencies.[15]

In the beginning, small-loan lending was a sideline for those looking to make some extra money. Likely candidates to become engaged in this business were payroll clerks, who lent to employees; storage and warehouse men, who lent on the security of stored furniture; and pawnbrokers, installment furniture dealers, lawyers, bank clerks, insurance agents, and real-estate brokers.[16]

But small-loan lending very quickly became a big, if quiet, business. Because small loan offices required little in the way of start-up capital (especially for salary loan lending), successful lenders quickly branched out to form chain offices in other cities. In 1890, the founder of what would become the Household Finance Corporation, Frank J. Mackey, operated fourteen loan offices from Omaha to Newark. In the East Daniel H. Tolman ran a chain of offices that numbered over sixty by the turn of the century. About the same time, John Mulholland, whose first Kansas City loan office opened in 1893, controlled over one hundred loan offices spread throughout the country.[17] In 1900, Tolman and Mulholland operated more chain offices than any of the retailers who would become famous as chain store innovators, with the one exception of the Great Atlantic and Pacific Tea Company, which operated nearly two hundred stores.[18] In other words, the illegal small-loan business is an uncredited pioneer of the chain-store movement.

Unlike the A&P, small-loan businesses were not exactly eager to draw public attention. For this reason it is hard to tell the exact extent of their business. But as noted in Chapter 1, a reputable estimate made in 1911 concluded that in cities with a population of over thirty thousand, one out of five workers borrowed from an illegal lender in the course of a year.[19] The number was greater in manufacturing cities. In New York City, an investigation in 1911 by Commissioner of Accounts Raymond Fosdick determined that 35 percent of the city's employees owed money to illegal lenders.[20]

The illegal loan business was the predictable result of a great need for consumer loans and lawmakers' refusal to recognize that need. There can be little doubt that usury laws hurt the very people they were intended to protect. The cheap money that poor borrowers could not get did not help them. The money they could get was not made cheaper to borrow or easier to find because it came from underground channels. Some of the illegal lenders were honest businessmen who simply wanted to run a profitable lending operation. But the illegality of the business did not attract the most reputable businessmen. The rule of business for many lenders was to charge the highest rate the market could bear. Unfortunately for borrowers, "what the market could bear" was often extended through chicanery and outright intimidation. Hence, the popular name for illegal lenders: "loan sharks."

One example suffices to show why illegal lenders were loathed and despised. In October 1891, a widow in Philadelphia, whose sole source of support was the income of her two children, borrowed $75 from an illegal lender. According to records later recovered from the lender, over the next two years the woman paid $7.50 a month on her loan, eventually paying the lender $142.50 for the original loan of $75. But even then the loan was not repaid, given the terms of the illegal contract that had been signed. In the winter of 1893–94, as the country slipped into a recession, the widow's daughters lost their jobs and the woman was forced to default on seven straight monthly payments. When the daughters were rehired in May, the widow was informed by the loan office that she now owed seven months' interest, or $52.50, as well as the original principal of $75. All told, she was asked to pay an additional $112.50, after having already paid $142.50. With this impossible demand staring her in the face, the woman finally determined to seek out help. She told her story to the representative of a local relief committee, who intervened on her behalf with the lender. Under threat of legal action, the lender was pressured into canceling the rest of the widow's debt. But he refused to refund the usurious interest that had been charged. Free of her monthly burden of payments, the woman declined to pursue the matter further.[21]

Incidents like this were probably not "typical" of the average small loan, but neither were they uncommon. Stories about the victims of loan sharks circulated among social workers and dotted the pages of city newspapers. Brimming with pathos, greed, and tales of urban ugliness, stories about the loan sharks were the perfect thing to create a public scandal and, not incidentally, boost circulation. Between 1887 and 1905, investigative reports on the "loan shark evil" were carried out by newspapers in Kansas City, Milwaukee, Providence, Toledo, and Boston. Outrage provoked by the newspaper articles led to public and semipublic investigations of loansharking in Philadelphia in 1893–94, and in Atlanta in 1903.[22] Everywhere the elements of the problem were the same: working-class people with emergency needs for cash were being victimized by the high rates, bullying tactics, and legal deceptions of unscrupulous lenders. But while publicity gave to the victims a measure of public sympathy, it offered no solutions. High-rate lending was not going to be shamed out of existence.

Attacks on loansharking in the press inspired urban reformers to think of ways to deal with the problem. Various plans were put forward for establishing low-rate lending agencies, all of them based on philanthropic principles. Some agencies were formed as straight philanthropic ventures; that is, they offered no financial return to the public-minded citizens who contributed to the agencies' loan fund. The Hebrew Free Loan Societies were of this type, as were various loan funds sponsored by employers. In many cases, loans from these lenders were offered interest-free. The other type of philanthropic loan agencies added a touch of business to their altruism, operating on the principle of "philanthropy + 6 percent." They also derived their loan fund from charitable contributions, but promised contributors a return on their investment, never to exceed 6 percent. These "remedial loan societies," as they were often called, were important progenitors of the personal finance business.[23]

The first remedial loan society, the Collateral Loan Company of Boston, opened its doors in 1857. It operated as a pawnbroking establishment. The first remedial loan society to lend on chattels was Boston's Workingmen's Loan Association, established in 1888. But the largest and most influential remedial loan society in the country was the Provident Loan Society of New York City. The idea for the Provident came from a pair of reform-minded citizens, one an attorney, the other a young banker. James Speyer, the banker, drew up a proposal in early 1893 for a lending agency that would be modeled after the municipal pawnshops of Europe, which he had observed firsthand. His idea came to life during the recession of 1893–1894. Members of the Charity Organization Society raised $35,000 for a loan fund, including contributions from Cornelius Vanderbilt and Percy Rockefeller. Robert W. deForest, president of the society, was persuaded to become the chairman of the organization. Against opposition from commercial pawnbrokers and moneylenders, the Provident Loan Society was incorporated by the state legislature in April 1894 with the help of favorable publicity in the city's newspapers. In its first full year of operation, the Provident made over twenty thousand loans on pawns, averaging eighteen dollars each. To its sponsors, the Provident Loan Society was a semiphilanthropic investment. The return on their contributions could never exceed 6 percent, and the trustees had the option of voting to pay no earnings at all. To its borrowers, the Provident showed a business face, operating as a normal pawnshop. But the Provident boasted one important distinction: interest on loans was held to 12 percent per annum, which was one-third to one-half the legal rate charged by pawnbrokers in New York City at the time. The low rate was made possible by the society's semiphilanthropic capital fund, its unpaid directorate, its very large volume of business, and its efficient management. Inspired by the example of the Provident Loan Society, public-minded financiers in other cities established lending agencies run on similar principles. In 1909 fifteen such societies met in Buffalo, New York, to organize the National Federation of Remedial Loan Associations (NFRLA).[24]

The philanthropic and remedial loan societies became a seedbed for the ideas that later would grow into successful alternatives to loansharking. But in the late nineteenth and early twentieth centuries, they were no more effective in solving the problem of illegal lending than the publicity campaigns run by the newspapers. The philanthropic agencies had unstable careers and suffered from haphazard management. The semiphilanthropic agencies compiled a better record, but their loans amounted to a drop in the bucket. They neither drove interest rates down through the force of competition, nor reached the neediest, and hence riskiest, borrowers.

Borrowers were blocked from an adequate supply of cash credit for small loans by state legislators who refused to take the necessary steps to put small "consumptive" loans on a legal basis. But in 1884, the legislature of New Jersey became the first to provide state support for small-loan businesses. Over the next twenty years nine states experimented with various ways of regulating charitable and small-loan lending. Different rates were tried, different-sized loans were regulated, and various types of lending organizations, such as pawnbrokers and philanthropic lenders, were granted special considerations. But none of the experiments set a rate high enough to allow for a legal small-loan business. Most legislators remained indifferent to the need for consumer credit. Even those sympathetic to reform drew a line at rates far too low to sustain a small-loan lending business.[25]

At the turn of the twentieth century, then, cash credit for small loans was a weak spot in the American industrial economy. Usury laws prevented capital from flowing smoothly into the small-loan business, and forced the lending that did exist into illegal channels. The problem was not being remedied by stiffer laws, occasional indictments, and newspaper headlines. Nor were attempts to inject competition into the business through philanthropic lending working, either. Experiments with statutory reform were steps in the right direction, but still much too tentative.

Why, in the face of arguments marshaled by Blackstone, Bentham, and others, and contrary to the example of European states that repealed their usury laws after 1854, did so many American states retain the usury laws on their books? Part of the answer had to do with pressure from loan sharks to preserve the status quo. Illegal lenders resisted reform of the usury laws because they rightly recognized that no state was willing to sanction the rates they needed to stay in business. By itself, this explanation does not go far enough, because it does not account for why loan sharks in the United States were more successful in opposing usury reform than their counterparts in England and on the Continent. Hence, historians of the small-loan business have tended to blame restrictive usury laws on a public ignorant of the needs of the urban small borrower. It is argued that populists favored usury laws because farmers had "a lack of understanding" about the way small-loan lending worked, and why it required rates higher than the tried-and-true 6 percent.[26] Robinson and Nugent argued that since most loans in the nineteenth century were long-term agricultural loans, the outlook of the rural debtor community prevailed over the business viewpoint of the urban trading community, which favored legal support for low-interest loans.[27]

But why would legislators refuse to distinguish between what were really two separate businesses, the long-term mortgage loan business and the consumer small-loan business? It is hard to avoid the conclusion that usury laws in the United States were supported less by the public's ignorance of basic economic principles than by general opposition to the idea of "consumptive" borrowing. Even the supporters of remedial lending harshly criticized the "extravagance" and "wastefulness" of the industrial worker that drove him or her into the hands of the loan sharks. "Consumptive" borrowing was firmly proscribed by the Victorian money management ethic. If the highest virtue in the money ethic was hard work and saving, the lowest vice was borrowing money to pay for mere "consumptive" cravings (the exception being borrowing for necessities in the case of true emergencies). From this point of view, reforms in the usury laws would result in a larger, more wide-open small-loan industry, which would lead to more borrowing for "consumptive" purposes, more unnecessary household debt. In other words, usury reform ran counter to the code of propriety held up by the Victorian money management ethic, and that was why usury laws stayed on the books so long. Accordingly, when progressive reformers in the early twentieth century fought to change the laws so as to establish a legitimate small-loan lending industry, they were very careful to justify small-loan lending in the language of the Victorian money management ethic.

CHAPTER 3

Arthur Ham and the Fight for Legal Lending

The American credit system at the turn of the century can be summarized this way: people who had money could easily borrow more, while people without money found it difficult to borrow at all. More precisely, businessmen could call on bankers for their business and personal needs, while blue-collar and lower-level white-collar workers were forced to borrow money from shadowy lenders, at high rates, under illegal conditions. This state of affairs compromised democratic standards of fairness, and reformers of the Progressive Era were not blind to it. In the early decades of the twentieth century reformers from a variety of circles joined together in a major effort to democratize credit. They successfully worked a major overhaul in the usury laws, and thereby created the legal foundation for the rise of consumer finance companies.

The campaign got started in the summer of 1909 when the Russell Sage Foundation turned its attention to the problem of small loans. It was a magnificent irony that the organization taking the lead in the fight to legalize small-loan lending was named in honor of a man who possessed not a shred of sympathy for the needs of indigent borrowers. Once, when Russell Sage was asked if he favored measures to help the poor, the flinty railroad tycoon responded: "There are persons who ought never to have money. . . . Poverty is the only salvation of such men because in that state they can be to an extent restrained by the community."[28] The remark was completely in character. No one ever gainsaid the judgment of Fiorella La Guardia on Russell Sage, that he was "one of the meanest skinflints who ever lived."[29]

Over the course of a long career of swindles, speculations, and sharp financial maneuvers, Sage built up a sizable fortune of $65 million. It was a fortune undiminished by the spirit of philanthropy. "He wanted money; he got it; he kept it," read the obituary for Sage in the business-minded *New York Post*.[30] But upon his death in 1906, Sage's entire fortune transferred to his wife, Margaret, who immediately began to give away her new millions. Un-

124

like her husband, Margaret Sage possessed a large sympathy for the poor. She was personally involved in works of charity and counted among her friends many of New York City's leading advocates of philanthropy and social reform. One of them was Robert W. de Forest, president of the Charity Organization Society since 1888, president of the National Conference of Charities and Correction in 1903, and Mrs. Sage's personal lawyer. On his advice, Margaret Sage in 1907 incorporated the Russell Sage Foundation for the purpose of "the improvement of social and living conditions in the United States of America."[31]

With an endowment of $10 million, the new foundation was modeled after the example of the Carnegie Institution and Rockefeller's General Education Board. Thus, it would not disburse its income in direct forms of aid. Rather, in typical progressive fashion, Margaret Sage and the foundation's trustees intended the foundation to be a fact-finding agency that would assist social scientists to track down the systemic roots of society's "larger and more difficult problems," so that other agencies could then effect the remedies.

The foundation showed an early interest in the credit problems of small borrowers. A small amount of the original endowment was invested in certificates of contribution to the Provident Loan Society of New York, the remedial loan society that de Forest had helped organize during the depression of 1893–1894. In 1909 the foundation stepped up its commitment when the small-loan problem was added to its investigative agenda. The impetus for this move came from W. Frank Persons of New York's Charity Organization Society. Persons had been employed by Margaret Sage in 1907 to administer her personal charities. In the next two years, over sixty thousand letters addressed to Mrs. Sage and asking for personal assistance passed across Persons' desk. So many of the appeals involved complaints about illegal lenders that Persons segregated these letters into a special file. At some point he brought the file to de Forest's attention, and in August 1909, the board of trustees of the Russell Sage Foundation voted to begin an exploration of the problem. A young graduate student was hired "to make a study of the Remedial Loan Associations in this country, to give advice to societies already established as to methods of work, and to give advice to those who wish to know about the formation of such societies."[32]

The graduate student was Arthur H. Ham of Columbia University. Only twenty-six years old, Ham already knew more about small-loan lending than almost any other person outside of the business. Ham was introduced to the subject while at Columbia, where he was selected for a fellowship awarded by the Bureau of Research at the New York School of Philanthropy. The fellowship, funded by the Russell Sage Foundation, asked students to choose a subject for study from a list of topics drawn up by the foundation's trustees. Ham chose the subject of chattel mortgage loans. His choice was perhaps inspired by his classmate Clarence Wassam, also on a Russell Sage fellowship, who was then completing an impressive study on wage assignment lending. The studies were the first in a long series of Russell Sage publications in the field of small loans.[33]

Both men concluded that small-loan lenders were causing a great deal of hardship among people of modest means, overburdening borrowers with unreasonable interest charges in gross violation of the law. This much had been said before, by newspaper reporters and social workers. But in the studies by Wassam and Ham, hearsay and melodrama were replaced by a more careful approach to investigation that avoided dramatic language and hyperbole. Both studies condemned the avaricious behavior of the illegal lenders, but they also made a stab at accumulating hard evidence to document the secretive workings of an underground business. Lengthy appendixes included office forms, financial statements, account book pages, lists of the occupations of borrowers, copies of state laws, and other materials relating to the legal, economic, and operating procedures of the illegal lenders, making their studies indispensable sources of evidence for later historians. Both studies pointed out that current attempts to solve the small-loan problem were doomed to failure. What reformers failed to recognize, suggested Wassam and Ham, was that the problems of the small borrower would only be addressed when a new small-loan industry based on remedial principles was freed from the impossible burden of the usury laws. Wassam's *The Salary Loan Business in New York City* (1908) and Ham's *The Chattel Loan Business* (1909) called for large, coordinated efforts to eliminate illegal lending, efforts that would combine publicity, competition from philanthropic lenders, and regulatory legislation.

Coordinated efforts require a coordinator. From the day he signed on with the Russell Sage Foundation in 1909 until leaving in 1917 to work for the War Savings Division of the U.S. Treasury Department, Arthur Ham fulfilled this role. Working out of an office provided by the Provident Loan Society, Ham also functioned as general secretary for the National Federation of Remedial Lending Associations. After a year of promoting the cause of remedial lending, in 1910 Ham was made director of the Russell Sage Foundation's newly established Division of Remedial Loans. From this position, Ham quickly became recognized as the nation's preeminent expert on the small-loan problem, and a tireless crusader against the loan sharks.

For the next eight years, Ham dedicated himself to what he described as "the campaign against the loan shark." The struggle to replace the illegal lending companies with a new type of credit system went through two phases. Before 1916, Ham and the remedial reformers took the lead; after 1916, leadership passed to reformers *within* the ranks of the lending business. In the earlier period Ham and the reformers of the NFRLA followed a double-barreled strategy that aimed, in something of a reversal of Gresham's law, to displace the "bad money" of illegal lenders with the "good money" of remedial lenders.

When Ham spoke of a "campaign" against the loan shark, the choice of a military metaphor indicated what he thought about illegal lenders. Simply put, they were to be eliminated. Following a strategy of unconditional victory, Ham and the early reformers made no distinctions between, on the one hand, moneylenders who simply wanted to run a profitable business and therefore might be allies in an effort to pass fair and just regulatory legislation and, on the other hand, unscrupulous lenders who used extortion, threats of violence, and legal chicanery to exploit the poor. Rather, illegal lenders of whatever character were lumped together and portrayed as cruel, rapacious Shylocks who made an evil living off the miseries of others. They were, in Ham's words, "sharks, leeches and remorseless extortioners," "usurious moneylenders" with "an arrogant disregard of human rights."[34] In 1912 Ham wrote and produced a motion picture about the perils of borrowing that was released in commercial theaters to good reviews. *The Usurer's Grip* took attacks on the "loan shark evil" to new heights.[35] But even these were surpassed the following year when Ham wrote a series of publicity pamphlets (never printed) under the collective title *The Green-Back Peril*. Individual titles in the series were *I. In the Maw of the Thing*; *II. In the Thing's Den*; and *III. On the Trail of the Thing*.[36] Ham's scorn for illegal lenders of whatever stripe characterized the first phase of the campaign against illegal lending.

In order to eliminate the loan sharks, Ham and the Division of Remedial Loans pursued an aggressive strategy of prosecutions and publicity.[37] In the first year of his appointment, he examined the available records of some of New York's three hundred illegal small lenders and succeeded in getting four licenses revoked and legal action taken against two other companies. Allegations of extortion were investigated and equitable settlements arranged. Ham widened the scope of his activities by calling on others for help. New York's Legal Aid Society provided voluntary legal help with prosecutions, the defense of victims, and the arrangement of test cases to be carried to the Court of Appeals. The loan sharks were dealt a major blow when Ham convinced the leading employers of New York City to stop discharging employees who got in trouble with illegal lenders. Previously, the threat of informing the boss had been the lenders' greatest security. In addition, several landlords were convinced that loan sharks were not acceptable tenants, and the daily newspapers were lobbied to refuse to accept advertising from illegal lenders. Perhaps Ham's greatest victory was convincing the district attorney of New York County to appoint a special prosecutor in charge of usury cases. The first man to fill this position, Franklin Brooks, handled more than one thousand cases of usury in just five months.[38]

Ham and the remedial reformers understood that attacking the illegal lenders was like weeding a potato patch: as soon as weeds are picked, new weeds spring up. Thus, they paired their negative strategy of attacking the loan sharks with a positive strategy to put remedial lending societies in their place.

Proponents of remedial lending approached the borrowing needs of workers with equal measures of sympathy and paternalism. Borrowers were promised dignified treatment and low rates of interest. But more than that, remedial lenders dedicated themselves to providing expert financial guidance and advice on how to develop good financial habits. This kind of service, the remedial reformers pointed out, had been sorely lacking with the loan sharks. A speaker at the 1909 meetings of the NFRLS castigated loan sharks for their part in corrupting the working class:

> [The usurer's] golden promises extend to the improvident, the thoughtless, and the covetous. Does a man wish for a summer vacation at the seashore or mountains? The loan man will provide the means. Does he wish to make Christmas presents to his family and friends, or perchance buy a watch for himself? The loan man is again his friend, his ministering angel. Does he owe "the butcher, the baker, the candlestick maker"? Here is his resource for paying his bills without trouble to himself and with the easiest of requirements for future settlement.[39]

Needless to say, remedial lenders promised borrowers a different kind of "help."

In fact, publicity put out by the remedial reformers often made it seem as if financial "guidance" was their major social service. Speaking to the National Conference of Charities and Corrections in 1911, Arthur Ham observed that the backbone of the illegal lending business was made up of loans to city workers who usually had "no cause to borrow except a fancied need." From Ham's point of view, many of the loan shark's so-called victims were actually "victims of their own improvidence and extravagance," easy suckers who fell prey to the alluring advertisements of the loan sharks. According to Ham, here was an opportunity for social workers to help stop the spread of the "borrowing germ," by supporting remedial loan societies in their work of "rehabilitating" the financial habits of low- and medium-income households. For these families, the task of the remedial lending societies was to lend money, of course, but more than that, "to discourage ill-advised borrowing, to give helpful advice, to encourage thrift and saving." "The most important part of the work," he continued, "is the creation of habits of thrift that often result in savings accounts after the loan is paid."[40] In his report on the chattel lending business published some years before, Ham had written approvingly of the St. Bartholomew's Loan Association of New York City, which "never makes a loan unless it is thought to be a good thing for the applicant, no matter how valuable the security may be."[41] Somehow, it never occurred to Ham or the other reformers that what they viewed as education others might view as paternalistic meddling. They would soon discover that many borrowers chose a lender based on criteria other than low rates.

In 1909 Ham corresponded with persons in 125 cities who were interested in establishing remedial loan societies. That year, the membership of the NRFLA stood at fourteen. Six years later, the group numbered forty, the largest it would ever get.[42] The increase was made possible more than anything else by Ham's work in the area of legislative reform.

In order to stay in business, even semiphilanthropic lending agencies had to charge more than 6 percent interest per year. The first remedial loan societies obtained special exemptions from the regular usury laws, but this kind of enabling legislation was difficult to obtain, and not a promising way to expand the number of societies. Hence, in June 1911, Ham proposed to the NRFLA that it pursue the passage of a model loan law that would provide for state supervision and control of small-loan companies, and set a rate of interest fair to both borrower and lender.[43] The problem lay in determining what a fair rate of interest was. If everyone agreed that 1,000 percent or 100 percent or even 50 percent was too much, what exactly was a fair rate? To find out, the Division of Remedial Loans in 1911 funded and organized the Chattel Loan Society of New York, a lending agency that would serve as a laboratory for determining the "scientific" rate needed to operate a viable small-loan business. Ham had previously argued that 2 percent was probably a fair rate of interest. But experience gained from running the Chattel Loan Society led to the conclusion that societies wanting to return 6 percent to investors would have to charge 3 percent a month on their loans.[44]

This conclusion was seconded by the results being obtained from legislative reform. In the state houses publicity for the campaign against the loan shark paid off in a big way: except for public utilities, state legislatures after 1909 gave more attention to regulating small loan lending than any other business activity. In the year ending June 1913, sixty bills were introduced in twenty-four states. Many more would come later.[45] Increasingly, Ham and the Division of Remedial Loans became preoccupied with legislative battles. After 1911, Ham was increasingly called upon to offer expert advice in states where reformers were fighting to amend the usury laws and establish a system of remedial lenders. The laws varied widely in their details, and in their success at making it through the legislative process. By 1913, experience with both good and bad bills had accumulated to the point where Ham felt ready to draw up a list of requirements for a model lending law. This first attempt to define a model law included the following provisions: licensing and bonding for all lenders charging more than the banking rate, a maximum rate of 2–3 percent per month with no additional fees allowed, state supervision of records, adequate penalties, the consent of wives and employers to assignment of wages, and copies of the law to be given to borrowers. Remedial reformers immediately began plans to lobby the model law.[46]

In every state where Ham's provisions were introduced into the legislature, they met with determined opposition. Some legislators objected to any rate over the banking rate. Illegal lenders argued that 2 percent a month was impossible and 3 percent unreasonable. Until 1914 the illegal lenders successfully parried every attempt by reformers to pass laws that would crowd out the high-rate lenders with their own low-rate remedial societies. In every case proposed bills were either defeated in their entirety or amended so that they lacked one or more of the key provisions drawn up by Ham. Without enforcement provisions or the prohibition on additional charges, laws passed in the early stages of the campaign for legal reforms amounted to little more than enabling laws for remedial lenders. They did nothing to eliminate the loan sharks.[47]

Nevertheless, by 1914 Arthur Ham and the remedial reformers could take satisfaction in the progress that was being made. In a case that received widespread attention in the fall of 1913, D. H. Tolman, owner of one of the nation's largest lending chains, was convicted of usury in New York and sentenced to six months in prison. The Tolman sentence sent shock waves throughout the lending community, because previous usury convictions had generally resulted in small fines, the surrender of illegal interest charges, or an overnight jail stay for an office clerk. Tolman canceled $500,000 worth of debts and moved his offices out of the state.[48]

In January 1914, a new and even more aggressive district attorney stepped in to take charge of the usury bureau in New York City. Walter S. Hilborn, formerly employed by Gimbel's Department Store to defend their employees against loan sharks, was handpicked by Ham for the new job. In the first nine months after Hilborn took the job, wage assignments against city workers fell off by a third.[49] More good news came in March 1914, when in New Jersey the illegal lenders were defeated for the first time in the legislative arena. The Egan Act, drafted and lobbied by Arthur Ham, was the first lending law based on the provisions of the NFRLA model law.[50] Two months later, on 5 May 1914, the last loan shark advertisement disappeared from the last New York City newspaper to allow illegal lenders to run ads in its classified section.[51] With this abundance of good news, both Ham and Hilborn claimed at the end of 1914 that the era of the loan shark in New York City was over. Ham reported that not one of the illegal lenders operating in the city when the Division of Remedial Loans was organized was still in business.[52] This could not be said of other cities, but the trend was encouraging.

What happened to the illegal lenders? Their story is harder to tell, because they left so few sources. But it is clear from what happened after 1914 that the campaign against the loan shark split the lending community into two camps. One group, composed mostly of wage assignment lenders, continued to fight all attempts to legislate into existence a reconstructed version of their small-loan business. Wage assignment lenders charged the highest rates in the lending business, because their loans were the smallest. They had no hope that legislators would ever legalize the rates they charged. The other group, which included most of the larger chattel mortgage lenders, was prepared to make a separate peace with the credit reformers. As loan bills began to multiply in the state legislatures, these lenders organized themselves into state and local associations for the purpose of influencing legislation in their favor.

The formation of these associations marked the emergence of a new voice of reform, one now articulated from within the lending business. On 19 April 1916, cash lenders from five states met in Philadelphia to organize the American Association of Small Loan Brokers (AASLB). The purpose of their organization, in the words of its first chairman, was to "standardize, dignify and police the small loan business."[53] The organizer of this meeting was Clarence Hodson of the Beneficial Loan Society, a company that would soon become one of the two giants in the business. In the first year, 325 lending companies signed on as charter members of the new association. Significantly, Arthur Ham, the bête noire of the loan sharks, attended the second day of the organizational meeting.

Ham began his career hostile to all illegal lenders. But when he recognized that the members of the AASLB were serious about reforming the business from within, he moderated his position. The model small-loan law favored by the AASLB was very close to the one championed by Ham and the NFRLA. On this basis, cordial relations between the reconstructed lenders and the remedial lenders were quickly established. From September to November 1916, representatives of the AASLB, the Division of Remedial Loans, and the NFRLA met several times to hammer out a model small-loan law that would be acceptable to all parties. The only real sticking point was the rate of interest. A compromise of 3.5 percent without fees was finally adopted.[54]

The fruit of these negotiations was the Uniform Small Loan Law, which became the basis for legislative action in the future, and the foundation for legal small-loan lending in the United States. Defining the small-loan business in terms of loans of three hundred dollars or less, the Uniform Small Loan Law conformed to the provisions set forth by Arthur Ham in 1913, with the exception of a slightly higher interest rate.[55] Though the Uniform Small Loan Law was bitterly opposed in every state where it was introduced, its chances for success were greatly enhanced by the combined forces of the remedial reformers and the reconstructed lenders. The uniform draft was introduced into the legislatures of four states in 1917, becoming law in Illinois, Indiana, and Maine. Amendments were later made to the draft several times as its sponsors fine-tuned its provisions. By 1932, twenty-five states had some version of the Uniform Small Loan Law on their books.[56]

Agreement on the Uniform Small Loan Law marked a watershed in the history of small-loan lending. Its significance was twofold. To begin with, it strengthened the cause of credit reform by bringing together two formerly implacable enemies. Like many philanthropic lenders, H. A. Cone, the director of Detroit's Provident Loan Society, held a dim view of the character of the loan sharks he was trying to drive out of business. But when Cone began meeting with Detroit's reformist elements in the lending community, he was surprised to find that his potential new allies in the campaign against the loan shark were "for the most part young men of good standing," giving "courteous treatment" to customers and only wanting a little education in order to convince them that regulated lending was a good thing."[57] In just this way, the Uniform Small Loan Law brought together philanthropic reformers and reform-minded lenders, dispelling their prejudices against each other and strengthening their common cause.

Second, the success of the Uniform Small Loan Law closed the door on the remedial reformers and their original strategy for credit reform. In retrospect it is clear that the NRFLA's strategy could not succeed. The problem was simply too big for a philanthropic solution. The NRFLA never numbered more than 40 societies, while in 1916, the first year of its existence, the AASLB enrolled 325 members. That same year the Executive Committee of the NFRLA voted to allow members to join state associations affiliated with the AASLB.[58] Eventually, the remedial lending societies either suspended their operations or were sold to commercial lenders. The Russell Sage Foundation sold its Chattel Loan Society to the Household Finance Corporation in 1925.[59]

Thus ended the first phase of the campaign against the loan shark, which was also a campaign to democratize credit for American workers. After 1916 leadership of the campaign shifted from philanthropic reformers to the "reformed" small-loan lenders themselves.

FROM LOAN SHARKS TO INDUSTRIAL LENDERS

The legalization of lending was a giant step forward toward the creation of a legitimate consumer loan industry. But it was only a first step. Decades of publicity against "the loan shark evil" had fixed in the public mind a negative opinion of small-loan lenders. In the popular estimation they ranked somewhere in between bail bondsmen and bookmakers. Lending came out of the shadows with passage of the Uniform Small Loan Law, but social acceptance lagged. Consequently, changing the public image of the lending business became the number one priority of the newly established small loan industry.

From the very beginning, licensed lenders found themselves besieged and beleaguered. Prejudice against them ran high in the courts, in the legislatures, in banking circles, in some newspapers, among the public, and, of course, among the unreconstructed illegal lenders, whose continuing activities made trouble for the entire loan industry. "We are resigned to abuse and misrepresentation," sighed the lead editorial of the first issue of the *Loan Gazette*, the trade journal of the American Association of Small Loan Brokers.[60] A defensive tone would mark the public voice of the personal finance companies for a long time to come. Probably no other business in America ever felt so misunderstood, or so craved the public's esteem.

To counteract their poor public image, the American Association of Small Loan Brokers followed the lead of other American businesses and embarked on an ambitious program of professionalization. Forming a trade association was the first step in this process.[61] In 1916, the year the association was founded, eight hundred business-related associations existed in the United States, many of them already two decades old. In functional terms, the associations disseminated information, established uniform procedures, ostracized offenders, and generally endeavored to show the public that the business of their members was "sound." Small-loan lenders departed from the pattern of other associations only in this respect: whereas most trade associations hoped that their internal reforms would obviate the need for external governmental regulation, the licensed lenders could hardly take such a position. Their business, after all, depended on state supervision of rates, charges, and terms. Rather, small-loan lenders intended to use state regulation as a weapon in the fight against their rivals, the illegal lenders, who were also their worst public relations problem. State control, then, was necessary. Constantly lobbying for the Uniform Small Loan Law, small-loan lenders were friendlier to state regulation than most other small-business organizations.

At the end of its first year the American Association of Small Loan Brokers numbered 325 members. Thirteen years later, in 1929, there were 1,008 members, or 29 percent of the licensed lenders in the country. A higher percentage belonged to the state associations.[62] By their own estimation, the members of the associations were "the best men engaged in the business." Most were chattel mortgage lenders, operating the larger agencies, often chains. The lenders banded together to protect their interests, but the real vitality of the associations stemmed from the solidarity they afforded to otherwise isolated businessmen who faced an overwhelmingly hostile public. Thus one of the objects of the association was to provide "occasions for pleasant and profitable social and business intercourse."[63] The primary goal of the association was to provide a "fair and dignified" financial service that the lenders judged to be as essential to the economic health of the country as that provided by banks and insurance companies. The task remained to persuade others to this opinion. "We must prove to the public," urged George W. Kehr, the first president of the AASLB, "that we are clean and decent and deserving their respect and confidence. When this is accomplished the business will be as highly regarded as any other financial institution."[64]

The first order of business for standardizing the industry and improving its stature was to decide on a public identity. Before the national association was formed various names were used. Early state regulations referred to "petty loan brokers," "personal loan brokers," "money lenders," and "industrial bankers." The first pick of the association, "small loan brokers," was already an anachronism when it was chosen, and hardly the thing to assure the public of the lenders' perfect honesty. "Brokering" was a ruse used by many lenders before the Uniform Small Loan Law to enable them to circumvent state usury laws. Claiming to be brokers for out-of-state loan offices, lenders had argued that their home state's usury laws did not apply to them. In 1916, the *Loan Gazette* canvassed association members for suggestions for a more appropriate name. "Licensed lenders" received the most votes.[65] In the following year, the association adopted the name it would use throughout the 1920s, the American Industrial Licensed Lenders Association ("Licensed" was dropped in 1921). The trade journal in turn became *Industrial Lenders News*.

Having settled on a name, the association worked hard to "elevate the tone" of the small-loan business. The job began with internal policing. Most licensed lenders honestly intended to operate in accordance with the law. Their integrity received frequent notice in reports filed by state supervisory boards.[66] But some lenders, whether through guile or the force of old habits, violated the spirit of the law, if not its letter. Clarence Hodson of the Household Finance Corporation warned his fellow lenders that the licensed but unreformed lenders needed "close watching for little abuses out of keeping with the spirit of anti–loan shark legislation."[67] Moral suasion and the threat of ostracism were used to weed out old business practices from the days when money cost 1,000 percent interest. Agencies were advised to move their offices out of second-floor rooms at the top of narrow, dark stairs. Attacks on competitors were discouraged. Standardized business forms were made available, tailored for the law in each state. Daylight business hours were recommended. As *Industrial Lenders' News* pointed out, the old practice of staying open evenings and holidays suggested "the spirit of the spider awaiting the casual fly."[68]

Advertising in particular came under the association's scrutiny. Advertisements were more important than anything else in shaping the public's general image of the loan business. In the days of illegal lending, advertisements could be counted on to contain false information, crude design, and frank appeals to the acquisitive spirit within workers. Promising "Quick Money" and "Easy Credit," the old ads encouraged debt for increased consumption, particularly at holidays, and preyed upon the guilt of parents who wanted to provide nice things for their children. Since this kind of "reason why" advertising was common in businesses outside the small-loan field, it was hard to weed out. Hodson reported to the association in 1917 that undignified advertisements required the state committees "to do considerable disciplining." Ads, handbills, and circulars were, in fact, censored by the state committees. Christmas ads in particular were frowned on.[69] The association did what it could to suggest new themes and ideas. Lenders were encouraged to switch their appeals away from greed and consumer desire toward the "higher" human emotions, such as sympathy for the weak, attachment to home and family, and honest pride in work. "She Helps Support Her Sick Father" was the headline of an ad for the Beneficial Loan Company, held up by the association as a model for others.[70]

Internal policing was helpful, but a bigger problem lay outside the ranks of the licensed lenders. The number of unreconstructed lenders who continued to do business in defiance of the laws was quite large. At the end of the 1920s, Evans Clark estimated that the unlicensed lenders still lent more money than the licensed lenders or any other small-loan agencies, and dealt with perhaps a million more customers than the licensed lenders.[71] In fact, after the initial victories of the credit reformers between 1914 and 1920, loan-sharking made a comeback in the early 1920s. Salary loan lenders, the most vocal opponents of the Uniform Small Loan Law, devised a subterfuge to help them escape the provisions of state regulatory laws. Now they claimed not to lend money at all but merely to "buy" some portion of a worker's wages. Buying $6.25 of wages, the worker received only $5.00, making the transaction effectively a loan. Recast as "salary buyers," many loan sharks moved back into states they had formerly abandoned.[72]

To meet this threat, the licensed lenders tried a variety of methods, beginning with moral suasion. "The task ahead," outlined the national treasurer, W. G. Wood, in 1916, was for the "better lenders" to "educate the weak ones, the spineless fellows, the unprincipled, don't-give-a-darn-for-anyone-but-themselves cusses operating in the business now, at a higher standard of principles."[73] Others used less provocative language to convince illegal lenders to come under the banner of licensed lending. "Many loan sharks," Clarence Hodson charitably observed, "are efficient in credits, collections, and service in the small loan business . . . most of them would prefer to do business on a lawful and mutually fair basis."[74] Hodson was always careful to speak of the "so-called loan shark evil" and the "so-called loan sharks." According to Hodson, in the states that passed the Uniform Small Loan Law about half of the loan sharks eventually became licensed lenders.[75]

As for the others, they either went out of business, moved across state lines into unregulated territory, or, after 1918, switched their operations to salary buying.[76] With their own fragile image in danger of being shattered, the state and national associations acted vigorously to oppose illegal lenders who caused trouble. In states with some form of the Uniform Small Loan Law, the association depended on members to report cases of illegal lending, and employed the law firm of Hubachek and Hubachek to conduct prosecutions.[77] In Missouri the association formed a "Vigilance Committee" charged with the task of exterminating the state's loan sharks. Missouri was a haven for salary buyers because of its proximity to several of the earliest regulated states. The association hired Charles Napier, a Chicago attorney well acquainted with small-loan lending, to head the Vigilance Committee. Napier's principal strategy, modeled on effective campaigns against salary buying in Chicago and Detroit, was to work in concert with the state's better business bureaus to convince employers not to honor contracts written up by the salary buyers.[78] Despite the work of the Vigilance Committee and of the Russell Sage Foundation's Remedial Lending Division, Missouri's loan sharks successfully fought off an adequate small-loan law until 1939.[79]

Loansharking would cast a shadow on the small-loan business until well into the 1930s. In the hope that the public could be educated to distinguish between loan sharks and legitimate licensed lenders, the association worked to make its members "clean and decent." But the image problems of the personal finance business could not be rectified by professional standards alone. Professionalism addressed concerns about the character of the men behind the loan desk. But it left unaddressed concerns about the character of the loans themselves, or about the character of the customers asking for loans.

In fact, the scandal of loansharking was only partly responsible for the poor reputation of small-loan lending. In addition to having a shady past, small-loan lending was also burdened with handicaps built into the nature of the business itself. One was the way in which the economics of commercial lending rubbed against the grain of commonsense notions about justice and equality. To most outsiders, it was not immediately obvious why smaller loans required higher interest rates than large loans. Even when the principles of the business were explained, there was no convincing some that the Uniform Small Loan Law was not a clever green light for lenders to fleece the public.[80]

But more significant than public concern over interest rates were concerns about the commodity moneylenders were selling, which was debt. In 1916 money at interest did not yet occupy the same mental category as other consumer commodities. Automobiles, radios, refrigerators, and vacation trips fairly shouted their status as consumer *goods*. But debt incurred for such things had more of the trappings of a consumer *evil*. Consumer debt, in other words, was a hard sell. Most loans extended by small lenders bailed households out from financial emergencies. This caused another kind of image problem for lenders. A debt to the loan agency was an admission that things had gotten out of hand, that something had gone terribly wrong. This put small lenders in the same class of business as mortuaries and other enterprises associated with times of distress. Such businesses could not hold sales, offer money-back guarantees, or advertise with the same freedom available to other businesses. In view of all the limitations inherent in their business, licensed lenders faced an uphill battle in their struggle for public esteem. The only way to level the field was to change the way people thought about small loans.

Therefore, in addition to fighting loan sharks and policing the unreformed elements within their own ranks, licensed lenders made justifying their business a top priority. Like the medieval scholastics who, centuries before, had devised an elaborate defense of the church's position on usury, the industrial lenders fashioned an *apologia* for themselves. It was a modest defense compared with that of the scholastics but no less fervent. The lenders' *apologia* called on familiar code words and ideas from the Victorian money management ethic to communicate to the public that the small-loan business was no threat to conventional values. If small-loan borrowing was commonly associated with misfortune and foolishness, the leaders of the industry attempted nothing less than to destroy these images and replace them with more appealing ones.

The lenders' defense of their business was couched in a rhetoric that Daniel T. Rodgers has called "the language of social bonds."[81] During the Progressive Era, ideals of social harmony became popular as many Americans turned away from the excessive individualism of late nineteenth-century Social Darwinism. The new emphasis was on "industrial harmony" and "the common good," examples of the key words and phrases in the new rhetoric. Idioms such as these focused attention on the unities of the nation, and provided defenders of licensed lending with a flexible and compelling rhetoric for explaining and justifying their business. All

Americans, the thinking went, were in the same boat—they all needed credit. "Men in all walks of life find it necessary to borrow money," read an ad sponsored by the Indiana Association of Industrial Lenders. "The capitalist calls upon the banker, the manufacturer could not operate successfully without an established line of credit, the merchant must have money beyond his capital to meet his obligations, likewise the industrial worker is called upon to meet some unusual and unexpected expense and must find some source of relief."[82] Statements of this sort rested their persuasiveness on the public's willingness to believe that all men were brothers, that the needs of the worker were not so different from the needs of the capitalist. At the height of the social gospel's influence, many wanted to believe this.

But the language of social bonds ran headlong against the language of the Victorian money management ethic, which denied that all borrowers were morally equal. In the Victorian mindset, merchants and workers might be brothers, but the former got credit easier than the latter for good reason. Merchants and capitalists *made* something with their money; workers *consumed* the fruits of their loans. In 1917 this distinction was still the common sense of the matter.

Thus, when the association in that year chose to call its members "industrial" lenders, it indicated how the early licensed lenders responded to this objection. They made no attempt as yet to justify consumptive borrowing. Rather, they tried to redefine the nature of their loans in terms acceptable to the Victorian ethic. Calling themselves "industrial" lenders helped in several ways, depending on the audience. For moralists, the name was intended to suggest that the emergency loans needed by workers were not the result of individual folly but a consequence of the industrial system. For potential customers, it was hoped that "industrial" lending would appeal to their identity as workers, to suggest that here was a business with the needs and interests of the worker in mind. For the general public, "industrial" loans would be associated with images of productivity, hard work, and the progress of modern life.

A new name was just the opening move in a campaign to redefine the lending business. Members of the state and national associations actively sought out opportunities to publicize their business, using speeches to business and social groups, newspaper and magazine features, and their own trade publications to get their points across. The most common feature of their business propaganda was the "success story." These stories were designed to emphasize one critical point: the productive nature of small loans. Beginning with descriptions of the misery of unfortunate borrowers, the lenders' success stories narrated how legal cash lenders helped borrowers to escape the industrial conditions that lay at the root of their economic misfortune. Very often the stories ended with the borrower an independent businessman or businesswoman.

As with so much of the lenders' *apologia*, the technique of the success story originated with Arthur Ham and the remedial reformers. Addressing a national conference of social workers in 1911, Ham described the way in which remedial loan societies distinguished "unnecessary" from "legitimate" borrowing. According to Ham, remedial lenders investigated a potential borrower's habits and character in order to make sure that loans would be "a valuable experience to the borrower." To illustrate his point, Ham offered examples of what remedial lenders would consider "legitimate borrowing." In one case, a widow with children to support used a loan from a remedial lender to find employment for herself and lift her family into "comfortable circumstances." In another case, a worker used a small loan to bridge the income gap between jobs. The experience of repaying the loan taught him the habit of putting aside money every month, so that after the loan was repaid, he started a savings account and became a stockholder in a loan association. In a third case, a worker borrowed fifty dollars to buy a small grocery stand. Several more loans enabled him to expand his business until eventually he become a "prosperous grocer . . . [reaching] out in other directions."[83] Stories like these passed almost verbatim into the lore of the industrial lending business.

The way lenders represented their business, the primary use of a small loan was to help workers become independent producers. Advertisements often called upon such republican themes. An ad sponsored by the Illinois Industrial Lenders Association featured a smiling woman under the caption, "She Saw the Opportunity / We Furnished the Money." Hers was another success story:

> She started making candy at home and selling it to the neighbors to earn some extra money.
>
> The demand was such as to encourage her to start a retail store downtown. She needed money but had no banking connection. We were impressed with her opportunity and furnished the money—a small amount which was paid back in monthly installments out of profits.
>
> Today she enjoys a reputation second to none in the candy business with several well-established stores—and incidentally a bank account of no mean proportions.[84]

Not all success stories ended with the borrower running his or her own business, but most did. If they did not always lead to financial independence, small loans were often characterized as helping borrowers to find a good job, to buy necessities for cash at a significant discount, or to establish the financial discipline that led to a savings account. It was this "investment feature" that state senator John Dailey of Illinois, speaking to the annual convention of the American Industrial Lenders Association in 1920, noted as "a striking characteristic" of the loans made by small lenders. Dailey echoed the line that the lenders were working hard to encourage. "Men and women in great numbers," he told the lenders, "are borrowing small sums to go into little businesses, to furnish rooms for renting, and to buy homes on the installment basis, the initial payments frequently being the money received from you."[85] In this way was a new image for small-loan lending spread in the public realm.

In addition to success stories, licensed lenders took another tip from the remedial reformers and presented themselves as conservative defenders of traditional financial values. Did the loan sharks prey on people's materialistic desires? "The job of the industrial lender," counseled the president of a Beneficial office in New York, "is to get people out of debt and teach them to budget their earnings and save."[86] Did installment credit threaten the morals of the country? "The success and prevalence of installment houses," argued a licensed lender, "indicate the existence of unhealthy credit conditions among the working classes which can be remedied only by the encouragement of thrift and by credit facilities for the unusual case."[87] Was advertising creating a nation of spendthrifts? "Our advertising," urged another, "must not be directed against the habit of thrift, or tempt people to spend money that should be saved."[88] This kind of financial conservatism was motivated in part by self-interest. As Clarence Hodson explained it, "The person who would borrow money for risk or extravagance would not likely be in a position to repay his installments."[89] Moreover, lenders did not want to do anything that invited the censure of legislators, employers, newspapers, and the public. But it was also true that the licensed lenders really believed in their own rhetoric. As practical businessmen with a "scientific grasp of the credit problem," they also liked to think of themselves as apostles of thrift.

Representing their loans as productive loans, and picturing themselves as defenders of the Victorian money ethic, licensed lenders attempted to turn the traditional view of moneylenders on its head. Since the medieval era moneylenders had been popularly perceived as degenerate parasites. But licensed lenders figured that they deserved to be placed among the ranks of American *producers*. As one of them asserted in *Industrial Lenders News*, "The industrial lender, by enabling the laborer to procure his needed tools, the petty merchant his stock and vehicles, the farmer his implements, seeds, and live stock, is an important cog in the wheel of production."[90] Thus, whether speaking to others or among themselves, the early credit reformers justified their business with the argument that they turned the "ambitious and industrious" into independent producers, and the helpless debtor into a thrifty saver.

Having used the language of social bonds to establish that all Americans needed credit, and the language of the Victorian financial ethic to show that industrial borrowers used their credit just as productively as wealthy capitalists, the last argument in the lenders' apologia was a simple appeal to fairness. As the lenders liked to point out, in the absence of a small-loan industry the great majority of Americans had no access to the credit they deserved.

145

Was this justice? As Benjamin Blumberg, a lender in Terra Haute, Indiana, argued, "It has not been *fair* to the community at large that the bankers have restricted their credit only to the wealthy, the manufacturer, and the influential merchant. It has not been fair to the laborer, wage earner, renter, school teacher, and stenographer. Your merchants and manufacturers cater to all alike, you provide hotels, newspapers, food, etc., for all alike. Why not loans?"[91] Accusing monopolies and "the interests" of denying "the people" their rights was an old tradition in American politics, and standard language during the Progressive Era. But the licensed lenders particularized their grievances in a way that harkened all the way back to Andrew Jackson's war on the Bank of the United States. Indeed, credit reformers once again made banks the adversary. Banks lent money at 6 percent, but only to the wealthy. As a joke making the rounds of lenders about this time put it, "A bank is the place for a poor man to put his money so that a rich man can get it when he wants."[92]

The unfairness of the American credit system looked even worse when comparisons were made to Europe. France and Italy had their hundreds of *monts-de-piété*, Germany its cooperative banks for farmers and workers. Small-loan lenders pictured themselves as the superior American solution to the workers' need for credit.[93]

How successful were the licensed lenders in convincing the public that their business was sound, their loans productive, and their customers industrious? There were many "publics," and not all responded in the same way. On the one hand, industrial loan companies received the endorsements of state regulatory commissions, social welfare agencies, church organizations, labor unions, chambers of commerce, and better business bureaus.[94] On the other hand, ignorance and outmoded impressions abounded. For their national convention in 1931, the association invited Albert E. Wiggam, a prominent after-dinner speaker of the day, to deliver an evening address. Wiggam reported to the conventioneers that when he searched for information about the industrial lending business, he found that "scarcely a sociologist or economist or industrial leader or politician knew anything about it."[95] Four years later, the president of the Ohio Finance Company, Charles W.

Wild, complained that "too many still look upon us as a sort of left-wing brother-in-law of the racketeer."[96] It was in the nature of the business that lenders would never enjoy the same esteem as doctors and clergymen. On the other hand, as developments in the 1920s would show, they did their part in helping to change the way Americans thought about borrowing and debt in general.

COUNSELORS TO THE CONSUMER

The 1920s were boom years for small lending. But growth was not limited to numbers. If in the early years of the business industrial lenders portrayed themselves as saviors of the honest poor and financiers for aspiring capitalists, developments of the 1920s inspired a new identity. Industrial lending gave way to "personal finance," and small-loan lenders began thinking of themselves as "counselors to the consumer."

Surveying the field of mass finance in 1930, Evans Clark wrote of "the most spectacular changes" taking place in the business of small-loan lending.[97] Fifteen years earlier the licensed lending business did not exist. In 1916, the first year of the association, loans outstanding at the end of the year totaled $8,251,000. By the end of 1929, this figure had mushroomed to $255 million. The total business in loans for that year was perhaps as high as $500 million.[98] Loans increased with the onset of the Great Depression, though not as much as might be expected. The first reliable figures for the loan volume of personal finance companies are M. R. Neifeld's computations for 1930. Neifeld conservatively estimated that licensed lenders in 1930 extended $354 million in loans. Assuming an average loan of $140, he concluded that in the twenty-six states covered by the Uniform Small Loan Law, licensed lenders in the course of a year reached 2.6 million families, or one-eighth of the population.[99]

At the close of July 1932, state supervisory agencies licensed 3,667 personal finance companies, up from 600 in 1923.[100] Of these, about one-third of the "more socially-minded element" were members of the national association, and almost half belonged to state associations.[101] Ninety percent of the association members' business was conducted on a chattel mortgage basis, and most of these were organized into several large chain office corporations. The oldest of the chains was the Household Finance Corporation, founded in 1878 by Frank J. Mackey of Philadelphia. The largest chain was the Beneficial Industrial Loan Corporation. The Beneficial was formed in 1929 when three large loan companies merged to form a new corporation. The new company operated 263 loan offices in 228 cities, extending $58 million in loans in 1929. In 1932 Household and Beneficial accounted for about 30 percent of the licensed lending business. Only 44 percent of all licensed lending companies were individually owned and operated.[102]

With numerical growth came transformations in the nature of small-loan lending. Some of the change documented itself. For example, in 1928 the Household Finance Corporation became the first lending chain to enhance its loan capital by selling stock to the public through an established, nonaffiliated underwriter. Opening one hundred new offices in the next five years, Household reduced its interest rate from 3.5 percent to 2.5 percent by refusing to make any loans under one hundred dollars. Since larger loans were generally made to borrowers with larger incomes and assets, this was a sign that the larger chains at least were going after a new kind of borrower, leaving less well off borrowers to illegal lenders willing to take the higher risk.[103]

Along these same lines, in 1929 the American Industrial Lenders Association changed its name to become the American Association of Personal Finance Companies. This decision made official what many lenders had known for some time: the business of lending money had moved well beyond its origins in the field of social work. By the late 1920s, small-loan lenders felt constrained by the image of their businesses as remedial institutions for meeting the problems of industrial life. "Personal finance" took the emphasis off industrial workers as the client field for the business, and moved the emphasis toward consumers in general. It also implied that debt could have a wider range of uses than simply the meeting of industrial emergencies, and that it might, indeed, be a normative state.

Who borrowed from small-loan lenders, and why? Did borrowers and their reasons for borrowing change between World War I and the Great Depression? Lenders spoke of changes in both. The credibility of their beliefs would be enhanced if change could be detected in the loan records of lenders over the course of the decade. Unfortunately, this is not possible.

Meticulous loan records were kept, and they were occasionally made public, but the problems involved in comparing the data make it hard to draw persuasive conclusions.[104] In addition to company records, several investigative studies of the small-loan business were made between 1922 and 1939. But their helpfulness is also severely limited because their results are not directly comparable. With regard to who borrowed, these studies used different classification schemes to establish the occupations of borrowers. The best that can be said on the basis of investigative studies is that throughout the 1920s licensed lenders' customers were neither the impecunious poor nor members of the professional and managerial classes, but were solidly blue-collar or lower-level white-collar workers, with certain occupations appearing to be overrepresented: transportation workers, public employees, newspapermen.

As for why people borrowed, the same problems of categorization present themselves, along with one more. It is very difficult to pin down why borrowers borrow. The reasons given by borrowers may have no connection at all to the real source of their difficulties. And who is to say what is a proximate cause of financial emergency and what is the actual cause? For all these reasons, developments in the small-loan business during the 1920s are not possible to verify with statistical evidence.[105]

In the absence of hard data, we are left with the testimony of the lenders themselves, and with the record of their adjustments to the changing nature of their business in the 1920s. Unlike their counterparts in the installment credit field, small-loan lenders did not encourage change, they reacted to it. Sensing change among their borrowers, they groped their way toward new understandings of lending and borrowing.

The subject of a changing business first came up at the annual convention of the National Federation of Remedial Loan Societies in 1920. Charles F. Bigelow, manager of a loan society in Providence, Rhode Island, sparked a heated discussion when he reported that his loan office was lending to "a new class of poor." In the past, Bigelow reminded his audience, remedial lending societies had lent to a class of people "deprived of the advantages of training and education." But since World War I, his loan company was interviewing fewer wage earners and more of what he called "Mr. Average Salaried Man," "that rather intellectual but meek and worried looking individual." These new "middle-class" borrowers wanted more money on better articles of security: antique furniture, Oriental rugs, paintings, Liberty Bonds, stocks, and automobiles. Bigelow raised the question of whether remedial loan societies were performing the same social service they had originally been set up to accomplish. He wondered aloud whether "their capacity for good has not virtually ceased." This sobering thought was answered in the negative. "The new borrower," argued Bigelow, "may not yet suffer for the bare necessities of life, but . . . he is subject to all the needs of the old borrower and there are added needs which arise from his social position." The "new poor" would have to be served by someone, making the future of the small-lending business brighter than ever before.[106]

Bigelow's presentation provoked what the secretary of the meeting termed "a decided conflict of views." Significantly, no one denied the claim that borrowers seemed to be wealthier than before. That much was undeniable. The real issue centered on what the new type of borrowers wanted to borrow for. Six of the agencies represented at the session indicated that they lent money to buy automobiles. Others objected to this practice, arguing that remedial loan societies were not in business to lend money for the purchase of "luxuries." This led to debate over whether the automobile was a luxury or a necessity. The meeting broke up without reaching a consensus. Judging by the discussion, remedial lenders welcomed the rising affluence of their borrowers, but felt apprehension about betraying the social service ideals they espoused.[107]

Four years after this meeting, the St. Bartholomew's Loan Association of New York City, a charter member of the NRFLA, closed its doors for good. It was a profitable business, but the trustees of the company decided that it "was no longer fulfilling the intention of its founders," because no "deserving borrowers" remained to be helped. It was the opinion of the trustees that the rising affluence of the city's workers lessened the need for remedial lending. Workers were still experiencing financial emergencies, but now, reported the trustees, it was the fault of their own acquisitiveness, not the industrial system.[108]

Other remedial loan societies were more willing to accommodate the different needs of more affluent borrowers. As the remedial lending societies were absorbed into the licensed lending business, discussion continued there of the changing nature of small loans.

Gradually, a consensus began to form that what was bringing more and more people through the loan company's front door was installment buying. It had always been true that most borrowers wanted to use their loan to refinance existing debts, in order to consolidate various obligations and get relief from pestering collectors. But whereas formerly people owed doctors, druggists, grocers, and illegal lenders, now it seemed as if most refinancing went toward paying off bills for automobiles, radios, refrigerators, and other goods sold on the installment plan.

The most forceful expositor of this view was Franklin W. Ryan, a frequent contributor to *Industrial Lenders News* and a trained economist working in the small-loan field. Based on personal observation and his study of loan office records, Ryan argued that the spectacular increase in the small-loan lenders' business in the 1920s was directly traceable to "the American worker's habits of getting into debt." More specifically, it was "the aggressive sales tactics of installment houses" that explained the expansion of the small-loan industry. In support of his argument, Ryan cited statistical studies investigating the reasons why people borrowed money. These studies generally put the percentage of loans made to consolidate existing debts at anywhere between 50 percent and 75 percent.[109] Ryan's discussions with loan office managers confirmed that most of the existing debt being refinanced was installment debt on automobiles, washing machines, radios, vacuum cleaners, and other durable consumer goods. As for the remaining percentage of loans that went to pay for current needs, Ryan claimed that many of these loans entered the books because "the customer is already obligated so heavily by installment debts and other open account debts that he has to come to us for any pressing emergency." Loan offices, Ryan pointed out, do not create debt. They simply provide financial relief to people already in debt. And the type of debts Americans were carrying was tilting increasingly toward retail installment debt.[110]

Not everyone agreed with Ryan. M. R. Neifeld, statistician for the Beneficial Management Corporation, avowed that only 3–4 percent of all personal finance loans were made to "conserve instalment purchases in danger of forfeiture because of delinquency." But this amount is so low as to strain all credibility. Neifeld based his figure on a study that took at face value borrowers' stated reasons for obtaining a loan. This undermines the validity of the figure considerably. Moreover, Neifeld made the claim within the context of a larger argument about the "productive" nature of industrial loans. He wanted to show that customers of the personal finance companies were not the kind of debtors who put having an automobile ahead of having food on the table or saving up for a small business. Still clinging to an outmoded justification for small-loan lending (one long ago dropped by other lenders), Neifeld had good reason to want to minimize installment debt refinancing.[111]

Given the loud outcry in the 1920s over rising personal indebtedness, Ryan's argument about installment debts was certainly motivated by a desire to shift the blame for rising debt from personal finance companies to retailers. Nevertheless, his point still stands: as installment debts accounted for an increasing share of the debt burden of American households, the desire to rescue equity invested in consumer durable goods drove an increasing number of debtors to the door of the small-loan lender. The rise of retail installment buying was changing the economics of the household, and small-loan lenders were well situated to observe the change taking place.

In response to this trend, small-loan lenders discovered a new identity for themselves. In their previous identity as "industrial lenders," they had characterized their loans as financial bridges to

help workers make it across the gaps in income common in industrial life. But by 1930, small-loan lenders referred to their work as
"personal finance," and their rhetoric was heavily salted with the
new ideal of financial service. "When we lend to a borrowing
worker," explained Ryan to fellow lenders in 1928, "we become
his financial advisor. We teach him to budget his income and expenditure. We teach him thrift. When he has paid us off, he has
never had to borrow again because we have taught him the basic
principles of household finance."[112]

Lenders had always claimed to teach the values of thrift and
saving, but the new ideal was broader than that. Through brochures, movies, exhibits, and one-to-one personal advice, licensed
lenders now gave instruction in budgeting, investing, and debt-
load management.[113] As the director of social research for the
Connecticut Association of Personal Finance Companies noted in
1935, "Very little is being done outside our line of business to
educate people in the ways of credit. . . . The responsibility gravi-
tates fairly and squarely to our shoulders."[114] "Our immediate
task," urged Burr Blackburn of the Household Finance Corporation's Consumer Education Department, "is not so much the lending of money as the improvement of the financial management of
families." Blackburn continued with a metaphor that was in almost universal use at the time. "I think I can confidently predict
that within a very brief period of time we will no longer be thought
of as 'moneylenders' but as financial physicians to the American
family."[115]

"Financial advisers," "financial doctors," "Doctor Family Finance," "counselors to the consumer"—these were the metaphors
used by small-loan lenders to reassure the public, and themselves,
that a steady diet of consumer credit would not bloat the country
with too much indebtedness.[116]

Sharing in the growth of the small-loan industry were the historic
makers of small loans: pawnbrokers and illegal lenders. But while
both saw their loan volumes grow in the 1920s, their businesses
were in eclipse. For working- and lower-middle-class Americans,
the new moneylenders of choice no longer lent money out of seedy

Figure 9. Branch office of the General Finance Corporation.
In the 1920s and 1930s, small-loan lenders moved from small, cramped
offices at the top of a dark flight of stairs to bright, modern office spaces as
they tried to recast their public image from greedy moneylenders into friendly
counselors for the consumer. (Chicago Historical Society, ICHi-21981)

second-story offices, or tumbledown storefronts cluttered with pawns. By the early 1920s an entirely new small-loan industry had come into existence, intent on expansion, hungry for respectability, and specializing in financial aid for the consumer.

Important sources for consumer credit, personal finance companies were not originally intended to be safety nets for those falling off the high wire of consumerism. In fact, the founders of the cash credit industry set themselves squarely against the making of "consumptive" loans. Instead, they envisioned their businesses helping impoverished workers achieve the financial security of independent producers. This was an older American dream. Its time was past.

In the 1920s the reformers and progressive businessmen who organized the small-loan industry watched the nature of their business change dramatically. What they intended never materialized, while unintended consequences abounded. Hoping to salvage republican producerism, small-loan lenders instead became the salvagers of a new American dream. The new dream acquiesced to wage labor. It was financed by debt. But it hoped for liberation and fulfillment through a culture of abundance.

❊ CHAPTER 4 ❊

Hard Payments:
The Rise of Installment Selling

RETAIL installment credit developed along a different trajectory than small-loan lending. In fact, the motivation and consequence for one were very nearly the inverse of the other. The lenders who built up the personal finance business were philosophically opposed to consumerism, but the financial service they provided became an important component of consumer culture. By contrast, the debt merchants who built up installment selling were proud to consider themselves founders of a mass-consumption society. But their method of credit enforced financial disciplines on consumers that were no less effective than the ideals of the Victorian money management ethic.

The installment plan was the preeminent symbol of debt during the credit revolution. It superseded older symbols of debt from the Victorian era, such as the mortgage deed, the credit book of the retail merchant, and the three golden balls of the pawnbroker. From these forms of credit installment credit differed markedly. The essential feature of installment credit is its system of repayment, which requires partial payments to be made at stated intervals until a loan of money or goods is fully repaid. This type of repayment scheme contrasted vividly with single-maturity mortgage loans, which required borrowers to pay only periodic interest charges until, at a contracted interval, the entire principal came due in one lump sum. It also differed from open-book credit, which left repayment to be negotiated between seller and borrower. As compared with pawnbroking, installment credit operated very much like pawning in reverse: installment buyers, instead of giving up the future use of a good in exchange for money in the here and now, gave up the future use of income in exchange for the immediate use of a good. The pawn loan required a sacrifice; borrowers had to give up something to get something. But the installment plan required sacrifices, small acts of renunciation on a continual basis until the debt was entirely repaid. If "buy now" provided pleasure for a moment, "pay later" enforced budgetary disciplines over a period of months and years. Billions of monthly installments paid on time since the credit revolution are a record less of hedonism than of how abundance came to be regulated in the American culture of consumption.

From 1910 to 1930, the practice of buying goods on installment credit expanded enormously. Once despised as a plebeian form of credit, installment credit "trickled up" the social ladder to become part of the middle-class way of life.

ALADDIN'S LAMP: THE ORIGINS OF INSTALLMENT CREDIT

Legally and practically, installment credit is a recent financial device, an invention of the mid- to late nineteenth century. But the idea of liquidating debts with partial payments is very old, its historical roots indiscernibly buried in the origins of credit in general.[1] By the fifteenth century, credit practices involving partial payments were common enough to have infiltrated the English language. "Estallement," a loanword from the Normans meaning "to fix," described the action taken by nobles who wished to pay debts to the crown in annual payments, or townsmen who desired to spread out tax assessments, or borrowers who wanted to pay back loans a little at a time based on annual rents of real estate. In 1641, when the Pilgrims consolidated their "heavy burthens" to London creditors, they arranged to pay their debts with four annual payments, which, in legal contracts of the time, were termed "estallments."[2]

As a retail marketing device, installment credit first appeared in the late eighteenth century. Advertisements of the day testify that credit terms involving partial payments were used occasionally to finance horses and farm implements in the United States, and mirrors, chests, and other home furnishings in London.[3] The English method of "hire purchase" apparently originated with a countess who, in 1830, convinced a furniture dealer to allow her to rent suites of furniture in the Parisian fashion, but with the proviso that she retain an option to buy. Likening her idea to "Aladdin's lamp," the countess urged its adoption on all her friends.[4] In the United States, Cowperthwaite and Sons, reputedly the first furniture retailer in New York City, sold furniture on installment terms within five years of opening its doors in 1807. The practice quickly spread to competitors.[5] At about the same time Eli Terry of Plymouth, Connecticut, accepted installment payments for his twenty-five-dollar wooden clocks, which were sold by itinerant agents on horseback from New York to Boston.[6] The nature of these goods, along with the conservative terms of the contracts, make it seem likely that the first American users of installment credit were people of known character and with the financial means to meet their obligations.[7]

In the early nineteenth century, partial payment credit was not nearly as important in retail trading as it was in other applications. As a matter of fact, from 1800 to 1820 the largest installment seller in the United States was the national government. Under the Land Act of 1800, the government sold 19.4 million acres of northwest public lands on terms calling for a downpayment of one-fourth of the purchase price and the balance due in equal payments two, three, and four years after purchase.[8] In 1828 Noah Webster's *Dictionary of the English Language* defined "installment" with examples drawn entirely from the commercial world, where, according to Webster, it was "not unusual" for businessmen to pay large contracts in installments.[9] During this period, installment schemes were often used to raise business capital. The Rhode Island Aquidneck Coal Mine advertised in the New York *Evening Post* of 8 February 1811 that it offered four hundred shares of stock to the public for sale at $150 a share, one-fourth to be paid down, and the balance due in six, twelve, and eighteen months. Webster noted that such stock-selling arrangements were "customary."[10]

Though partial payment credit had a place in the early national credit system, it was the exception rather than the rule. Open-book, single-maturity, and short-term demand obligations predominated. Only gradually did a legal, social, and economic superstructure sufficient to support mass installment credit come together.

This happened in the mid-nineteenth century, as the world of goods available to people changed dramatically in their lifetimes. In 1800 the average farm family counted among its material possessions only a few well-worn pieces of furniture, bedding, some kitchen implements, shoes, homemade clothing, some essential tools, a firearm, and perhaps a wagon. Most families lived in a world of goods that had remained essentially unchanged for centuries. But as the nineteenth century wore on, people found themselves confronting a wholly new world of goods, one rendered dramatically different by advancing technology. Old ways of doing things were challenged by new, technologically complex farm and household appliances. The new goods displayed obvious advantages, but their expense presented problems. In fact, they were so expensive that normal credit instruments provided scant help. Better to stick with the tried and true and spend money on other things. To meet this type of sales resistance, manufacturers and retailers of the first durable, technologically complex household goods found that partial payment credit made all the difference.

Thus, many rural Americans became acquainted with installment buying when they made the transition from the hand to machine age of agriculture. In 1850 most farmers used tools only slightly improved since biblical times. At the critical moment of harvest, cereal farmers faced a formidable bottleneck in production as they raced against time to reap, thresh, and winnow their crop before it was ruined by exposure to the elements. Limits on the scale of production spurred efforts on both sides of the Atlantic from the late eighteenth century on to find ways to mechanize the harvest. Inventions proliferated. From 1840 to 1890, American farmers were introduced in rough succession to hundreds of different types of threshers, reapers, self-raking reapers, harvester-binders, automatic wire binders, automatic twine binders, and, finally, the combined harvester-thresher, or "combine." During this period, mechanized harvesting machines reduced the man-hours required to harvest an acre of grain from twenty hours to one.[11]

Farmers needed little convincing to see the advantages of mechanical farm implements. Buyers weighed their choices among the many models available, taking into account matters of reliability and of price. The machines were not cheap, especially the ones with a reputation for quality. In the mid-1840s, when a prosperous farm might gross an income of $300, the price of a McCormick reaper was $100. Credit for the expensive machines was a matter of course, but traditional terms of agricultural credit were not much help. For most farmers, the new machines cost too much to be paid off in full after one harvest.[12]

The solution proved to be installment credit. The first wall-hanger advertisement for the J. I. Case Threshing Machine Company announced in 1848 that the price for a Case thresher ranged from $290 to $325 on terms of $50 down, $75 due 1 November, $100 due 1 January, and the balance due the following October.[13] In the same year Cyrus McCormick experimented with two-payment installment terms. With his reapers costing $100 to $160, McCormick recognized that the only way most farmers could buy a machine would be if they were allowed to pay for it out of the profits it made them. Moreover, he must have worried that owners of small farms would find it tempting to pool resources and share a reaper, as was commonly done with threshers. Thus, beginning in the early 1850s, McCormick instructed his agents to offer the popular Virginia reaper for sale on "liberal terms." McCormick asked for a down payment of $35 on a $125 machine, with the balance due on 1 December. Sales shot up, but McCormick felt the drain of extending credit to customers. To improve his own financial strength he offered attractive discounts for cash purchases, but two-thirds of his customers preferred to buy on credit. According to McCormick's grandson and biographer, installment credit was "the most important innovation introduced into his selling system." Other implement dealers followed McCormick's lead.[14]

Farm implement credit was an installment "plan" in only the loosest sense. Downpayments were often reduced to make a sale, or waived altogether. Agents reported that farmers were reluctant to sign formal credit agreements, and unable, or unwilling, to pay their balances on time. Collections sometimes stretched out over a year and a half. This led to losses that, by later standards, were high, around 3 to 5 percent.[15] Fierce competition forced the liberalization of terms; for manufacturers the experience of granting credit became highly frustrating. "To term an American farmer dilatory in regard to the payment of his bills," wrote one of Case's early bookkeepers, "is arrant flattery."[16] Nevertheless, most farmers paid when they could. In this way, the farm implement industry played a significant role in introducing late nineteenth-century farmers—the majority of the American population—to the idea of installment buying. A half century later their experience would be remembered and studied by American automobile manufacturers.

Urban Americans had no use for reapers. They learned about installment credit through other buying experiences. Some learned about it through the example of the building and loan associations. As described in Chapter 1, these societies were first organized in Philadelphia in 1831. By 1897 building and loan associations enrolled 1.6 million members in 5,872 associations, lending money in every state, with loans of over a half-billion dollars outstanding. Most houses in the nineteenth century continued to be financed with single-term mortgages, but the highly regarded building and loans introduced an increasing number of home buyers to a form of credit known as the "sinking-fund loan." The sinking-fund loan allowed members to pay for a home, a lot, or expensive home furnishings with regular monthly payments that covered dues to the society, interest on the loan, and assorted fees. Significantly, the monthly dues payments were called "installments."[17]

Buying a house was one thing, furnishing it another. Furniture dealers were among the first retailers to use installment credit as a means for increasing sales. Not much is known about furniture marketing in the nineteenth century. Still, scattered evidence suggests that furniture sets, pianos, and organs could be bought on installments in larger cities. Newspaper advertisements promised "easy terms," and records of chattel mortgages indicate that people took advantage of these offers.[18]

While furniture dealers and building associations quietly introduced many people to the idea of installment terms, one household appliance in particular became synonymous with installment credit. This was the sewing machine. Led by the example of the I. M. Singer and Company, the sewing machine industry was largely responsible for popularizing the installment plan on a national scale.

Sewing machines were the first durable, technologically complex household appliances to find a national market. The first bulky machines integrated a dozen or so essential mechanical features into one large intricately designed apparatus. Since each of the essential mechanisms was independently devised by a number of inventors between 1790 and 1855, the early years of the sewing machine industry saw dozens of small manufacturers competing against each other in a bitter patent war, each working to assemble a better machine than the others, by legal means if possible, illegal when necessary. After many suits and countersuits, the owners of the important sewing machine patents agreed in 1856 to a patent-sharing arrangement. Patents were cross-licensed among the major firms and other manufacturers were required to pay a license fee of fifteen dollars per machine for the privilege of using the essential patents. The resulting "sewing machine combination" was the first patent pool in American business. It included the three largest manufacturers—the Wheeler and Wilson Manufacturing Company, the I. M. Singer and Company, and the Grover and Baker Sewing Machine Company—and Elias Howe, who built only three machines in his life but whose lock-stitch patent was indispensable for machine sewing. By 1859, the combination had sold over 100,000 machines; by 1877, when the original patents expired and the patent pool came to an end, over half a million machines were being sold each year.[19]

After the spinning jenny and the plow, *Scientific American* considered the sewing machine to be "the most important invention that has ever been made since the world began."[20] American women must have thought so. Before the sewing machine, sewing garments by hand was slow, tedious work. To make the average shirt required 20,620 stitches; at 35 stitches per minute, a competent seamstress completed one shirt in ten to fourteen hours of labor.[21] At home, where most clothing was made before the Civil War, the drudgery of hand-sewing was mitigated by the companionship of the sewing circle, but no remedy existed for the smarting eyes, tired back, and aching fingers brought on by hours of sewing—until sewing machine agents began selling their machines. A sewing machine operating at three thousand stitches per minute could assemble a shirt in an hour or less, and with neater results. In fact, machine production of garments transformed the social meaning of clothing in the nineteenth century, making stylish, handsome clothing available to virtually everyone. It also fostered the organization of a large garment industry that could boast of fit and durability as well as style. Very quickly the production of clothing, especially men's apparel, was removed from the home and relocated to the factory and sweatshop. Thus were fulfilled the early predictions of *Scientific American*, that the sewing machine would create a "social revolution."[22]

In 1862 three out of four new sewing machines were bought by garment manufacturers.[23] But from the beginning sewing machine manufacturers recognized that the garment industry was not their largest potential sales market. Rather, their largest market was to be found among those whom a contemporary chronicler described as "the six millions of families, most of whom mean to have a sewing-machine when they can afford it."[24]

Affordability was a big problem. The earliest sewing machines cost as much as $300. By 1860 the big three manufacturers offered domestic sewing machines in a range of $50 to $150; $65 was the minimum price for a machine of good quality. Even this was a lot to pay in a single amount at a time when the average family income was around $500.[25]

The price barrier was heightened by the fact that sewing was women's work. How was a woman to convince her husband to lay out a large sum of money for a machine that only promised to accomplish more easily what women had been doing just fine for thousands of years? From the point of view of some husbands, $65 was too much to pay for a device that promised greater convenience but not increased income. Some men even doubted that women possessed the ability to operate a complex device like the sewing machine. To meet this objection, manufacturers redesigned the large, bulky machines of the 1840s into smaller, lighter machines with polished metal surfaces, elaborate ornamentation, and cabinets of fine woods. Machines like these, epitomized by the popular Singer "New Family" model, were clearly intended for female operators. In this way women and their husbands were persuaded to think of a sewing machine as an article of furniture, something found in the best sitting rooms right alongside the piano.[26] But neither feminized designs nor the use of female demonstrators in elaborate dealer showrooms addressed the largest barrier to buying a sewing machine. Sewing machines were priced out of the mass market.[27]

Credit for breaching the price barrier is given to Edward Clark, the business manager and marketing wizard of the I. M. Singer and Company.[28] "Why not rent a sewing machine to the housewife and apply the rental fee to the purchase price of the machine?" suggested *I. M. Singer & Co.'s Gazette* in 1856. The company newspaper felt sure that this plan of purchase would reassure husbands who feared their wives wanted to run them into debt.[29] The idea for the plan was Clark's, although Clark, unlike company historians, never claimed credit for inventing the idea of installment selling itself. In fact, in the 1850s, monthly payment plans were being advertised by five piano dealers in New York City, whose showrooms were located next door to the Singer Company headquarters on Broadway.[30] Most likely inspired by their example, Clark instituted in 1856 a scheme whereby suitable buyers could purchase a Singer sewing machine for five dollars down and the balance, plus interest, in monthly installments of three to five dollars. I. M. Singer, the flamboyant president of the company, referred to the plan as "hire-purchase."[31]

Success followed immediately. In the year after the introduction of installment credit, Singer's sales tripled. By 1867, installment selling enabled Singer to surpass its closest competitor, the Wheeler and Wilson Company. By 1876, Singer sold 262,316 machines, more than twice as many as its nearest rival, and about as many as sold by all other competitors combined.[32]

Eventually the cash price of the popular Singer New Family sewing machine fell to thirty dollars. Still, most buyers preferred to pay forty dollars on the installment plan. Singer allowed agents a surprising latitude to experiment with terms and collections. This led to a progressive liberalization of credit terms, as competition from other agents forced Singer salesmen into bidding wars over lower down payments and extended repayment schedules. The company experimented all through the 1870s and 1880s with various credit systems, finally settling in the 1890s on a basic policy of requiring weekly payments of one dollar. By that time, sewing machine agents, including Singer's, were notorious for their aggressive, "dollar down, dollar a week" tactics.[33]

People objected to installment salesmen, not to the installment plan itself. Singer's success with this new form of credit inspired other manufacturers and retailers of consumer durable goods to begin selling on installments. For example, in 1872, Dwight Baldwin, a retailer of quality pianos in Cincinnati, Ohio, hired several former sewing machine agents to become salesmen in his growing piano company. Selling on installments allowed Baldwin's branch outlets to sell pianos without making heavy investments in stock of merchandise—they simply turned in cash or buyer's contracts to the parent company. It also encouraged moderate-income customers to "buy up," that is, to buy a Steinway for credit when they could only afford a cheaper name brand for cash. According to one historian of the piano industry, the adoption of installment selling made the D. H. Baldwin and Company one of the leading piano firms in the country.[34]

By 1880, installment selling had a firm foothold as an American marketing practice. Its legal status was defined about this time. In English law relating to "hire purchase," the transaction between seller and buyer represented not a contract of sale but an agreement to rent with the option to buy. In this arrangement, ownership of rented goods remained with the dealer until the renter paid a previously agreed-on purchase price.[35] In contrast to this straightforward approach, installment credit in the United States inclined toward a method known as the "conditional sale." Conditional sales left the question of ownership more ambiguous than with hire purchase. In a conditional sale, when a commodity changes hands from seller to buyer, all rights of possession, use, and incidents of ownership transfer to the purchaser. In this sense, the commodity "belongs" to the buyer. But to protect the seller's interests, conditional installment sales have either imposed a mortgage on the goods as security for the loan or left in the hands of the seller sufficient "title" to permit repossession of the goods in the event of default on contracted installments. In the late nineteenth century, state laws on installment credit varied. But in cases of default the seller was usually allowed not only the right of repossession but also the right to pocket all previously paid installments.[36]

By 1880, household budget strategies continued to rely on open-book and single-term credit, but certain goods were well known for being sold on the installment plan, particularly mechanical farm implements and sewing machines. Houses, furniture, and pianos were also sold this way. All of these goods were expensive. But they were also highly desirable, contributing to the fulfillment of Victorian ideals of production, domesticity, and the higher life. The principal buyers were men with good credit reputations, who had steady jobs, who were rooted in the community, and who were not subject to discrimination based on race and ethnicity. This last characteristic of installment buying changed dramatically in the last decades of the nineteenth century.

GROWTH AND STIGMATIZATION, 1880–1915

In the years preceding the credit revolution, retail installment credit ceased being a novelty and became something of a disgrace. As installment selling spread beyond its original retail fields, and as installment buying spread extensively among marginalized groups, the installment plan acquired a reputation for being the folly of the poor, the immigrant, and the allegedly math-impaired female.

The expansion of installment credit in the late nineteenth century cannot be tracked with statistics, but without a doubt it did expand. The appearance of new terms offers one record of its increasing public profile. The vocabulary of credit grew to include "installment plan," "installment house," and "installment men," phrases that first appeared in big city newspapers across the country in the late 1870s and 1880s. By 1910 installment credit already functioned as a metaphor to describe how other things worked, as in a *Saturday Evening Post* description of "beaver dams . . . built on the instalment plan."[37] References to installment credit begin to appear in the works of novelists and short-story writers around the turn of the century. A character in Charles M. Flandrau's *Harvard Episodes* (1897) notes that "a piano or a set of Kipling" could be bought on the installment plan, "or any old thing." Likewise, in Charles Fort's *The Outcast Manufacturers* (1909), two working women explain their stylish clothing with the airy admission, "You can get anything on the installment plan nowadays."[38]

What lay behind this expansion? The driving forces behind the expansion of installment credit were the same developments remaking the whole of American life in the late nineteenth century, especially immigration, urbanization, and industrialization. Immigration vastly enlarged the domestic market for goods, as each pot and pan left behind in the old country had to be replaced. Coincident with the expanding market for goods, urbanization played a role in the rise of installment buying by creating social conditions that encouraged people to communicate through the clothes they wore, the way they decorated their homes, and the way they emulated the consumption patterns of those around them. "Keeping up with the Joneses" was hardly limited to city people, but cities provided the largest stage for social emulation.

Industrialization was the basic economic fact behind the rise of the installment plan. To begin with, the reorganization of production increased the output of durable consumer goods. In 1850, the low level of consumer durables production left Americans spending only 2 percent of their income on durable goods. But by 1880 this ratio had risen to 11 percent, a ratio approaching twentieth-century levels.[39] Already by 1879, in terms of the share of total commodity production, the production of consumer durable goods equaled that of producer durables. After 1879, while the population grew at 1.3 percent per year, production of consumer durables increased at an average annual growth rate of 4.7 percent. This was faster than the growth rate of producer goods, and much faster than the production of consumer perishables.[40] As the supply of consumer durables increased, industrialization also promoted a new credit system for consumers by displacing the traditional calendar of agricultural income that had existed for centuries. When income came once a year at the harvest, single-payment loans were the most appropriate method of credit, due in full sometime after the harvest. But wage earners typically received weekly income; for them, single payment loans required financial discipline in the form of being able to save weekly income, a discipline many did not have and that was never required of farmers under the old system. A third contribution of industrialization was that as workers switched to a new calendar of income, wage income between 1860 and 1920 rose at about 1.3 percent per annum. In other words, the real wages of American workers doubled over the period, which was not enough to enable workers to buy goods such as furniture or sewing machines for cash, but was just enough for some workers to gain a margin of disposable income that could be applied to regular credit payments.[41] In all these ways, late nineteenth-century industrialization, immigration, and urbanization created the necessary conditions for the development of installment credit.

Sketching the late nineteenth-century development of installment credit, a pioneer in the field of consumer credit described it as an expansion on three fronts: new fields of merchandising, new geographic areas, and lower-income groups.[42] These trends can be seen with the sharpest resolution on a local scale, in Boston, Chicago, and New York.

In Boston the use of installment credit to purchase new types of goods spread quickly in the last two decades of the century. In 1870 the only household article available on installments had been the sewing machine. But thirty years later, when the Massachusetts Bureau of Statistics of Labor (MBSL) made an investigation of changing conditions in the city's retail trades, it was noted that "the instalment houses frequently carry everything necessary to furnish a tenement, for example, furniture, clocks, bedding, stoves, pictures, cutlery, plated ware, etc."[43]

According to the MBSL study, the introduction of installment selling into the city's furniture trade created "a distinct branch" of the business. The bureau categorized Boston's furniture stores into six classes of business, ranging from small antique dealers who sold for cash to wealthy patrons, to secondhand furniture shops that sold almost exclusively for cash to the very poor. Between these extremes stores of several classes competed for the business of those with low to moderate incomes. About half of these stores sold high-grade furnishings mostly for cash, while the other half, mostly large firms occupying an entire building and employing ten to twenty workers, sold a variety of grades primarily on the installment plan. In these "installment houses" three-quarters or more of the goods were sold via partial payment credit. "Many of their customers," recorded an MBSL investigator, "are unable to pay in full at time of purchase."[44] This description indicates that the installment furniture houses catered to those having a small margin of disposable income but very little cash savings, probably skilled workers and lower-middle-class buyers.

But in turn-of-the-century Boston installment selling was hardly limited to the sale of durable goods like furniture. It was also common in the garment trades. By 1899 clothing for men and women could be bought on weekly payments terminating sixty days from the time of sale. Since clothing had little or no resale value, clothing retailers could not protect themselves with the conditional sale or lease system developed in the sewing machine and furniture trades. The installment clothier's only protection was his own judgment; he could afford to sell only to reliable customers, and only in amounts within the customer's probable resources. If sickness or unemployment interfered with payment, clothing dealers simply waited for their money. Explaining why they assumed such a risk, store owners told investigators that their customers deserved credit and rarely skipped payments. "Under the credit system," one store owner told the MBSL, "having incurred an obligation, they endeavor to meet it. In our experience they will pay their bills before spending money for pleasure or otherwise." By 1900 terms had relaxed to the point that down payments were not always required.[45]

Installment credit spread to the clothing business because of stiff competition from department stores. In Boston, the rise of department store retailing compelled single-line retailers to adopt installment credit as a last resort to preserve their businesses. The arrival of mass retailing seriously threatened the viability of small single-line shops. To begin with, department stores made enticing appeals to shopper's imaginations. Department store merchants self-consciously employed alluring advertisements, elaborately designed exteriors, and festive interior environments to transform the dull chore of shopping into an adult fantasy experience, an amusement comparable with visiting a museum or traveling to foreign lands. But in addition to massaging consumer passions, mass retailers also calculated to meet some very practical concerns. They advertised—if not always delivered—the lowest prices in town. They could offer low prices on quality goods because they bought in volume, used cost-accounting procedures, and adhered to strict cash-only policies.[46] Faced with competition from department stores, single-line retailers reluctantly struggled to redefine their businesses. Many chose to exploit the one weakness in the department store selling strategy: the insistence on cash. "We were forced into the instalment business," complained one furniture store owner to an agent of the MBSL. Selling department store goods on "easy payments" was the only way that he and many others like him could stay in business.[47]

A growing desire for high-quality clothing also contributed to the spread of the installment plan among clothiers. A store owner in Boston observed that workers demanded "clothing of a style and quality superior to that formerly worn on special occasions."[48] The desire for better clothing had something to do with rising standards for public dress, but it also reflected the changing requirements of the workplace in late nineteenth-century American cities. "In every sort of position," observed an investigator in Pittsburgh, "the clothing . . . is of increasing importance."[49] This was especially true for job seekers, because employers gave preference to workers whose street clothes gave evidence of thrift and reliability. In this situation workers had two choices. If they wanted to stay out of debt they could buy cheap used clothes for cash from a pawnbroker or secondhand clothing store. Or they could buy better-quality clothing on an installment clothier's sixty-day plan. This unhappy choice was the "Scylla and Charybdis" of the industrial working woman, according to one investigator.[50]

An instance of the latter choice is described in William Dean Howells's *The Minister's Charge* (1886). Lemuel Barker, a young man who has come to Boston to make his fortune, soon realizes that his country clothes are a little too rustic for the social requirements of his new job. Entering a shop "on a degenerate street, in a neighborhood of Chinese laundries," Barker looks longingly at a new suit of fancy clothes. Admitting that he cannot afford the suit, Lemuel is informed that "he might pay for it on the instalment plan, which the proprietor explained to him." Besides hinting at the low social respectability of installment buying, Howells's vignette illustrates the psychology of installment buying. It allowed people of very small means to "buy up," that is, to purchase new clothing—or furniture, or other goods—of better style and quality than what they could afford with cash only.[51]

According to the MBSL report, the installment system was "said to be increasing in all our cities."[52] This was true. After 1880 large installment houses opened in Indianapolis, St. Louis, Kansas City, Milwaukee, and Seattle. But no western city was more receptive to the growth of installment houses than Chicago, where the Spiegel House Furnishings Company established itself as the leading "credit merchant" in the country.

Why Chicago proved to be such a hotbed for the growth of installment financing is laid out in Upton Sinclair's classic novel of immigrant life, *The Jungle* (1906). In this work of "realistic" fiction, Sinclair described in vivid detail the hard life of an immigrant family of twelve who left a peasant village in Lithuania for the crowded stockyard district of Chicago's Packingtown.[53] Sinclair intended the Rudkus family to represent the hundreds of thousands of immigrant families who migrated to Chicago in the late nineteenth century, turning the small village of 1840 into a leading metropolis of 1.5 million in 1900. Like the Rudkuses in *The Jungle*, these families arrived in need of basic household furnishings, clothing, and implements. Like the Rudkuses, many were also entering the life-cycle stage where growing families increase their purchasing in order to keep up with expanding material needs. Also like the Rudkuses, Chicago's immigrant population tended to have little or no savings. But during upswings in the business cycle, they did command a relatively stable income from their work in the stockyards and the mills. The combined factors of need, a lack of savings, and weekly paychecks created a situation well suited for installment credit. As was the case elsewhere, Chicago's immigrant working-class families were judged to be good credit risks by the city's new installment house merchants.[54]

In *The Jungle*, Upton Sinclair described in detail how an immigrant family went about outfitting a home. First there was the buying of a house, which in the Rudkuses case involved nerve-wracking negotiations in a foreign language with strangers, resulting in an installment mortgage on a modest clapboard house ($300 down, the balance of $1,200 to be paid at $12 per month, plus additional hidden charges of interest, insurance, and tax assessments).

But this great step up the social ladder only led to another challenge: the need to furnish the house. This problem absorbed "every instant of their leisure." A member of the family sees a bright advertisement, featuring two little birds building themselves a home. "Feather your nest," urges the ad, promising that seventy-five dollars is all it takes to fully outfit a four-room house. In Sinclair's words, "The particularly important thing about this offer was that only a small part of the money need be had at once—the rest one might pay a few dollars every month. Our friends had to have some furniture, there was no getting away from that; but their little fund of money had sunk so low that they could hardly get to sleep at night, and so they fled to this as their deliverance." There is more counting up of resources, more deliberations pro and con, more unfamiliar contracts, but finally the Rudkus family becomes the owner of a parlor set of four pieces, a bedroom suite, a dining room table and four chairs, a toilet set "with beautiful pink roses painted all over it," an assortment of crockery (one plate cracked), and assorted utensils. For the next few days the fixing-up of the home is "a never-ending delight," until it became "quite wonderful to see how fine the house looked."[55]

Sinclair did not identify the sponsor of the "Feather Your Nest" advertisement. If he had, it might have been the Spiegel House Furnishing Company, which by 1906 was Chicago's leading installment house. Spiegel originally sold high-quality furniture for cash, but the company's bankruptcy in 1892 encouraged the owners to look for new approaches. Impressed by the success of Chicago's pioneering installment houses, Modie Spiegel, son of the founder, copied the methods of the "borax" houses (described in Chapter 1) and reorganized the company as a retail house catering to immigrant families like the Rudkuses. Spiegel's borax methods were simple but effective. Low-priced furniture was bought at wholesale and marked up 100 percent. Half- and full-page advertisements ran frequently in the daily newspapers. "Clearance" sales were held on a regular basis. Inside the store, creative displays added imaginary qualities to displayed goods. Most important, aggressive, high-pressure salesmanship aimed to convince customers that Spiegel furniture represented a superior value.[56]

Sales at The Spiegel House Furnishings Company's three stores were brisk. In 1904 the company established a mail-order department and began extending its credit to customers nationwide. The decision to get into mail-order selling was prompted by requests from out-of-town customers who wanted Spiegel to send them goods via the U.S. Post Office—on the same terms of credit offered in the store. These customers could have traded with Sears and Montgomery Ward, the established mail-order giants, but both companies made a point of selling only for cash. Sensing a possible niche for itself in the mail-order trade, Spiegel in 1904 cautiously mailed out a small catalog to people living within a hundred-mile radius of Chicago. The response was overwhelming. In just two years the mail-order department at Spiegel took in twice the business of Spiegel's retail stores, and the Spiegel mail-order empire was off to a dramatic, if chaotic, start.[57]

Figure 10. Advertisement for a borax house from the Chicago
Tribune, 3 November 1889. Stores selling cheap goods on
"long easy payments" made it easier for working-class families
to oufit themselves with consumer goods.

From the beginning, Spiegel mail order emphasized installment credit. "We Trust the People—Everywhere" announced the first catalog. The benefits and terms of installment credit were explained on the catalog's first page. "For the first time in the country's history," trumpeted Arthur Spiegel's cover letter, "a high-class furniture house extends installment credit to the nation." Appealing to the "great army of wage earners," the Spiegel catalog sympathized with working people, especially those in small towns, who found their purchasing limited by meager stocks, high prices, and the fact that both local dealers and mail-order businesses "MAKE YOU PAY CASH for goods." But Spiegel customers were promised "all the time you need to pay." In actuality, most customers were allowed twelve months' credit. Moreover, the catalog tactfully left unmentioned something that the company's biographers have pointed out: that the cost of running a credit business elevated Spiegel's prices 5–25 percent over prices in the Sears catalog. Nevertheless, Spiegel's claim that installment selling was "a boon to wage earners" found an audience. Mail-order sales for 1906 totaled about $1 million, with sales made in every state in the Union and in southern Canada as well. Along with sellers of sewing machines and farm implements, Spiegel played a leading role in spreading the installment plan to every town and village across the country.[58]

Thus, installment credit in the late nineteenth century spread to more parts of the country just as it had spread to new classes of merchandising. In addition, it also spread to lower-income groups. In New York City, civic reformers fretted that installment buying was endemic among people of small means.[59]

Concerned about this development, in 1903 New York's Legal Aid Society commissioned an investigation of the city's installment trade. Directed by Henry Mussey, a graduate student at Columbia University, the study found that a "remarkable development" of installment selling had made it possible to obtain virtually anything and everything on the installment plan. "Indeed," wrote Mussey, "one may buy a house and furnish it from top to bottom with every article of necessity, convenience, and luxury he desires; he may clothe himself and his family; he may deck himself with jewelry and all sort of articles of adornment; he may go abroad, and having seen Paris, he may die and be buried—all on the installment plan. And all this is no mere pleasantry, but sober fact."[60] Mussey distinguished between three types of installment businesses. Most large American cities had what he called a high-grade and low-grade installment business. In addition to these, a "fake" installment business operated in New York City, discrediting installment credit in general, and making the installment plan "a hissing and a by-word."[61]

The high-grade installment business was distinguished by dealers whose reputation, methods, and clientele gave them a modicum of respectability. High-grade retailers sold house furnishings, pianos, sewing machines, and books on the installment plan, but the lion's share of the business was in furniture. According to Mussey, it was a "well known fact" that almost every furniture dealer in New York City sold goods on the installment plan, even though terms were not generally advertised. But some firms, including Cowperthwait and Sons, who had started the installment furniture business in 1807, made much of the way they sold house furnishings—usually medium and cheaper grades—on installments. The high-grade businesses showed a conservative selectivity in granting credit. Ninety percent of their customers were wage earners and men on salary, while 10 percent were small-business people. African Americans were excluded. Terms were moderate and delinquencies rare. When customers procrastinated with payments, creditors responded with leniency. In cases of repossession some businesses credited customers with the money they had already paid in, a practice that made business sense, though it was not legally obligatory. According to Mussey, the high-grade piano businesses sold only to customers "well up in the financial and social scale"; hence, problems of default and repossession with them were "almost unheard of."[62]

The fast-growing underside of the installment business presented a striking contrast. Unlike the high-grade business, which was dominated by a small number of large firms, the low-grade trade was conducted by a large number of small enterprises, numbering perhaps two hundred dealers. In New York City their activities were confined to the Lower East Side, where they sold to lower-income households a wide range of goods that included virtually everything except groceries, pianos, and books. Broadway tailors made clothes to order for a dollar a week; steamship tickets could be had for a few dollars a week; hats for young women could be bought for fifty cents a week. Mussey cited a typical advertisement: "Dealers in Cloaks, Clothing, Rugs, Extension Springs, Wringers, Albums, Lace and Chenille Curtains, Table Covers, Furniture, Jewelry, Pictures, etc. Weekly or monthly payments taken. Please send postal card and I will call." The quality of goods ranged from shoddy to medium grade. But all were sold at prices that reached three and four times the cash value of the goods.[63]

The most remarkable characteristic of the low-grade business was the prominent role it gave to peddling. Each day on the Lower East Side five thousand to ten thousand peddlers went about their rounds, carrying goods from house to house or bringing customers into the stores. Most were recent immigrants from eastern Europe. One type of peddler was the "custom" peddler, a man with no affiliation to any particular store, but who carried on a highly personalized trade with customers in his home neighborhood. Custom peddlers acted as middlemen between local retailers and the huge tenement blocks of potential customers, buildings filled with immigrants who were uncertain about American shopping procedures and eager to get advice from someone who spoke their language. On the strength of a hundred dollars in credit from their retail suppliers, custom peddlers offered in turn extremely flexible credit terms to their customers, usually without written contracts, always counting on the strength of personal relationships to guarantee their risk. In contrast to the custom peddler, a larger group of peddlers contracted to work for a particular installment house. Known as "pullers in," this type of peddler went from apartment to apartment looking for customers who would consent to being escorted back to the store. If a sale was made, "pullers in" made the delivery and collected the weekly payments. Finally, a third class comprised peddlers who operated as their own walking stores, buying goods from wholesalers and then selling on installments in their own name. Whatever the type, most peddlers dreamed of working their way up to become installment house dealers.[64]

Installment peddlers guided decision making on such matters as furnishing a new apartment, buying a wedding dress, and locating cemetery plots. The impression they made on immigrant families was often a strong one, as reflected in later reminiscences of life on the Lower East Side of New York. In one memoir, Samuel Chotzinoff recalled how in 1899 his mother bought a flowered silk table-cloth from a peddler for nothing down and ten payments of twenty-five cents a week. After that experience, she "could not resist" buying more on the installment plan, everything from furnishings to Chotzinoff's piano lessons. Since Chotzinoff's father "professed to abhor the credit system," he was kept in the dark about the weekly payments. Chotzinoff's role in this deception was to stand on the street corner each week in order to intercept the collector before he came to the door.[65]

In a memoir by Marie Jastrow, an entire chapter is devoted to the subject "Buy Now, Pay Later—Mama Discovers an American Custom." As Marie remembered it, Mrs. Jastrow never lost her amazement that in America people could buy things "without the money to pay right away." Marie's mother became friends with a custom peddler named Finkelman, who sold her curtains, linoleum, furniture, dishes, and clothing on weekly payments ranging from ten to fifty cents a week. Like Chotzinoff's father, Mr. Jastrow also frowned on this kind of buying—until Mrs. Jastrow explained to him that buying on the installment plan meant they could furnish their house without touching their nest egg of savings. After that, Mr. Jastrow was "quite impressed" with Finkelman's credit plan, "because bank accounts remained intact."[66] According to Andrew Heinze, who has studied the role played by peddlers in the Americanization of Jewish immigrants, "the practice of installment buying initiated newcomers into the possibilities of immediate acquisition and familiarized them with the impatient optimism that characterized the American consumer."[67]

On the whole, installment peddlers conducted their business honestly. But Mussey's investigation into installment selling in New York found that the low-grade installment business shaded imperceptibly into a thoroughly disreputable installment business that scandalized the entire practice of installment selling. Mussey termed this the "fake" installment business. Specializing in jewelry, the fake installment business employed fraud and intimidation of the worst kind. Mussey believed that Italians came in for the worst treatment, because they had a reputation for being fond of jewelry and because they were generally unaware of their rights under the law.[68]

A typical swindle worked in the following manner. Fake installment agents would arrange to visit the home of an immigrant family while the husband was away at work. Once inside the home, the agent would bring out an assortment of watches, lockets, rings, phonograph players, and other cheap goods, with vast exaggerations as to their worth. On terms of twenty-five and fifty cents a week, goods were sold at prices two to twenty times their real value. But the ultimate aim of the fake installment salesman was to make a contract that could be used to defraud the buyer. A variety of means were employed so that customers were unwittingly tricked into "breaking" their contracts. Thus, contracts were often made in pencil, so that agreed-upon terms of twenty-five cents a week could later be changed to one dollar a week. In another common practice the collector simply failed to appear on one of the scheduled days for payment. After a few weeks of "missed payments," the dealer would then descend upon the confused customer, accuse her of missing a payment, and demand immediate cash payment in full. Often he would get his money. But if not, the dealer would file suit, and then arrange for the customer never to receive a summons to appear in court. The court would then enter a judgment in the dealer's favor, leading to the arrest of the luckless buyer. During the year 1901, Mussey found in New York City's Second and Fourth District Courts over nine thousand cases involving fake installment dealers. This was one-sixth of the total case load in these courts. The previous year, 594 people were locked up for failure to pay installment debts.[69]

The fake installment dealers accounted for a very small portion of the total retail installment business. Nevertheless, Mussey noted that "the ordinary observer lumps all the [installment] business together as ill-concealed robbery."[70] This was true even in cities untouched by the fake installment business. Certain "fake" methods, especially the charging of exorbitant prices for shoddy goods, were not limited to dealers who used the full system of "fake" tactics. After 1880, the installment plan became increasingly stigmatized for genteel Victorians as a sign of poverty and improvident living.

Distaste for installment selling appears in the first entry for "installment plan" in an American dictionary. In 1889 *The Century Dictionary* defined it as "a system adopted by some traders in substantial articles, such as furniture, sewing-machines, pianos, etc., by which the seller retains the ownership until payment, and stipulates for the right to retake the article, without return of some or any part of what has already been paid, if the buyer makes default in any instalment."[71] With no reference to installment credit's key attribute, the scheduling of partial payments, this definition is less an explanation of the installment plan than it is a statement of the lexicographer's disapproval. But it accurately reflected middle-class opinion of the time.

It is hard to find direct contemporary evidence for middle-class attitudes about installment credit around the turn-of-the-century. Milan Ayres, a leading credit analyst in the 1920s, suggested why when he recalled, "People who made such purchases didn't talk about them. Installment buying wasn't considered quite respectable."[72] But commentators living in the credit expansion of the 1910s and 1920s uniformly testified to the low status of installment credit. According to Ayres, in the late nineteenth century the only things that a "self-respecting, thrifty American family would buy on the installment plan were a piano, a sewing machine, some expensive articles of furniture, and perhaps a set of books."[73] C. W. Tabor, author of a text on home economics, reported that even this type of buying was furtively conducted, as many installment firms used "plain and unmarked wagons" to deliver their goods, so that customers would be spared the humiliation of having an installment company's wagon pull up in front of their door.[74] Wilbur Plummer, an economic historian, remembered that "buying on the installment plan was considered one of the lowest forms of debt that one could contract—it was looked down upon socially. It was considered an arrangement for persons who were poor, improvident—not able to take care of their own affairs. They needed a collector to tell them under threats how to dispose of their money on pay day."[75] As indicated by Ayres, middle-class people used installment credit in certain applications. But the class stigma of the installment plan encouraged them to uphold the ideal of cash buying. Cash buying provided a standard for distinguishing between life-styles that were acceptably "middle-class" and those that were not.

But the stigma that developed around installment credit involved more than class prejudice. It also involved assumptions about gender. In fact, the rise of installment buying in the late nineteenth century linked women and credit together to form one of the most prevalent images of the twentieth-century consumer culture, the image of the female credit abuser.

Before the mid-nineteenth century, the world of credit was almost exclusively a male preserve. But as women gained more control over the family budget, and as shopping became designated a "female" activity, women increasingly demanded and received retail credit. The notion that women could not resist buying things on credit originated with the popularity of buying sewing machines on the installment plan. In 1884, an editorial in *Scientific American* criticized "the curious processes of reasoning" by which women decided to buy a machine on installments. According to the writer, one of the "anomalies" of the sewing machine business was "a psychological fact, possibly new," that women "will rather pay $50 for a machine in monthly installments of five dollars than $25 outright, although able to do so." The implication was that women, unlike men, suffered from a latent instinct toward instant gratification that overturned their weak grasp of business arithmetic. But in the next issue of the magazine a female correspondent from Michigan rebutted the accusation, and in the process showed a woman's view of family politics. "She does it from policy," explained the reader, "for if she says, 'Husband, I wish $25 to buy a sewing machine with,' she expects a shrug of the shoulders, and is unable to obtain the money; but if she says, 'I can buy a sewing machine, and pay for it in monthly installments, only $5 each month,' perhaps she can get the coveted machine." In this interchange a woman got the last word, but it did not prevent speculation among men about the alleged psychopathology of the female credit user.[76]

The association of women with installment credit was sealed by the conjunction of two late nineteenth-century trends in the culture of consumption: the gendering of consumption as women's work and the spread of installment credit among retail dealers. Men continued to take primary responsibility for certain "productive" credit operations, such as farm credit and house mortgages, but installment contracts for household goods were usually signed by the female head of the house. This could lead to deceptive tactics if husbands disapproved of installment buying, as in the example of the Chotzinoffs.

Deception between the sexes is the theme of a *Harper's Monthly* short story of 1913 that further illuminates the gendering of installment credit in household finance by that time. "On the Instalment Plan," by Corra Harris, opens in a hardscrabble village of northern Georgia, where two weary women lean over the fence talking about their difficult lot in life. Like the other women in town, these women head up subsistence-level families whose wants far exceed their means. But the women of the town use installment credit to improve gradually the material lives of their families. The "easy payments" system has allowed them to purchase sewing machines, stoves, organs, and other furnishings from various itinerant agents and mail-order companies. "It costs more to get things on the instalment plan," admits one of the women. "But it's the only way for folks like us to get 'em," replies the other.[77]

The plot of the story revolves around what happens when an installment agent, who happens to be a widow, comes to town selling caskets—on the installment plan. Skeptical at first, the women of the town find their sales resistance weakened by the installment agent's smooth arguments. Who could deny that caskets would be needed at some future date? The offer of low monthly terms clinches the sales pitch. Caskets are ordered, but as with their other installment purchases, the women decline to inform their husbands of the specifics of the sale. Eventually the truth comes out when an overdue bill catches one husband's attention. The men reestablish control over how family budgets are run, the women learn a lesson, and the story ends happily. The moral of the story was twofold. First, the absurdity of buying caskets on credit demonstrated that there were indeed proper limits on the use of installment credit to make future "consumption" a present reality. Second, men were better able to see these limits than women.[78]

At the time this story appeared in print, installment credit was about to enter a new phase of development in which buying caskets on the installment plan would not seem so ridiculous. This time it would be men, not women, who wanted to overstep the "proper" limits of installment buying.

GROWTH AND LEGITIMIZATION, 1915–1930

After a century of quiet, steady growth, in the 1920s the installment plan became a fixture of American consumer culture. It lost its class stigma, and became the standard method for financing expensive household purchases. How this happened was summarized in an amusing "history" of installment credit that appeared in the June 1928 issue of the *Century Magazine*:

> Once upon a time there was a Bad Boy in the business world, and his name was Instalment Buying. He was cordially despised by his affluent brother Cash Down, and his more respectable cousin Charge Account. Good Society tabooed him, and only Poor Unfortunates had anything to do with this enfant terrible, who brought attachments, seizures and excessive interest rates wherever he went. To be seen playing with this rascal was to jeopardize your standing in the community, and to give a man the final rap on the sconce you had only to accuse him of having commerce with the Instalment Plan.
>
> Strangely enough, however, the Bad Boy grew up to be a fine member of society, and today leads the merchandising parade by many millions of dollars. He has changed his name, and now appears in the best circles as the Acceptance or Finance Plan. In this

guise he has saved manufacturers of automobiles, radios, furniture and clothing—to mention only a few of his activities—from many a sad and unprofitable season.

Scholarly economists and substantial financiers laud his works; books are written about him, philosophies evolved, and he is gradually taking his place as a mighty power in the land.[79]

Bad melodrama, but not such bad history. As a professor of finance noted, by the late 1920s "even the plutocrat might buy goods on the installment plan without having his social standing impugned."[80]

AUTOMOBILES ON TIME PAYMENTS

According to an early student of consumer credit, "the automobile was the great expansive agent for installment credit."[81] Statistics tell the story. By 1924, almost three out of four new cars were bought "on time." Of the total volume of retail installment credit in that year, $670 million, or more than half, represented auto installment paper. No other consumer durable good accounted for nearly as much consumer debt.[82] But if the automobile sold Americans on installment credit, it is also true that the installment plan sold most Americans their automobile. Without credit financing, the automobile would not so quickly have reached, and perhaps never have reached, a true mass market, and its impact on American life would have taken a very different course. Installment credit and the automobile were both cause and consequence of each other's success.

In most histories of the automobile, car financing is a minor detail. Pride of place is given to the production of automobiles, not to their marketing. Thus, automobile histories tend to focus on technological breakthroughs, innovations in factory production, and the vision of industry giants such as Henry Ford and William Durant. Of course, none of these things should be minimized. But if the history of the automobile is considered from alternate points of view, such as those of marketers, distributors, and consumers, new landmarks appear on the horizon. From the standpoint of car buyers, the greatest watershed event in the history of the automobile was not the invention of the electric starter, or the adoption of the moving assembly line, or even the introduction of the Ford Model T. In fact, it had almost nothing to do with the automobile manufacturers themselves. Rather, the key event was the discovery that automobiles could be bought on the installment plan.

This discovery was first made by individuals wanting to sell their secondhand automobiles. A market for used cars began to flourish around 1910, as car registrations approached the half-million mark. Wealthy car owners wanted to replace their older runabouts with more powerful and stylish newer car models. At the same time, people who were less well off saw in the used car market a good opportunity to buy a first car. But used cars still cost a lot of money, anywhere from $300 to $3,000. Recognizing this problem, sellers began accepting down payments of one-third to one-half the asking price for their car and the balance in monthly payments. In Chicago, installment terms like these first appear in the classified ads of the daily newspapers in 1909. A typical ad in June of that year offered a 1909 Overland for "$800 cash, balance monthly," while another ad announced "a new, up-to-date, moderate priced runabout, very desirable for doctor or city salesman, which I will sell on payments." Classified ads featuring installment terms increased in number into the 1910s, most often financing the sale of midpriced cars such as the Peerless, Benton 6, and Locomobile.[83]

Despite the vision of manufacturing pioneers like Ransom Olds and Henry Ford, the automobile at the beginning of its third decade of production was still a toy for the rich. In 1906, Woodrow Wilson, then the president of Princeton, predicted that the automobile would bring socialism to America, because everyone wanted a motorcar but only the rich could afford one.[84] It was in fact the case that most manufacturers produced for a wealthy class of buyers who could well afford to pay cash for their cars. Indeed, from 1899 to 1909 the average price of motorcars increased, from $1,559 to $1,719.[85] The prevalence of body styles labeled "brougham," "stanhope," and "landaulet" led Alfred P.

Sloan Jr. to label this period of automobile history the "class market" era.[86]

In Sloan's periodization, the class market yielded to the "mass market" in 1908, the year Henry Ford rolled out the first Model T. But in 1908 Ford's vision of a "car for the great multitude" was one thing, and reality another. In its first year of production the touring version of the Model T cost $850. After increasing to $950 the following year, the price of a Model T then declined, but even the 1916 sticker tag of $360 put the Model T beyond the means of most budgets. At the 1916 price, a Tin Lizzie cost the average industrial wage earner almost half a year's income, while a white-collar accountant had to write a check for one-fourth of a year's salary.[87] With all the claims on a family's income, the high cost of even low-priced automobiles put up a significant barrier to the creation of a true mass market for automobiles.

For this reason, the mass-market era for American automobiles did not begin when Henry Ford rolled out the first Model T. Rather, it commenced when automobile dealers began experimenting with installment credit as a way of selling cars to people who could not afford to pay cash for them. In Chicago, three years after individuals began offering "terms to suit buyers," retail dealers placed their first advertisements offering automobiles on "easy payments."[88] On the Pacific Coast, between 1910 and 1915 dealers experimented with both open-account and installment credit. It seems that in most cases they lent their own money.[89]

But in 1910 few dealers could afford to extend credit to customers. On the contrary, most of them badly needed credit themselves. Unlike in the farm implement, piano, and sewing machine industries, in the automobile business dealers were expected to bear the burden of distribution costs without any help from the manufacturer. Car manufacturers refused to send stock on credit; standard terms dictated that dealers put up a deposit on orders and cash on delivery. To get into the business a prospective dealer had to make a beginning with either his own cash savings or a loan from a local banker. After the first purchase of stock, running the dealership was, on paper, a matter of taking cash from customers and handing it over to the manufacturer for more deliveries of stock. But it was really more complicated than that. Customers wanted credit. The dealers wanted a larger sales volume than a cash-only policy allowed. And manufacturers, to save on storage costs, wanted to send larger consignments of automobiles than dealers could afford to buy. Caught between the cash policy of the wholesale trade and the need for a credit policy in the retail trade, dealers stood in a vulnerable position.

They could get little help from local bankers. Auto loans violated every traditional canon of safe, sound, commercial banking. Repayment schedules were too long, and the loan itself, being made for a consumer good, was not self-liquidating through a return of profits. So in 1913 the sales finance company was created to solve the problem of credit for customers and dealers. Sales finance companies acted as intermediaries between banks, sellers, and customers. While the banks supplied the finance companies with capital, the finance companies supplied credit to dealers, so that the dealers could extend credit to their customers. For sellers this method of raising money on the basis of promises to pay from customers had a long history. "Accounts receivable financing" had formed the basis of many nineteenth-century enterprises, such as cattle loan companies, equipment trusts, and commercial credit companies. Beginning in 1905, credit companies were organized that specialized in the financing of businesses engaged in the installment selling of consumer goods, such as books and pianos. Impressed by the service these credit companies offered, a San Francisco wagon seller named L. F. Weaver proposed to organize a similar arrangement for country merchants who found it difficult to sell wagons and buggies on credit. The automobile caused a slight change in plans. In 1913 Weaver established the first sales finance company to help car dealers sell their stock to customers on credit.[90]

In 1915 Weaver's company was joined by a much larger and more ambitious finance company, the Guarantee Securities Company of Toledo, Ohio. Guarantee established the model that future sales finance companies followed. Not only did the company finance the retail side of the dealer's business, but Guarantee also lent money to dealers to buy automobiles from manufacturers at

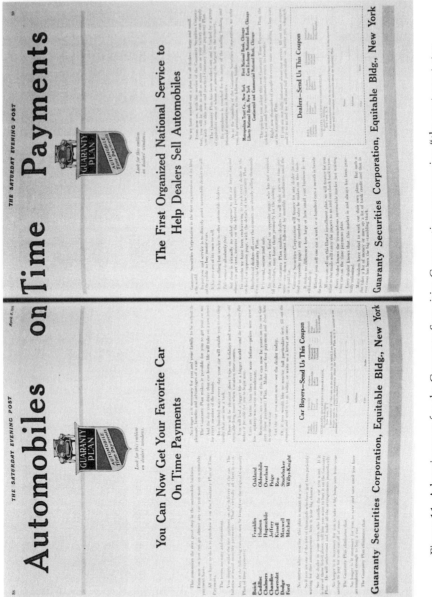

Figure 11. Advertisement for the Guaranty Securities Corporation announcing "the next great step in the automobile business": a nationwide plan for installment financing.

wholesale. Guarantee devised the practice of "floor-planning" dealers' stock, an arrangement that allowed dealers to store automobiles in their showrooms even though legally the cars belonged to the finance company. In the beginning, Guarantee financed the dealers and customers of the Willys-Overland Company exclusively. But swamped with business in its first year of operations, the company reorganized itself, moved to New York, increased its capital, and after 1 April 1916, made its credit available to all makes of cars. Taking out a double-page advertisement in the 8 April 1916 issue of the *Saturday Evening Post*, the Guarantee Securities Corporation announced to the public the arrival of "Automobiles on Time Payments."[91] The ad campaign attracted the notice of dealers and manufacturers, who now began to look more seriously at the credit financing of their automobiles.

In January 1916, an attempt was made to organize a single giant finance company under the directorship of the major automobile manufacturers. But the project never got off the ground. Some manufacturers objected in principle to the idea of selling their cars on installments, while others were simply too preoccupied with production matters to take this aspect of marketing seriously.[92] The Guarantee advertising campaign inspired a number of entrepreneurs to enter the sales finance business, but the major manufacturers resented what they felt was a threat to the control of their industry. The treasurer of a competing sales finance company recalled that the manufacturers exerted "considerable pressure" to have the Guarantee ads discontinued.[93]

The reason for the manufacturers' indignation is outlined in an important and revealing memo written by Edward Rumely, an independent financial consultant, to Edsel Ford of the Ford Motor Company. Dated 14 April 1916, Rumely's long, confidential memorandum was directly inspired by the Guarantee advertising campaign.[94] "The automobile industry will pass from a cash to a time basis," predicted Rumely. "Because of certain facts of human nature," continued the memo, "there are always more people who will buy when they can pay for a thing gradually in the course of the next six months, than there are people who have the cash in their pockets to buy outright." But if this was the nature of things for customers, Rumely argued that installment selling could benefit manufacturers, too. It could be used to solve the problem of slow demand in the winter, which was a major problem for the auto industry. To deal with it, either factory production had to slow down when demand fell off, which was a waste of capital equipment, or dealers had to take up the burden of storing automobiles that could not be sold for several more months, something few could afford to do. But, argued Rumely, if dealers had access to credit financing, then they would be able to buy automobiles the year round, thereby smoothing out factory production.[95] Moreover, it was clear that if Ford wanted to expand the market for cars, credit for the customer was the answer. Since customers wanted it and because dealers and manufacturers needed it, Rumely looked for "the most gigantic unfolding" of credit services in the near future. The only question was, Who would be the lender?

Drawing on the historical example of the farm implement industry, Rumely argued that Ford should stay out of the lending business. Implement manufacturers carried the notes of customers, and the results were not encouraging. Farmers took advantage of the impersonality of the manufacturer's loan to procrastinate with their payments. When they could not pay, they lied about supposed defects. Manufacturers got caught up in competition with each other and had to fight a constant temptation to liberalize terms. According to Rumely, in 1916 over half of the working capital of the farm implement dealers was tied up in loans to customers. Ford should stay out.

Nevertheless, Rumely warned against letting companies like the Guarantee Securities Corporation command the field of automobile sales finance. Eventually, Rumely feared, the installment finance companies would be forced by their own bankers to concentrate their loans on one or two favored automobile companies. What if Ford was left out?

The solution outlined in Rumely's memo accurately foreshadowed later developments. Rumely suggested that the Ford Motor Company organize a banking company that would be separate from Ford yet still under its control. The new finance company would discount the notes of both customers and dealers. Borrowing an idea from Willys-Overland, city purchasers would be given terms of 25 percent down and monthly, bimonthly, or quarterly installments with short maturities, while farmers would buy notes maturing after the fall harvest. "Now is the time to act," argued Rumely; "when the field is occupied, it will be difficult to make a new start."[96]

But Ford did not act. Henry Ford thoroughly disapproved of installment buying, and scotched every attempt by Edsel to act on Rumely's advice. Ford did not publicly express his views on install-ment credit until some years later. But his antipathies toward bankers, borrowing, stockholders, and most other aspects of fi-nancial capitalism were already well known. Distaste for install-ment credit followed naturally. Ford's convictions found their way into an article that appeared in the *Ford Times* two years before Rumely's memo. After reviewing the huge scale of production at the Ford Motor Company, the author concluded that "a business so vast as this could not be conducted on a credit business. Every Ford car is sold cash."[97]

Every Ford car was sold for cash—to the dealer. But already in 1914 Ford dealers were selling the Model T on installment credit arranged by local finance companies. In 1919, Edsel Ford esti-mated that at least 65 percent of Ford cars and trucks were being sold on a time payment basis. "I also feel," he wrote the president of a sales finance company, "that the time payment plan will be-come more important as time goes on."[98]

In 1920, when one out of every two cars in the world was a Model T, Henry Ford felt that the future for his company looked bright. But by insisting that Ford cars be sold for cash, he author-ized one of the more important factors that triggered the decline of the Ford Motor Company in the 1920s.[99]

Unlike Ford, the managers at the General Motors Corporation held fewer grudges against the credit mechanisms demanded by industrial capitalism. Early in 1919, John J. Raskob proposed to his fellow executives that General Motors create a credit financing arm to be controlled by the parent manufacturing company. Echo-ing Edward Rumely, Raskob argued that selling cars on the in-stallment plan would increase company sales and stabilize factory production. In addition, it would enable GM to compete with Ford in the low-priced automobile market. The low monthly payments of an installment plan would help dealers convince middle-income customers to substitute the greater comfort, power, and style of a Chevrolet or Oldsmobile for the basic transportation of a Model T. Raskob did not have to convince Alfred P. Sloan, then a vice-president in charge of the accessory department. Sloan had earlier been one of the directors of the Guarantee Securities Company. With the above ideas in mind, the General Motors Acceptance Corporation (GMAC) was set up in March 1919.[100]

The formation of GMAC began the boom period in automobile finance. In the spring of 1917 there had been about a dozen sales finance companies that lent to finance automobiles; by 1922 the number had risen to 1,000, and by 1925 the number of sales finance companies peaked at 1,600–1,700. A survey in 1926 showed that combined these companies lent a total of almost $4 billion. Still, 90 percent of automobile loans were financed by the oldest and largest companies: GMAC, the Commercial Investment Trust Corporation, the Commercial Credit Company, Hare & Chase, the Merchants and Manufacturers Securities Corporation, the Industrial Acceptance Corporation, the National Bond and Investment Company, and the Pacific Finance Company.[101] The larger companies offered both wholesale and retail aid, while the smaller companies tended to limit themselves to retail credit. Apparently no companies specialized in wholesale credit only.[102]

Finance companies extended credit in the following manner. When a customer was ready to buy, the dealer sat down with the buyer to explain the transaction, complete a credit application, and sign a contract stipulating the terms of the deal. Most installment terms asked for one-third of the price down, and the balance in six to twelve monthly payments. The twelve-month limit was not arbitrary. Repair bills after the first year often ran so high that finance companies were afraid car buyers would be disinclined or unable to pay their remaining notes. Security for the loans was given in the form of a chattel mortgage or a conditional sales contract. After the paperwork was completed, the dealer would call his sales finance company over the phone, a credit check would be

Figure 12. Advertisement for the General Motors Acceptance
Corporation, from *American Magazine*, March 1925. In an effort
to persuade middle-class buyers of the respectability of buying
an automobile "on time," this series of GMAC ads featured
understated prose and illustrations of well-to-do people in dignified
settings—such as the young couple seen here, signing on the dotted
line for their installment purchase of a General Motors automobile.

conducted in a matter of hours, and the deal would be sealed or denied. To make sure that the dealer screened applicants with care, risk was distributed between the finance company and the dealer through a variety of risk-sharing arrangements.[103]

Competition was fierce, especially between the hundreds of smaller companies. This led to a progressive liberalization of terms. Initial payment schedules of twelve months were lengthened to two years and longer, and dealers were courted with offers that relieved them of all risk when selling a car on credit. Moreover, many manufacturers made it a quiet practice to award subsidies to the major finance companies for contracts on the manufacturer's cars. These developments inspired the banks that capitalized the finance companies to insist that a professional organization be created to police the finance companies' own ranks. The National Association of Finance Companies was formed in 1924 to lobby for conservative business methods. Its annual conventions were well attended, and its pronouncements generally ignored.[104]

In retrospect, the ballooning of consumer debt for automobiles seems like an inevitability. It was not. Theoretically, people could have saved money in order to buy a car, and some did: throughout the 1920s 25 to 40 percent of Americans in any given year continued to buy cars for cash. Most cash buyers were wealthy.[105] Middle-class people, on the other hand, soundly rejected the cash ideal when it came to buying a car. The Ford Motor Company learned this the hard way.

In 1923, the Ford Motor Company showed no obvious signs of the decline that lay just ahead. Production of the Model T had increased steadily each year since most factories had shut down in the disastrous postwar recession. In 1921, Ford manufactured 56 percent of all cars sold in the United States. Two years later, Ford's share of the market was still rising, if slightly, to 57 percent. The Ford strategy of providing basic transportation at the lowest prices was obviously working.[106]

But as some executives at Ford well knew, the foundation of prosperity for the nation's leading automobile company showed serious cracks. To begin with, Ford no longer owned the low-

priced car market. Using the same production techniques pioneered by Ford, General Motors and other companies were also
turning out cars in the low-price range. But in terms of technology,
comfort, and style, their cars boasted significant advantages over
the Model T. Thus, from 1921 to 1922, Chevrolet production increased 220 percent, while Ford's rose only 27 percent.[107] Second,
the Model T was beginning to lose ground to the sale of used cars,
because buyers saw that they could purchase a better used car at
about the same price as a Ford. Finally, an "installment effect"
could no longer be ignored. As GM installment sales rose from
33 percent of new cars sold in 1919 to 46 percent in 1923, Ford
managers could see that customers were using monthly payment
plans to buy expensive cars they could not afford for cash. Ford
cars could be financed by local finance companies, but the General
Motors Acceptance Corporation had the advantage of visibility
and customer confidence, if not better terms. Soberingly, none of
the problems facing Ford could be met by further reductions in the
price of the Model T. By 1923, the margin of profit on a Ford car
had sunk to about two dollars per unit. Unless the company
wished to sell cars at a loss, it was clear that a new strategy was
needed for increasing sales. Marketing, long neglected at Ford,
would have to be brought back into play.[108]

Accordingly, in 1923 Ford pumped life into a dormant advertising department. More important, the company created a much bal-
lyhooed alternative to the time payment plan. The Ford Weekly
Purchase Plan, unveiled on 7 April 1923, sounded like an installment scheme, but its method was radically different. Under the
Weekly Purchase Plan, a customer was invited to select a body
style at his local Ford dealer, then begin a savings plan with the
dealer by making a "down payment" of as little as five dollars. The
dealer took the money and all future weekly payments to a local
bank where it was deposited in the purchaser's name and drew interest for the buyer. Depositors were allowed to skip deposits, and
the money could be withdrawn in the event of emergencies. When
the purchase price of the selected automobile had been accumulated, the customer took delivery on the car. It would be difficult to

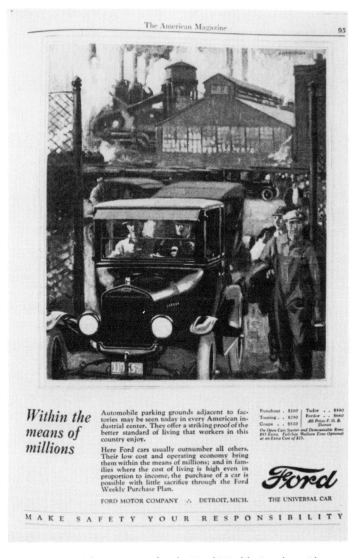

Within the means of millions

Automobile parking grounds adjacent to factories may be seen today in every American industrial center. They offer a striking proof of the better standard of living that workers in this country enjoy.

Here Ford cars usually outnumber all others. Their low cost and operating economy bring them within the means of millions; and in families where the cost of living is high even in proportion to income, the purchase of a car is possible with little sacrifice through the Ford Weekly Purchase Plan.

FORD MOTOR COMPANY ∴ DETROIT, MICH.

Runabout . $260
Touring . . $290
Coupe . . $520
Tudor . . $580
Fordor . . $660
All Prices F. O. B.
Detroit

On Open Cars Starter and Demountable Rims
$85 Extra. Full-Size Balloon Tires Optional
at an Extra Cost of $25.

Ford

THE UNIVERSAL CAR

MAKE SAFETY YOUR RESPONSIBILITY

Figure 13. Advertisement for the Ford Weekly Purchase Plan, from *American Magazine*, June 1925. Ford's alternative to installment selling required automobile buyers to save in advance for car purchases. In the ideal world of Ford represented in this ad, everyone benefits from the Ford Weekly Purchase Plan. The workers walking home can feel good about saving "with little sacrifice" for their future car purchases; the workers driving home benefit from "the better standard of living" they enjoy free and clear of debt; while Ford itself is a public benefactor working to preserve old-fashioned thrift while bringing its automobiles further "within the means of millions."

imagine a starker alternative to the idea of "buy now, pay later." The Ford Weekly Purchase Plan promoted the most conservative conceptions of thrift, savings, and delay of gratification.[109]

The Ford Weekly Purchase Plan was intended to give people in the $1,000 to $2,000 income bracket the necessary external support they needed to save money over an extended period. Obviously anyone might simply have established his or her own savings account, but as a Ford promotional brochure observed, most savers ended up frittering away their small accumulations "with nothing to show for it."[110] Edsel Ford, Kenneth Kantzer, and William Ryan became convinced the plan would work after studying the popular Christmas Club plans organized by various banks across the country. In 1922 Americans wanting to save money for Christmas presents had saved $190 million this way.[111] In addition, it was hoped that the Ford Plan would appeal to people who shared Henry Ford's twin beliefs in the necessity of the automobile and the virtues of the Victorian money management ethic.

Apparently, not enough people believed in the latter to save the Ford Plan from embarrassing failure. In the first eighteen months of the program only 400,000 people enrolled, and of these only 131,000 persevered to take delivery on cars (less than a month's regular sales). The Ford Plan fell apart for several reasons. Because there was nothing in the Weekly Purchase Plan to interest the dealers, they failed to promote it. In addition to this, customers found it hard to stick with the plan. "We often had to refund [deposits]," explained one Ford dealer. "After people would get $50 or $75 they would want a vacation or something and they would withdraw it."[112]

But fundamentally the Ford Plan failed because most car buyers entertained ideas about consumer finance considerably more sophisticated than the simple notions about thrift espoused by Henry Ford. What seemed like thrift to Ford seemed like waste to others. In the minds of many, the costs and benefits of saving to buy a car were no different than those associated with buying other expensive durable goods. While saving to buy a house, one had to pay rent. While saving to buy a refrigerator, one had to pay the ice man. While saving to buy a ring, a suitor might lose his prospective

Figure 14. Advertisement for Chevrolet's "6% Purchase Certificate," from *Literary Digest*, 21 March 1925. Chevrolets could be purchased with GMAC installment credit, but the Ford Weekly Purchase Plan inspired Chevrolet to offer its own "save before you buy" plan. But unlike the Ford Weekly Purchase Plan, the Chevrolet 6% Purchase Certificate encouraged prospective buyers to save up for only part of the cost of their automobile, then pay down the balance in monthly installments.

fiancée. In the same way, while saving to buy a car, people either had to pay money for other forms of transportation or go without the benefits provided by an automobile. Why not, many reasoned, take advantage of an installment plan to pay as you use, thus avoiding the costs of *not* owning a car? This line of reasoning gained converts all through the 1920s, though some were slow to catch on. Boosting Henry Ford for president, a reporter in 1923 wondered, "Will the historian of the future look back upon this $5-for-a-Ford plan as one of the most astute maneuvers in the history of American politics?"[113] On the contrary, the Ford Weekly Purchase Plan was such a miscalculation of what the public wanted in automobile financing that Henry Ford later disclaimed any responsibility for the plan.[114]

With the failure of the Weekly Purchasing Plan, and with the loss of market leadership to General Motors for the first time in 1926, Ford finally was forced into the credit business. Introducing in late 1927 the long-awaited Model A, Ford announced in early 1928 the creation of a Ford-sponsored installment sales finance company, the Universal Credit Corporation. Ford justified its belated entry into the consumer finance business as one more step in its long-range goal of integrating all aspects of automobile production "from the mines to the consumer." It was a step that came too late to help Ford regain its market leadership.[115]

FINANCING OTHER CONSUMER DURABLES

Elsewhere in the 1920s, the same story that played out between General Motors and Ford was repeated in other fields of merchandising. The results were always the same. By 1930 virtually all retailers of durable goods had developed their own time payment credit systems.

Henry Ford was not the only businessman who, against all business sense, opposed installment selling. With few exceptions, the nation's major department stores and mail-order houses had built up their businesses in the late nineteenth century by boasting of the price advantage they enjoyed because they only sold for cash.

In its 1910 catalog, Sears, Roebuck and Company delivered a stern lecture on the folly of installment selling. "Don't buy on the Installment Plan," editorialized the catalog, "it costs too much in the end."[116] Macy's department store in New York City, the self-proclaimed "largest department store in the world," angled for customers with a plainspoken slogan that claimed "No One Is in Debt to Macy's."[117]

But businessmen who opposed installment selling could not deny the bottom line: it worked financial wonders, and at very little risk to retailers. In 1927, bad debt losses as a percentage of total credit sales were only 1.2 percent. This amount of loss hardly counted for anything when it was considered that credit customers bought more goods than cash customers.[118]

By the early 1930s virtually all retailers of durable goods offered various credit plans. Sears quietly abandoned its cash policy very early—in 1911. According to the company's historians, the mail-order company was deluged by so many requests for time credit that Sears officials feared they had to sell on installments or suffer a serious loss of business. "Easy Payments" were first offered in 1913 on pianos, farm implements, cream separators, gas engines, vehicles, and encyclopedias. "No Money Down" became the catalog's policy in 1917 on a wider assortment of durable goods, everything from unassembled houses to "Bible lovers' books." By 1927, the most prominent feature in a Sears advertisement was usually the monthly payment.[119] Montgomery Ward waited until 1921–22 to begin inconspicuously installment selling.[120] Apparently, the postwar recession stimulated a vast wave of installment selling, as department stores, hardware stores, appliance stores, jewelers, quality clothiers, and other retailers scrambled to stay ahead of competitors.[121] All through the 1920s credit plans sprouted like mushrooms, as retail merchants converted charge accounts into time payment plans that masqueraded under a variety of names such as "planned charge account" and "junior account."[122] Later, the onset of the Great Depression would prod Sears, Montgomery Ward, and the larger department stores to offer for the first time almost anything they sold on installments.[123]

In a 1924 survey of newspaper advertisements featuring install-ment credit, a Washington economist found at least one store in the nation that sold candy and nuts on the installment plan.[124] But more typically, sellers of perishables and inexpensive durable goods were among the installment plan's most ferocious critics. John Stiers, an official with the Houston Trunk Factory, warned his fellow businessmen that the popular "Budget Plans" and "Club Plans" were in reality "instruments of destruction."[125] Business-men and women in the clothing, construction, and provisioning trades feared that goods bought on the installment plan took money out of their cash registers. Their point of view was stated by the chairman of the board of the International Shoe Company when he alleged that, "In order to possess nonessentials, many families are cutting down on essentials, setting a less nourishing table, buying fewer shoes, and skimping on living quarters." This was a common observation in the 1920s. In their "Middletown" study, Robert and Helen Lynd quoted one woman as saying, "We'd rather do without clothes than give up the car." Another respondent said the same about food, and the Lynds noted that twenty-one families in Muncie, Indiana owned a car, but no bath-tub. Recently, Martha Olney has used econometric analysis to show that in the 1920s American households did indeed use the installment plan to shift their spending toward expensive durable goods. Apparently, grocers, shoe store owners, and doctors had some good reasons for disliking installment selling.[126]

But it was hard to argue with a tidal wave. From just over a half-billion dollars in 1910, the annual volume of retail install-ment credit rose to about $7 billion in 1929.[127] According to a Department of Commerce retail credit survey for 1928–30, sales on installment credit accounted for only 9.2 percent of total retail sales (open-account credit accounted for an additional 32.2 per-cent).[128] But most durable goods were bought "on time." By 1930, installment credit financed the sales of 60–75 percent of automo-biles, 80–90 percent of furniture, 75 percent of washing machines, 65 percent of vacuum cleaners, 18–25 percent of jewelry, 75 per-cent of radio sets, and 80 percent of phonographs.[129]

He Makes Only $3,000 a Year, but Is Worth $112,290!

"I was a victim of debtor's cowardice," confessed a remorseful debtor in a *Saturday Evening Post* testimonial of early 1922. The author recounted how promises of easy credit had led him on a fruitless quest to keep up with the Joneses. But having sunk deep into debt, the day came when this self-described "coward" had to face the truth—easy credit had sapped his courage to say no to consumer passions. Like an alcoholic publicly confessing his helplessness, the recovered debtor desired to tell his story to others, to warn them before they, too, fell prey to the "pay-by-the-month system." The testimonial's prosaving, antidebt message said nothing new about the morality of debt. The novelty lay in the intended audience. "I am not writing for deadbeats and crooks," wrote the repentant "coward." "I am not writing for the ineffectuals, for failures, or for people ground down by poverty," he continued. Instead, the author declared, "I am addressing myself to the financially middle-class young man and woman—the 40 percent of our American population—because I believe that at one time or another most of that class suffers from debtor's cowardice."[130]

Did the middle class in the 1920s suffer from "debtor's cowardice"? Survey results at the end of the 1920s showed that as many as one out of two American families was purchasing one or more items on the installment plan.[131] Who were these families?

National data on the social makeup of installment buyers are not available for years before the mid-1930s. But in 1927, Wilbur Plummer, an economic historian and a widely respected credit expert, believed that the largest proportion of people using installment credit was to be found in the lower-income groups. He based his opinion on a trade journal study of 532 families in a city of 60,000. The study found that 40 percent of those in "the poorer parts of town" bought on an installment basis; 25 percent of the middle-class families bought goods in this way; and 5 percent of the "well-to-do" used installment credit.[132] A few years later

Plummer amended his view. He continued to believe that the greatest number of installment debtors were from the poorer classes. But more significantly, it was also the case that the greatest amount of installment debt by far was owed by the middle class and the upper layer of skilled workers. In other words, the massive expansion of installment credit in the 1920s was largely a middle-class phenomenon.[133]

Plummer's view is supported by strong circumstantial evidence. For one thing, most of the volume of installment debt was used to finance goods that had a clear middle-class bias. In 1926, the goods accounting for the greatest volume of credit outstanding were:

1. Automobiles (50 percent of total)
2. Household furniture (19 percent)
3. Pianos (7 percent)
4. Sewing machines
5. Phonographs
6. Washing machines
7. Radio sets
8. Jewelry
9. Clothing
10. Tractors[134]

Automobiles accounted for over half the total of installment debt, yet automobiles were not often found parked next to the homes of lower-income families. Figures on automobile ownership in the 1920s have recently been surveyed and analyzed by Frank Stricker. His conclusion is that in 1929 the average working-class family probably had about a 30 percent chance of owning a car, and an unskilled worker, much less than that. On the other hand, the average nonfarm family had a 50 percent chance of owning a car. When Jessica Peixotto studied the budgets of academic families, she found that almost six out of ten reported owning an automobile.[135] If most car buyers were middle-class people, and if up to 75 percent of all new cars were sold on installments, and if the automobile accounted for more than half of all installment debt, then most of the increase of installment credit in the 1920s was extended to people in the middle income groups.

Credit marketers understood this trend and worked to amplify it. After World War I, advertisements for extended credit rarely used the phrase "installment plan" and avoided stigmatized phrases like "easy payments." Instead, credit marketers appealed to middle-class notions of propriety with offers of "budget plans," "club plans," "thrift accounts," "preferred buyers plans," and, most commonly, variations on "time payments." Not all retailers made installment credit the focus of their store advertising, but one who did was Julian Goldman, owner of a large chain of eastern department stores. Goldman's ads typically featured men in business suits and fashionably dressed women in furs. While this was an old strategy for appealing to those with dreams of upper-class status, the ad copy explicitly addressed middle-income customers. "He makes only $3,000 a year," blazoned one Goldman ad, "but is worth $112,290!"[136]

If the greatest percentage of all credit users comprised low-income households, they used their credit to buy less expensive durable goods, such as washing machines, phonographs, and radios. By contrast, middle-income Americans who converted to installment buying were most likely to purchase expensive durable goods on the installment plan, such as automobiles, electric refrigerators, and expensive furniture. This pattern has recently been confirmed by a local study of Chicago workers in the 1920s. "It was middle-income people, not workers," writes Lizabeth Cohen, "who made installment buying such a rage in the 1920s, particularly the salaried and well-off classes who anticipated larger incomes in the future."[137]

The first hard national data on consumer credit that are available cover the year 1935–36. It clearly shows that by then installment buying had become a middle-class practice. Sponsored by the National Bureau of Economic Research, the study found that the households most likely to use installment credit were those in the income range of $1,250 to $3,000. Of the poorest families in the survey, those with incomes under $500, only 12 percent used installments. But the frequency of debt rose with successively higher income levels, peaking at 32 percent for those families in the $1,750–2,000 bracket. The study also determined that wage

Figure 15. Advertisement prepared for the Julian Goldman Stores, Inc. According to the ad, "Jim Jones," a middle-class everyman, can expect to earn $112,290 over the rest of his working life. "Wouldn't it be nice," the ad suggests, "if Jim could use some of that money now?"

earners used installment credit slightly more than professionals, but that professionals borrowed larger amounts. In addition, city people were more likely to be installment debtors than farmers.[138]

REGULATED ABUNDANCE

The legacies of the installment plan have been various and profound. Most studies of installment credit have concentrated on its economic significance.[139] By augmenting consumer buying power, installment credit tremendously expanded the manufacturing and retail base of the national economy, to the point that today the sudden removal of credit buying from the economy would cause immediate economic collapse. Such a scenario is hard to imagine, and to keep it from happening the Federal Reserve, through its manipulation of interest rates, uses consumer installment credit as a valve to regulate stable economic growth. Measurable in dollars and cents, the economic effects of installment credit attract the attention of many analysts, but the installment plan's other legacies have been no less important.

Installment credit generated a psychology of affluence that contributed immensely to the spirit of the Roaring Twenties. It financed a middle-class consumer society even as it erased one of the sharpest prescriptive boundaries of middle-class identity, the boundary between life-styles based on thrifty cash buying and life-styles built on improvident "consumptive" debts. This last point loomed large during the credit revolution. Maxwell Droke, an early apologist for consumer credit and author of *Credit: The Magic Coin of Commerce*, remembered that in his youth the only people who bought on the installment plan were "the poor, the shiftless, and the improvident." Writing in 1930, Droke found that things had changed. "Today," he observed, "when a man pays cash for his winter overcoat, we raise a mildly surprised eyebrow. 'What's the matter; can't he get credit?'"[140]

But if installment credit made the middle class a debtor class, it does not follow that it also made it an improvident, careless, and profligate class. Installment credit seems like "easy credit," and sometimes it has been marketed that way. But it is not easy. A Boston clothier said as much in 1899, when investigators inquired whether installment customers paid their bills: "Having incurred an obligation, they endeavor to meet it. In our experience they will pay their bills before spending money for pleasure or otherwise."[141] As evidenced by the low rates of delinquency and default, most installment borrowers, for the duration of their repayment periods at least, have been forced to live on a budget, reduce or cut out expenditures on momentary fancies, put aside money for the monthly installment note, and work hard in order to guarantee an income supply.[142] In other words, their consumerism has not only been bolstered by the installment plan, but held in check by it as well.

The kind of discipline enforced by installment credit involves the renunciation of many small desires for the purpose of enjoying a few expensive ones. It preserves the relevance of old ideals such as thrift, frugality, and planning, while differing in a key respect from the discipline imposed by the Victorian ethic of money management. When confronted by the temptations of consumer capitalism to spend, spend, spend, Victorian culture expected individuals to discipline themselves. But most could not do this, even in the nineteenth century when the culture of consumer desire was yet relatively undeveloped. By the 1920s, when the artfulness of merchants and advertisers had made America truly a Land of Desire, very few could practice the Victorian precepts of thrift in order to save in advance for the things they wanted, even when what they wanted was an automobile, one of the most ardently desired consumer goods ever sold to the public. The need for a new kind of discipline was made dramatically clear by the failure of the Ford Weekly Purchase Plan. The external discipline imposed by installment payments became the answer to what Edward Rumely in his memo to Edsel Ford referred to as "certain facts of human nature." The fact was—and is—that in a market crowded with sellers, if people were to purchase durable goods with lasting value they would need the authority of written contracts, the discipline of regular payments, the supervision of credit bureaucracies, and ultimately the threat of embarrassment, harassment, and repossession by bill collectors. Compared with the internal discipline of Victorian thrift, the external regimen of savings imposed by installment credit expects less of people. But in terms of investment in durable goods, it accomplishes more.

"They Turn Your Promise into Cash" was the title of a 1927 article in *Collier's Weekly* based on an interview with John J. Raskob, the first chairman of the General Motors Acceptance Corporation and therefore one of the founding fathers of the credit revolution. But nothing Raskob said in the interview was as perceptive as the illustration accompanying the article. The artist, Clive Weed, borrowed a familiar image from the world of credit marketing and represented installment credit as a bridge. Over the bridge marched the masses, from a gray world of crowded tenements and wash hanging on the line to a splendid world of modern skyscrapers and tree-lined parkways. The tenements represented "Hand to Mouth Living." The bridge was labeled "Bank-Controlled Easy Payments." And the beautiful city was the land of "Regulated Abundance." Regulated abundance was the greatest legacy of the installment plan.

The regulating function of installment credit has generally gone unnoticed. It has always been overshadowed by another, more obvious legacy of the installment plan: its ability to nullify time by taking the wait out of wanting. With installment credit, future time is packaged into month-long segments that are "bought" for the price of interest so that an automobile or some other consumer good can be enjoyed in the present. This aspect of installment credit was most apparent to its first users, who dubbed installment financing as "buying on time" and "time buying." Due to installment credit, the most popular commodity in American consumer culture is time. The way that it obviates the constraints of time has made it easy for critics of installment credit to overlook the regulating disciplines of periodic payments. Condemning installment credit for the way it marketed "instant gratification," critics in the 1920s provoked a crisis of legitimacy for the credit industry that inspired new, more positive ways of thinking and talking about credit for consumption.

PART THREE

GETTING CREDIT:

THE LEGITIMIZATION OF CONSUMER DEBT

*

CHAPTER 5

From Consumptive Credit
to Consumer Credit

In the United States, credit for consumers was twice invented. It was invented the first time between 1910 and 1925, when licensed lenders and enterprising retailers made installment financing available to millions of credit-hungry consumers. But in the mid-1920s their initial success at bringing an entirely new credit system into being was soured by a crisis of legitimacy. As debt levels rose, so did public anxiety over what was disparagingly termed "consumptive" credit. A loud chorus of critics alleged that the installment plan was a grave threat to public morals and a harbinger of economic catastrophe. Fierce opposition to the whole business of "buy now, pay later" alarmed the makers of the credit revolution. They feared a counterrevolution that would slow the growth of their business and perhaps even lead to restrictive government regulation. As it was, many who bought goods on the installment plan felt embarrassed to admit it.

In hindsight, it appears that the critics of consumptive credit were trying to sweep back the tide with brooms. But in the 1920s, the propriety of credit for consumers was very much in doubt. The credit revolution had started with small loan lenders seeking a legal business and retailers looking to increase sales. The revolution picked up speed when millions of people took advantage of credit plans to buy automobiles and other durable goods. The revolution could not be considered over, though, until they had learned to feel good about it. Debt was a moral condition. Accordingly, new types of credit required moral justification.

In the late 1920s, what had already been invented as a practice was invented a second time as an idea—the concept of "consumer" credit. When economists and credit marketers succeeded in reinventing "consumptive" credit as "consumer" credit, they accomplished more than just a change of vocabulary. They achieved a significant victory in their struggle against Victorian objections to "consumptive" debt and gave consumer installment financing a moral base to accompany its existing legal and institutional foundations. More broadly, the shift to "consumer" credit also signaled a decisive moment in the maturation of American consumer culture. Before this time, consumers had not been considered worthy of credit—either of loans or of honor. So when consumers got credit, they got it in both senses of the word. As individuals they got access to their future earnings; as a class, they won a public seal of approval for being consumers.

THE LATEST ALLY OF THE DEVIL

In the late nineteenth century, credit for consumption attracted little notice. Its growth was capillary and secretive; its problems and portents were overshadowed by recurring crises in the more developed systems of agricultural and commercial credit. Victorians frowned on the idea of credit for consumption, but it was not viewed as a threatening problem.

This inattention began to change around the turn of the century, when the first alarm bells were rung by those involved in the home economics movement. Domestic educators and urban reformers were the first to notice the widespread use of consumption credit because they were the first investigators to penetrate the private world of household finance. Using budget studies and retail surveys, and benefiting from countless hours of classroom discussions and informal interviews with housewives, home economists compiled the first accurate reports of household money management as it was actually practiced. It did not escape their attention that important changes were taking place in the nation's personal credit structure. What they learned, they publicized, the better to educate women in their new role as "buyer," "spender," and "guardian of the purse."[1]

To their dismay, what home economists learned was that many families carried a heavy load of debt—the wrong kind of debt. In

1899 Edith Elmer Wood was "horrified" to discover "how wide-spread among our people is the habit of going into debt." It was not home mortgage or farm credit that Wood found so disturbing. Rather, it was installment debt. Her research into family finance convinced Wood that installment selling "lured thousands to ruin," encouraging people to buy what they could not pay for and making debt "the curse of countless families." This was not all. In Wood's mind, the most astonishing thing about modern indebtedness was that it had spread well beyond the poor and the irresponsible. Modern debtors, she discovered, were "upholders of the law and pillars of the church."[2]

Like Wood, most home economists strongly disapproved of installment credit. Not that they opposed all forms of credit for consumption. "The most sensible of women want credit, and have a right to it," advised Marion Foster Washburne, referring to the convenience of retail book credit. Indeed, the stress home economists placed on "putting the home on a business basis" made it hard for them to be against all forms of credit, since businesses depended on borrowed money. But installment buying was another matter because it violated all the rules of economic efficiency for the home. In Washburne's words, the partial payment system was "a trap for the newly-married." It lured young couples into debt for ephemeral things such as shirts, collars, hats, and holiday vacations. It was used to sell goods of dubious quality. Its cost was high. It was a disguise for unscrupulous selling methods, which forced buyers into debt over their heads and caused them to lose both their goods and the money paid in on them. Washburne urged young men and women to learn from the mistakes of the "large proportion of the adult population" constantly indebted to "loan companies, installment houses, and clothing concerns." Echoing Wood's sentiments, Washburne found the "evils" of installment buying to be "fairly appalling."[3]

Attacks such as these reverberated elsewhere, especially in popular fiction. A spate of short stories examining household debt appeared in the mass-circulation magazines beginning in 1904.[4] But the author who beat the tocsin loudest was the popular novelist and short-story writer Irving Bacheller. Through his writings,

Bacheller popularized a point of view on the new credit system that many took as the common sense of the matter, in his own day and for many years after, even down to the present. Bacheller's treatment of credit is the best place to look for understanding why consumption credit inspired so much abuse in the 1910s and 1920s.

In the first decade of the twentieth century Irving Bacheller was America's best-selling spokesman for the simple values of rural life. He was a writer from the "b'gosh school" tradition, which expressed folksy wisdom in a regional dialect (in Bacheller's case, the "b'gosh" and "b'gum" heard in the North Woods of New England). Beginning with *Eben Holden* (1900), Bacheller's fictional heroes followed in the footsteps of Artemus Ward and anticipated Will Rogers, thus bridging the gap between the two most famous exemplars of American country-style wisdom.

In 1910 Bacheller introduced the public to a new cracker-barrel philosopher, a character with the unsubtle name of Socrates Potter. "Soc" Potter was a country lawyer and indefatigable dispenser of droll epigrams and homespun philosophy who first appeared in a short story in *Harper's* satirizing contemporary spending habits. The story generated such a positive response that Bacheller expanded it into a novella titled *Keeping Up with Lizzie*. *Lizzie* briskly sold over 100,000 copies in 1911, a great success. Encouraged, Bacheller followed up in 1912 with *"Charge It!" Or, "Keeping Up with Harry*.[5] The two stories captured the popular imagination. They inspired a popular comic strip (*Keeping Up with the Joneses*) and tagged the Ford Model T with a popular nickname ("the Tin Lizzie").[6] More significantly, Bacheller's stories popularized the notion, already evident in Mark Twain's *The Gilded Age*, that the youth of America were turning away from the sensible money morals of their elders.

Keeping Up with Lizzie and *"Charge It!"* told of efforts to restrain fashionable extravagance among the sons and daughters (the "heirastocracy") of the affluent middle class. Both stories worked as parables condensing current economic trends into the small circle of a Connecticut village.

In *Keeping Up with Lizzie*, a young woman with high social ambitions corrupts the life of an entire community through her fondness for reckless spending. Lizzie is the pretty daughter of the town's leading grocer, a thrifty and prosperous man. He sends his daughter to a fashionable school where Lizzie is educated in the ways of accumulation and display. Not to be outdone, the town's other grocer sends his son Dan to Harvard, where he is tutored by the sons of rich men in various subjects but mostly in how to keep up with Lizzie. When the two youths return home they engage in a spending competition that gradually draws in the entire town. Prices go up as shopkeepers tax the community in order to fund their free-spending children. The standard of living ratchets endlessly upward. Everyone becomes hopelessly mired in debt. Scales are fixed, homes are mortgaged, bankruptcies are declared. Finally, a young cashier at the bank, after embezzling $18,000 in a vain effort to keep up with Lizzie, blows his brains out with a pistol.

With the moral and economic well-being of the town in ruins, Socrates Potter steps in to save the day. Through bread-and-butter living Potter has saved up enough capital and common sense that he can bail out a town, even an entire nation, of prodigal debtors. Potter gives fatherly lectures to Lizzie and Dan. Dan repents of his prodigality and returns to the simplicity of life on the farm. Lizzie is redeemed through marriage to Dan. The townsfolk quickly reverse course so as to keep up with Lizzie in her new life of downward mobility. Inflation, bankruptcies, and moral corruption become things of the past.

As a morality tale, the message of *Keeping Up with Lizzie* was plain and unambiguous: Americans were courting disaster because they were living beyond their income. Bacheller continued the theme in *"Charge It!"* Addressing a young bride who charged up $6,000 in purchases over the eight months of her marriage, Socrates Potter admonished:

> Credit is the latest ally of the devil. It is the great tempter. It is responsible for half the extravagance of modern life. The two words "charge it" have done more harm than any others in the language. They have led to a vast amount of unnecessary buying. They have developed a talent for extravagance in our people. They have

created a large and growing sisterhood and brotherhood of dead-beats. They have led to bankruptcy and slow pay and bad debts. They have raised the cost of everything.[7]

Inflation can be a difficult concept to understand, but Bacheller made it simple. In his view, macroeconomics was a function of micromorality. All economic problems boiled down to clear-cut moral choices undertaken by individuals. If people were thrifty and not wasteful, if they saved more than they spent, if they went without instead of going along, that is, if they conformed to the Victorian ideal of the productive life, then the economy would be all right. But if people spent their lives engaged in comparing, envying, shopping, and spending, that is, if they acted like consumers, then the game was up.

Despite his thunderous denunciation of credit, Bacheller made it clear that traditional credit was not the problem. After all, how does Lizzie's beau get into farming? Socrates Potter lends him the money, *immediately after giving him a lecture on the evils of debt.* In Bacheller's mind there was no contradiction. Traditional credit flowed through safe channels. It was kept within bounds by the personal relations of the rural community. It opened out into a sea of expanded wealth and fortune. It was "productive." But credit in the city was strikingly different, which aroused suspicions. "Boys have been leaving the farms an' going into the cities to be grand folks," grumbled Socrates Potter. Urban credit was impersonal, without visible restraints. Urban credit was seductive, its temptations pushed without shame. Urban credit was elective in that wage earners, unlike farmers, could draw on a regular income to make cash payments at stores. Most of all, urban credit was wasteful. It went for goods that were used up rather than goods that produced income. Viewed in this way, rising consumptive debt signified the rise of a consumptive society, where people spent more time and energy using things up in the pursuit of selfish pleasure than producing things for the common good.

An article published in *McClure's* two years after *Keeping Up with Lizzie* shows that Bacheller's archetypical criticisms of consumption credit resonated with others. In "What Every Grocer

Knows: Fifteen Years' Observation of the American Housekeeper by a Grocery Clerk," the author related what he saw when he transferred from a village country store to a grocery in a medium-sized city. The "new world" of the city described by the clerk was a world of social emulation, of keeping up with the Joneses, of institutions like department stores that actively goaded people into contracting more debt. This was the first thing he noticed about city people: "Here folks were living on what they hadn't got yet. It was cash or go without in the old village; here everything was charged; there weren't 15 percent of the people who paid cash and got cash discounts." Beyond a general unthriftiness, the grocery clerk also noticed that with city families it was women who spent the income of the family and women who ran up the bills. Unlike country women, city women seemed to have "no exact idea of money." Playing the role of Socrates Potter, the clerk claimed that the only thing saving most of his customers from financial ruin was his own prudence in extending them credit.[8] If the clerk's report is an accurate record of one man's experience, it certainly cannot be relied on for an accurate picture of family finance at the time, either rural or urban. On the other hand, it is a faithful adaptation of the point of view expressed in *Keeping Up with Lizzie*.

New Anxieties about Debt

The disapproval of installment credit shown by domestic educators and moralists like Irving Bacheller marked the beginning of a crescendo of credit criticism that reached peak intensity in the mid-1920s. Anxiety about debt, of course, was nothing new in American history. But the new criticism differed from the old in several important ways.

One thing new was who was being held responsible for the nation's descent into debt. When the credit system was largely agricultural and mercantile, critics of debt were generous in assigning responsibility for thriftlessness and extravagance. The vices leading to bankruptcy were found in all social groups, though it was recognized that immigrants were thriftier than natives, while men received harder treatment than women for running their families into debt. During periods of high anxiety about debt, such as in the decade before national independence, in the panic of 1839, and again in the farm mortgage crisis of the late 1880s, moralists assumed it was men who speculated, men who ran up gambling debts, men who bought too much from merchants, and men who overreached themselves when purchasing property.

The critics of consumption credit, however, focused on a different target. In Bacheller's *Keeping Up with Lizzie*, the morals and prosperity of an entire community are almost destroyed, along with a man's life, for want of prudence in a woman's life. But Bacheller did not invent the notion that women were irresponsible users of credit; he reflected a view that was already common. As early as 1897 an English visitor reported to his home newspaper: "In New York, almost everybody lives above his income. Women, *many people will tell you*, are especial offenders."[9]

The feminization of credit criticism reflected important social and cultural currents. The proximate cause stemmed from women's new role as consumers. In the early stages of monetarization women often were not deemed capable of handling money. But as society became fully monetarized many of the productive roles formerly assigned to women—raising chickens, churning butter, making clothing, and the like—were removed from the home and women increasingly assumed the role of buyer and spender. "Women are the real spenders of the civilized world," observed Belle Squire, a home economist, in 1905. "The stores are filled with women, not men, shoppers. It is the women who do the marketing, who buy the groceries, the milk, the ice, the family stores, the children's clothes, and their own. As society is at present constituted, the spending of money, in the majority of cases, falls to the women."[10] Given this social context, consumer credit in the very beginning was women's credit. Credit was extended to married women on the basis of their husband's earning power and character, but women signed for the purchases. In 1914 a banker who was an authority on credit estimated that at least 80 percent of personal credit was extended to women.[11]

This was a step forward from the days when husbands gave small allowances to their wives, or disbursed money only in response to particular requests. With more access to money and more control over spending, some women found the consumer role emancipating. But the increased financial power acquired by women ran up against limits. No sooner had women gained access to store credit than the female sex was stigmatized as being constitutionally unable to manage debt. Thereafter the female credit abuser became a popular and enduring figure in the lore of consumer culture.

Those who spoke for American women tried to dispel this image, but with little success. Indeed, sometimes they reinforced it. Margaret Sangster, the editor of *Harper's Bazaar*, argued that the remedy for bankruptcy in wage earners' families rested "almost entirely with women to apply."[12] Her view made sense only where women exercised complete control over the family's spending, a rare enough case; at any rate Sangster's view hardly encouraged men to share responsibility for household debts. Other domestic educators may have unwittingly contributed to the image of the credit-crazed female shopper when they argued, as they often did, that society was not giving women the same level of training in the spending of money as it gave men in the making of money. Given this imbalance in education, Belle Squire admitted that "thoughtless women are likely to gather the impression that the adornment of their persons and the beautification of the home are the chief ends of money-spending." Squire labeled "absolutely false" the opinion that all financial failure was traceable to women, but at the same time she doubted whether women were "more economical" than men, as some maintained. She blamed female thriftlessness on the modern store with all its alluring temptations.[13] But in a public culture dominated by men the tendency grew strong to blame consumer debt on the inherent weakness of women.

Even today the contentions are familiar. Women cannot resist the temptation of a sale. Women lack knowledge of the value of a dollar. Women charge first, ask questions later. But, then as now, the case against women would always be selective and anecdotal. When automobile credit became the largest single component of

consumer credit, the fact that this type of debt was largely contracted by men should have disabled the notion that consumption
credit was women's credit. But it had no effect. The focus merely
shifted to retail store credit, and then, in the 1950s, to credit cards.
Retail store credit remained the province of women, but the low
rates of default on this kind of credit consistently demonstrated
that women were exemplary credit users.

Even as the new criticism of credit focused attention on women,
many critics softened their reproach by recognizing that women
moved in a social context more conducive to borrowing. This was
another difference from older criticisms of credit, which tended to
lay blame for running into debt squarely on the individual. But
criticism of consumptive credit looked beyond the individual
debtor to the modern urban environment. It allowed that the impersonality of the city greatly stimulated impulses for emulation,
conspicuous consumption, and overspending. Retailers in particular came under heavy fire for the way in which they tempted shoppers to buy more on credit than they normally would with cash.
"The great stores of the city put a premium upon extravagance by
their persistent invitations to open credit accounts," wrote one
critic in 1908.[14] "Look over the advertising pages of the papers of
any city," fumed Margaret Sangster, "read large sign-boards along
the streets, and there you find invitations to women to furnish their
houses and feed their families with 'just one dollar down.' The
impression created on the unthinking mind is that philanthropic
souls engaged in this credit business offer everything from a piano
lamp to tea with chromos, and ask nothing in return but a casual
dollar and the chance to make happy homes."[15] It was "modern
social forces," argued Belle Squire, that tempted women to
"stretch the $1,000 income to a $2,000 scale." But in her opinion,
the pressure women felt to expand their horizon of wants could be
traced back to one particular source, the modern store. There,
Squire protested, "the weak are allured with promises of credit."[16]

A third feature of the new criticisms being leveled against credit
was its amplification of the myth of lost economic virtue, insisting
that modern indebtedness represented a departure from the high
moral standards—and practices—of previous generations. The

charge, then, was backsliding: the American character was changing for the worse. "Our moorings are gone," lamented Belle Squire. "Extinct as the bison," said another of thrift. Society was suffering a "break down," declared Walter Rauschenbusch, the prominent Protestant clergyman and theologian of the social gospel movement, who feared that installment credit was reducing Americans to "the moral habits of savages who gorge today and fast tomorrow."[17] This theme of declension was not new, but in the decades of the credit revolution it achieved a currency it had not obtained before.

In addition to mythologizing the past, forgetting that previous generations of Americans had been no strangers to debt, the rhetoric of credit critics intensified. Credit for consumers was sneered at as "an absurd policy," "a rapidly growing evil," "the first step toward national bankruptcy." "The menace of installment buying" represented "a species of speculation" that would lead to "inflation of the worst kind." "The monster" sent people "plunging on the stock exchange," trapping them in "a morass of debt." "The false mirage of consumers' credit" lured people into "an orgy of buying." "The morphine of credit" reduced society to a state of "economic slavery," a "dollar-down serfdom." The most popular allegation: people who bought on credit were "mortgaging the future."

The language of the critics was extreme, to say the least. What fears lay behind it?

Beware of the Slimy Coils of the Installment Evil

One reason for the desperate tone of the criticisms leveled against installment credit lay in the fact that, for the first time, important structures of social authority were lending credibility to the practice of buying goods on credit. Foremost among these credibility structures was the law, always an important shaper of public culture, which increasingly sanctioned consumer debt as state after state adopted the Uniform Small Loan Law.

Another powerful social authority promoting the idea of credit buying was advertising. In a recent survey of 1,800 advertisements in *Ladies Home Journal* from 1901 to 1941, Martha Olney found that credit terms were *not* an important marketing strategy. However, it was different in other media, especially in large urban newspapers. For example, Julian Goldman, owner of the Goldman's chain of department stores, one of the largest retail empires in the country in the 1920s with sixty department stores scattered across the eastern half of the country, made credit the focus of his company's newspaper advertising. In a book he wrote to explain, justify, and document his own role in making credit terms part of the service ideal of department store retailers, Goldman recalled that the credit expansion of the early 1920s was spurred on by a massive national advertising campaign in 1921. "In the leading newspapers of every American city," Goldman recalled, "in the small town press from coast to coast, and in the multitude of weekly publications of rural America, there blossomed out the most colorful of all advertising campaigns, arousing an unexampled interest." In Goldman's opinion, the selling of consumer credit was "a brilliant chapter in the history of newspaper advertising."[18]

The new "debt mode of life" also received support from people's own prior experience with installment credit. A contributor to one of the numerous published debates over installment buying in the 1920s remembered that while growing up on a "midwest wilderness farm" he had come into contact with the installment plan on five occasions: "first, when my mother bought her sewing machine; second, when my father bought his reaper; third, when the family purchased a piano; fourth, when I bought my first good suit . . . ; and fifth, when I purchased my *Encyclopaedia Britannica* in place of the college education that was beyond my reach."[19] By 1920 most people had experimented with occasional installment buying. Doubtless, the positive experience of this one man was shared by others.[20]

Alarmed by the changing legal environment, confronted by the propaganda of credit marketers, and vexed by the positive previous experiences many Americans had with installment buying, critics of consumption credit turned to the traditional strategies of the lost cause. That is, they mythologized the past and grew shrill.

The archetypal criticism of Irving Bacheller was also employed as a cover by various groups with special complaints of their own against installment selling. The fact was, certain people's oxes were being gored. This was certainly the case with savings bankers. Claiming that installment buying was diverting money from their vaults, they were among the first to join the chorus of opposition against consumption credit. "Can any one view the vast expansion of retail credit throughout the country with other than alarm?" asked A. L. Mills, the president of the First National Bank of Portland, Oregon.[21] Bankers had other reasons for objecting to consumer credit. Eight of them were listed in a 1926 prize essay in *Banker's Magazine*. Among other things, installment credit was said to destabilize the business cycle by encouraging manic spending in pursuit of a "false" standard of living. Bankers feared that when the inevitable decline in the business cycle next occurred, people would find all their discretionary income tied up in debt repayment. This would cause consumer spending to fall off drastically, thus deepening the downward spiral of recession.[22]

Not lacking certitude in their views, bankers in the 1910s did what they could to stop the rising tide of consumer debt. Direct action was not an option; bankers did not yet supply the capital that put consumer lenders in business. But they could use their authority as the nation's captains of finance to speak to public opinion. Savings bankers used the nation's two thousand school banking programs to teach the gospel of thrift to future savers. In five states they succeeded in making thrift education compulsory in the public schools.[23] Another important venture was the American Society for Thrift, organized in 1914 by Simon W. Straus, a mortgage banker. Straus was an energetic propagandist for the virtue of putting one's pennies in the bank, organizing an International Congress for Thrift in San Francisco in 1915, and publishing a magazine called *Thrift*. Straus and other bankers involved in the thrift movement preached the gospel of thrift through schools, churches, and national clubs and organizations. Beginning in 1919, bankers joined with the YMCA in promoting observance of

National Thrift Week. During that week, the Sunday morning sermon hour was viewed as prime time for propagating messages of thrift. Ministers received sample sermons on thrift in conservative, liberal, and middle-of-the-road versions. The message to fundamentalist congregations was plain and unvarnished: "Thriftlessness—debt—mars and stains the soul."[24]

David M. Tucker has shown that the bankers' belief in thrift rested to a large degree on self-interest. When the United States entered World War I in 1917, the need for money to finance the war inspired the government to become a major proponent of thrift and opponent of consumer spending. For two years the government's War Savings Division inculcated thrift by every means possible, using the schools, the churches, and a national advertising campaign to shame Americans out of the habit of living beyond their means. Bankers might have been glad to have a new partner in their crusade for thrift, but they were not. Government savings bonds were a competing business. Bankers became "the enemies" of the War Savings Division, and did all they could to oppose its savings program.[25]

When the armistice was signed, the War Savings Division was quickly dismantled, and the banking community again shouldered the responsibility to preach thrift and oppose consumption debt. The governor of the Federal Reserve Banks, George W. Norris, used his position in the mid 1920s as a bully pulpit for denouncing installment selling.[26] A few bankers declined to participate in the crusade against credit, either because they had large mercantile customers or because they were supplying capital to sales finance and personal finance companies. But the majority remained vocal in opposing credit. One statement in particular was a favorite when speaking to the press. The installment seller, said Alex Dunbar, vice-president of the Bank of Pittsburgh, was "an *economic traitor* to his country."[27]

Bankers and representatives of organized labor rarely saw economic issues in the same way. But on the issue of credit buying they lined up on the same side. Labor officials took a dim view of the rising indebtedness of the rank and file. Officials of the International Typographical Union found the "root of the evil" in the tremendous growth of installment buying among union members. A statement issued by the union accused "insinuating sales-men, trained in selling-psychology and in 'credit desire,' abetted by wives jealous of neighbors' display" of "constantly waiting to take the breadwinner in a weak moment and unload something on him."[28]

Like the savings bankers, union officials had obvious reasons for opposing consumer credit. The worker overloaded with install-ment payments might find it hard to keep up union dues. He might be more inclined to suffer long and stand much. In the event of a strike he would need more help from the union's strike fund than the worker with no debts and credit to spare. Strikes might become harder to call. To strike would mean not only the loss of income but also the possible loss of automobile, radio, vacuum cleaner, furniture, and house—along with the installment money already paid for them. Labor officials understandably grew concerned when propagandists for American business boasted that consumer credit was doing more to "Taylorize" American workers than all the plans of all the efficiency engineers put together. A writer in *Forbes* went so far as to compare workers with installment debts to a donkey with a wisp of hay fastened in front of his nose. "The man whose pay envelope is all spent before he gets it is a discon-tented soul," observed the writer. "He has the divine discontent. His face may get wrinkled, his hair may turn grey, the fillings may come out of his teeth—but *he has something to work for!*" The author thought this was a good thing. Labor thought differently. "Pernicious rot," retorted a letter to the editor. "Dollar-Down serfdom," responded a spokesman for the labor position.[29]

Was consumer credit wielded as an instrument of social control, a concoction by business interests to solidify their hegemony over workers? Hardly. In fact, American business was deeply divided over the issue of credit for consumption.

When manufacturers were asked in a 1926 opinion survey whether they favored the sale of merchandise on the installment plan, 18 percent said "sometimes" and 72 percent said "no." Al-most all agreed that credit for the sale of clothing and food was irresponsible.[30] Some of the most virulent attacks on consumer credit came from manufacturers and retailers of perishable and semiperishable goods. George F. Johnson, president of the Endicott Johnson Corporation, one of the largest shoe manufacturers in the country, called the installment plan "the vilest system yet devised to create trouble, discontent, and unhappiness among the poor." Demonstrating that a deep sympathy for the poor did not preclude a healthy appreciation for his own bottom line, Johnson reckoned that installment buying was "just about a thousand times worse than the old 'liquor habit'; meaning, it creates more unhappiness, misery and discontent."[31] Johnson was joined by other shoe manufacturers and sellers of inexpensive goods in thinking that the national economy was a zero-sum game, where a dollar to the installment seller was a dollar taken out of the cash registers of other stores. Following this line of reasoning, both the National Grocers Association and the National Hardware Association issued statements condemning installment selling. In addition, the *Philadelphia Retail Ledger*, representing the point of view of small retailers, consistently opposed installment credit, labeling it "an alcoholic stimulation," a source of "financial indigestion," an "open sesame to desires and a continual inducement to 'forget the price.'"[32]

The clothing industry and the larger department store chains showed more ambivalence. Their view was expressed by B. J. Cahn, chairman of the board of B. Kuppenheimer and Company, when he said that while he personally opposed installment selling because it encouraged people to live above their means, and while he regretted the extra burdens of time and expense it placed on the retailer, there was really no getting around installment selling if retailers wished to stay in business. A similar position was taken by Theodore F. Merseles, president of Montgomery Ward and Company.[33]

But not all businessmen followed the dictates of the bottom line when forming their opinion of consumer credit. Henry Ford resisted installment selling long after it became obvious that his stand was not helping the Ford Motor Company retain its dominance of the automobile market. And in New York City, where store after store jumped on the credit bandwagon, advertisements for the nation's most renowned department store proclaimed throughout the 1920s, "No one is in debt to Macy's!"

Others also bucked the trend in their trades. One of the most fervid campaigns against credit buying was conducted by Zindler's Clothing Store, a Houston dry goods emporium selling men's and boys' wear to working- and lower-middle-class customers. For fourteen weeks in the spring and summer of 1926, Zindler's supplemented its weekly one-page advertisements in the Houston *Chronicle* with a series of large, dramatically illustrated "public service" advertisements dedicated to a single theme: the folly and immorality of buying "luxuries" on credit. The first ad explained Benjamin Zindler's motivation for sponsoring the series: "In view of the rapid spreading of installment buying propaganda . . . , it is our duty to point out the inevitable pitfalls and dangerous miry places in the path of the habitual installment buyer." There is no reason to doubt Zindler's sincerity, but more than "duty" was involved; the strategy behind so-called institutional advertising is that when a business can be linked in the public mind with a high-minded message in accord with popular sentiment, then the profits of that business can only be helped. In any case, the messages of the ad were not at all subtle. "Beware of the Slimy Coils of the Installment Evil," warned one of the ads, which illustrated the fate of those who violated "the law of economics by leasing their salaries for things beyond their means" with a drawing of the terrible end of Laocoön, the Trojan priest of Neptune, and his sons, being drawn to their deaths in the bottom of the sea by "the slimy coils" of serpents represented as "the installment plan." The text warned that if readers did not return to "self-denial, conservative living, and consistent saving," their "buying passion" would lead them into the coils of the "unmasked oppressor called DEBT." Later advertisements in the series pictured installment credit variously as a great chasm of debt at the end of "easy pay road," as a hideous octopus dragging its hapless victims down to the "abyss of debt," and as a pack of wolves menacing the front door of the American home. The antidebt, procash buying message proved to be more profitable for Benjamin Zindler than for Henry Ford. Zindler told the *Philadelphia Retail Ledger*, which reported on the campaign,

227

Figure 16. Advertisement of Ben Zindler's Sons Clothing Store, Houston, Texas, from the Houston *Chronicle*, 13 May 1926. Part of a series of ads criticizing the "Easy Pay Plan," installment credit is here pictured as a "wolf gnawing at the latchstring of a man's home and happiness."

Are You a Victim of the Installment System?

He is, indeed, a foolish diver who ventures into the fathomless depths of the sea without first arming himself with the proper weapon for defense against his most dreaded and most fearful enemy—the octopus. Should the diver be attacked by this pirate of tropical seas, unerring aim and precisive stroke with the dagger are his only means of freeing himself from the holey, fleshy, sucking sessils embedded in the long tentacles of this unsightly thing.

Is it not of equal importance for those who are plunging and diving in the sea of experience to protect themselves against the results so frequently imposed by the Partial Payment System? Buckle on the armor of self-denial, wield the knife of common-sense cash buying, and you'll see the old MORTGAGE OCTOPUS weaken and relax under the power of your offensive.

The Installment Plan—when not associated with the commonalities of the term, like the eight-arm monster—has its commercial value. As quoted in a previous advertisement, "we find no fault with the using of any method which enables men to build and own their homes," for it is this type of citizenship that has made America great. But when the promoters of installment credit extension forget the good purposes for which the plan was instituted and employ it as a scheme to sell a man more than he can afford, we believe it is time to use the hypodermic of public opinion in combating that FREEDOM-ABSORBING SYSTEM.

Pay Cash---It Pays!

BEN ZINDLER'S SONS
CORNER CONGRESS AND FANNIN

See Our 7-Column Ad Tomorrow

Copyright, 1926, by Ben Zindler's Sons

Figure 17. Advertisement for Ben Zindler's Sons Clothing Store, Houston, Texas, from the Houston *Chronicle*, 24 June 1926. This ad admits the installment plan has a "commercial value" for productive purposes such as buying a home, but the message of the illustration takes a more uncompromising line against consumer indebtedness: a victim of installment selling wields "the knife of common-sense cash buying" against the "holey, fleshy, sucking sessils embedded in the long tentacles of . . . the old MORTGAGE OCTOPUS."

that business at his store increased 20 percent in a single month after the campaign began.[34]

In addition to those with a material interest in opposing consumer credit, the ranks of the credit critics were swelled by people who had no financial stake in the issue: social workers, home economists, politicians, academic economists, newspaper editors, and clergymen. Public figures who spoke out against the new credit system included the economist Thomas Nixon Carver, Mary Hinman Abel, editor of the *Journal of Home Economics*, Secretary of Commerce Herbert Hoover (he compared the installment buyer to "a man walking around with a hole in his pocket"), and Henry Ford. The most dogged critic came from an unexpected quarter, from Senator James Couzens of Michigan, the automobile state, whose economic boom in the 1920s owed a lot to installment credit. "I believe more harm is being done to the development of our country through widespread installment buying than any other one cause," said the senator, whose numerous speeches and writings against credit indicate he thought of himself as something of a Socrates Potter for his times. But he was not alone in spreading gloomy forecasts of doom. C. Reinold Noyes of the Merchants National Bank in St. Paul, Minnesota, predicted in 1927 that a period of business depression was only two years away, and warned that the "national habit" of "financing prosperity on next year's income" was "today the most dangerous situation in the body economic." A former businessman writing in H. L. Mencken's *American Mercury* was less apocalyptic, but no less foreboding. He feared that the ultimate price of easy credit would be "the breaking down of the whole morale of the nation."[35]

THE ROOT OF ALL FEARS

As opposition to installment credit mounted, defenders of credit marshaled the contrary facts. Yes, it was true that credit sales had ballooned, but the volume of cash sales remained huge, dwarfing credit sales.[36] Moreover, savings bank deposits were up, and more were investing in life insurance than ever before.[37] To refute the claims of aggrieved shopkeepers, apologists for credit pointed out that sales of cosmetics, toiletries and other nondurable goods were increasing, so retailers of perishables had no real cause for concern. As for the charge that credit led people to live beyond their means, it was easy to say, but hard to prove, that people were spending more than they were making. Bankruptcy courts did not seem to be crowded. And defenders of credit buying asked whether there was any real proof, beyond anecdotes, that goods bought on installments forced parents to deprive their children of food and clothing. Reflecting on such questions, George Horace Lorimer of the *Saturday Evening Post* realized the true nature of the problem raised by consumption credit. "The meat in the coconut of the question," wrote Lorimer, "lies in the utility of the articles purchased on installments. It is the purpose of purchase and the quality of the article, not the form of payment, that is decisive." In other words, credit selling and buying was not the real issue.[38]

In their calmer moments, critics of credit buying admitted the truth of Lorimer's insight. "The objection is not to instalment selling as such," acknowledged Thomas Nixon Carver. "The practice of selling merchandise to be delivered at once and paid for in installments is neither new nor in itself objectionable," granted the American Bankers Association. "No rational person wants to condemn all installment sales," conceded Senator James Couzens.[39] Such statements always ended in "but." But what? "There is no quarrel," spelled out J. George Frederick, "with purchase on a time-payment basis of *productive, useful goods. . . .* But there is much debatable ground as to such usefulness and productivity, and so large a number of items that can be included if one is free and easy in one's interpretation, that a sense of financial soundness is easily lost in the lure of 'a dollar down.' "[40] The real issue, in short, was not that people were using credit, but that they were using it to buy the wrong things: nonproductive things; luxurious things; consumptive things. Men and women were using credit to become consumers.

Lurking behind all the criticism of consumer credit was a fear that Americans, particularly men, were using credit to become free-spending, nonproductive, effeminate consumers, a significant departure from traditional male identities. It is revealing that the ambitious anticredit campaign sponsored by Zindler's Clothing Store was conducted by an establishment selling to men and boys. All of the victims in the series were illustrated as men, and the "venomous thing" that threatened them was not debt itself but consumptive debt. As one of the advertisements explained:

> We do not censure the man who buys a home on an anticipated income. . . . Neither do we find fault with him because he obtains home furnishings on the same plan. But when in quest of perpetual happiness, this same well-meaning fellow, without thought of his earning capacity, drifts headlong into the ever gripping clutches of the so-called "Easy Pay" buying habit, he will realize, sooner or later, that the MONSTER has a mortgage on his future.

Another Zindler ad praised the kind of debt that "enables men to build and own their homes" as a "type of citizenship," indeed, as one of the things "that has made America great." But credit employed for luxuries beyond people's means was described as a "FREEDOM-ABSORBING SYSTEM."

It seems clear that much of the abuse heaped on consumer credit in its early years stemmed from a perception that credit buying aided and abetted an important transformation in male identity that many found odious. As the Zindler's ads insinuated, credit buying was inconsistent with male character ideals of independence, self-reliance, and thrift, ideals that defined the "true American" man. Traditionally, the worth of a man had been measured by his ability to provide and produce. Now, installment credit was creating a society where men competed to consume and carouse. That was the real issue.

To get this point across, Senator Couzens of Michigan told a favorite story about "the menace" of installment buying. It involved a young soldier just returned from the war. Married, the soldier loved his wife and twin babies dearly. One day, while looking in a jewelry store window, a desire burst upon the soldier to buy his wife some gift as a token of his deep affection for her. A smooth-talking clerk convinced him that a brilliant diamond ring

232

could be had with only a little money paid down. So the soldier bought the ring. But before he could complete the "little easy payments" on the diamond, one of the babies died. The family was just scraping by, so, in order to pay for the funeral, the soldier sold the ring, even though it was not really his to sell. The deception was discovered. The owner of the jewelry store had the soldier arrested and sent to prison for two years. While in prison, the soldier's wife and other baby also became sick and died. Racked with grief and remorse, the imprisoned man contracted tuberculosis and died. It was a true story, according to Couzens, and the moral was obvious: "The man who buys on the instalment plan risks more than mere loss of money." What did he risk losing? The soldier and his family lost their lives to tuberculosis, which, in the 1920s, was still known as "consumption." Death by consumption—that was the threat.[41]

The disease metaphor shows up again in a letter to the editor of *Forbes* magazine, written by a man who understood what was ultimately at stake in the rise of credit buying. "Probably the greatest economic and moral infections we have today, are the result of this broadcasting of the idea that a spendthrift and worthless debtor, even though he has a 'silk shirt' on his back, is the worthwhile citizen that makes the wheels go round. "Easy come, easy go,' shades of Benjamin Franklin, what a national motto!"[42] The central issue, then, ran straight to the heart of male and national identity: what did it mean to be an American man? Was he the sturdy producer, the man who worked and saved and used credit to invest in his future? Could he possibly be the unmanly consumer, the weak-willed spender and buyer, the dandy or social parasite who used credit to squander away the hope of tomorrow? Many thought not. "If anything is un-American," concluded one critic, "surely that is!"[43]

It is well known that the 1920s witnessed the first act of a cultural struggle between traditionalists and progressives that would continue intermittently for the rest of the century. The Kulturkampf would be fought over many issues—women's rights, prohibition, civil rights for minorities, the relation between church and state, abortion. Consumption credit was an early battleground where Americans struggled to clarify the moral status of the consumer in their society.[44]

A Cloud of Unrespectability

The critics of credit buying put up a spirited fight. But the more that people were warned of the dangers of consumptive debt, the more they seemed willing to "buy now, pay later." From 1920 to 1926, the percentage of the nation's households who bought an automobile on the installment plan rose from 5.4 percent to 12.2 percent. By 1926 two of every three cars sold were bought on credit. Over the same period, outstanding consumer debt nearly doubled (in constant dollars), while household debt as a percentage of income rose from 4.68 to 7.25 percent.[45] Clearly, more people were using consumer credit every year, and those who used it used it more.

But the increase in household debt does not mean that the critics were totally ineffective. Failing to stanch the flow of debt, the critics succeeded for a long time in controlling the language of debt and credit. People certainly experimented with installment buying, but in light of what the critics said about consumer debt, the experience left many feeling uneasy. Evans Clark, author of the first general survey of the new consumer credit industry, testified in 1928 that the average person buying a car "would much prefer to have one's neighbors think the purchase had been made outright, in cold cash." Clark averred that the pleasure of a new automobile bought on the installment plan was often tinged by "a cloud of unrespectability."[46]

It is hard to know what people thought about installment buying. Statistics register the use of credit, but say nothing of the intentions and rationalizations that accompanied the decision to go into debt. Opinion surveys would be more informative. But polling was in its infancy in the 1920s, and the surveys made of the public's opinion of credit buying are hardly conclusive. One poll in 1926 found that while almost half the respondents thought installment selling was "a good idea" in general, more than three out of four felt that their neighbors used the installment plan entirely too much. This ambivalence suggests that credit users brushed off the critics' condemnation of debt for themselves, but listened to the critics when judging their neighbors.[47]

Another poll, also conducted in 1926, found that 23.9 percent approved of installment buying, while 26.4 percent disapproved. The feelings of the remaining 49.7 percent were mixed.[48] This survey probably gets closer to the truth. Most people's opinions about credit buying were neither deeply held nor particularly clear-cut. Most people had habits rather than convictions, vague notions rather than settled opinions. Often, the same person harbored conflicting feelings, as their comments in the survey reveal: "Going into debt for luxuries is wrong. . . . But instalment buying helps the family on a small income to raise its standard of living." "Instalment buying costs too much money. . . . But instalment buying means that the seller will service his product if it breaks." "Instalment buying is perfectly fine, in moderation. . . . The instalment plan is going to be the ruin of the country."[49] Out of the swirl of such impressions people made up their minds. Which thoughts were activated and hardened into convictions depended a great deal on the language available for people to use when expressing their thoughts.[50] That language began to change in the 1920s.

DEFENDERS COME FORWARD

Through the mid-1920s most opinion leaders were critics of consumption credit. But in the late 1920s credit buying gained more support.

The shift in viewpoint of opinion leaders is easy to date. It occurred suddenly and noticeably in 1926 and 1927. The evidence is scattered in many places. For example, in 1926 *Forbes* published an article recognizing the benefits of the installment plan. There was nothing unusual about the article, except for its sheepish tone. The author was public relations counsel for the National Thrift Committee![51]

Similar about-faces took place in larger and more influential organizations. In 1926 and 1927 both the American Bankers Association and the American Federation of Labor published official reports on the installment buying phenomenon. Whereas both groups had previously expressed marked hostility to installment buying, now they gave cautious approval, concluding in almost identical reports that credit for consumption had "a proper place" in the nation's economy.[52]

The shift was very apparent in the middle-class magazines. In May 1926, after years of railing against debt and extravagance, the conservative George Horace Lorimer gave the seal of approval of the *Saturday Evening Post* to installment buying.[53] In the *American Magazine* the reformation of editorial opinion was both abrupt and comic. In 1915 the magazine started a new column featuring testimonials from readers on the problems of personal money management. Month after month, year after year, "The Family's Money" reported how families escaped the clutches of the bill collector through rigorous budgeting, sacrificial saving, and adoption of the pay-as-you-go, make-do, and do-without systems of living. But in 1926 the curtain was brought down on the orthodoxy of thrift. In the February column a reader timidly advanced the notion that some types of debt might be good for the family budget, since debt forced people to set aside dollars for valuable goods instead of wasting them on luxuries of the moment. In March, another testimonial offered the heretical notion that "it is often by spending money that you make money!" And in July "H.L.F." was allowed to tell his story. He and his family had followed a program of elective austerity for years. Pinching pennies had done little for them, he admitted, except to put wrinkles in their foreheads, provoke a lot of quarrels, and prevent them from enjoying the finer things of life. During a heated argument over whether the budget would allow tickets to a violin concert, husband and wife hit on a novel solution to the cash-flow problems so often featured in the "The Family's Money." They would "burn the blamed budget book." As his wife lit a fire, H.L.F. cranked up the phonograph and put on "America."

In his own words, "When 'America' reached that line, 'Let freedom ring,' I let out a whoop and threw the book into the flames. 'There she goes, Bobby!' I shouted. 'And maybe your college education and your whole future has gone with her; but we can't help it!' As I said, we have been free ever since." A few months later "The Family's Money" was discontinued. The editors, presumably, were setting Americans at liberty to go into debt all they wanted.[54]

Of course, not everyone took their lead from the editors of the *American Magazine*. But what arbiter of cultural propriety had more authority than the president of the United States? In 1926, President Calvin Coolidge, that exemplar of New England thrift and frugality, whose life and sayings seem to have been taken from the pages of an Irving Bacheller novel, gave his cautious approval to installment buying. In an interview making page-one headlines around the country, Coolidge scoffed at the dire warnings of the credit critics. In his mind, installment credit was far preferable to "the old way of running up a bill at the store."[55]

E.R.A. Seligman and a New Language of Credit

Until the late 1920s, critics and apologists alike used the same terms when talking about credit. They spoke of "consumptive debtors," "consumptive" and "consumption lending," and "consumptive credit agencies." But in 1927 a new set of idioms for talking about debt and credit emerged. The new language of credit lifted from consumption its association with disease and made debt for consumer goods seem proper, legitimate, and worthwhile. Now "consumptive" credit was reinvented as "consumer" credit.

As explained in Chapter 1, the classical theory of credit distinguished between two broad categories of credit based on the motivation of the borrower. "Productive credit" financed business enterprise where the motivation was profit. "Consumptive credit" financed the household economy where the motivation for borrowing was the satisfaction of personal wants. In the language of the classical theory, productive credit was superior to consumptive credit because it added rather than subtracted from the supply of wealth. Coincidentally, it paid for itself, whereas consumptive credit represented a drain on personal resources.

The person most responsible for altering the classical language of credit and debt was E.R.A. Seligman, the most erudite economist of his generation and one of the chief architects of the modern American system of public finance. In 1927 Seligman published a massive, two-volume study of installment selling. *The Economics of Instalment Selling* became the definitive vindication of credit for consumption, or, as Seligman termed it, "consumers' credit." Seligman's views on the new credit system gained a wide hearing, both because of the timeliness of the subject and because of the eminence of the author.

Born in 1861, eleven days after the fall of Fort Sumter and named for its defender, Edwin Robert Anderson Seligman was the son of Joseph Seligman, the prominent Jewish banker and rival of J. Pierpont Morgan. Tutored as a child by Horatio Alger Jr., Edwin grew up in Wall Street circles, but when he graduated from Columbia College at age eighteen, the prospect of entering the family banking business no longer interested him. After four years abroad in Berlin, Heidelberg, and Paris, Edwin returned home in 1882, entered Columbia's newly formed School of Political Economy, and received in 1885 the Ph.D. and LL.B. Seligman remained at Columbia for the next four decades, becoming the first McVickar Professor of Political Economy, chairing the Department of Economics for many years, and retiring in 1931.[56]

Early fame came to Seligman in the field of public finance. His groundbreaking theories on taxation were published in numerous editions and widely translated abroad. In the United States, Seligman's influential writings laid the groundwork for tax reform in New York and other states, for the national income tax legislation of 1913, and for the decision of government officials in the 1920s to base the nation's tax revenues on the personal income tax rather than, as in European countries, on a value-added sales tax.

But if public finance lay at the center of Seligman's interests, it did not define the circumference. His hundreds of publications ranged freely across history, economics, and public law. Among other contributions, Seligman helped found the American Economic Association (which he served as president from 1902 to 1904), edited the *Political Science Quarterly* for many years, and late in life served as editor in chief of the *Encyclopaedia of the Social Sciences*. An active participant in the politics of local, state, and national reform, Seligman epitomized the service ideal prevalent among university professors in the Progressive Era, always ready to answer the numerous calls for technical assistance from government officials, legislators, and taxpayer associations. In the obituary he wrote for his friend and colleague, Wesley Mitchell recalled that Seligman's productivity was "a marvel" to everyone who knew him, and that his opinions were greatly valued by many in the worlds of government, academia, philanthropy, business, and banking.[57]

Since Seligman was an economist, it seems natural he would have been interested in an economic subject like credit buying and selling. But before Seligman published his study of installment credit, economists of his generation showed slight interest in the subject of household credit. Immersed in the world of theory, and conditioned by both classical and Marxist economics to view production as superior to consumption, they stood aloof from the economic world of the consumer.[58]

For their failure to join the crusade against consumptive credit, economists were mocked and derided by critics of the new credit system. Seligman, a public-minded academic, took this criticism personally. After reading a particularly scornful article in a popular magazine proclaiming the "bankruptcy" of theoretical economics, Seligman felt impelled to investigate installment credit as a way of demonstrating his profession's "competence to deal with an important practical problem."[59]

But there was more to it than that. At some point in 1925, the board of directors of the General Motors Corporation became concerned about the mounting criticism of installment selling.

General Motors was a pioneer in the field of automobile install-ment credit, having established in 1919 the General Motors Accep-tance Corporation, the leading sales finance company in the credit business. Company officials worried that negative publicity about installment credit reflected poorly on General Motors, and might even dampen future automobile sales. They probably also worried that the critics might be correct in some of their views. The sugges-tion was made by Seward Prosser, chairman of the board of the Bankers Trust Company, that General Motors could benefit from having a reputable and independent expert look into the matter and give advice. If the researcher concluded that installment selling was ushering in a new era of economic growth and posed no real danger to either the economy or public morals, then General Motors could take credit for having pioneered such a progressive credit device. If, on the other hand, the researcher concluded that installment selling was getting out of hand and ought to be dis-couraged, then GMAC could stiffen its credit terms (thus reap-ing the profits of a sounder credit policy), while presenting itself to the public as a benevolent guardian of the nation's spiritual and economic health. Either way, General Motors would reap the benefits of what management consultants today call a "win-win" situation.[60]

John J. Raskob, chairman of General Motor's Finance Commit-tee, approached Seligman for the job. Both men were active in re-form circles. Each knew the reputation of the other. But the invita-tion from Raskob was somewhat unusual. Who, a few decades earlier, could have imagined John D. Rockefeller inviting a promi-nent Harvard professor to make a study of the trust movement in American industry? The cooperation between Raskob and Selig-man signaled a new willingness between university economists and corporate business to forge closer relationships.[61]

Obviously, the new type of venture posed problems for schol-arly objectivity. As a leading spokesperson for the right of univer-sity professors to speak their minds freely (Seligman authored the American Association of University Professors "General Declara-tion of Principles," a founding statement on academic freedom),

Seligman took this issue seriously.[62] He asked for and was granted two assurances: that he would have unlimited access to the complete records of GMAC and General Motors on the subject of automobile installment financing, and that he would be completely free to form his own conclusions, and publish them, if it turned out they contradicted the views of the General Motors board of directors.[63]

If a study commissioned by General Motors had its problems, Seligman also saw its possibilities. Hard data on credit buying were almost nonexistent at the time. The promise of access to the records of GMAC must have been tempting. Seligman was determined to show that the "science" of economics could make an authoritative contribution to the clamor over credit buying, and perhaps even resolve it.

Having accepted the project, Seligman assembled a team of researchers and began investigating whether the opposition to installment credit was justifiable. His team immediately ran into the same trouble that doomed the Census Bureau investigation of 1890: data on private debt and credit were extremely difficult to come by. Some of the needed records did not exist, because businesses and individuals did not keep them. Other records existed, but finding them would require a well-funded effort carried out over many years with the help of hundreds of investigators. Seligman realized that a truly accurate and comprehensive study would require the sponsorship of the national government. In the meantime, he and his team did the best they could with what they had.

Seligman settled on a research strategy based on five sets of factual inquiries.[64] In the first of these, "the consumers' study," researchers analyzed credit data provided by the clothing, furniture, jewelry, and hardware industries, looking for credit trends that varied according to region, size of community, size of store, and changes over time. A second investigation, "the merchandise study," attempted to document the history of installment selling in several key industries, particularly with regard to automobiles, furniture, pianos, books, and jewelry. A third line of research was

241

based on questionnaires completed by automobile dealers who used GMAC financing. The purpose of this "dealers study" was to find out what percentage of automobiles was sold on credit, as well as other facts about the business of selling cars. A fourth investigation, "the repossession study," examined the records of GMAC in order to make generalizations about the causes and prevention of consumer delinquency. The fifth study also made use of the records of GMAC. This "depression study" examined a business depression caused by a coal miners' strike in Pennsylvania's anthracite coal region in 1925. It was hoped that a case study of this event would forecast the fate of debtors and creditors when general business conditions turned sour. Completion of all five studies took the better part of a year. All five were major pioneering efforts in the statistical study of consumer credit.

Armed with the unprecedented information turned up by these studies, Seligman intended to lift the public discussion of credit selling to a higher level. In his view, the problem with the critics and propagandists alike was that they based their views on "the interests, the fears, the desires, or the prejudices of the individuals concerned."[65] He was correct. But Seligman had his own prejudices, well hidden behind his scholarly pose of objectivity. For example, he believed in progress. As a follower of Simon Patten, Seligman believed that human development depended not on making peace with limits but on multiplying human wants. He believed that increased production was the key to social progress. He believed it was good that modern society based itself on "the economy," an agent of change having no ultimate objective in mind beyond an infinite series of new commodities.[66] Assumptions like these did not guarantee Seligman would endorse installment credit, but they disposed him to favor it. Ultimately, these deeply shared assumptions would incline most people to favor it.

After almost a year of analyzing GMAC documents and gathering data on the larger field of credit selling, Seligman wrote up his results, which were published in 1927 as *The Economics of Instalment Selling*. Avoiding the ambivalence that marked earlier study documents on credit put out by the American Bar Association and American Federation of Labor, Seligman came out unequivocally in favor of the "business revolution" transforming household credit. Installment selling, Seligman wrote, had "come to stay." Minus a few "improper practices" already being eliminated, he concluded, consumption credit ought to be recognized as "constituting a significant and valuable contribution to the modern economy."[67]

To support his verdict, Seligman advanced four arguments. The first was historical. Critics implied that installment credit was a brand new innovation, but Seligman reminded people otherwise. The valuable information he amassed on the history of credit made him the first real historian of consumption credit. The story he told was a polemical refutation of those who believed that credit for consumers was a radical idea. Seligman argued instead that the extension of credit to the consumer was not a repudiation of the past, but an organic development squarely in line with the centuries-old development of credit in general. Credit, he observed, had evolved through successive systems of pawnbroking credit, agricultural credit, and commercial credit. Now, the "final form" of credit was at hand: consumption credit.[68]

There is scant evidence to support such a stage theory of credit. But Seligman succeeded in his larger purpose, which was to show that every new credit innovation advanced through predictable stages of public opinion. First it met with unqualified opposition, then after awhile came cold acceptance, and then came warm if belated recognition of the innovation's unquestioned value.[69] This was a rhetorical masterstroke. Without calling anyone names, Seligman tarred the critics of consumption credit as economic cranks, putting them in the same class of people as the zealots still writing tracts against interest, banks, and paper money.

After this lengthy historical prelude, Seligman advanced three more contentions to show why opposition to installment credit was unfounded. First, he argued that the opponents of installment selling rested their case on "a woeful poverty of economic analysis."[70] In other words, their theory of credit was shallow and fallacious. Second, in terms of the effect of credit buying on the individual, Seligman found that the critics exaggerated the pernicious effects and ignored the positive effects. Finally, he endeavored to show that the alarmists who feared installment selling jeopardized future business conditions were wrong. Rather, argued Seligman, installment selling provided a great stimulus to the nation's economic growth.

The Economics of Instalment Selling was a massive two-volume work of economic analysis, a treatise of numerous parts, books, and chapters. It amassed a wealth of statistical data, which included among other findings the first reliable estimate of the total volume of installment debt in the country. Pegging it at $4.5 billion for the end of 1926, Seligman showed that previous estimates were wildly exaggerated.[71]

But the heart of Seligman's book did not rest on statistical data. The largest burden undertaken by Seligman was a direct frontal assault on the standard nomenclature people used to evaluate installment credit. "We must avoid old shibboleths," wrote Seligman, "and refuse on the one hand to be led astray by the magic of the word credit, or on the other hand to lift our eyebrows or to shrug our shoulders because of the idea that in some way so-called consumption credit is unsound as compared to production credit."[72] In a way that poststructuralist critics might envy, Seligman skillfully deconstructed the categories of "luxury" and "necessity," "saving" and "thrift," "consumptive credit" and "productive credit." This was not all. Seligman even denied that consumption and production were the best categories of analysis for clear thinking about economic activity. With this bold stroke, he opened the door for new ways of talking about credit for consumers.

The work of deconstruction began with a simple problem: what to call the category of credit to which installment credit belonged? "Consumptive credit," argued Seligman, was a meaningless term. "Consumptive credit" was literally nonsensical, because most goods bought on installments were not actually destroyed or used up. Pursuing the point further, Seligman suggested that the correct term for describing the opposite of "productive credit" ought to be "nonproductive credit." But this was not satisfactory either, because "productive credit" was a meaningless term, too. All credit

244

was productive, contended Seligman, in the sense that all credit either stimulated or allowed borrowers to do things which otherwise they could not have done. The traditional categories of credit, then, needed to be rethought.[73]

In place of the traditional nomenclature, Seligman recommended a "simpler" set of terms. It was fairly obvious, he argued, that certain kinds of credit were advanced to producers for purposes of production, and that other kinds of credit were advanced to consumers, to increase their standard of consumption. Hence, Seligman proposed that "the better terms" for describing credit would be "producers' credit" and "consumers' credit."[74]

This was verbal sleight of hand, and Seligman knew it. It begged the question of how to tell the difference between a producer and consumer, between acts of production and acts of consumption. Therefore, Seligman's exercise in linguistic recoding forced him to make a more ambitious revision of classical economic theory.

In classical economics a rigid line was drawn between production and consumption. Production was defined as activity that created new commodities or income. Consumption was activity that depleted or destroyed the wealth gained by production. Social welfare was thought to be advanced when human energies were applied to increasing production. Thus, in a common application of the principle, workers were urged to put their spare income in savings banks where it could be lent out to industry to finance future production, rather than spending it on "luxury" purchases, which amounted to a robbery of the future for the sake of ephemeral present satisfactions. Eventually, as the consumer and industrial revolutions swept through Great Britain, France, and the United States, production in popular usage came to mean work done for wages or profits in a business organization. Consumption meant everything else. Improving on Adam Smith, Karl Marx and other nineteenth-century economists considered that consumption itself could be "productive" or "unproductive." Productive consumption described the use of goods that exerted a direct, positive effect on production, such as eating a square meal. "Unproductive consumption" referred to consumption that hindered or had no effect on production, such as eating cakes and truffles. Thus, while Adam Smith had written that the goal of all production was consumption, Victorian producerism maintained something of the opposite.

The assumption that production and consumption were distinguishable spheres of activity, and that it was better to produce than to consume, lay at the heart of Victorian moral thinking on economics and its proscription of consumptive debt. It was this kind of thinking that moved Thomas Nixon Carver to believe that "the active criminal" was "superior" to "the passive glutton," because the former had a productive mind while the latter had only consumptive passions. He gave thanks (in 1928) that the United States had more criminals than gluttons—the opinion of a man whose home had never been burglarized.[75]

But Seligman disagreed. Like Simon Patten before him, he wondered whether it continued to make sense to disparage consumption. The classical preference for production made sense, he argued, in the late eighteenth and early nineteenth centuries when the doctrines were formed. At that time, the gearing up of the industrial revolution urgently required that society amass capital in order to expand the industrial machinery of business enterprises. But now, Seligman contended, the old doctrine of thrift-for-production was actually injurious to society. With "the material base" of abundance secured, continued adherence to the production ethos only meant that an enormous surplus of material goods was being created. Industries would eventually have to cut back on hours and wages unless people could be convinced to stop saving and start spending, thus soaking up all the goods being produced in such mass quantities. With the threat of overproduction looming over the modern economy, it was high time, averred Seligman, "to question the truth of the widely accepted maxims of former days."[76]

Seligman had one particular maxim in mind. It was an assumption more than a maxim, so basic to the Victorian worldview that it rarely needed stating. This assumption was that production and consumption were distinguishable spheres of activity, as self-evidently different as day and night. On the basis of this assumption rested the principle that it was better to produce than to consume, as well as all the related beliefs of Victorian producerism.

Seligman undermined the Victorian fetish with production by denying the categories that inspired it. In literal terms, he pointed out, the categories of production and consumption made no sense at all because it is physically impossible either to create or to destroy anything. "Man can create nothing material," he reasoned. "He can only impart motion to particles of matter and so arrange them that in their new form they may gratify some desire." The same was true of consumption, as nothing can be truly "destroyed." The old categories were useful, argued Seligman, only in the limited sense that consumption refers to that part of the cycle of goods where wealth is enjoyed while production refers to that stage where wealth is assembled.[77]

Hence, for Seligman, production and consumption dissolved into a larger category, namely, utilization. In the broadest economic sense, Seligman believed that production and consumption could not be sharply distinguished or one valued over the other, because both involved a calculus of utilities versus costs, with the outcome of the equation frequently unpredictable. Acts normally considered to be "production" might result in a deficit of utilities, as in the case of a poorly run business. What producers really hoped to accomplish, argued Seligman, was not the literal creation of new matter, but a surplus of utilities over costs. If the creation of new utilities was in excess of the costs required to create them, then an act of production had taken place. Producers, then, could be carpenters, painters, and factory owners, or, just as likely, novelists, poets, and orchestra conductors. The producer's "real income," argued Seligman, was fundamentally a "psychic income," the production of utilities. Continuing in the same vein, Seligman went on to observe that many activities in the suspect category of "consumption" produce huge surpluses of social wealth, such as the furnishing of a comfortable home, the eating of a healthful diet, and the securing of "the finer wants that are developed by civilization." To speak of "consuming" a material good, his analysis went, is not to refer to the physical destruction of an object, but to the using up of "the evanescent utility" the article affords at a particular time. In this way the concept of utility gave to production and consumption an essential unity. The conclusion followed that the classical distinction between consumption and production was less sharp than normally conceived, because the results of both activities were not inherently good or bad. Production might be beneficial to society, or it might be destructive. The same with consumption.[78]

To distinguish good utilization from bad, Seligman proposed that, whether in production or consumption, the utilization of wealth resulted in one of four different outcomes. He suggested that an activity such as shoveling coal, whether it was done by a stoker working on a locomotive or by a man in his home basement, might increase the surplus of utilities over costs, balance utilities and costs, diminish the surplus, or bring about a deficit of utilities compared to costs. Seligman labeled these categories of utilization "creative," "neutral," "wasteful," and "destructive."[79]

Previously, economists had distinguished between productive and unproductive consumption, but Seligman's classification scheme, in addition to being more refined, departed from older theories in this crucial respect: his theory of utilization recognized the social benefits of *immaterial* satisfactions. By contrast, when other economists justified some consumption because it was productive, what they meant was that the act of consumption resulted in an addition of actual material goods or money. But Seligman urged that production could not be limited to such physical results. In his new theory, real productive surpluses could result in new goods, more income, or a surplus of "pleasurable sensations." Spending money on a vacation, then, was prima facie no more or no less justifiable than putting money in a savings account. "The real secret of life," Seligman counseled, was not to blindly pursue "production" while renouncing "consumption." Rather, it was to pursue "the productive utilization of wealth, as in the positive utilization of all our opportunities." This was the true road of moral progress.[80]

Seligman's excursion into economic theory was a long detour away from the subject at hand, which was the wisdom or folly of installment selling. But his new theory of utilization had important implications for thinking about installment credit. The new theory took the ground out from under the critics who attacked the installment plan because it represented "consumptive credit" as opposed to "productive credit," something destructive as opposed to something creative. In light of Seligman's doctrine of utilization, buying an automobile with credit was neither more nor less legitimate than using credit to purchase raw materials for a factory. In either case, the economic question to be asked was whether the loan financed a productive or neutral utilization of wealth, or whether it contributed to a wasteful or destructive utilization. Buying a car on the installment plan could be a wise choice. Buying raw materials for a factory could, in certain situations, be a destructive choice.

Seligman's theory of utilization erased the boundaries of the old, simple distinction between production and consumption. It replaced the old categories with new ones declaring the moral equivalence of consumption and production, consumer credit and producer credit. The fourfold scheme of utilization was confusing and forgettable, but the idea of a moral equivalence between consumption and production resonated well with many who never read *The Economics of Instalment Selling*.[81]

"A VINDICATION FOR INSTALLMENT PAYING"

The Economics of Instalment Selling was an important book not because it was read by many people but because it was read by a few people who were in a position to influence many others. Reviews were generally positive. W. R. Plummer, Seligman's only rival in knowledge of the subject, called it "exceedingly useful." It is "a vindication for installment paying," wrote a reviewer for *World's Work*, while in the *New York Times* Evans Clark breezily pronounced installment buying "absolved by a high priest of the academy."[82]

Not surprisingly, the credit industry welcomed the support of an "objective" outsider. Credit men in the pages of *Industrial Lenders News* immediately began the work of appropriating and translating Seligman's views for popular consumption. In one case an author lifted whole passages on utilization theory from Seligman without attribution.[83]

Seligman's ideas were spread by other popularizers, too. Among them was Julian Goldman, the East Coast department store magnate. His book on credit selling, *Prosperity and Consumer Credit* (1930), cited lengthy quotations from Seligman, while his defense of consumer credit went almost point by point through Seligman's argument. But probably no one was more pleased with Seligman's final product than the company officials at General Motors. In an autobiography written many years later, A. P. Sloan Jr. credited Seligman for melting the opposition of bankers, businessmen, and the general public to installment selling.[84]

Admitting that it is difficult to pin down the impact a text makes on readers, it is still hard not to agree with Sloan. A college debate handbook published in 1929 noted that the number of articles published on the subject of installment buying dropped precipitously after 1927.[85] For a while, at least, the critics of consumer credit were driven from the pages of middle-class magazines and journals of opinion. In money management advice books, writers moved away from outright condemnations of consumptive credit. After Seligman it became more common to list the advantages and disadvantages of the various kinds of consumer credit.[86]

Seligman did not begin the attack on Victorian producerism and the Victorian money management ethic, nor did he finish it. His defense of installment selling built on ideas that were already circulating, and, as a magnifying glass focuses light, he combined them together into a potent challenge to older ways of thinking. The result was that, after Seligman, the way people talked about debt and credit was never the same again.

In the first place, Seligman brought new terms into existence while pronouncing the last rites on others. The most obvious shift was from "consumptive" to "consumers'" or "consumer" credit. It would be hard to underestimate the meaning of this shift in terms. "Consumptive" credit smelled of disease. It prejudged a loan of money or goods as destructive and socially wasteful. "Consumer" credit made no such judgments. On the contrary, it explicitly recognized the consumer as a person worthy of trust. It quietly presumed that consumers were people worthy of respect.

In addition to coining the term consumer credit, Seligman also introduced the important concept of "pay as you use." Critics of "consumptive" borrowing frequently complained that the principle of "buy now, pay later" discouraged the building up of character by elevating the desire for immediate gratification over the traits of self-control and perseverance. This charge was usually sidestepped in credit marketing, which countered with installment buying's other advantages. But Seligman met the charge head on. "Buy now, pay later," he argued, was a misrepresentation of the true facts about installment buying. It was only under the old system of book credit, he explained, that consumers really postponed the act of repayment until *after* they enjoyed the use of a good. But with the installment plan, he pointed out, where a reasonable down payment was followed by periodic payments, consumers in actual practice pay *in advance* for the satisfactions they enjoy from the use of commodity. Since all durable commodities possess a bundle of utilizations which consumers enjoy, not all at once, but a little bit at a time, "the ordinary purchaser really pays in each periodic installment for something which he will utilize in the future."[87] The concept of "pay as you use" seemed obvious once it had been said. Seligman was the first to say it.

Following from the idea of "pay as you use," Seligman advanced a redefinition of the concept of "savings" that in time became accepted wisdom among most economists. Critics of consumer credit complained that installment credit encouraged people to spend more and save less. Consumptive credit, they said, turned individuals into spendthrifts, and injured society by reducing the supply of capital available for investment. Propagandists for credit responded by pointing to the rising deposits in savings banks during the 1920s. Rejecting this defense as irrelevant, Seligman urged instead a reconsideration of what it meant to "save."

In classical theory and in the Victorian money management ethic, the discipline of saving referred to one thing: putting money in the bank. Seligman suggested there was a broader way to think about it. If it was true that consumers utilized a durable good not all at once but over an extended period of time, then it followed that income used to purchase at one time a good whose utilities would not be used up until a future date really amounted to a form of "saved" income. Viewed this way, buying an automobile was an act of "saving" just as much as putting the purchase money into a savings account. All that had to be considered was whether the automobile represented a wise investment for the consumer.[88]

To this it could be objected of course that consumer borrowers hardly "save" money relative to cash buyers who save up for their purchases, if only because the former *pay* interest for the credit they use while the latter *earn* interest from their savings account. But with regard to savings, Seligman considered the psychological implications of consumer credit to be very important. Following the lead of credit propagandists, he argued that installment credit increased not only consumers' capacity to save but also their desire to save. This had always been recognized as true for home ownership. Give a man a home mortgage, it was held, and he will work twice as hard. Now Seligman applied the same reasoning to credit for furniture, automobiles, and other durable goods. If having a car or a radio contributed "satisfactions of a purely psychical nature," Seligman asked, "will not the possession of the durable commodity actually increase the ability of the individual to make renewed and augmented exertions?"[89] The family with car payments to make would be forced to work hard to make the payments and, through the new leisure opportunities provided by the car, enabled to work hard. Presumably, they would also be less likely to fritter away paychecks on frivolous, nondurable expenditures. The result would be increased savings, whether defined as money in the bank or money invested in durable goods.

Having redefined the concept of savings, Seligman also did what he could to inter the remains of the concept of "luxury." Like a mutant from a horror movie, this hoary old concept refused to die no matter how many bullets of logic were fired into it. The *moderate* position on installment buying in the mid-1920s held that installment credit was "all right for necessities, but not for luxuries."[90] This way of thinking was long outmoded, argued Seligman, who saw himself as finishing the work of those who long ago had planted dynamite in the cracks of the classical and medieval view that luxuries were inherently vicious. Hume and Voltaire, for example, had shown it was foolish to think that it was always wrong to indulge in costly, sensual consumption. Luxury, they pointed out, was a relative term, in the sense that every modern person wore socks and thought nothing of it. More recently Simon Patten and other modern economists held up the relativity of luxury as a positive good, in the sense that the desire for costly things set in motion the wheels of ingenuity, capital, and production, resulting in higher wages, a higher standard of life, and the transformation of yesterday's luxuries into necessities. The progressive argument, in short, said that the desire for luxuries brought about a higher stage of civilization.

Yet in the 1920s these ideas had not percolated very far beyond a thin stratum of intellectuals. Debate over installment credit almost always ended up with attempts to establish the dividing line between luxuries and necessities; the uncertain frontier between them was represented by the automobile. Seligman, with his theory of utilization, plowed under the whole luxury-necessity dichotomy one more time. Viewed his way, to call something a "luxury" was a statement of fact, not of value. Whether it was right or wrong to purchase a costly or sensual commodity depended on whether the purchase maintained or increased the individual's surplus of utilities over costs, as opposed to diminishing or destroying the surplus. In the final analysis, Seligman added, a truly free society would let the individual decide for himself.[91]

By the time Seligman drove his nail into the coffin of the ancient dichotomy of luxury-necessity, most economists were ready to drop the concept of "luxury" from economic analysis. A reviewer for the *Harvard Business Review* praised Seligman's chapter on the hollowness of the luxury-necessity dichotomy as "one of the best in the book."[92] Seligman's brief for a "demoralized" analysis of consumption was followed by Harvard's N. R. Danielian, whose 1929 paper on the theory of consumer credit began with the curt statement, "we are interested in this discussion in purely economic and not ethical facts."[93] Outside academia the moral connotations of luxury would fade away in time, though never disappear completely.

WISE BORROWING AND FOOLISH BORROWING

Seligman's formal, academic approach to consumer credit was quickly translated into more popular idioms by the credit industry. In the retail world, no one worked harder to popularize Seligman's ideas than Julian Goldman.

Goldman had been in the dry goods business since opening his first store in 1916. From the beginning, he wanted to sell quality goods on credit. At the time, however, stores catering to middle-class buyers typically sold on a cash basis. Store owners might make convenience charge accounts available to qualified customers, but there was little interest in using credit to sell goods. High-pressure credit selling was a feature of the so-called borax stores, which had been serving the low-income market since the 1890s. But Goldman did not want to be in the borax business. Determined to grow his business by tapping the large middle-class market, he resolved to do all he could to make credit buying a respectable practice.

The difficulty was that the advertising messages of borax-type credit stores were crassly materialistic, their newspaper ads emblazoned with promises of "EASY CREDIT" and "BUY NOW—PAY LATER!" This was "bait," thought Goldman, "not business," and he chafed at the bad name it gave his business. Dissatisfied with this kind of appeal, Goldman found an alternative in 1928 when he read Seligman's *The Economics of Instalment Selling*.

Seligman had argued there was "an essential similarity between production and consumption." Seizing on the value of this equation, Goldman launched a new advertising campaign in 1928 that aimed to bring Seligman's ideas to the masses. One of the ads in the campaign featured drawings of two people: a businessman at his desk, looking out his office window upon a bustling factory he presumably owned or helped to manage; and a stylish

Figure 18. Advertisement prepared for the Julian Goldman Stores, Inc. Goldman capitalized on the message of E.R.A. Seligman's pioneering study of consumer credit, using ads such as this to encourage consumers to think of consumption as a form of production, and therefore deserving equal access to credit.

young woman, wrapped in a beautiful floor-length fur coat. The text read:

> "A Factory or a Fur Coat {. . . both of them may be bought on credit}."
>
> A big manufacturer wants to put up a new building. He borrows the money, giving the lenders his notes, which fall due every three months or six months. He pays for his building on time, with installments.
>
> A young girl buys a fur coat at our store. She pays one-third of its cost at once, and the balance at her convenience within three months.
>
> What is the difference in these transactions?
>
> Nothing—except size!

This advertisement, appearing in newspapers all over the East, effectively translated Seligman's convoluted arguments into language and images that everyone could understand. There was no difference, it proclaimed, between buying a fur coat and investing in a physical plant, no moral distinction to be drawn between consumption and production. Indeed, the ad referred to the woman in a fur coat as a "good business woman"—because she financed her "business" in "the only modern, practical way." Moreover, the ad made the buyer of a fur coat appear to be one of the busiest busy beavers in a production-oriented society, because buying a "[fur coat] keeps people at work, pays another salary, puts more money in circulation." The fur coat and the installment plan were defined as integral parts of a prosperous, happy, hard-working, and better-looking business civilization. It was a very different image of "consumptive" debt than that presented by the Zindler's ads in Houston only two years before.

The consumer as a businessman or businesswoman was a prevalent theme in all the advertisements from Goldman's 1928 campaign. In one ad, readers were invited to think of their households as "You Not Inc., The Biggest Business in the World," and therefore deserving the highest of credit ratings. In another ad, Goldman presented a picture of his ideal credit customers, "Jim Jones" and "Mrs. Jim." The couple were described as hard-working, middle-class Americans, interested in style, but demanding good value—in other words, citizens who represented the best qualities of Americans as defined by traditional producerism. They were forward-looking (at age twenty-seven, Jim was already interested in buying life insurance), trustworthy (they had already repaid obligations on a car and house furniture), thrifty (they were buying a bond on the installment plan), and economical (Mrs. Jim always looked for "rock-bottom prices" on the "finest workmanship"). The advertisement portrayed consumption in the same terms as Seligman described it—when done well, said the ad, consumption was really a form of productive work.

Like Goldman, small-loan lenders found much to like in Seligman's work. In the trade journals of the personal finance industry, Seligman was quoted, imitated, and plagiarized extensively in the years following publication of *The Economics of Instalment Selling*. Here is advice from one credit man to his colleagues about what to say in their advertising now that the old theory of credit had been "exploded": "Just as it is sound for a government to obtain credit to defend itself in war, or a railroad to borrow money to build its right-of-way, so it is sound for a human being to use credit to obtain articles that increase his productivity, his well-being, and his happiness." The new principle, he advised, was not to distinguish productive credit from consumptive credit, but "wise borrowing and foolish borrowing." These would become the core terms of the new way of thinking and talking about debt and credit.[94]

WE DO LEND FOR PRODUCTION

The ultimate importance of Seligman's economic theory went far beyond his changing the terms employed in the language of credit and consumption. More sweepingly, Seligman's justifications for consumer credit were part of a larger attempt to legitimize consumption and the consumer in general. Seligman's views are worth examining because the mental path he went down to vindicate consumption points in fruitful directions for understanding how consumer culture became a popular expression of American culture.

The underlying objection to consumer credit was really an objection to consumption as a valued activity, particularly for men, and to the consumer as an appropriate identity for the American citizen. Consumption was regarded as women's sphere of activity, and so it followed that the consumer was viewed as weak-willed, as sensuous, as someone who lived for the pleasure of the moment, who found it hard to make sacrifices and to think ahead, who used things up, instead of making tangible contributions to society's wealth. The consumer, in short, lacked what Victorians valued above all else: "character."

When J. Pierpont Morgan told the 1912 Pujo Committee investigating the financial power of Wall Street that "the first thing" in getting credit was not money or property or connections but "character," he gave businessmen and credit marketers a phrase they never tired of repeating, that "credit was a matter of character." Thus, if consumers were going to get credit, they would have to acquire some measure of character, some allotment of social worth to use as collateral. But how could consumers get credit in the moral sense of the word? How could social attitudes regarding the value of consumption be adjusted to harmonize with the fact of the consumers' rising significance? Seligman found a way. He removed the stigma of consumption by showing it was possible in many ways for the consumer to be a producer, for consumption to be a form of production.

There was, said Seligman, "an essential similarity between production and consumption."[95] Both activities utilized wealth in the interest of increasing human satisfaction. Consumption did not have to mean a destructive frittering away of society's wealth. If done well, consumption and consumership could be a "productive utilization" of wealth, a form of work, of labor, of valuable production. This was easy to see in cases where consumers used durable goods to make something new or to increase their money income—as with women who bought sewing machines on installments and made their family's clothes, or the man who took up woodworking as a hobby. But Seligman's notion of productive utilization went farther. It stretched the aura of production to cover what consumers did when they spent their money for the creation of "immaterial wealth." If buying a consumer good produced a measure of relief from the pressure of work, if it contributed to health and well-being by providing positive mental diversion, if it broadened the mind or brought the lonely into contact with friends, then spending and using and enjoying things represented a surplus of utilities over costs; in short, it was a productive investment of wealth.[96] This was, to borrow a phrase from the French theorist Michel De Certeau, "production without capitalization."[97] But it was production nonetheless. It was the production of a satisfying life.

"The ultimate aim of all economic activity," Seligman argued, was the "'production' of satisfactions."[98] Thus if consumption was the production of satisfactions, consumers might be producers after all.

The value of this way of thinking was immediately recognized by credit marketers. Credit for the "production" of satisfactions—here there was a way to baptize the new in the language of the old, as they had already done by labeling the installment plan a "thrift plan" or "budget account." Seligman's idea was clearly expressed—more clearly than Seligman himself expressed it—in an article appearing in *Industrial Lenders News* one year after publication of *The Economics of Instalment Selling*. The article opposed the contention that lending to consumers was a bad economic policy. The author, Franklin W. Ryan, argued that most people misunderstood the real nature of production. Production did not stop, he argued, when goods reached the shelves of dealers. Production continued when the buyer made a purchase. By helping individuals make their purchases, Ryan maintained that consumer lenders made an important contribution to the process of production:

> We lend money to the worker to buy bread and meat and other groceries and in so doing we help produce or increase human energy which after all is nearly all there is to production. We lend to help

him buy clothes to help him put his human energy to work. We lend
to buy him coal because this helps increase his human energy. We
lend to buy school books because with the right knowledge, the ef-
fectiveness of human energy is increased. If what he buys increases
his happiness, his better frame of mind makes his energy more effective and he becomes a more valuable citizen.

The most wasteful kind of lending of all, argued Ryan, was "productive" credit lent out for purposes of stock speculation. The old
distinctions between production and consumption and productive
credit and consumptive credit were "claptrap." The truth, Ryan
insisted, was that "we *do* lend for production and the part of the
productive process that we finance is the most important part
of it."[99]

Through the 1920s the credit industry continued to be painfully
aware of the lingering shame and embarrassment that tainted its
"product" and its business.[100] Despite the blessing of E.R.A. Seligman, public attitudes changed slowly.

In 1937, ten years after *The Economics of Instalment Selling*
was published, the keynote speaker at the annual convention of the
American Association of Personal Finance Companies was M. R.
Neifeld. Neifeld was a logical choice. An economist and loan in-
dustry insider, he was also the author of *The Personal Finance
Business*, the most comprehensive study ever made of the econom-
ics of small-loan lending. The program committee knew that when
Neifeld spoke, lenders would listen.

At the convention, Neifeld began his speech by recognizing that
"the people have discovered debt as a mode of life." This was a
great accomplishment, comparable, Neifeld thought, with the discovery of a new mode of production in the industrial revolution.
But the present was no time, he cautioned, for lenders to coast
along on the strength of yesterday's accomplishments. Neifeld
warned his audience that a critical problem loomed over the credit
industry. It was a problem of cultural lag: public attitudes about
debt still lagged behind the explosive growth of the consumer
credit industry. "Many of us," Neifeld observed, "have not quite
outgrown father's feeling about debt. We use consumer credit of

the twentieth century for twentieth century purposes, but think of it by the standards of the horse and buggy age."[101]

Neifeld was probably right. People had discovered debt "as a mode of life," but not everyone had yet discovered how to feel good about it. Perhaps not everyone ever would. But a moral base for consumer credit had been worked out, a base sufficient enough for most people to justify their use of consumer credit. As for an economic base, this was being tested by the Great Depression, even as Neifeld spoke.

Consumer Credit
in the Great Depression

THE GREAT DEPRESSION put consumer credit to a decisive test. The Depression tested the entire American economic system, putting corporate capitalism on trial until its capacities were proved during the prosperous years of wartime production. But unlike the overall economy, consumer credit did not need a war to save it. The 1930s were prosperous years for consumer credit agencies. They prospered not by lending to the unemployed and destitute, but by expanding services to people who were fortunate enough to hold on to their jobs. Thus, during the bleak years of the Great Depression the logic and legitimacy of consumer credit was perfected, not destroyed; the popularity of consumer borrowing was enhanced, not diminished; and consumer credit acquired the institutional makeup that, after the Depression and another world war, would make so many American dreams come true.

1929: Now We Test Installment Selling

In 1926, the featured speaker at the annual convention of the Wholesale and Retail Credit Men's Association analyzed the state of the installment credit business with a joke just then making the rounds. The speaker hoped that everyone was as optimistic about the installment selling business as the man "who jumped off the Woolworth Building in New York." As the jumper passed the twentieth floor, a man looked out a window and shouted, "How are you?" Came the reply: "All right, so far."[1]

All right, so far—not a bad characterization of the state of the consumer credit industry in the late 1920s. During the boom years all branches of consumer credit had expanded. A growing demand for loans swelled the business of the smaller branches in the credit industry—credit unions, industrial banks, "Morris Plan" banks (early pioneers in consumer lending that lent on security of two endorsers)—and the oldest branches as well: pawnbrokers, loan sharks, and remedial agencies. But the agencies that prospered above all others were the agencies that led the way in the credit revolution. Personal finance companies expanded as more and more states sanctioned the small-loan business through regulations based on the Uniform Small Loan Law. Installment sellers also made out well in the late 1920s. By 1929 they basked in the glow of endorsement after endorsement, from economists and presidents and even, at last, from Henry Ford himself. Taken together, the total volume of consumer credit continued to swell, past $7 billion in October of 1929. In that year, consumer credit seemed all right. So far.

Then came the deluge. When the stock market collapsed in late October 1929, it brought to an end the longest binge of speculative investment in the nation's history. For observers no less than investors, the crash was a momentous event. In the opinion markets of the day it set off something like the Oklahoma Land Rush, everyone rushing to stake out a theory that made sense of it all.

In the weeks following the crash, blame for the disaster was attributed to hundreds of causes. The list ranged from the immutable laws of God to inadequate ticker-tape technology. It did not go unnoticed that much of the spree had been financed "on margin," a broker's euphemism for the installment plan. Buying on margin meant that investors borrowed money from their brokers in order to buy new stocks, expecting to repay the loans with the profits made as stocks climbed in value.[2] A good idea, investors thought, assuming the market would head upward for eternity. But when it reversed course dramatically on "Black Thursday" and "Black Tuesday," the investors and brokers who relied heavily on margin trading found themselves wiped out.

In addition to margin trading, two other factors were favorite targets for blame: installment selling and the American people's love of luxury. These were said to have created the necessary climate of profligacy for stock market speculation. Early in

November, Leroy D. Peavey, president of the Babson Statistical Organization, an organization whose stock in public opinion rose considerably after Roger Babson accurately predicted both the timing and the extent of the stock market debacle, told a national radio audience that the causes of the stock market crash boiled down to a combination of two factors: irresponsible investment trusts, which built up the market on a flimsy base of highly inflated stocks, and greedy investors, who felt free to operate on the principle of "buy now, pay later." Peavey claimed that this latter "class of gamblers" included "millionaires and elevator boys," the same people "who [had] been buying on instalments automobiles, radios, fur coats, vacuum cleaners, mechanical refrigerators, and many other things, essential or otherwise."[3] Peavey's allegations against installment selling, and others like it, inspired legislators to troop to the podiums in their state houses and denounce the installment selling of stocks. In Congress legislation was introduced to outlaw the buying of stocks on the "easy payment plan." Some did not think this went far enough. A letter writer to the *New York Times* demanded, "Why not include property, automobiles, radio, and washing machines, by heck?"[4]

This kind of sentiment sent jitters down the spine of the credit industry. For a long time both friends and enemies of the industry had predicted that the real test of consumer credit would come when the business cycle turned downward.[5] Those hostile to consumer credit declared that a recession would show up weaknesses in the consumer credit structure. Critics described scenarios in which a business recession sent workers rushing to the credit retailer and small-loan agency, hoping to borrow money to maintain their accustomed level of spending during periods of unemployment. Loan companies, it was predicted, would act shortsightedly, expanding their business through risky loans to the jobless. For workers, new obligations would be piled on top of old obligations, new loans would be taken out to pay off other loans, leading them to overdose on debt and collapse into bankruptcy, pulling the entire consumer credit structure down with them. Defenders of consumer credit doubted this scenario could happen, but no one knew for sure. Only a business slowdown would show who was right.

By January 1930, business was definitely entering a "dull" period. Following the lead of other business and government leaders, spokesmen for the credit industry put up a brave front. Milan Ayres of the National Association of Finance Companies brushed off concerns about the future of installment selling, claiming to harbor "regret" that the business slowdown was "so slight" it hardly amounted to a real challenge at all. But others outside the industry were more honest. "Now We Test Instalment Selling," proclaimed the 4 December 1929 issue of *Business Week*.[6]

PASSING THE TEST

The depression which followed the 1929 crash pushed individuals, families, and the economy as a whole to the breaking point. Unemployment rose from 3.2 percent of the work force in 1929 to a high of 25 percent in 1933. By that time, perhaps another quarter of the labor force was only partially employed, while in some cities and regions the unemployment rate reached as high as 90 percent. Everywhere, but especially in heavy industry and among unorganized workers, wages dropped.[7] The crisis presented a stiff challenge to the new system of consumer credit.

But to the surprise of many, consumer debt did not soar with the unemployment rate. Nor did the business crisis cause a general debtor's crisis, though in individual cases hardships were severe. Instead, to the satisfaction of most analysts, it was demonstrated that consumer debt followed the business cycle, in the manner of retail sales. In bad times, people borrowed less, not more.

Thus, when the economy stalled in late 1929 and began to nosedive in 1930, consumer debt followed. The total volume of consumer debt fell from $7.6 billion in 1929 to a Depression era low of $3.9 billion in 1933. Debt as a percentage of income also fell, from 9.34 percent to 8.71 percent, and lower the following year.[8]

But this general deflation of consumer credit was not uniform throughout the credit industry. Aggregate statistics hide an important difference between the two broad types of consumer credit: retail installment credit, which people use to increase their standard of living; and cash credit, a countermeasure for people facing economic emergencies.

In the beginning, the only consumer debt to decline was installment credit and retail charge account credit. In the three years following the crash, outstanding debt for automobile loans fell 75 percent below the 1929 total, following a substantial decrease in automobile sales in general. The drop in debt for other durable goods and for retail open-account credit was not so extreme, but still substantial.[9]

What happened was that the prospect of reduced wages or unemployment made buyers extremely conservative. Except among the wealthy, nonessential consumption was drastically curtailed. In their follow-up study of Middletown, made ten years after their original 1925 study, Robert and Helen Lynd reported that a negative buying psychology prevailed among the town's workers. From 1929 to 1933, jewelry sales in Middletown dropped 85 percent; building materials, 82 percent; motor vehicles, 78 percent; candy and confectionery sales, 70 percent; furniture, appliances, and radios, 69 percent; men's and boys' clothing, 67 percent; and restaurants, 63 percent.[10] As belts were tightened, debts incurred during more optimistic days were paid off. For most people this did not take too long. On 1 January 1930, the average automobile note had only 4.65 months left to run.[11] Thus, from 1930 through 1932, more people paid off their loans than made new installment purchases. The result was a large deflation of consumer installment credit.

Surprisingly, very few installment debtors found it impossible to meet their obligations. Delinquent accounts became more common after 1929, and more people defaulted entirely, but the rates for delinquency and default remained very low, especially when compared with those for commercial loans. As of June 1930, delinquent accounts (past due over thirty days) for the nation's four largest automobile finance companies amounted to only 0.5 percent of the total value of loans. This was a considerable increase from a year earlier, but still remarkably low.[12] And delinquency only rarely led to outright default and repossession. In the late 1920s, the rate of default on automobile loans had been stabilized at slightly less than three in one hundred automobiles sold on installments. In 1932, the worst year of the Depression for defaults, only five out of one hundred automobiles bought on installments ended up being repossessed.[13] Though undoubtedly a misfortune for those affected, this increase was neither sharp nor dangerous for the credit system in general.

In fact, losing a car or some other durable good to repossession was something installment buyers strained hard to avoid. This was partly due to the great value people set on their automobiles—"People give up everything in the world but their car" was a refrain the Lynds heard again and again in 1935.[14] But it also had to do with the nature of the installment plan. Under the law, installment sellers owned a prior lien on installment goods. This meant that if the buyer defaulted on payments and the merchandise was repossessed, buyers lost the good *and* the money they had paid in. Thus, default usually meant the loss of a substantial investment of money.

For this reason, before giving up and admitting defeat, installment buyers who found themselves unemployed or with reduced income made use of every strategy available to make payments on their car or radio or refrigerator. In desperate circumstances, installment debtors scraped up money by scrimping on food, clothing, and other expenditures, by borrowing from friends and relatives or against their life insurance, and by letting other debts accrue—to the doctor, the dentist, the grocer, and the landlord.[15] Early in 1932, the Emergency Relief Bureau of New York City canvassed 6,304 families in "urgent" need of help but too proud to apply for organized relief. Most were in debt; the average debt per family was $224. The investigators found that 81 percent of the families lacked food, 88 percent were behind on rent, 63 percent were behind on life insurance premiums, 50 percent had borrowed the full value of their life insurance, 74 percent had borrowed from relatives or friends, and 23 percent sold or pawned furniture to buy food. For an unknown but certainly large number of Americans, the scramble to keep ahead of the bill collector was the main business of life in the 1930s. It left a psychological scar on an entire generation.

Very often, urban workers who had fallen behind on installment payments visited a small-loan lender, perhaps for the first time. Thus, in the early years of the Depression, consumer cash lending displayed a different pattern than consumer installment credit. Whereas the latter went down, the former went up.

In 1930, the Beneficial Corporation and the Household Finance Corporation, the nation's two largest personal finance companies, increased their lending over the past year by 12.8 and 18.8 percent, respectively. Household opened twelve new offices that year; Beneficial opened sixty-eight.[16] Receivables—that is, debts due—ballooned in the early years of the Depression, almost doubling in two years, from $132 million in 1929, to $203 million in 1930, to $226 million in 1931. But 1931 was the high point for cash lending, after which it too began to decline. Using 1929 to signify an index of 100, M. R. Neifeld calculated that the outstanding loan volumes of regulated small lenders for 1930–1934 were 104.8, 111.8, 99.6, and 92.0, respectively.[17] Pawnbrokers and loan sharks did more business, too. But all cash lenders saw their loan balances contract after February 1931. That month, the federal government promised veterans of the Great War they could borrow up to 50 percent of the value of their upcoming bonus certificates, otherwise not due to be paid until 1945. Walter Waters, a leader in the Bonus March, remembered that most of his men applied for the loan.[18]

Those who obtained money from a cash lender could consider themselves "lucky," because more people wanted loans than received them. In 1931, one Household Finance office processed applications from 540,000 people who came to ask for a loan; only 302,871 went home with money in a loan envelope.[19] Looking at the accounts of one of the larger lending companies, M. R. Neifeld found that from 1928 to 1931 the percentage of successful loan applications declined, from 74 percent of all applications to 53 percent.[20] Most unsuccessful borrowers were turned down because they lacked visible income. Denied a loan at the personal finance company, the unemployed turned for help to the original consumer lenders: pawnbrokers, illegal lenders, and friends and relatives.

There was another reason personal finance companies saw more would-be borrowers in their offices. Continuing a trend that began in the 1920s, successful borrowers increasingly used cash loans to pay off installment contracts. Thus, the low rate of default on installment loans in the Depression is not evidence that installment payments were "easy." In many cases, individuals who ran into trouble with installment buying got out of it the hard way: by shifting their debt load from one creditor to another. Many in arrears went to cash lenders for help.

This trend is clear from loan company records. The "cause" of a borrower's distress is difficult to ascertain, and personal finance companies used different reporting methods for determining it. Thus, in 1931, reports of how many people borrowed cash from a personal finance company to pay for other debts varied from a low of 14.2 percent of borrowers in the case of one company, all the way up to 85 percent for another.[21] The low figure belonged to the Beneficial Loan Company, which reported an increase in this type of borrowing from 9.6 percent of their loans in 1929 to 14.2 percent in 1931.[22] For the period 1934–1937, the National Bureau of Economic Research estimated that between 25 and 75 percent of personal finance company loans were used to refinance miscellaneous existing debts.[23] Whatever the precise number, it is hard to avoid the conclusion that many consumer debtors borrowed from Peter to pay Paul, shifting their debt load to save their investment.

This practice was both expensive and nerve-wracking. In Studs Terkel's oral history of the Great Depression, Anna Ramsey described how her father, "a frugal man," had to "scrounge and scrape" to keep up the mortgage payments on a building he bought just before the crash. Ramsey's father borrowed money from a "well-known loan company" very frequently. "Oh, the tension in the house," she recalled, "when Pa used to scramble around trying to get enough money to pay that installment loan. That was the one degrading thing I remember."[24] Though overall the consumer debt volume fell with the onset of hard times, experiences like Anna Ramsey's left many people with an aversion to being in debt that would stay with them the rest of their lives.

Ramsey's father fell behind on payments to the loan company, but he was not forced to default. Nor were the overwhelming majority of people who borrowed from personal finance companies and then fell behind on payments. Delinquencies and losses were higher with cash lenders than with installment sellers. But they were never so high as to threaten the lending business or frighten away investors.

A study of finance companies in seven states by M. R. Neifeld revealed that in 1930 about one in seven accounts was in arrears at any one time.[25] This figure is close to that reported by the Household Finance Corporation. Loan delinquencies at Household Finance rose from 9.22 percent of the total value of their loans in 1929, to 10.48 percent in 1930, to 13.55 percent in 1931, to 19.43 percent in 1932, to a Depression era high of 21.08 percent in 1933.[26] While some of this delinquency represented "technical delinquency" (i.e., people who missed their payment deadline by only a few days), it still shows that those who borrowed cash money from personal finance companies were finding it harder to repay on time than those repaying installment loans on automobiles.

But while many debtors slipped behind in payments, very few defaulted and had their merchandise repossessed. Household reported that only 1.02 percent of its loans in 1930 were charged off as bad debts, while the Beneficial Loan Corporation repossessed only 0.025 percent of its chattel mortgages.[27] Leniency was the policy of small-loan lenders. They threatened repossession but rarely followed through. Repossession simply was not profitable, because the value of repossessed goods rarely amounted to the full purchase price. From the loan agency's point of view, more money could be made if the terms of repayment were extended. In addition, regulated firms were eager to build up a reputation for being fair, public-spirited companies.

In spite of widespread misery in the early and bleakest years of the Great Depression, the specter of a general debtor's crisis never materialized. Looking back at the early 1930s, the Census Bureau in 1940 reported that "consumers did not repudiate debts en masse . . . but merely tightened their belts until they could pay what they owed and then buy more."[28] This made consumer credit a much safer investment than cash in commercial banks. Lenders and installment sellers in the early 1930s complained that business was down, but they looked to their long-term interest. They did not try to expand on the basis of risky loans to the unemployed. Thus, consumer credit agencies suffered far fewer losses than expected, causing much less stress to the credit industry than critics had feared. Only two small finance companies failed in the first year of the Depression—a fact that caught the eye of astute commercial bankers, who were losing money hand over fist on other business investments.[29]

Consumer Constipation

After the 1929 crash, the quick deflation of consumer debt put to rest some fears about the viability of a consumer credit economy but stoked others. It became progressively clearer that a business recession was not going to harm the credit structure itself. But what about the effect of consumer credit on the overall economy? Were consumer debts a malignant cancer on the body economic? Having made the boom bigger, was consumer debt now making the depression deeper?

In 1930 and 1931, as the economy refused to respond in the way that President Hoover and others insisted it should, many in the business world blamed the delay of economic recovery on what an advertising trade journal called "consumer constipation."[30] The public had suddenly stopped buying. Why? Some blamed the public's stinginess on fear, but others claimed it was not a matter of attitude or choice. Those arguing the latter view contended that "frozen" buying power was a consequence of the "overextension" of installment credit in the late 1920s. In other words, the chickens of consumer credit had finally come home to roost. According to the theory of "frozen credit," people were not buying automobiles in 1931 because in 1931 people were straining to scrape together enough income to pay off the debts of 1929. Installment credit had saturated the market for automobiles, radios, and other durable goods, and now people were waking up with a bad financial hangover. This raised a troubling question. As one commentator put it, "Has business been obliged to rest on its oars until people who mortgaged their earnings a year or more in advance should have time to pay off their installments and start over again?"[31]

The frozen credit theory owed much to the "underconsumption" school of economic thought. In the late 1920s, underconsumptionists such as William Trufant Foster and Waddill Catchings argued that a business recession was inevitable and that the only thing delaying its onset was the phenomenal rise of installment selling. Disagreeing with E.R.A. Seligman, the underconsumptionists argued it was a mistake to think that consumer credit enlarged consumer buying power. The only thing that could really enlarge purchasing power, according to Foster and Catchings, was higher wages. In their view, consumer credit caused merely a temporary spurt of production, an economic boomlet which would last for awhile and then be followed by a period of retrenchment as consumers were forced to begin using income to pay off accumulated bills. The underconsumptionists were fuzzy about when precisely the "saturation point" for installment buying would be reached. But they had no doubts that a time of reckoning would come. When a recession commenced after the 1929 crash, of all economists the underconsumptionists were the least surprised. For a while, the onset of a recession added credence to their theories.[32]

Taking their cue from the underconsumptionists, critics of consumer credit in the early years of the Depression argued that "frozen purchasing power" was a barrier to recovery. The *New Republic* had carried the banner of underconsumptionism in the 1920s, and now it promoted the theory of frozen credit. In June 1931, it published an article by Isador Lubin, an economist at the Brookings Institution, who expressed surprise at "how little attention" had been given to consumer credit's role in the Depression. According to Lubin's estimates, the average person in 1930 owed 30 percent of earnings for consumer debt. "Thus," concluded Lubin, "it is not improbable that a considerable portion of the wages which would otherwise have gone toward the purchase of new shoes, and clothes for the family, toward new radios or automobiles—will go instead toward canceling bank loans now out-standing against instalment paper." What this meant, feared Lubin, was that the present sluggishness would not follow the pat-tern of past depressions, when consumer credit was not a factor. This time, massive indebtedness was throwing a wet blanket on economic revival. Recovery, he predicted, would be very gradual, if it happened at all. Lubin speculated that worsening unemploy-ment would leave people without sufficient income to afford the down payments for a new round of installment selling. As a conse-quence, the economy would remain stuck for a long time.[33]

Of course, it did remain stuck for a long time. Despite the New Deal, the economy remained moribund for the rest of the decade, until it was revived after 1941 by wartime production and massive government spending. But was consumer credit responsible? N. R. Danielian of Harvard University set the bold tone for all succeed-ing analyses when he wrote in an article of 1929, "As it appears, consumers' credit affects economic welfare both negatively and positively. It is difficult to say which way the balance lies." Econo-mists, then and now, could not agree on what role consumer credit played in prolonging the Great Depression.[34] But in the realm of public debate in the 1930s, the defenders of consumer credit had the more convincing arguments.

Milan Ayres, statistician for the National Association of Fi-nance Companies, responded quickly to the indictments of Lubin and other "frozen credit" theorists. Ayres corrected Lubin's esti-mate of the burden of debt on the average consumer. It was an outrageous exaggeration to say it amounted to 30 percent of in-come, argued Ayres; it was more like 5 percent, he estimated (the best recent calculation puts it at 9 percent).[35] But more important, according to Ayres, was that installment contracts signed in 1929 were long paid off by 1931. At the time of the crash, the average remaining maturity on auto loans was only 4.65 months. Even if one assumes that some debtors paid off installment loans by borrowing from personal loan companies, plenty of time had passed for old consumer loans to have been liquidated. Thus, Ayres concluded, consumer debt could not be blamed for prevent-ing people from buying more goods. The sources of the public's tightfistedness lay elsewhere. His final argument was convincing: all through the boom and the bust, the ratio of installment buying to total retail buying stayed about the same. Cash buyers who owed nothing were spending just as conservatively as people in debt up to their ears.[36]

Many continued to believe that too much credit had "frozen" consumer buying power, but in the Depression calls for a return to a cash-oriented economy went unheeded. Other voices clamored for more credit, not less. By the time Franklin Delano Roosevelt called for a "new deal" for the American people, many analysts and businesspeople considered consumer credit to be a key, not a barrier, to full recovery.

Now You Can Owe Macy's!
—and the Government and the Banks, Too

During the Depression, the consumer credit system picked up important new support from three *entrants* in the field of consumer lending. These were retailers who had previously stayed out of the credit business, the national government, and the nation's commercial banks.

As might be expected, retailers and installment finance companies took the view that consumer credit could nurse the country back to economic health. Beginning in 1933 installment finance companies led a revival of consumer credit that lasted through the end of the decade. Retailers joined them, having learned in the depression of 1921 that installment selling brought more customers in the door, who tended to buy more merchandise when shopping on credit.

After three years of decline, financing for durable goods picked up again in 1933. Automobile sales sparked the expansion. From a low of $356 million in 1932, outstanding automobile paper rose to $1.4 billion by 1936. Thereafter automobile loans grew more slowly, dipping substantially in the slump of 1937–1938. But just before the downturn, and then again at the end of 1939, the volume of auto loans reached its highest mark up to that time.[37] The significance of the rise in auto loans is that it outpaced the rise in total automobile sales. In other words, more people were buying cars on credit in the 1930s than ever before. Liberalized terms helped. For example, in 1935, the Universal Credit Company announced a "$25 a month plan" for Ford automobiles. This plan made it possible to stretch out the period of repayment for some models longer than twenty-four months, a period unheard of in the 1920s.[38] Competition among finance companies led to the further reduction of down payments and the progressive lengthening of contracts.

The same trend was at work with other consumer durable goods, which also contributed to the credit boom of the 1930s. Mechanical refrigerators, washing machines, oil burners, and vacuum cleaners were especially popular with the buying public, and were heavily promoted by public utility companies. Seeking to increase demand for electricity, public utility companies began liberalizing terms on household electrical appliances as early as 1930. On one plan, an electric refrigerator costing between $200 and $300 could be bought for as little as $10 down, the balance to be paid in eighteen months.[39] All together, loan volumes on household durable goods more than doubled between 1933 and 1939, from $799 million to $1.6 billion.[40]

The spread of installment selling to more and more items, one of the pronounced trends of the 1920s, continued unabated during the Depression. In July 1930, Montgomery Ward and Company used ten million flyers and full-page advertisements in 650 newspapers to announce that for the next sixty days, all items in its catalog (except for groceries) would be available on time payments. "We consider it a constructive move to stimulate consumer spending," explained George B. Everett, the company president. Sears responded before Christmas by lowering its installment terms by 20 percent across the board. All together, the four major mail-order companies increased installment sales fourfold between 1932 and 1937.[41] Other retailers followed suit. The list of stores and businesses that inaugurated installment credit schemes included Cunard Steamship Lines (1932), Chicago's The Fair Store (1935), Philadelphia's Wanamaker's (1938), and numerous other department stores, furniture stores, clothiers, sporting goods dealers, and jewelers.[42]

It was apparent to most retailers that installment credit accounts offered definite advantages over open-book charge accounts. With installment credit, the seller received partial payments on a regular basis. This meant that when a buyer ran into trouble and was forced to negotiate with creditors for a rescheduling of debts, the installment seller had already received part or even nearly all the value of the purchased goods. Moreover, installment sellers by law owned a prior lien on "bought" goods. Open-book sellers, by contrast, got lumped with other creditors at the time of bankruptcy and received only a proportionate share of the salvage. Finally, the evidence showed that installment purchasers were better payers than charge account buyers, doubtless because of the threat of repossession hanging over them.[43]

Still, one prominent retailer resisted the trend toward installment selling—Macy's, arguably the nation's premier department store. While other stores jumped on the installment selling bandwagon, Macy's refused to surrender its proud slogan, which was as unusual in the late 1930s as it had been in 1851: "No one is in debt to Macy's!" In order to compete successfully against credit-granting stores, the store emphasized in its advertising that no one could match Macy's low prices on high-quality goods. "Macy's sells for 6 percent less because we sell only for cash," boasted Macy's advertisements. Whether this was true or not, store officials understood that some loyal Macy's customers wanted the convenience of a charge account. For them, Macy's introduced in 1902 its "Depositor's Account" program. Under this plan, the "D.A." customer deposited a sum of money in Macy's bank—an incorporated state bank—and was issued a numbered card which could be used to "charge" purchases against the account. Macy's signed up a good number of D.A. customers, but in the long run, the system worked about as well as Henry Ford's Weekly Purchase Plan.[44]

And it met the same fate. On 9 October 1939, Macy's declared an end to its rearguard action against credit selling. On that Monday, Macy's customers were invited to apply for "Cash-Time" privileges. "Cash-Time," the first store-sponsored credit plan in Macy's history, made everything in the giant department store (except wines and liquor) available on the installment plan. The idea for Cash-Time came from Beardsley Ruml, Macy's treasurer (later known for his "pay-as-you-go" federal tax plan of payroll deductions). Like Henry Ford a decade before, Ruml and other Macy's executives eventually had to face up to the writing on the wall, or, more precisely, the writing in the newspaper: "For Complete Credit Convenience—Let's Go To Gimbel's!"[45] To survive in a credit-oriented economy, Macy's had to scuttle the cash-only policy that was the store's oldest and best-known tradition. To save face, Ruml gamely tried to contextualize the new policy as a step back to the future. Macy's would continue to offer low "cash prices," but Cash-Time buyers would pay for the service of installment buying through a service charge assessed on each installment purchase. The rate: six cents on ninety-four cents of merchandise, with up to sixteen months to pay.[46]

The name of Macy's credit plan followed in the well-worn grooves of previous retail credit propaganda. "Cash-Time Service," Macy advertisements matter-of-factly explained, "simply means cash-over-a-period-of-time." Ads and brochures for the new credit plan intended to reassure customers that buying on credit at Macy's was the right thing to do. But by 1939, it was probably the officials at Macy's who needed reassuring the most. Customers had been demanding credit from Macy's for years. It was the store officials who were most concerned with the problem of how to come up with an installment plan that would "logically supplement" the store's cash policy.[47]

The decision by Macy's to adopt installment selling made newspaper headlines across the country—but only because Macy's was the last of the major department store retailers to capitulate to the credit revolution. Store retailers, along with installment finance companies, had been pioneer institutions in the credit revolution of the 1920s. The revolution now continued in the 1930s as two new credit-granting institutions committed themselves to building up a consumer credit system. These were the national government and commercial bankers.

The national government had been in the credit business for a long time. In the nineteenth century it granted easy terms to stake homesteaders; later, in 1916, it established a system of banks to extend reasonable credit terms to farmers who needed help climbing up out of tenancy to ownership. But it never seemed like a popular idea for the government to grant credit to city dwellers, who, after all, would use it for "consumptive" purposes.

When the idea was finally put forward seriously, it was precipitated by the mounting economic crisis of 1931–1932. As historians have argued for some time now, Herbert Hoover, reviled in his own day as a "do-nothing" president, responded to the crisis by doing more to involve the government in the economy than any previous peacetime executive. Part of his recovery plan, in theory at least, aimed to increase household borrowing power.

One reason why the recession of 1930 ratcheted into the Depression of 1932 was that commercial lenders, looking out for the interest of their depositors, became too scared to do what bankers are supposed to do: make loans. To get them back in the lending business, Hoover initially tried moral suasion, always his preferred policy. This did not work. A series of White House conferences followed, in which Hoover and his advisers inched toward proposals that involved the federal government in the nation's non-agricultural credit system. The plan that touched most closely on consumer credit involved the establishment of a large network of federal mortgage discount banks, called the Home Loan Bank System, which would be to mortgage lenders what the Federal Reserve was to commercial lenders. The intent was to liquify the nation's building and loan associations, and force the nation's insurance companies and savings banks to take more active lending policies, in order to supply desperately needed funds to the real-estate and mortgage markets. The plan as originally envisioned never made it to Congress, due to opposition from the lenders whose interests were affected. But the Federal Home Loan Bank System was finally enacted in July 1932, with a dozen banks and $125 million in capital.[48]

For Hoover, it was too little, too late. Only three applications for loans were granted in the first two years of the program—out of forty-one thousand applications. Hoover, true to his principles, never intended the program to aid those who needed credit the most. But this measure, along with the Reconstruction Finance Corporation and the Emergency Relief and Construction Act, established important precedents for larger government lending programs in the next administration.[49]

When Franklin Delano Roosevelt assumed office, he arrived in Washington having made no promises that the government would continue Hoover's lending programs, much less float new ones. Before certain audiences, in fact, Roosevelt had campaigned for a balanced budget and accused Hoover of "overregulating" the economy. But in the Hundred Days and following, Roosevelt's New Deal quickly seized on consumer credit as an engine that could help pull the nation out of depression. By 1935, M. R. Neifeld could boast before an approving convention audience, "The New Deal has thoroughly endorsed the use of credit as part of the recovery program."[50]

The New Deal supported consumer credit with several kinds of initiatives. One type involved direct government lending. The very first consumer credit program operated by the government was the Electric Home and Farm Authority (EHFA), incorporated in 1933 as a subsidiary of the Tennessee Valley Authority (TVA). EHFA was the brainchild of David E. Lilienthal, director of the TVA, whose father was a retail merchant in Indiana. Perhaps the son learned from the father the value of extending credit to customers. TVA's electric utility plants hoped to have many customers, but the only home appliances owned by most people in the Tennessee Valley were washboards and iceboxes, neither of which required great amounts of electricity. Through EHFA, Lilienthal hoped to encourage people to buy electrical appliances and thereby build up the load on TVA electric power systems. The EHFA bought low-cost refrigerators and other appliances from manufacturers, then made them available to the public through local utility companies. The appliances were sold on installment contracts that allowed repayment in three to four years. Purchases were billed by the utility company, but EHFA served as the actual lender. Though EHFA's director, Jesse Jones (formerly head of the National

Recovery Administration), prevented the program from lending aggressively nationwide, EHFA credit did successfully increase demand for electricity in the Tennessee Valley. For the first time the federal government was directly competing with private consumer lenders.[51]

Another program involving the national government in direct consumer lending was the New Deal's Farm Credit Administration (FCA). Through the Farm Credit Act of 1933, FCA established a Central bank and twelve regional banks to loan money to farmers' cooperatives, which in turn were authorized for the first time to lend money to farmers for consumption purposes, such as buying an automobile or refrigerator. Previously, federal credit aid to farmers had been limited to the production and marketing of crops.[52]

The most active direct lending program established by the New Deal expanded on the foundation built by Hoover's Federal Home Loan Bank Board. The Home Owners' Refinancing Act of 1933 responded to a crisis in the nation's mortgage credit system that had only grown worse since 1931. Distress in the real-estate market stemmed from two causes. The first was mounting unemployment, which sent many homeowners into foreclosure. The second was the disarray of the banking system. As bank failure followed bank failure, and as delinquent commercial investments left bankers with insufficient deposits, bankers were in no mood to issue much-needed second mortgages to individuals with standard five-year mortgages, whether they could afford to make house payments or not. In desperation, many states in 1930–1933 proclaimed moratoriums on foreclosure proceedings. But when the banking system approached collapse in early 1933, the Roosevelt administration stepped in to do something to stabilize the real-estate finance markets. The Home Owners' Refinancing Act was the first step.

The act took Hoover's Federal Home Loan Bank Board and made it more effectual through establishment of a subsidiary lending arm called the Home Owners' Loan Corporation (HOLC). HOLC lent low-interest money to families in danger of losing their homes to foreclosure. In this way, HOLC made it a national policy that the government would encourage widespread homeownership (for some more than others; through the invention of "red-lining," HOLC institutionalized and worsened the racial discrimination that already existed in lending). In the first two years of HOLC lending, more than a million troubled mortgages were serviced with loans totaling over $3 billion. Forty percent of eligible mort-gagees sought help from HOLC. By 1936, when HOLC suspended its active lending program, one out of ten mortgages in the country was assisted by a HOLC loan.[53]

As Kenneth Jackson points out, HOLC dramatically affected private money management because "it introduced, perfected, and proved in practice the feasibility of the long-term, self-amortizing mortgage with uniform payments spread over the whole of the debt."[54] The twenty-year mortgage, along with "revolving" in-stallment credit at department stores, gave real substance to a phrase coined in the 1920s to describe what Americans were adopting in the credit revolution: "the debt way of life."

Through the New Deal, direct government lending became an important element in the nation's credit structure. But the New Deal gave the consumer credit system crucial indirect backing as well.

According to its historians, the credit union movement profited immensely from passage of the Federal Credit Union Act in 1934. Credit unions are banks run on a cooperative basis for the benefit of their members, extending low-cost loans on the basis of pooled savings. In 1930 a thousand credit unions were organized in thirty-two states, but the movement lost momentum during the general banking crisis of the Depression. Edward A. Filene, the eastern retail merchant and father of the American credit union move-ment, tried to coax President Roosevelt and other Washington offi-cials into coming up with federal funds for an extensive national network of credit unions, but was rebuffed at every turn. Roy F. Bergengren, director of the Credit Union National Extension Bu-reau and the movement's other tireless promoter, had better suc-cess with his plan. Bergengren found congressional support for legislation that simply provided for the incorporation of credit unions in any state of the union. Bergengren's plan received the enthusiastic backing of President Roosevelt, who as governor of New York had signed that state's first credit union legislation. Most senators did not know what a credit union was, but the Federal Credit Union Act passed with the president's blessing. Within a year, over one hundred credit unions a month were being organized, with six thousand new members signing up weekly.[55]

The twenty-year home mortgage established by HOLC received further federal support in 1934, when the National Housing Act established the Federal Housing Administration (FHA). FHA was intended to do two things: to create jobs in the very depressed housing industry, and to repair, modernize, and replace the existing stock of homes in order to "bring them up to the standard of the times."[56] Unlike the HOLC, the FHA did not involve the government in direct lending. Rather, the government aimed to induce private lenders to loan money to home buyers and homeowners by guaranteeing the lenders against loss through an insurance fund capitalized at $200 million. The carrot worked very well, and lenders loosened their purse strings quickly. By the end of 1937, FHA insurance had stimulated over a billion dollars of mortgage credit for new homes. New construction starts went from 93,000 starts in 1933 to 530,00 in 1940, an increase almost entirely attributable to FHA-backed loans.[57]

FHA was even more successful in revamping the entire mortgage credit procedure. Second mortgages, costly commissions and renewal fees, and widely varying interest rates became things of the past. In their place stood a system offering twenty-five- and thirty-year amortized mortgages, with a downpayment of 10 percent or less, based on standardized appraisals and careful consideration of the buyer's ability to pay.

In addition to home mortgages, FHA also insured about half a billion dollars in loans for modernization purposes by 1937, which very directly stimulated consumer credit agencies. Under Title I of the FHA, lending agencies could count on federal insurance to back up loans for modernization purposes of up to $2,000 (a year later, the ceiling was raised to $50,000). Through the 1930s, FHA continually broadened its definition of "modernization" improvements, so that eventually the government guaranteed loans for the purchase of electrical refrigerators, automatic gas and oil heaters, and other household equipment, as well as the refurbishing of bathrooms, kitchens, garages, and other general construction upgrades. Support for this kind of modernization lured new lenders into the consumer installment credit market. By 1935, insured modernization loans were being extended by eleven thousand commercial banks, several hundred installment finance companies, a hundred or so industrial banks, and a handful of other agencies. Seventy-five percent of the modernization loans were for $300 or less.[58]

One other New Deal measure provided indirect but significant aid to consumer credit. In June 1933 Roosevelt decided that the nation's banking crisis demanded a policy of government insurance for bank deposits. The Federal Deposit Insurance Corporation (FDIC) helped stabilize the nation's banking system by reassuring small depositors that the money they had tucked away in a bank vault was safe. But FDIC had another legacy as well. It freed commercial bankers from their ingrained allegiance to the principle of liquidity, which mandated large cash reserves and only short-term "call" loans in case depositors should make a run on the bank. In this way, the FDIC program brought to the support of consumer credit one of its former, and most vocal, opponents: commercial bankers.

In the credit-mad 1920s, the lot of the conservative banker was described by H. L. Mencken as "the immensely painful one of a good Presbyterian in Hollywood."[59] Bankers opposed consumer credit for a variety of reasons, ranging from self-interest in the case of savings bankers to ethical scruples in the case of individual moralists. But the fundamental reason why bankers refused to lend to consumers had to do with conventional wisdom about how banks should operate. In the orthodox banking confession, deposits were sacrosanct. Nothing was allowable that might jeopardize the depositors' trust. This cardinal principle ruled out loans to consumers on two grounds. First, because "consumptive" loans were considered risky. Consumers typically had no collateral to offer; nor were they typically planning to invest the loan in profitmaking enterprises that would erase the debt. Second, and more important, loans to consumers were almost always long-term loans, whether five years as with real-estate mortgages, or six months to one year as in the case of automobile installment contracts. Long-term loans tied up money. What if the need should arise to satisfy a number of depositor's demands for their money? Consumer loans could not be "called." Thus, short-term, thirty-day "call" loans to commercial enterprises were the banks' main outlet for investment. Experience with this one type of loan bred conservatism. Other types of loans, such as mortgage and consumer loans, even if perfectly "safe," were considered to be too much trouble for too little return.

Of course, exceptions were always made. A personal loan might be made, quietly, to a valued customer. Then, in the early 1920s, a handful of bankers began to challenge orthodox banking procedures. In 1920, a bank in Bridgeport, Connecticut, advertised small loans to individuals; four years later a Jersey City bank opened the first small-loan department in a commercial bank.[60] Other banks experimented with consumer lending as it became increasingly obvious that the risks in this line were much exaggerated, and as local opportunities for commercial and agricultural loans soured. By the end of the decade, the percentage of bank loans made to households (both personal and mortgage loans) increased from less than 6 percent in 1922 to more than 9 percent. Rolf Nugent counted 208 personal loan departments in banks in 1929, up from 6 in 1923.[61]

The quiet shift in banking practice came into public view in 1928, when the nation's largest commercial bank, the National City Bank of New York, announced the opening of a personal loan department. City Bank was prepared to lend money in amounts ranging from fifty to one thousand dollars for family needs, home improvements, personal emergencies, and property charges to borrowers who agreed to open a compound-interest savings account and could provide the names of two cosigners. President Charles E. Mitchell spoke reassuringly to fellow bankers that City Bank was merely trying "to make closer contact with the people of the city and, specifically, those individuals minded to thrift." But the new loan department's circular took a different line: "Sometimes it may be as important to borrow money as it is to save money."[62] According to one reporter, in the weeks following the opening of City Bank's personal loan department, City Bank fielded inquiries from twelve hundred banks across the country requesting full details of the department's operations and procedures.[63]

Due to government support for household credit, the very small trend of the 1920s was now amplified in the 1930s. When the FDIC put government insurance behind 98.5 percent of all bank deposits, the specter of a mass run on the banks was eliminated, and the banker's need for liquidity along with it. When the FHA insured home loans, bankers were attracted to the prospect of low-risk, long-term mortgages, as well as the higher-interest, short-term home improvement loans.

Even these programs might not have been enough to motivate bankers to learn a complicated new type of lending, except that, as a result of the Depression, commercial opportunities for loans all but dried up. From 1932 to 1936, bank loans dropped almost $11 billion, while their deposits increased over $3 billion.[64] This change, combined with the excellent record of small-loan companies and finance companies in the Depression, made consumer loans look increasingly attractive.

Hence, while there were 208 banks making consumer loans at the time of the crash, seven years later the number had tripled to 685.[65] At the end of the 1930s, banks still lent less money than before the Depression—$16 billion in 1939, down from $36 billion in 1929—a sign of how seriously the Depression affected business investment. But the proportion of bank loans going to households had risen dramatically, from 9 percent in 1929 to over 20 percent in 1939.[66] In that year commercial banks surpassed small-loan companies in the total amount of personal cash loans extended, becoming for the first time the nation's largest lender of cash loans. The following year, 1940, commercial banks also became the largest lenders of consumer installment credit, surpassing the installment finance companies, which in the 1920s bankers had supplied with capital. Today, commercial banks remain the most important institutional cash lenders in the consumer credit system.[67]

Compared with other consumer lenders, banks had distinct advantages. For borrowers with status aspirations, the solidly respectable "First National" or "First City" bank lent prestige as well as money. More important, banks had in their deposits a cheap supply of loan capital. This permitted them to charge a low 6–8 percent annual rate of interest. If competition with other lenders did not force bankers to charge this rate, state usury laws did: unlike licensed small-loan companies, the business of banking fell under the states' general usury laws. Of course, the low rate of interest charged by bankers made small-loan agencies nervous. It raised questions all over again about the personal finance company's need for an interest rate of 30–42 percent a year.

However, it became quickly apparent that banks and personal finance companies were not competing in the same loan market. When National City Bank opened its personal loan department in 1928, *Industrial Lenders News* showed little alarm, but advised its readership that "no competition exists between bankers and industrial lenders."[68] With the bank's usual demand for two cosigners and an account of deposit, the less affluent and the less well connected were discouraged from applying to banks for a loan. In addition, the fact that state regulations allowed much higher loan size limits for bank loan departments (up to $3,500 in New York, as compared with $300 for licensed lenders), showed that the loan market was effectively segmented into two parts. Lending records indicate that banks served loan customers who were mostly white-collar and professional, while personal finance companies continued to cater to industrial wage earners (skilled workers particularly), schoolteachers, civil servants, and office and clerical workers.[69] Once small-loan lenders realized that bankers were not entering into direct competition with them, they welcomed the conversion of their fiercest critics. By the end of the 1930s, bankers had not only become the most important retailers of loans but were leaders in the continuing public relations campaign on behalf of consumer credit.[70]

ROADS NOT TAKEN

In view of the great outcry over installment selling in the 1920s, it is surprising how little opposition was voiced when the federal government and the banking industry got behind consumer credit during the Depression. Virtually the only disagreements to be heard were from those disappointed that credit had not been increased through more radical measures.

Late in 1933, before the credit measures of the first New Deal began to show an effect, scare talk about national indebtedness— similar to what swept the country in the late 1880s and led to the first national census of private debt in 1890—circulated freely all over the country. Officials in Washington heard complaints that the nation's consumers were overloaded with debt, that workers coming back to work were being unmercifully dunned for loans piled on while they were unemployed, and that many retailers were going under because their capital was tied up in uncollectible credit accounts. To study the problem, a committee of experts was appointed by the Consumer Advisory Board, a division of the National Recovery Administration. Chaired by Gardiner C. Means, the committee roster read like a who's who of consumer credit analysts from within and without the industry. Included were Evans Clark of the Twentieth Century Fund; Rolf Nugent of the Russell Sage Foundation; Leon Henderson, then with the NRA but formerly with Russell Sage; William O. Douglas, then of Yale Law School; and several other representatives of various credit industries and associations. Since the committee was allotted no funds for its investigation, it made use of extensive contacts with philanthropic foundations and government agencies to carry out its instructions.[71]

While the committee worked, and while officials of the various consumer credit institutions trooped in and out of the capital to share their views, rumors circulated that the federal government was about to enter the consumer credit field on a scale so large it would dwarf the credit programs of the Hundred Days. "The idea," speculated *Business Week*, "is to make these loans, if the plan is approved, to any person of good character who has a job and wants to spend, in advance of income, on permanent improvements of property, legitimate purchases in keeping with his income, etc., the money to be repaid out of pledges of a portion of salary definitely allocated by the borrower."[72]

Fuel for such speculation came from a number of sources—frightened lenders probably started it. But it was encouraged by supporters of various plans to nationalize the credit industry. One of these was the nostrum of "social credit," a British import with the support of highly trained economic theorists such as the poet Ezra Pound and the novelist William Carlos Williams. Formulated by a Scotsman named C. H. Douglas, social credit took a new tack on the old problem of how to raise wage incomes to an equivalency with the prices of goods. Classical theory maintained that purchasing power must always balance prices; but clearly it did not. Addressing this problem, social credit excoriated capitalism for allowing economic power to fall into the hands of a few financiers. At the same time, it mocked socialism for believing there was magic in state ownership. What Major Douglas proposed in the theory of social credit was a monetary reform to fix what he perceived to be a simple error in the accounting system of society, an error that prevented incomes from matching prices.

The monetary reform envisioned by social credit called for consumers to be issued credit not on the basis of their own collateral or productive capacity, but on the basis of social credit—the wealth and productive capacity of the nation. This would remove control of credit from the grasp of the oligarchic financiers and restore it to the people, thereby breaking loose the logjam preventing the flow of purchasing power. The appeal of social credit, then, aside from its shallow clarity, lay in the way it promised middle-class consumers something for nothing, without doing away with private property. The scheme found enough supporters in Alberta, Canada, that a social credit movement controlled the government there from 1935 to 1938.[73]

Social credit made little headway in the United States, where it had no constituency large enough or powerful enough to push it through the political process. No more successful were nationalization schemes advocated by Bronson Cutting, the Progressive senator from New Mexico, and Father Charles E. Coughlin, the popular radio priest. The only nationalized credit plan to receive serious attention in Washington was a plan called "the Community Credit Plan," put forward by a New Haven, Connecticut, lawyer, Edgar L. Heermance, with support from at least some members of the National Retail Credit Association. The prospectus for the Community Credit Plan laid out a succinct case for government control of credit: "The Voter is a Consumer, and the Average Consumer is today a Debtor." Assuming the "frozen credit" theory of the underconsumptionists, Heermance argued that the only way to unfreeze retail credits and start the wheels of industry turning again was for the government to pool the debts of the nation's consumers. Once this was accomplished, the government could then proceed to pay off preferred creditors up to 50 percent of the total amount of debt, and then arrange for consumer debtors to pay off their newly reduced debts to locally organized community credit corporations. The Community Credit Plan appealed to some retail creditors because it promised an immediate cash infusion into the retail industry. It had a practical appeal, too, in that it drew from the functioning examples of local credit pooling organizations that already existed in ten major cities.[74]

Plans for large-scale government intervention in the consumer credit industry ran up against two obstacles. The first was the self-interest of existing credit agencies, which were well represented on the Consumer Advisory Board committee. The second was the committee's finding that the alleged debt crisis was largely exaggerated. In fact, the committee reported to the president that quite a few less people were in debt in 1934 than in 1929 at the height of New Era prosperity.

President Roosevelt, for his part, had an eye on the next election and how he might overcome conservative opposition to the New Deal. Debtor's crisis or no debtor's crisis, the president was eager to see programs that made more use of the private sector, less use of public money and government controls. Hence, the committee's final report led to two initiatives very much in the spirit of the New

Deal's middle-of-the-roadism and social scientific rationalism: the Federal Housing Administration, with its program of guaranteed home mortgages, and Rolf Nugent's painstaking, pioneering study of the social and economic aspects of consumer credit, published in 1939 as *Consumer Credit and Economic Stability*.[75]

The Great Depression left many with bad memories about being in debt. Scrimping to make payments, avoiding creditors, sitting in the banker's chair, hat in hand—these are the kind of memories that surface when people recall the hard times of the 1930s.

But in 1935, when Robert and Helen Lynd interviewed the people of Muncie, Indiana, many Middletowners expressed frustration with the old savings-oriented proscriptions of the Victorian money management ethic. "Never again!" was the response of a large group of people to the way the Depression wiped out their painfully acquired savings accounts.[76] With the added pressure of government and business propaganda for consumer spending ("Spending Will Win the War against Depression!"), along with the creation of government-sponsored social security for the retirement years, incentives to save were further reduced. In this way, the Great Depression further encouraged the doctrine of "spending to save," so crucial to the legitimization of consumer credit.

Beyond its effect on attitudes, the Great Depression provided the moment for the full validation of the consumer lending industry. Surviving this test of its viability, and picking up important new allies in commercial banking and the government, consumer credit agencies solidified their claim to being important financiers of the American dream. The credit system built by these agencies in the 1920s and 1930s would, after the interregnum of World War II, expand consumer debt so enormously that, years later, the period of the credit revolution would often be remembered as the age when "people never went into debt and lived within their means." But there was never such a time. The rise of consumer credit followed a long-standing American tradition of going into debt to bring unattainable dreams within reach.

In 1927, E.R.A. Seligman predicted—correctly—that "consumers' credit" had "come to stay." Knowing many would be dismayed by his prediction, he offered a consoling thought. "Beefsteaks and eggs," he reassured readers, "will probably never be sold on installments."[1] Seligman was a good forecaster, but not a perfect one.

Today, a half century after the credit revolution, not only can steak and eggs be purchased on the installment plan, but so can every item found in a supermarket—from motor oil to comic books, from asparagus to zucchini. And this is not the half of it. The significance of consumer credit is now measured by the fact that for middle-class people it has become virtually impossible to live the American dream *without* access to credit payment methods, as anyone knows who has placed a phone order from a catalog or tried to pay cash for a rental car. The business writer was hardly exaggerating who said, "To have one's credit cards canceled is now something akin to what being excommunicated by the Medieval church meant."[2] A difference between church membership then and access to credit now is that church membership was never a right. But Americans seem to think access to credit is.[3]

The necessity of access to credit is not new in American life. But since 1940, building on the foundations laid during the credit revolution, consumer lenders have continued to develop new methods and uses for credit. The story of consumer credit since 1940 can be summed up in a single word: *more*.

More credit, to begin with—unbelievably more credit. Since 1945, when wartime credit restrictions had lowered the indebtedness of American consumers to $5.7 billion, the volume of consumer debt has climbed to the unimaginable height of $1.266 trillion in July 1998.[4] Statistics do not speak intelligibly for themselves, but these shout to be heard.

Translated, the figures testify to a host of things today's debtors take for granted that either did not exist or were not widely available fifty years ago. More methods, for example: "revolving" credit plans, charge cards for travel and entertainment, the all-purpose credit card in its many varieties—gold cards, platinum cards, the legendary "black" card, affinity cards—offering both retail credit and instant cash loans, to the point that credit cards today are the most widely accepted means of payment in the American marketplace. There are more lenders: gasoline companies, commercial banks, insurance companies, large retailers, suburban pawnbrokers, third-party payers (Diner's Club, Carte Blanche, American Express), and nonbank credit card issuers (Fingerhut, General Electric, AT&T, Sears, Ford, General Motors). There is more publicity for credit: commercials for "credit-fixers" crowd the airwaves on afternoon and late-night TV, community-sponsored credit workshops abound, and mailboxes are stuffed with bankcard solicitations (over a billion were sent out in 1996). There are more government regulations: uniform annual percentage rates (APRs) that make loan comparisons possible, standard nationwide procedures for resolving billing disputes, maximum liability for unauthorized credit card purchases, protection from abusive debt collectors and their odious practices (late-night phone calls, collectors posing as government agents, humiliating shakedowns before neighbors and co-workers), conspicuous advertisement of credit card interest rates and annual fees, the length of the grace period before interest is charged, and the maximum finance charges for cash loans and late payments. More people today are considered worthy of credit: single women, married women using their own name, African Americans and other racial and ethnic minorities, college students, teenagers, children, people with less than top-notch B and C credit ratings. And there is still more that is new: credit counseling agencies, tax deductions for interest on certain forms of consumer credit (most recently, home equity loans), and new idioms and phrases—"Put it on the card." "Got any plastic with you?" "Honey, we're maxed out." These are but some of the post–World War II products of the historical developments described in this book.[5]

Fifty years of headlines in the periodical press show that consumer credit has never lacked for nervous critics:

Harper's, 1940 (when consumer indebtedness was $5.5 billion): "Debt Threatens Democracy"

Business Week, 1949 (when consumer indebtedness had doubled to $11.6 billion): "Is the Country Swamped with Debt?"

U.S. News & World Report, 1959 (when consumer debt had tripled again to $39.2 billion): "Never Have So Many Owed So Much"

Nation, 1973 (when consumer debt had quadrupled again to $155.1 billion): "Mountain of Debt"

Changing Times, 1989 (when consumer debt had increased another fivefold to $795 billion): "Are We over Our Heads in Debt?"

U.S. News & World Report, 1997 (when debt stood at $1.2 trillion): "In Debt All the Way Up to Their Nose Rings (Generation X)"

After examining a half century of such articles, the historian who reads in his newspaper "Credit-Card Debt Could Be the Plastic Explosive That Blasts the Economy in '97" can be forgiven for calmly turning to the sports page. As Yogi Berra says, it's déjà vu all over again.

The recipe for conventional analysis of rising consumer credit is much the same today as it was in 1957 and in 1927. It begins with the unhappy tale of how a "typical" middle-class family fell thousands of dollars in debt as it struggled to keep up with the Joneses. Then comes the observation that American consumer debt is larger than the combined gross domestic product of six or seven foreign countries. There follows a paragraph of handwringing over the demise of the "Puritan ethic," followed by finger-pointing at bankers and retailers for the indiscriminate issuance of credit cards to teenagers, toddlers, dead people, and the occasional house pet. Then comes a litany of specific worries: first, that generous credit leads to overbuying, which leads to inflation, which causes recession, which brings on a wave of defaults and repossessions, which aggravates the recession, and so on (a kind of economic domino theory). Second, that installment credit is deceptively expensive, as the rhythm of regular payments lulls consumers into a state of appalling ignorance about the total cost of their loans, until all that matters to most of them is the size of the monthly payments. Third, that consumer credit has turned America into a nation of bank-rupts (in 1996 over one million households filed for bankruptcy protection) and pleasure-loving hedonists increasingly bereft of the capacity to discipline desire and postpone gratification. It is an old and tired analysis, its chief merit being that stories about profligate spenders up to their eyeballs in debt still sell magazines and attract viewing audiences for television news shows.

Americans themselves do not take the critics very seriously. Ex-horted to cut up their credit cards, they react like earlier Americans responded to the harangues of Father Abraham, who, Poor Rich-ard tells us, "heard it, and approved the Doctrine, and immediately practiced the contrary." Perhaps today's consumers are mindless hedonists. Or perhaps they know other analyses of consumer credit more in tune with its essential nature.

The developments in consumer credit over the years since the credit revolution only reinforce my argument in this book that the principal significance of consumer credit is the way it regulates and ultimately limits the hedonistic qualities of consumer culture. This claim would be incredible if consumer credit were merely the key to instant gratification. But consider the "hedonism" of modern consumers financing the American dream with consumer credit.

In 1924, an unnamed woman of Muncie, Indiana, described for anthropologists Robert and Helen Lynd how credit and debt af-fected her family's life. Forty-two years old, the wife of a pipe fitter and mother of two high school boys, the woman proudly ticked off her family's major assets: a $6,000 bungalow ("built . . . by a building and loan like everyone else does"), electric washing ma-chine, electric iron, electric icebox, vacuum cleaner, and a $1,200 Studebaker, which the family had just used for a vacation trip to Pennsylvania—taking in Niagara Falls along the way. It was clear in the interview that possessions such as these brought real plea-sure to the woman and to her family, but pleasure exacted its pay-ments—literally. When the monthly bills exceeded her husband's income, off to work the woman went, doing cleaning six days a week in one of the city's public institutions. She expressed no re-grets to the Lynds about working outside the home; now that her boys were older, she had no desire to lay about the house all day enjoying her leisure and possessions. At first, "the mister" objected to her working outside the home, but the spur of regular monthly payments had a marvelous effect on his mind, and he eventually came around. So off to work she went. Throughout the interview, the woman made it clear she thought of herself more as a worker than a consumer. "I feel if I can't give my boys a little more all my work will have been useless," she told the Lynds.[6] If we want to call this woman a "hedonist," it must at least be admitted that her diligent labor made her "hedonism" a peculiar variant.

A generation later the same pattern is on display again in the lives of a middle-class family profiled in *Life* magazine. In the early spring of 1962, as part of a series on personal money management, *Life* sent a writer and photographer to the home of Dave and Betty Jacobs of Bluffton, Indiana, a "hard-working" young couple whose financial adventures were typical of "millions of young Americans much like them, who want what they want when they want it." Their story, wrote the author of the essay, offered "an ingenious object lesson in modern American living," where the central lesson to be learned was how to operate a household in debt as "an agreed-on way of life."[7]

As a designer at Bluffton's Franklin Electric, Dave brought home a monthly salary of $511—very good money for a middle-class wage earner at the time. To this amount Betty contributed $63 more, money earned by taking care of two young boys whose parents worked away from home. Before the Jacobses even sat down to their monthly financial "summits," $50 had already been taken out of Dave's paycheck for taxes and social security, and another $87 removed by the Franklin credit union to help pay off a loan used to furnish the Jacobses' new house. After these automatic deductions, the Jacobses faced the sober reality of an additional $16,000 in home mortgage and consumer debts. In the hard light of these inescapable demands the couple's take-home pay quickly melted away. The check for the house mortgage was written first, for $161. Then life insurance and hospital insurance took $26. The operating costs for the car Dave used to commute to work skimmed off an additional $30. Then the other bills took their cut: a car loan, a cash loan for new storm windows and a

Figure 19. The consumer's lament: there's always too much month
at the end of the money. When a photographer for *Life* magazine
captured this moment in the lives of Dave and Betty Jacobs, clearly the
thrill of buying things on credit had yielded to the more sobering
and lasting reality of a pile of installment bills.

fireplace, minimum payments on revolving "budget" accounts at
Sears and Montgomery Ward. When all the bills were paid, $92
was left for that month's food and household expenses, and $41
for "whooping it up." For these 1960s consumers, whooping it up
meant paying for doctors' bills and haircuts, grass seed and fertil-
izer, an infrequent movie and a daily newspaper, ballet lessons for
their daughter and an occasional golf game for Dave, and dona-
tions to their church. The kids got toys—on Christmas and for
birthdays. The house was full of books—checked out from the
local library. Betty got a new coat at Christmas, and lingerie, and
a carpet sweeper—which Dave paid for by working overtime every
day for two months, and putting aside his $2 a month allowance
for cigarettes and coffee breaks. In spite of such sacrifices, the
Jacobses' spending exceeded their income each month by about

$31. How this could be pulled off was explained by the writer who interviewed them: "Like millions of other young American couples, [the Jacobses] live beyond their income but not beyond their credit, staving off perpetual immanent disaster with the aid of check books, installment plans, easy terms and the optimistic conviction that, as Dave Jacobs says, 'We'll make it somehow. Things will always be better—maybe a lot better.' "[8]

Looking at the budget numbers alone, the Jacobses appear to be reckless, pleasure-loving hedonists; each month they spent more money than they earned. But such a view is misleading, much like looking down from an airplane upon towns and cities below—the details are all lost, and people do not look like the human beings they are. On closer inspection, the Jacobs do not look like stereotypical hedonists at all. To be sure, they expected a high standard of living and were susceptible to viewing consumption as a therapy for what ailed them. But if this is hedonism, it is certainly a strange sort of disciplined dissipation, for the Jacobses lived by an incredibly tight regimen of forced savings that caused their unsatisfied wants to far outnumber the wants that got satisfied. So, for example, when an income tax refund in the amount of $331 arrived in the mail, Betty did not get the new dress she wanted, and there was no family vacation. Instead, all but $20 went to pay off debts the couple owed. Even as these debts were paid off, others were contracted. For the Jacobses then, as for millions of other households, the pattern of using almost all their monthly income to satisfy bills for consumer credit meant their life differed from the hedonist's endless succession of pleasures. Judging from the worry lines on Dave and Betty's faces, it appeared to be more of an "endless series of nibbles, pinches, and bites."[9]

The pattern of using a large share of monthly income to pay off consumer debts was given a name in 1956 by business writer William H. Whyte Jr., who called it "budgetism." As White defined it, "budgetism" was "a person's desire to regularize his income by having it removed from his own control and disciplined by external forces."[10] Budgetism was different from the budget keeping advocated by Victorian financial advisors. Then, the standard module in household finance was the week; now, as creditors geared everything to a thirty-day cycle, couples sat down once a month to pay bills, chew pencils, and discuss strategies for staying afloat. But the larger difference was the locus of discipline. With the Victorians self-discipline was everything. In spite of encircling temptations from an incipient culture of consumer desire, they felt confident in their powers to exercise restraint and discipline their desires all by themselves. But the first generations actually to grow up in a full-fledged culture of consumption knew better than to trust their internal restraints. Bombarded by mass marketing, modern consumers of the 1950s needed all the help they could get. Their problems with self-discipline were effectively remedied by the "budget" plans of consumer credit.

Installment payments are an expensive proposition, as critics never tire of pointing out. Why have not more people saved on interest charges by doing what Victorian money managers once urged: build up a constantly replenished saving fund and "borrow" from themselves interest-free? Whyte had the answer: "We're sure we'll pay back the bank, but we couldn't be sure we'd pay ourselves back."[11] The Ford Motor Company stumbled over this way of thinking back in the 1920s when its experiment with the Weekly Purchase Plan ended in failure. If there are no serious consequences to letting one's money dribble away on the endless array of goods and services proffered by the agents of consumer desire, it becomes hard to stick to a budget. But installment payments take care of this problem, ensuring that money is directed toward more durable, or at least more expensive, goods and services. "The beauty of budgetism," Whyte pointed out, "is that one doesn't have to keep a budget at all. It's done automatically."[12]

Whyte astutely perceived that the popularity of installment buying was not solely due to a desire for instant gratification, but also owed something to people's desire for budgetary controls. This is the point so frequently missed in conventional analyses of consumer credit. "The suburbanites," Whyte observed, "try to budget themselves so tightly that there will be no unappropriated funds, for they know these would burn a hole in their pockets."[13] Consumer credit is expensive credit, but the consumers he interviewed seemed willing to pay for the peace of mind that came from carefully charted debt payments, for the sense of stability that came from a rational, orderly household budget. At any rate their rigidly budgeted lives were a far cry from that of unbridled sybarites. "What is striking about the young couples' march along the abyss is the earnestness and precision with which they go about it. They are extremely budget-conscious. They can rattle off most of their monthly payments down to the last penny; even their 'impulse buying' is deliberately planned. They are conscientious in meeting obligations, and rarely do they fall delinquent in their accounts."[14]

Whyte could not shake his belief that indebted Americans were "true prodigals," but he had to admit it was a strange sort of profligacy they practiced. They lived "eminently respectable" lives in "sober suburbia," where there were "no pink Cadillacs, no riotous living." They were "homeowners; they go to church; from one-third to one-half have gone to college; more will send their children to college, and about 65 per cent of them vote Republican." If they had any discipline at all in their lives, and if they were not living in the poorhouse, Whyte concluded it was all due to "budgetism, the opiate of the middle class."[15]

In Whyte's "budgetism" we have a key for unlocking the greatest puzzle of the American dream. American dreams have come true by dint of the marvelous productivity of consumer capitalism. But what prevents the acquisitiveness required of model consumers from sabotaging the discipline required of workers in the capitalist system of production?

Awareness of this puzzle goes all the way back to the Puritans, but no one has explored it in more depth than sociologist Daniel Bell in his richly rewarding analysis of "the cultural contradictions of capitalism." Beginning with the widely accepted premise that consumer society is a hedonistic society, Bell worked his way to his famous argument that capitalist societies have developed a "radical disjunction" between the economic and cultural realms of life, a disjunction that brings the United States to "the hinge of history" where a society's shared moral purpose evaporates and social decline sets in. Bell explained the contradiction as follows. In the world of work, people are expected to march to the rhythms of rationality, efficiency, and productive maximization. Because the goal in the work realm is high levels of production, and because competitive markets ensure that this goal must be kept in mind at all times, employers demand that employees display character types marked by self-discipline, the delay of gratification, economizing, and restraint—behaviors exactly the opposite of those encouraged in the cultural realm. As Bell sees it, the cultural realm promotes and celebrates a gospel of self-gratification, self-realization, and liberation from externally imposed restraints. The cultural contradiction of capitalism then, is that Americans are expected to be both disciplined workers and liberated consumers. Bell believes that the asceticism that gave rise to a productive economy in the United States was long ago overwhelmed by the boundless acquisitiveness and hedonism unleashed by the culture of consumption, and by the installment plan in particular. "What then, can hold the society together?" is the question raised by his analysis.[16]

Bell's deepest concerns are beyond our scope here.[17] But his question concerning what holds consumer society together is directly addressed by the history related in this book. How has consumer capitalism survived the subversive doctrines of consumer culture, which would seem to wear it down: its libertinism, its insatiable devotion to "wants," its hedonistic concern with play, fun, pleasure, and leisure? How have people managed to balance the contradictory identities urged on them in the economic and cultural realms of society—those of disciplined worker and voracious consumer? In a society where suspicion of extravagant consumption is one of the oldest national traditions, whose founding political act involved the repudiation of what one colonial boycotter called "the baubles of Britain," a society that has always given intellectual assent to the ideal of "plain living and high thinking," how did Americans ever learn to feel good about debt-financed abundance?[18]

For some, especially the young, the disjunction between production and consumption is less resolved than it is embraced. "Work hard, play hard" is the watchword of middle-class youth, a schizophrenic way of being in the world that few can sustain past marriage and children.

For the rest of us, the cultural contradiction within capitalism is smoothed over with the aid of various social conventions. For starters, there is the way we manage our time, dividing the week into workdays and weekend, company time and personal time, so that it becomes easier, though by no means always possible, to confine the conflicting codes of conduct for the economic and cultural realms of life to their own separate time spans.[19] Contradictions between the two realms have also at times been managed through the social construction of stereotypical male and female roles, in which men were understood to be society's producers and women its consumers, an effective way of balancing discipline and desire that had the virtue of symmetry, if little else.[20] A third means of containing the hedonistic potential within consumer culture has been suggested by Elaine Tyler May, whose work on American family life in the cold war shows that "family-centered spending" was a popular way many tried to reconcile consumerism with traditional values.[21] These are but a few of the ways the unsynchronized gears of capitalist society have been adjusted so that they mesh at all.

But the most effective solution has been worked out at the precise point where the economic and cultural realms connect, and that is in the domain of household financial management. Practically speaking, the resolution of the tensions inherent in consumer capitalism is most evident in the way that consumer credit has preserved the relevance of key values inherited from earlier producer cultures. Far from causing the demise of thrift, consumer credit has actually worked to make most modern credit users at least as disciplined in their finances as the generations who lived before the credit revolution. The installment plan of repayment forces typical credit users to adopt disciplines of money management that would have impressed even Poor Richard. Poor Richard is well known for his disapproval of indebtedness, but his creator Benjamin Franklin eventually came to wonder, "May not luxury therefore produce more than it consumes if without such a spur people would be, as they are naturally inclined to be, lazy and indolent?"[22] Indolence is not an option for people living by the installment plan. The fact is, "easy credit" is really not all that easy. Installment credit imposes on borrowers financial regimens requiring discipline, foresight, and a conscious effort to save income in order to make payments on time. "Easy payment!" exclaimed an immigrant housewife to a journalist in 1912. "Hard payment it is! Easy payment with everybody workin' their nails out!"[23]

Some borrowers have succumbed to the allure of "buy now, pay later" and been overloaded with debt. This has been a real problem.[24] But historically the numbers who are delinquent with payments or default on their loans have been very small compared with the numbers who pay their bills on time. Today, when consumer bankruptcies are at an all-time high and banks are forced to erase from their books 4.4 percent of their credit card loan balances from debtors who cannot pay (far above the percentage of charge-offs and delinquencies of other consumer loans), comment on the national "debt wish" is shrill to the point of being hysterical. Yet the more impressive fact remains that 95.5 percent of consumer debt gets paid.[25]

These statistics imply that most installment borrowers, for the duration of their repayment periods, have been forced to cut out expenditures on momentary fancies, put aside money for the monthly installment bills, and work diligently at one or more jobs to guarantee a dependable supply of income. Consumer credit has gratified some of their consumer desires, while reining in others. The installment plan then, has had the paradoxical effect of expediting the rise of a culture of consumption while limiting its potentially subversive effects on the economic realm of work and production. In the process, it has made it possible for people to think of consumption in the way that E.R.A. Seligman conceptualized it, as "the *production* of satisfactions."

It might have been different. As Gary Cross has pointed out, the original promise of industrialism was that it would bring people more time for leisure, not more money for goods. But the installment plan, by bringing expensive durable goods within reach of consumers, ensured that people living under conditions of abundance would continue to work more than play; to think of themselves as workers more than as consumers; and to consider their consumption more as a form of satisfying production—production

302

of identity, production of well-being, production of meaning—than of wasteful destruction. The importance of these outcomes for the legitimization of consumer culture cannot be overestimated. The culture of consumption offended Victorian moralists because it looked like the province of mere indulgence and excess. What Americans did on the installment plan was to transform consumer culture into a suitable province for more work.

The history of consumer credit reveals a truth known to all bargain hunters, coupon cutters, overtime workers, and, indeed, to anyone who has ever stayed up late working over personal accounts: life in a consumer society is a lot of work. A bumper sticker sums it up accurately: "I owe, I owe; it's off to work I go!"

✻ *Notes* ✻

INTRODUCTION
CREDIT, CONSUMER CULTURE, AND THE AMERICAN DREAM

1. "Ask Marilyn," *Parade*, 10 August 1997, p. 5.

2. *Saturday Evening Post*, 15 August 1959.

3. The artist, Constantin Alajalov, was born in Russia and trained at the University of Petrograd before emigrating to the United States as a young man. His work appeared frequently in national magazines in the 1950s and 1960s. Originally, he intended to paint the young couple dreaming about castles in the air, then changed his mind. In a note about the cover, an editor denied the charge of "cynicism": "It takes as much moon magic to create a two-car domicile as it does to whip up an air castle."

4. James Truslow Adams, *The Epic of America* (Boston: Little, Brown, 1932), pp. 405–406.

5. David Riesman, "Abundance for What?" *Bulletin of Atomic Scientists* 14 (April 1958): 136.

6. This is the definition used by the Federal Reserve Board, which reports monthly statistics of consumer credit. See Douglas Greenwald, ed., *The Encyclopedia of Economics* (New York: McGraw-Hill, 1982), p. 184.

7. "The American Dream," in Richard Maltby Jr. and Alain Boublil, *Miss Saigon* (Milwaukee, Wis.: Hal Leonard Publishing, 1991), pp. 87–96.

8. Randall Jarrell, *A Sad Heart at the Supermarket: Essays and Fables* (New York: Atheneum, 1962), p. 66.

9. Quote is by Kenneth T. Jackson, in "All the World's A Mall: Reflections on the Social and Economic Consequences of the American Shopping Center," *American Historical Review* 101 (October 1996) : 1111. For the best overviews of this rapidly expanding scholarship, see Jean Christophe Agnew, "Consumer Culture in Historical Perspective," in *Consumption and the World of Goods*, ed. John Brewer and Roy Porter (New York: Routledge, 1993), pp. 19–39; Robert Bocock, *Consumption* (New York: Routledge, 1993), pp. 10–33; Simon J. Bronner, *Consuming Visions: Accumulation and Display of Goods in America, 1880–1920* (New York: W. W. Norton, 1989), pp. 2–11; Robert M.

Collins, "David Potter's *People of Plenty* and the Recycling of Consensus History," *Reviews in American History* 16 (June 1988), pp. 321–335; and David Horowitz, *The Morality of Spending: Attitudes toward the Consumer Society in America, 1875–1940* (Baltimore: Johns Hopkins University Press, 1985), pp. xxi–xxviii.

10. Daniel Bell, *The Cultural Contradictions of Capitalism* (New York: Basic Books, 1976), p. xv.

11. A good introduction to the influence of Baudrillard and other theorists can be found in Robert Bocock, *Consumption* (New York: Routledge, 1993), pp. 53–75.

12. William Leach, *Land of Desire: Merchants, Power, and the Rise of a New American Culture* (New York: Vintage Books, 1993), pp. 10–11.

13. Jarrell, *Sad Heart at the Supermarket*, p. 67.

14. Those studying the United States have focused on the years between 1880 and 1930, though some see a "consumer revolution" happening in the colonies in the half century before Independence. Europeanists push the date for the arrival of consumer culture farther back, to seventeenth- and eighteenth-century France and England, perhaps even as early as fifteenth-century Florence. See Paul G. E. Clemens, "The Consumer Revolution: Now, Only Yesterday, or a Long Time Ago?" *Reviews in American History* 23 (December 1995): 574–581.

15. Warren I. Susman, *Culture as History: The Transformation of American Society in the Twentieth Century* (New York: Pantheon, 1984), p. xx.

16. Data in this and the following paragraph are from Board of Governors of the Federal Reserve System, *Federal Reserve Bulletin*, the selected years. The Federal Reserve also publishes historical charts summarizing data from the *Bulletins*. See Board of Governors of the Federal Reserve Board, *Federal Reserve Charts on Bank Credit, Money Rates, and Business* (February 1948), p. 22.

17. Estimates computed from Board of Governors, *Federal Reserve Bulletin* 83 (September 1997): A36; and from population statistics in George Thomas Kurian, ed., *Datapedia of the United States, 1790–2000: America Year by Year* (Lanham, Md.: Bernan Press, 1994), p. 30.

18. Daniel Boorstin, *The Americans: The Democratic Experience* (New York: Random House, 1973), pp. 422–428; Helena Flam, "Democracy in Debt: Credit and Politics in Paterson, New Jersey, 1890–1930," *Journal of Social History* 18 (Spring 1985): 439–462; Irving S.

Michelman, *Consumer Finance: A Case History in American Business* (New York: Frederick Fell, 1966); Alfred L. Malabre Jr., *Beyond Our Means: How Reckless Borrowing Now Threatens to Overwhelm Us* (New York: Random House, 1987); Hillel Black, *Buy Now, Pay Later* (New York: William Morrow, 1961).

19. Martha L. Olney, *Buy Now, Pay Later: Advertising, Credit, and Consumer Durables in the 1920s* (Chapel Hill: University of North Carolina, 1991).

20. Jarrell, *Sad Heart at the Supermarket*, p. 66.

21. Robert Lynd and Helen Lynd, *Middletown: A Study in American Culture* (New York: Harcourt, Brace, 1929), pp. 45–47, 278, 492.

22. Riesman, "Abundance for What?" p. 136; John Kenneth Galbraith, *The Affluent Society* (Boston: Houghton, Mifflin, 1958), p. 201.

23. Boorstin, *The Americans*, p. 426.

24. Daniel Bell, *The Cultural Contradictions of Capitalism* (New York: Basic Books, 1976), p. 66; Francesco M. Nicosia and Robert N. Mayer, "Toward a Sociology of Consumption," *Journal of Consumer Research* 3 (September 1976): 67–68; George Ritzer, *Expressing America: A Critique of the Global Credit Card Society* (Thousand Oaks, Calif.: Pine Forge Press, 1995), p. xi.

25. In a surprising turnabout, college-level history textbooks, which usually *summarize* the latest scholarship, have actually *anticipated* historical research on the subject of consumer credit. See James A. Henretta et al., *America's History*, 3rd ed. (New York: Worth Publishers, 1997), pp. 748–749; Carol Berkin et al., *Making America: A History of the United States* (Boston: Houghton Mifflin, 1995), p. 706; and George Brown Tindall and David E. Shi, *America: A Narrative History*, 4th ed. (New York: W. W. Norton, 1996), pp. 1331–1332.

26. Johan Heuzinga, "The Idea of History," in *The Varieties of History: From Voltaire to the Present*, ed. Fritz Stern (New York: World Publishing, 1972), p. 300.

27. Abigail van Buren, *The Best of Dear Abby* (Kansas City, Mo.: Andrews and McMeel, 1981), p. 242.

28. Robert Porter, "Public and Private Debts," *North American Review* 153 (November 1891): 610–612.

29. Evans Clark, *Financing the Consumer* (New York: Harper & Bros., 1930), p. 213.

30. See, for example, Jack Weatherford, *The History of Money* (New York: Crown Publishers, 1997), pp. 222–224; Paul Boyer, *Promises to*

Keep: The United States since World War II (Lexington, Mass.: D. C. Heath, 1995), p. 126; Douglas T. Miller and Marion Nowak, *The Fifties: The Way We Really Were*, excerpted in Robert Griffith, ed., *Major Problems in American History since 1945* (Lexington, Mass.: D. C. Heath, 1992), p. 223.

31. Raymond Goldsmith, *A Study of Saving in the United States* (Princeton, N.J.: Princeton University Press, 1955), p. 699. It is worth noting that the period 1920–1929 also saw home mortgage debt tripled, from $9.1 billion to $27 billion outstanding. See Leo Grebler, David M. Blank, and Louis Winnick, *Capital Formation in Residential Real Estate: Trends and Prospects* (Princeton, N.J.: Princeton University Press, 1956), pp. 443–445.

32. Olney, *Buy Now, Pay Later*, pp. 86–91, 96.

33. Ibid., p. 96.

34. Janet Ford, *The Indebted Society: Credit and Default in the 1980s* (New York: Routledge, 1989), p. 13.

35. Clark, *Financing the Consumer*, p. 7.

36. Paul F. Douglass, ed., "Consumer Credit: A Critical Analysis of Credit Agencies and of the Development of Regulation," *Annals of the American Academy of Political and Social Science* 196 (March, 1938): xi.

37. "What Is the Sound Limit of Installment Buying?" *Philadelphia Retail Ledger*, 1 April 1926, p. 10.

38. See Ernestine Wilder, *Consumer Credit Bibliography* (New York: Prentice-Hall, 1938). In her preface, Wilder apologizes for excluding many citations due to the "voluminous amount of material available."

39. Franklin W. Ryan III, "Family Finance in the United States," *Journal of Business of the University of Chicago* 4 (October 1930): 415. For similar comments, see J. M. Head, "Is the Installment Plan an Artificial Stimulus to Prosperity?" *Magazine of Wall Street*, 19 June 1926; *New Republic* 46, 7 April 1926: 186; and Julian Goldman, letter to John M. Glenn, 2 January 1928, Russell Sage Foundation Files, Box 166, Library of Congress, Washington, D.C.

40. Ryan, "Family Finance in the United States," p. 415.

41. Barbara A. Curran, *Trends in Consumer Credit Legislation* (Chicago: University of Chicago Press, 1965), p. 1; "Dumping the Assumption," *Isthmus*, 23 November 1990, p. 8.

42. For examples of the myth expressed in various contexts, see Senator Paul H. Douglas's memories in *In Our Time* (New York: Harcourt,

Brace & World, 1968), pp. 101–102; "The American Way of Debt," *Time*, 31 May 1982, pp. 46–49; *Business Week*, 30 October 1989, p. 18; James L. Clayton, "Why Can't We Hear the Distant Thunder?" *Vital Speeches*, 15 November 1984, pp. 92–93; Alfred J. Malabre Jr., *Beyond Our Means: How Reckless Borrowing Now Threatens to Overwhelm Us* (New York: Random House, 1987), pp. 6–7, 16–18, 123, 144; David Caplovitz, *Consumers in Trouble: A Study of Debtors in Default* (New York: Free Press, 1974), pp. ix, 1; Robert Nisbet, *The Present Age: Progress and Anarchy* (New York: Harper and Row, 1988), p. 90. For historians, see note 46.

43. Mark Twain and Charles Dudley Warner, *The Gilded Age: A Tale of Today* (New York: New American Library, Meridian Classic, 1985), pp. 64, 193, 184–185. The *Oxford English Dictionary*'s first reference to "charging" a credit purchase dates to 1889.

44. "Saving by Borrowing," *Saturday Evening Post*, 12 January 1924, p. 24.

45. Editorial, *New York Times*, 4 November 1923.

46. On nostalgia in the 1920s, see Jacqueline Fear and Helen McNeil, "The Twenties," in *Introduction to American Studies*, ed. Malcolm Bradbury and Howard Temperley (New York: Longman, 1981), pp. 195–196.

47. M. R. Neifeld, *Personal Finance Comes of Age* (New York: Harper & Bros., 1939), p. 4.

48. Preston William Slosson, *The Great Crusade and After, 1914–1928* (New York: Macmillan, 1930), p. 181.

49. Boswell's *Life of Johnson*, 13 April 1773.

50. William H. Whyte Jr., "Budgetism: Opiate of the Middle Class," *Fortune* 53 (March 1956): 133.

51. John Kenneth Galbraith, *The Affluent Society* (Boston: Houghton Mifflin, 1958), pp. 200–201, 206.

52. From $45 billion in 1958 to $1.266 trillion in July 1998. Credit figures from U.S. Board of Governors of the Federal Reserve System, *Federal Reserve Bulletin* 45 (February 1959): 188; and *New York Times*, 9 September 1998, p. C2. Population figures are from Kurian, *Datapedia of the U.S.*, p. 30.

53. Christopher Lasch, *The Culture of Narcissism: American Life in an Age of Diminishing Expectations* (New York: W. W. Norton, 1978), p. 53; David M. Tucker, *The Decline of Thrift in America* (New York: Praeger, 1991), p. 114.

54. Daniel Bell, *The Cultural Contradictions of Capitalism* (New York: Basic Books, 1976), pp. 21, 69–70. For similar claims made by historians, see Loren Baritz, who compares the "revolutionary" installment plan of the 1920s with Hugh Hefner's new sexual morality of the 1950s in *The Good Life: The Meaning of Success for the American Middle Class* (New York: Harper & Row, 1990), pp. 64, 72–73, 79, 80, 190; Thomas C. Cochran, *Challenges to American Values: Society, Business and Religion* (New York: Oxford University Press, 1985), p. 86; William E. Leuchtenburg, *The Perils of Prosperity, 1914–1932* (Chicago: University of Chicago Press, 1958), pp. 174, 200.

55. A bibliography on debt in early America could start with William Bradford, *Of Plymouth Plantation, 1620–1647* (New York: Random House, Modern Library, 1967), pp. 36–46, 93–96, 184–188, 194–200, 213–215, 399–403; T. H. Breen, *Tobacco Culture: The Mentality of the Great Tidewater Planters on the Eve of Revolution* (Princeton, N.J.: Princeton University Press, 1985), pp. xii–xiv, 93–106, 127–129, 161–175; David P. Szatmary, *Shays's Rebellion: The Making of an Agrarian Insurrection* (Amherst: University of Massachusetts Press, 1980), pp. 19–36; Arthur M. Schlesinger, *The Age of Jackson* (New York: Little, Brown, 1945), pp. 131–136; Allan G. Bogue, *Money at Interest: The Farm Mortgage on the Middle Border* (Lincoln: University of Nebraska Press, 1969); Lewis E. Atherton, *The Frontier Merchant in Mid-America* (Columbia: University of Missouri Press, 1971), pp. 142–153.

56. Baritz, *The Good Life*, p. 64.

57. A good introduction to Taylor's ideas is Samuel Haber, *Efficiency and Uplift: Scientific Management in the Progressive Era, 1890–1920* (Chicago: University of Chicago Press, 1964). Weber often used images of machines when describing the bureaucratic organization of capitalist industrial society. His famous prediction that the future under capitalism would be "an iron cage" appears in the final pages of *The Protestant Ethic and the Spirit of Capitalism* (London: Unwin Hyman, 1930), p. 181.

58. Philip Rieff, *The Triumph of the Therapeutic: Uses of Faith after Freud* (Chicago: University of Chicago Press, 1987), pp. 14–27.

59. Jackson Lears, *Fables of Abundance: A Cultural History of Advertising in America* (New York: Basic Books, 1994), pp. 10–11, 138, 159, 198, 206–207.

60. C. S. Lewis, *The Allegory of Love* (Oxford: Oxford University Press, 1936), p. 1.

CHAPTER 1
BEAUTIFUL CREDIT! THE FOUNDATION OF MODERN SOCIETY

1. Charles Farrar Browne [Artemus Ward], *Artemus Ward in London* (New York: G. W. Carlton, 1867), p. 71. Sixty-five years later during the Great Depression, versions of this joke were still making people laugh. See Sheffield Boardman, "Our Sixth Freedom—The Pursuit of Credit," *Vital Speeches*, 1 December 1960, p. 114.

2. Mark Twain and Charles Dudley Warner, *The Gilded Age: A Tale of Today* (New York: New American Library, Meridian Classic, 1985), p. 193.

3. Quoted in Janet Ford, *The Indebted Society: Credit and Default in the 1980s* (New York: Routledge, 1989), p. 13.

4. Edward Everett, *The Mount Vernon Papers* (New York: D. Appleton, 1860), pp. 167–168.

5. "The Credit System," *Banker's Magazine* 42 (May 1888): 832; U.S. Department of the Interior, Census Office, *Report on Real Estate Mortgages in the United States at the Eleventh Census, 1890* (Washington, D.C.: Government Printing Office, 1895), p. 102.

6. Census Office, *Report on Real Estate Mortgages*, p. 3. For analysis of the debt controversy, which centered on western farm mortgages, see *Banker's Magazine* 42 (January 1888): 502–503; Daniel R. Goodloe, "Western Farm Mortgages," *Forum* 10 (November 1890): 347–355.; and J. P. Dunn Jr., "The Mortgage Evil," *Political Science Quarterly* 5 (March 1890): 65–83.

7. "Private" real-estate mortgages included farm acreage, city lots, and some mortgages for commercial purposes, but excluded mortgage debt of "quasi-public" corporations, such as railroads and public utilities. Robert Porter, "Public and Private Debts," *North American Review* 153 (November 1891): 610–612.

8. Census, *Report on Real Estate Mortgages*, p. 102.

9. Estimate of debt per household computed from data on households in U.S. Department of Commerce, Bureau of the Census, *Historical Statistics of the United States from Colonial Times to 1970*, 2 vols. (Washington, D.C.: Government Printing Office, 1975), 1:41. Average annual wages for American workers is reported in *Historical Statistics of the United States*, 1:165.

10. Charles Barnard, "A Hundred Thousand Homes: How They Were Paid For," *Scribner's Monthly* 11 (February 1876): 479.

11. Quoted in Dorothee Schneider, "For Whom Are All the Good Things in Life?: German-American Housewives Discuss Their Budgets," in *German Workers in Industrial Chicago, 1850–1910: A Comparative Perspective*, ed. Hartmut Keil and John B. Jentz (DeKalb: Northern Illinois Press, 1983), p. 156.

12. Louise Bolard More, *Wage-Earners' Budgets: A Study of Standards and Cost of Living in New York City* (New York: Henry Holt, 1907), pp. 108, 268; Robert Coit Chapin, *The Standard of Living among Workingmen's Families in New York City* (New York: Charities Publication Committee, 1909), pp. 236, 245–246; Frank Hatch Streightoff, *The Standard of Living among the Industrial People of America* (Boston: Houghton Mifflin, 1911), p. 24–25.

13. New York Bureau of the Statistics of Labor, *Fourteenth Annual Report* (1896), pp. 802–803.

14. Alan Dawley, *Class and Community: The Industrial Revolution in Lynn* (Cambridge, Mass.: Harvard University Press, 1976), pp. 151–153, 168.

15. Peter Shergold, *Working-Class Life: The American Standard in Comparative Perspective, 1899–1913* (Pittsburgh: University of Pittsburgh Press, 1982), pp. 224–225. Dubofsky quoted p. 7.

16. Pawnbroking in the United States has no historian. For English pawnbroking, see Melanie Tebbutt, *Making Ends Meet: Pawnbroking and Working-Class Credit* (New York: St. Martin's Press, 1983); and Kenneth Hudson, *Pawnbroking: An Aspect of British Social History* (London: Bodley Head, 1982).

17. Champion Bissell, "A Study of Pawnbrokers," *Lippincott's Monthly Magazine* 53 (February 1894): 229.

18. In Elizabeth Ewen, *Immigrant Women in the Land of Dollars* (New York: Monthly Review Press, 1985), p. 159.

19. Chapin, *The Standard of Living among Workingmen's Families in New York City*, p. 233; More, *Wage-Earners' Budgets*, pp. 147–148.

20. Charles Barnard, "Pawnshops and Small Borrowers," *Chautauquan* 19 (April 1894): 72.

21. Peter Shergold, "The Loan Shark: The Small Loan Business in Early Twentieth-Century Pittsburgh," *Pennsylvania History* 45 (July 1978): 200. Shergold arrived at this number by relating population statistics of Philadelphia to W. R. Patterson's report on the volume of pawnbroking credit in that city in May 1898.

22. The following description is taken from several sources, including Helen Campbell, *Darkness and Daylight; or, Lights and Shadows of New*

York Life (Hartford, Conn.: Hartford Publishing, 1895), pp. 603–607; "Up the Spout," *Harper's New Monthly Magazine* 19 (October 1859): 672–677; "Pawnbrokery in New York," *Hours at Home* 7 (July 1868): 246–254; Barnard, "Pawnshops and Small Borrowers," pp. 70–75; Jonathon Gilmer Speed, "Pawnbrokers and the Poor," *Harper's Weekly* 36, 3 September 1892, p. 862; "How Nellie Lee Was Pawned," *Harper's New Monthly Magazine* 13 (September 1856): 500–503.

23. Edward Howland, "The Bankers of the Poor," *Galaxy* 3 (January–April 1867): 662; W. R. Patterson, "Pawnbroking in Europe and the United States," in U.S. Department of Labor, *Bulletin* 4 (March 1899): 273–275, 278–279; "Up the Spout," pp. 675–676; "People and Pledges that Come to a Pawnbroker," *Literary Digest* 69, 23 April 1921, pp. 48–50.

24. Information on the early history of pawnbroking can be found in Samuel W. Levine, *The Business of Pawnbroking: A Guide and a Defense* (New York: D. Halpern, 1913), pp. 8–25; and "Pawnbrokers and Loan-Offices," *Harper's New Monthly Magazine* 39 (June 1869): 125. Statistics are from Patterson, "Pawnbroking in Europe and the United States," p. 268; and Levine, *The Business of Pawnbroking*, pp. 30–32, 115. New York led the states, with one-sixth of the pawnshops. On money-lending in California, see H. C. Carey, *Of the Rate of Interest* (Philadelphia: Collins Printer, 1873), p. 7.

25. "Pawnbrokery in New York," pp. 247, 252; "The Loaners' Association in New York City," *Banker's Magazine and Statistical Register* 16 (September 1861): 212.

26. On family roles in the household economy, see More, *Wage-Earners' Budgets*, p. 28; and Ewen, *Immigrant Women*, pp. 101–109. On the pawnbroking "habit," see More, *Wage-Earners' Budgets*, p. 147.

27. Frank Tucker, *Proceedings of the National Federation of Remedial Loans* (Buffalo, N.Y.: n.p., 1909), pp. 25–26; Levine, *The Business of Pawnbroking*, p. 4; "Pawnbrokers and Loan-Offices," p. 126; "Up the Spout," p. 675.

28. Patterson, "Pawnbroking in Europe and the United States," p. 270. Reformers cited cases where rates went as high as 1,000 percent, but this was mostly the work of a disreputable fringe. For efforts by reformers to professionalize the lending business, see Chapter 3.

29. Patterson, "Pawnbroking in Europe and the United States," pp. 273–275; "Up the Spout," p. 676; Albert Bigelow Paine, "At the Sale of the Unredeemed," *Century Magazine* 69 (January 1905): 366; Shergold, "The Loan Shark," p. 201.

30. Patterson, "Pawnbroking in Europe and the United States," pp. 257–273; Levine, *The Business of Pawnbroking*, pp. 91–131; "The Greer Loan Association Plan," *Outlook* 49, 27 January 1894, p. 191.

31. Emerson W. Peet, "A Review of Provident Loan Societies," *Charities Review* 4 (February 1895): 181–190; Patterson, "Pawnbroking in Europe and the United States," pp. 280–310; Barnard, "Pawnshops and Small Borrowers," pp. 74–75; A. B. Mason, "Evils Growing Out of Extortionate Usury," *Charities Review* 4 (June 1895): 446–448.

32. "Pawnbrokers and Loan-Offices," p. 126.

33. Clarence Wassam, *The Salary Loan Business in New York City* (New York: Charities Publication Committee, 1908), p. 62; Arthur H. Ham, *The Campaign against the Loan Shark* (New York: Russell Sage Foundation Pamphlets, 1912), p. 1.

34. The secrecy of illegal lenders makes it hard to reconstruct their activities. The best historical summary of the small lending business is Rolf Nugent, *Consumer Credit and Economic Stability* (New York: Russell Sage Foundation, 1939), pp. 72–75. In this paragraph and in what follows, I rely heavily on two investigative studies sponsored by the Russell Sage Foundation: Wassam, *The Salary Loan Business in New York City*; and Arthur Ham, *The Chattel Loan Business* (New York: Charities Publication Committee, 1909). In addition, investigations into "the loan shark evil" were conducted in Philadelphia in 1893, Atlanta in 1904, and Massachusetts in 1911. More recently, Peter Shergold has documented the activities of loan sharks in Pittsburgh from records in city directories and police reports. See Shergold, "The Loan Shark," pp. 195–223.

35. Wassam, *Salary Loan Business*, pp. 12, 74–75; Ham, *Chattel Loan Business*, pp. 21–22.

36. The high figure can be found in Frank Marshall White, "The Crusade against the Loan Shark," *Munsey's Magazine* 50 (November 1913): 217–218. But Peter Shergold argues for lower rates on the basis of sworn statements given in Pittsburgh, 1908–1909, in "The Loan Shark," p. 216.

37. Ham, "The Campaign against the Loan Shark," p. 1.

38. Wassam, *Salary Loan Business*, p. 25; Ham, *Chattel Loan Business*, p. 17; Irving S. Michelman, *Consumer Finance: A Case History in American Business* (New York: Frederick Fell, 1966), p. 110.

39. Loan offices were more likely to be patronized by workers in certain trades due to word-of-mouth advertising and the loan shark's strategy of "targeting" selected markets. See Wassam, *Salary Loan Business*, p. 26. Ham's estimate is in "The Campaign against the Loan Shark,"

p. 1; compare with Shergold, "The Loan Shark," pp. 206–207. Quotation is from Shergold, "The Loan Shark," p. 202.

40. An alternate view can be found in Shergold, "The Loan Sharks," p. 201. Citing Robert Chapin's 1907 budget study of 318 families, Shergold argues that pawnbrokers served more affluent borrowers, whereas loan sharks served poorer workers who did not own expensive jewelry and watches. But Shergold overlooks the large number of pawnbrokers lending on clothes. Nor does his view take into account the more extensive data from loan offices that is compiled in Clarence Hodson, *Money-Lenders, License Laws, and the Business of Making Small Loans on Unsecured Notes, Chattel Mortgages, and Salary Assignments* (New York: Legal Reform Bureau, 1919), pp. 51–59, 77–84. Here, various loan office books report on the occupations of their borrowers. The largest sample, that of the Hebrew Free Loan Society of New York City, covers 24,330 borrowers. The Citizens' Loan Company of Cincinnati, lending half of its loans to workers, covered a sample of 2,700 loans.

41. Ads are from Wassam, *Salary Loan Business*, pp. 24, 44.

42. Russell Sage Foundation Files, box 34 (clipping file), Library of Congress, Washington, D.C. On other methods, see Wassam, *Salary Loan Business*, pp. 46–52.

43. The following information on the methods of small lenders is collated from Wassam, *Salary Loan Business*, pp. 14–16, 52–69; and Shergold, "The Loan Shark," pp. 209–211.

44. The adventures of these loan company employees are dramatized, rather heavily, in Forrest Halsey, *The Bawlerout* (New York: Desmond Fitzgerald, 1912).

45. Installment buying was "almost universal" among the families visited by Louise More. More, *Wage-Earners' Budgets*, 145.

46. Herbert Tetenbaum, "The Survival of the Installment Peddlar," *Journal of Retailing* 16 (February 1940): 11–13; Nugent, *Consumer Credit*, p. 68; Edwin R. A. Seligman, *The Economics of Instalment Selling: A Study in Consumers' Credit*, 2 vols. (New York: Harper & Bros., 1927), 1:19–22; Ewen, *Immigrant Women*, p. 170.

47. Nugent, *Consumer Credit*, p. 72. Nugent gives two explanations for the origin of the term "borax"; neither one is convincing. The explanations given here are from Louise Conant, "The Borax House," *American Mercury* 17 (June 1929): 169; and Pollack Foundation for Economic Research, *Pollack Pamphlet*, no. 41 (January 1941): 2. It should be noted that not all borax dealers remained on the disreputable fringe. The Spiegel Company, for example, began as a borax furniture company. See

Orange A. Smalley and Frederick D. Sturdivant, *The Credit Merchants* (Carbondale: Southern Illinois University Press, 1973), pp. 23–40.

48. Massachusetts Bureau of Statistics of Labor, "Changes in Conducting Retail Trade in Boston, since 1874," *Thirtieth Annual Report* (March 1900), pp. 49–56; Smalley and Sturdivant, *The Credit Merchants*, pp. 23–26.

49. Stuart Blumin, *The Emergence of the Middle Class: Social Experience in the American City, 1760–1900* (Cambridge: Cambridge University Press, 1989), p. 297.

50. Massachusetts Bureau of the Statistics of Labor, *First Annual Report* (1870), pp. 185–187.

51. Walter Post to his father, 20 July 1894, Walter Teller Post Papers, Minnesota Historical Society, Minneapolis.

52. Ira Steward, in Massachusetts Bureau of the Statistics of Labor, *Fourth Annual Report* (1873), p. 414.

53. Nugent, *Consumer Credit*, pp. 43–50, 83–86. See also Susan Strasser, *Satisfaction Guaranteed: The Making of the American Mass Market* (New York: Pantheon Books, 1989), pp. 68–71.

54. Robert A. Lynn, "Installment Credit before 1870," *Business History Review* 31 (Winter 1957): 415–424; Seligman, *Economics of Instalment Selling*, 1:16–17, 2:383–388; Craig Roell, *The Piano in America, 1890–1940* (Chapel Hill: University of North Carolina Press, 1989), pp. 100–101; Ruth Brandon, *Singer and the Sewing Machine: A Capitalist Romance* (London: Barrie & Jenkins, 1977), pp. 116–118; Illinois Bureau of Labor Statistics, "Statistics of Mortgages," *Fifth Biennial Report* (1888), pp. lxxxiv, xcvi; Minnesota Bureau of Labor, "Chattel Mortgages and Pawnbrokers' Loans," *Fourth Biennial Report* (1893–1894), pp. 18–29; *Harper's Bazaar* 23 (November 1890): 910.

55. Seligman, *Economics of Instalment Selling*, 1:15–18.

56. Walter Post to Charlie Post, letters between April 1895 and September 1896, Post Papers.

57. T. H. Breen, *Tobacco Culture: The Mentality of the Great Tidewater Planters on the Eve of Revolution* (Princeton, N.J.: Princeton University Press, 1985), pp. 23–30, 91–106. Friendly lending capitalized a fair amount of business in the antebellum period; Mary Ryan reports that one out of five businessmen in Oneida County, N.Y., got started on family credit. See her *Cradle of the Middle Class: The Family in Oneida County, New York, 1790–1865* (Cambridge: Cambridge University Press), p. 155.

58. Examples can be found in his *Indoors and Out; or, Views from the Chimney Corner* (Boston: Brown, Bazin, 1855), pp. 20, 104–105, 112, 114–123, 172, 216, 228, 302.

59. Freeman Hunt, *Worth and Wealth* (New York: Stringer & Townsend, 1856), pp. 129–130.

60. Ewen, *Immigrant Women*, pp. 113–115; Frank Shotoro Miyamoto, *Social Solidarity among the Japanese in Seattle* (Seattle: University of Washington Press, 1939), p. 75; William Mitchell, *Mishpokhe: A Study of New York City Jewish Family Clubs* (The Hague: Mouton, 1978), pp. 105–109; Shelly Tenenbaum, *A Credit to Their Community: Jewish Loan Societies in the United States, 1880–1945* (Detroit: Wayne State University Press, 1993), pp. 47, 145–152. Tenenbaum finds that credit extended by ethnic credit associations was used mostly for entrepreneurial purposes.

61. William Dean Howells, "Who Are Our Brethren?" *Century Magazine* 51 (April 1896): 934. For descriptions of friendly lending among the working class, see Massachusetts Bureau of Statistics of Labor, *Report* (1870), pp. 298–303.

62. Robert E. Park and Herbert A. Miller, *Old World Traits Transplanted* (New York: Harper, 1921), pp. 148–149.

63. H. L. Reade, *Money and How to Make It* (New York: John P. Jewett, 1872), pp. 558–566; "On Lending and Borrowing," *Frank Leslie's Popular Monthly* 28 (October 1889): 430.

64. Massachusetts Bureau of Labor Statistics, *Report* (1870), p. 188.

65. Ibid., p. 335.

66. Russell Conwell, *Acres of Diamonds* (New York: Harper & Bros., 1915), p. 19.

67. Barnard, "A Hundred Thousand Homes," p. 477.

68. William Taylor Adams [Oliver Optic], "The Savings Bank, or, How to Buy a House," in Hunt, *Worth and Wealth*, p. 267.

69. Sam Bass Warner, *Streetcar Suburbs* (Cambridge, Mass.: Harvard University Press, 1962), pp. 117–127.

70. H. L. Cargill, "Small Houses for Working-Men," in *The Tenement House Problem*, ed. Robert W. De Forest and Lawrence Veiller, 2 vols. (New York: Macmillan, 1903; reprint, New York: Arno Press, 1970), pp. 337–346.

71. "How We Saved for Our Home," *Ladies Home Journal* 20 (January–October 1903); D. M. Frederiksen, "Mortgage Banking in America," *Journal of Political Economy* 2 (December 1893): 204–210.

72. U.S. Commissioner of Labor, *Ninth Annual Report* (1893), pp. 15, 318; Frederiksen, "Mortgage Banking in America," p. 209.

73. H. Morton Bodfish, *History of Building and Loan in the United States* (Chicago: U.S. Building and Loan League, 1931), pp. 87–99; Barnard, "A Hundred Thousand Homes: How They Were Paid For," pp. 479–483; Horace Russell, *Savings and Loan Associations* (New York: Matthew Bender, 1956), p. 29.

74. Paul B. Trescott, *Financing American Enterprise: The Story of Commercial Banking* (New York: Harper & Row, 1963), p. 69, 178; J. Laurence Laughlin, *Banking Progress* (New York: C. Scribner's Sons, 1920), pp. 143, 158; Richard Sylla, "American Banking and Growth in the Nineteenth Century: A Partial View of the Terrain," *Explorations in Economic History* 9 (Fall 1971): 197–227.

75. Kenneth T. Jackson, *Crabgrass Frontier: The Suburbanization of the United States* (New York: Oxford University Press, 1985), p. 118.

76. Stephen Thernstrom, *Poverty and Progress: Social Mobility in a Nineteenth Century City* (Cambridge, Mass.: Harvard University Press, 1964), p. 120; "How We Saved for Our Home"; George K. Holmes, "The Concentration of Wealth," *Political Science Quarterly* 8 (December 1893): 590.

77. "How We Saved for Our Home," *Ladies Home Journal* 20 (July 1903): 27.

78. Ibid. For similar comments from other respondents, see the January issue, p. 19; February, pp. 20–21; April, pp. 26–27; June, p. 22; August, p. 26; and October, p. 22.

79. William Cobbett, *Advice to Young Men* (New York: John Doyle, 1831), p. 59.

80. Franklin Wilson, *Wealth: Its Acquisition, Investment, and Use* (Philadelphia: American Baptist Publication Society, 1874), p. 154.

81. Clarence D. Long, *Wages and Earnings in the United States, 1860–1890* (Princeton, N.J.: Princeton University Press, 1960), p. 68. On rising wages among skilled workers and white-collar workers, see Melvyn Dubofsky, *Industrialism and the American Worker, 1865–1920* (Arlington Heights, Ill.: AHM Publishing, 1975), pp. 13–19; Stuart M. Blumin, *The Emergence of the Middle Class*, pp. 272–273.

82. Lewis E. Atherton, *The Frontier Merchant in Mid-America* (Columbia: University of Missouri Press, 1971), pp. 143–146.

83. Laurence A. Johnson and Marcia Ray, eds., *Over the Counter and on the Shelf: Country Storekeeping in America, 1620–1920* (New York: Bonanza Books, 1961), p. 63.

84. Ibid., p. 62.

85. This report can be found in Paul H. Nystrom, *The Economics of Retailing* (New York: Ronald Press, 1915), p. 67.

86. See Edward Hungerford, *The Romance of a Great Store* (New York: Robert M. McBride, 1922), pp. 24–26; Boris Emmet and John E. Jeuck, *Catalogues and Counters: A History of Sears, Roebuck and Company* (Chicago: University of Chicago Press, 1950), pp. 264–265; David L. Cohn, *The Good Old Days* (New York: Simon and Schuster, 1940), p. 523; Norman Beasley, *Main Street Merchant: The Story of the J. C. Penney Company* (New York: McGraw-Hill Book, 1948), pp. 91–92, 219.

87. William Leach, *Land of Desire: Merchants, Power, and the Rise of a New American Culture* (New York: Vintage Books, 1993), pp. 123–127; Strasser, *Satisfaction Guaranteed*, p. 207.

88. *Outlook* 87, 21 December 1907, pp. 849–850.

89. George Fitch, *Credit World* 5 (May 1915): 30.

90. Robert P. Porter, "Public and Private Debts," *North American Review* 153 (November 1891): 614, 618.

91. Raymond Goldsmith, *A Study of Saving in the United States*, 3 vols. (Princeton, N.J.: Princeton University Press, 1955), 1: 699.

CHAPTER 2
DEBT IN THE VICTORIAN MONEY MANAGEMENT ETHIC

1. Obviously, this period is several decades longer than Queen Victoria's reign. But like a number of historians, I believe that "Victorian" is the best word to describe the official public culture that reigned in the United States in the nineteenth and early twentieth centuries. As John Kasson points out, America in this period "was governed by a strikingly coherent set of values, a culture in many respects more thoroughly 'Victorian' than the England over which Victoria reigned." See John F. Kasson, *Amusing the Million: Coney Island at the Turn of the Century* (New York: Hill & Wang, 1978), pp. 4–5; Thomas J. Schlereth, *Victorian America: Transformations in Everyday Life, 1876–1915* (New York: HarperPerennial, 1992), pp. xi–xii; and Daniel Walker Howe, "Victorian Culture in America," in *Victorian America*, ed. Daniel Walker Howe (Philadelphia: University of Pennsylvania Press, 1976), pp. 3–28.

2. Michael Chevalier, *Society, Manners and Politics in the United States* (1839; reprint, New York: Burt Franklin, 1969), p. 304. Nineteenth-century travelers gave the United States a reputation for being the

land of the "Almighty Dollar." For a sampling of views, see Alexis de Tocqueville, *Democracy in America*, 2 vols. (New York: Alfred A. Knopf, 1956), 2:228–229; Frances Trollope, *Domestic Manners of the Americans* (Gloucester, Mass.: Peter Smith, 1974), p. 301; Anthony Trollope, *North America*, 2 vols. (1862; New York: St. Martin's Press, 1986), 1:186–189; G. W. Steevens, *The Land of the Dollar* (New York: Dodd, Mead, 1897), pp. 1–4; Oscar Handlin, ed., *This Was America* (Cambridge, Mass.: Harvard University Press, 1949), pp. 94–95, 243, 273, 278.

3. Of course, money is an ancient fact of life. But in the rudimentary economies of ancient and medieval times, money was limited in both scope and complexity. See Fernand Braudel, *The Structures of Everyday Life: The Limits of the Possible*, vol. 1: *Civilization and Capitalism, 15th–18th Century*, trans. Sian Reynolds (New York: Harper & Row, 1981), pp. 436–478; and Karl Polanyi, *The Great Transformation* (1944; reprinted, New York: Octagon Books, 1975).

4. The colonial experiments with paper money were the first publicly sponsored paper money since China abandoned it in the fifteenth century. See Braudel, *The Structure of Everyday Life*, p. 452; and Eric P. Newman, *The Early Paper Money of America* (Racine, Wis.: Whitman, 1967), p. 7.

5. Baynard Rush Hall [Robert Carlton], *The New Purchase*, ed. James Albert Woodburn (Princeton, N.J.: Princeton University Press, 1916), p. 214.

6. Henry C. Carey, *Of the Rate of Interest and of Its Influence on the Relations of Capital and Labor* (Philadelphia: Collins, 1873), p. 7.

7. Wilbur C. Plummer, "Consumer Credit in Colonial Philadelphia," *Pennsylvania Magazine of History and Biography* 66 (October 1942): 390–393.

8. Robert H. Wiebe, *The Opening of American Society* (New York: Alfred A. Knopf, 1984), pp. 150–152, 298–303; Thomas D. Clark, *Pills, Petticoats, and Plows: The Southern Country Store* (New York: Bobbs-Merrill, 1944), pp. 78–79, 313–335.

9. E. Clavier and J. P. Brissot, *De la France et des Etas-Unis* (1787), quoted in Braudel, *The Structures of Everyday Life*, p. 447.

10. Albert Gallatin, *Considerations on the Currency and Banking System of the U.S.* (Philadelphia: Carey and Lee, 1831), p. 15. See also H. C. Carey, *Reconstruction: Industrial, Financial, and Political* (Philadelphia: Collins, 1867), pp. 58–59. For recent studies of barter and the self-sufficiency of early nineteenth-century rural communities, see Lewis E.

Atherton, *The Frontier Merchant in Mid-America*, University of Missouri Studies, vol. 55 (Columbia: University of Missouri Press, 1971), pp. 123–133; Richard L. Bushman, "Family Security in the Transition from Farm to City, 1750–1850" *Journal of Family History* 6 (Fall 1981): 240–242; Michael Merrill, " 'Cash Is Good to Eat': Self-Sufficiency and Exchange in the Rural Economy of the United States," *Radical History Review* 4 (Winter, 1977): 42–71. Mary P. Ryan found that barter was important even for industrial families in "the vortex of industrial development." See her *Cradle of the Middle Class: The Family in Oneida County, New York, 1790–1865* (Cambridge: Cambridge University Press, 1981), p. 47.

11. Hall, *The New Purchase*, pp. 214–215.

12. George M. Weston, *Banker's Magazine and Statistical Register* 37 (September 1882): 3; Charles W. Coulter, "Coulter Sees Credit Increase," *Personal Finance News* 24 (March 1940): 7.

13. These figures count money in actual circulation. There is no need to adjust figures to reflect changes in the price level, as I am only concerned with pointing out the increasing presence of money in American life. Figures from *Statistical Abstract of the United States* (Washington, D.C.: Government Printing Office, 1943), p. 277; Seymour E. Harris, *American Economic History* (New York: McGraw-Hill Book, 1961), pp. 82, 105; and J. G. Gurley and E. S. Shaw, "The Growth of Debt and Money in the United States, 1800–1950: A Suggested Interpretation," *Review of Economics and Statistics* 39 (August 1957): 258.

14. On the history of paper money, see Braudel, *The Structures of Everyday Life*, pp. 470–473; Newman, *The Early Paper Money of America*, pp. 7–12; Emanuel Coppieters, *English Bank Note Circulation, 1694–1954* (Louvain: Louvain Institute of Economic and Social Research, 1955), pp. 133, 140–141; and Robert Minton, *John Law, the Father of Paper Money* (New York: Association Press, 1975), p. 79.

15. New York *Evening Post*, 13 February 1836; quoted in Lawrence Frederick Kohl, *The Politics of Individualism: Parties and the American Character in the Jacksonian Era* (New York: Oxford University Press, 1989), p. 50; H. C. Carey, *Answers to the Questions: What Constitutes Currency?* . . . (Philadelphia: Lea & Blanchard, 1840), p. 1.

16. Calvin Fletcher, *The Diary of Calvin Fletcher*, ed. Gayle Thornbrough, Dorothy L. Riker, and Paula Corpuz, 8 vols. (Indianapolis: Indiana Historical Society, 1975), 2:221, 223, 350.

17. For antebellum monetary history, see Gilbert Courtland Fite and Jim E. Reese, *An Economic History of the United States*, 3rd ed. (Boston: Houghton Mifflin, 1973), pp. 155, 243–250; Arthur Cecil Bining and

Thomas C. Cochran, *The Rise of American Economic Life*, 4th ed. (New York: C. Scribner's Sons, 1964), pp. 407–408; Joel William Canaday Harper, "Scrip and Other Forms of Local Money" (Ph.D. dissertation, University of Chicago, 1948), pp. 8–19.

18. *North American Review* 102 (January 1866): 100. E. L Godkin reported that as late as the 1890s there was "confusion" abroad and at home over the complicated American paper money. See the *Nation 55*, (14 July 1892), p. 23. Arthur Nussbaum, a historian of the period's numismatics, concludes that "taken together, the money circulation of the period suffered from an exaggerated variety and confusion." See his *A History of the Dollar* (New York: Columbia University Press, 1957), p. 147; and Robert Friedberg, *Paper Money of the United States*, 4th ed. (Chicago: Follett, 1962), pp. 8, 15–25.

19. Tocqueville, *Democracy in America*, 2:228–229.

20. William Makepeace Thayer, *The Ethics of Success* (Boston: A. M. Thayer, 1893), p. 274.

21. Elizabeth Ewen, *Immigrant Women in the Land of Dollars: Life and Culture on the Lower East Side, 1890–1925* (New York: Monthly Review Press, 1985), pp. 23–24. Comparing the French money and credit system with that of the United States in the 1830s, Michael Chevalier concluded that France was "yet in a state of barbarism." Chevalier, *Society, Manners and Politics in the U.S.*, p. 351. England was more on a par with the United States.

22. Charles Saunders Peirce, "Evolutionary Love," *Monist* 3 (January 1893): 176.

23. For the distinction between esoteric and popular theories of money, see Thomas Crump, *The Phenomenon of Money* (London: Routledge & Kegan Paul, 1981), p. 29. Crump, an anthropologist, writes: "One should ask, finally, whether there is, in any sense, a popular theory of money. . . . In the world of primitive money—at least where it is sacred rather than profane—a cognitive system always exists at the popular level . . .; indeed, without it, the circulation of money would in a case of this kind have no function at all." The Victorian money management ethic, along with contemporary epistemological assumptions about money, constituted such a popular theory.

24. The best book on the money question is still Walter T. K. Nugent, *Money and American Society, 1865–1880* (New York: Free Press, 1968), pp. 3–4, 263–275.

25. John A. Rogers, *The Irrepressible Conflict* (Puyallup, Wa.: Rogers, 1892), p. iii.

26. Quoted in the introduction to William H. Harvey, *Coin's Financial School*, ed. and intro. Richard Hofstadter (Cambridge, Mass.: Harvard University Press, 1963), p. 4–5. In Hofstadter's estimation, Coin represented "the common man thinking."

27. "Even a cursory glance at the nineteenth-century novel reveals money to be that novel's most habitual obsession." John Vernon, *Money and Fiction: Literary Realism in the Nineteenth and Early Twentieth Centuries* (Ithaca, N.Y.: Cornell University Press, 1984), pp. 7, 9.

28. William Dean Howells, *The Quality of Mercy* (New York: Harper & Bros., 1892), p. 240.

29. Book review in *Graham's*, November 1841, in Roy R. Male, *Money Talks: Language and Lucre in American Fiction* (Norman: University of Oklahoma Press, 1980), p. 11.

30. William Dean Howells, *The Rise of Silas Lapham*, Library of America (New York: Literary Classics of the United States, 1982), p. 918.

31. On the moralization of Christianity, see James Turner, *Without God, without Creed: The Origins of Unbelief in America* (Baltimore: Johns Hopkins University Press, 1985), pp. 31–34, 64–72, 82–95, 126–132; and Robert T. Handy, *A Christian America: Protestant Hopes and Historical Realities* (New York: Oxford University Press, 1971), pp. 95–116.

32. Ralph Waldo Emerson, "Wealth," in *The Conduct of Life* (Boston: Riverside Press, 1904; reprint, New York: AMS Press, 1968), p. 90.

33. Washington Gladden, "Tainted Money," *Outlook* 52, 30 November 1895, p. 886.

34. John Mackenzie, *A Manual of Ethics*, 3rd ed. (New York: Hinds and Noble, 1897), pp. 32–33.

35. M. B. Anderson, *The Right Use of Wealth* (New York: n.p., 1878), pp. 6–7.

36. On the general influence of the Puritan plain-speech tradition, see T. J. Jackson Lears, "Beyond Veblen: Rethinking Consumer Culture in America," in *Consuming Visions: Accumulation and Display of Goods in America, 1880–1920*, ed. Simon J. Bronner (New York: W. W. Norton, 1989), pp. 75–97.

37. P. T. Barnum, "The Art of Money Getting," in *The American Gospel of Success: Individualism and Beyond*, ed. Moses Rischin (Chicago: Quadrangle Books, 1965), p. 58.

38. Philip Lindsley, *The Works of Philip Lindsley*, ed. LeRoy J. Halsey (Philadelphia: J. B. Lippincott, 1866), p. 394.

39. In 1900, the longest-running feature in the *Saturday Evening Post* was an advice column entitled "Your Savings." See Christopher Wilson, "The Rhetoric of Consumption: Mass-Market Magazines and the Demise of the Gentle Reader, 1880–1920," in *The Culture of Consumption: Critical Essays in American History, 1880–1920,* ed. Richard Wightman Fox and T. J. Jackson Lears (New York: Pantheon Books, 1983), p. 52. Tellingly, the most popular title for nineteenth-century magazine articles on money was, by far, "What Is Money?" See William Frederick Poole, *Poole's Index to Periodical Literature (1802–1881)* (Gloucester, Mass.: Peter Smith, 1958), pp. 860–861.

40. Benjamin Franklin, "Poor Richard Improved, 1758," in *Benjamin Franklin, Writings,* ed. J. A. Leo Lemay (New York: Literary Classics of America, 1987), pp. 1294–1303. Lewis J. Carey's count is quoted in Louis B. Wright, "Franklin's Legacy to the Gilded Age," *Virginia Quarterly Review* 22 (Spring 1946): 273. Paul Leicester Ford, historian and nineteenth-century bibliographer of Franklin, listed fifty-six pages of various editions of the "The Way to Wealth," and then gave up what was a hopeless task. He found it "impossible to find and note all the editions." See his *Franklin Bibliography* (Brooklyn, N.Y.: n.p., 1889).

41. Joseph Medill, *Benjamin Franklin, A Typical American* (Chicago: Benjamin Franklin, 1896), p. 18.

42. *Memorial of the Inauguration of the Statue of Franklin* (Boston: George C. Rand and Avery, 1857), pp. 113–114.

43. See Jacob Riis, *How the Other Half Lives* (1890; New York: C. Scribner's Sons, 1929), pp. 48–50, 104–107, 136–140, 144; Edward Bok, *The Americanization of Edward Bok* (New York: Scribner's & Sons, 1921), pp. 434–436; John R. Commons, *Races and Immigrants in America* (New York: Macmillan, 1907), p. 78; Laurence Franklin, "The Italian in America," *Catholic World* 71 (April 1900): 67–80; Robert Chapin, *The Standard of Living among Workingmen's Families in New York City* (New York: Charities Publication Committee, 1909), p. 235; Irwin Yellowitz, *The Position of the Worker in American Society, 1865–1896* (Englewood Cliffs, N.J.: Prentice-Hall, 1969), p. 82; Elizabeth Cady Stanton and Susan B. Anthony, *Correspondence, Writings, Speeches,* ed. Ellen Carol DuBois (New York: Schocken Books, 1981), pp. 42, 137, 248–249. It would be interesting to know more about the responses of African-Americans and native Americans to the money economy, but, in any case, African American leaders preached thrift and economy to rival the white moralists. See Alexander Clark, "Socialism and the

American Negro," in *The Annals of America*, vol. 11: *1884–1894: Agrarianism and Urbanization* (Chicago: Encyclopaedia Britannica, 1976), pp. 111–112; the "National Colored Labor Platform," in *The Annals of America*, vol. 10: *1866–1883: Reconstruction and Industrialization* (Chicago: Encyclopaedia Britannica, 1976), p. 222; Frederick Douglass, *Narrative of the Life of Frederick Douglass, an American Slave* (New York: Penguin Books, 1986), pp. 140, 147–149. The influence of Victorian culture on American ethnic and racial subcultures is discussed in Howe, *Victorian America*, pp. 518–519.

44. Benjamin Franklin, "Poor Richard Improved, 1758," p. 1302.

45. Daniel Wise, *The Young Man's Counsellor* (New York: Carlton & Phillips, 1854), pp. 41–42.

46. J. M. Austin, *Voice to Youth*, 2nd ed. (Utica, N.Y.: Grosh & Hutchinson, 1839), p. 29; Franklin, *The Autobiography of Benjamin Franklin*, in Lemay, *Benjamin Franklin, Writings*, p. 1369; Henry Ward Beecher, *Twelve Lectures to Young Men*, rev. ed (New York: D. Appleton, 1890), p. 12; Orison Swett Marden, *Pushing to the Front*, rev. ed. (1894; Petersburg, New York: Success, 1911), p. 863.

47. For more on the "culture of character," see Warren I. Susman, *Culture as History: The Transformation of American Society in the Twentieth Century* (New York: Pantheon Books, 1984), pp. xxii, 273–280; and Burton J. Bledstein, *The Culture of Professionalism: The Middle Class and the Development of Higher Education in America* (New York: W. W. Norton, 1976), pp. 134–135.

48. Quoted in P. T. Barnum, *Dollars and Sense* (New York: H. S. Allen, 1890), p. 383.

49. Ruth Miller Elson, *Guardians of Virtue: American Schoolbooks of the Nineteenth Century* (Lincoln: University of Nebraska Press, 1964), p. 251.

50. "About Money," *Eclectic Magazine* 44 (July 1886): 562.

51. Andrew Carnegie, "Thrift as a Duty," in *The Empire of Business* (New York: Doubleday, Page, 1902), p. 99.

52. B. R. Cowen, *Our Beacon Light* (Columbus, Ohio: Patrick, Gordon, 1888), p. 314.

53. Catherine A. Beecher, *The Moral Instructor, for Schools and Families* (Cincinnati, Ohio: Truman and Smith, 1838), p. 131.

54. Franklin Wilson, *Wealth: Its Acquisition, Investment, and Use* (Philadelphia: American Baptist Publication Society, 1874), p. 152.

55. John Todd, *The Young Man* (Northampton, Mass.: J. H. Butler, 1845), p. 205.

56. Franklin, "Poor Richard Improved, 1758," p. 1298. On the history of thrift, see David M. Tucker, *The Decline of Thrift in America: Our Cultural Shift from Saving to Spending* (New York: Praeger Publishers, 1991), pp. 1–15.

57. Marden, *Pushing to the Front*, p. 759.

58. Quoted in Mary Hinman Abel, *Successful Family Life on a Moderate Income* (Philadelphia: Lippincott, 1921), p. 173.

59. Beecher, *The Moral Instructor*, pp. 112–113.

60. Lydia Marie Child, *The American Frugal Housewife* (Boston: Marsh and Capen, 1829), p. 5; Emerson, "Wealth," p. 116. Franklin also urged the virtue of system, but he primarily referred to business accounts.

61. Thayer, *The Ethics of Success*, p. 357.

62. Emerson, "Domestic Life," in *The Conduct of Life*, p. 367.

63. Child, *The American Frugal Housewife*, pp. 1, 9.

64. Barnum, "The Art of Money Getting," pp. 48–49. Compare with Catherine Beecher, *The Moral Instructor*, p. 145.

65. See Marden, *Pushing to the Front*, p. 763; Cowen, *Our Beacon Light*, p. 314; Wilson, *Wealth*, pp. 146–147.

66. Child, *American Frugal Housewife*, pp. 6–7.

67. Maria Edgeworth, *Popular Tales* (London: C. Mercier, 1805), pp. 301–375.

68. Edwin A. Kirkpatrick, *The Use of Money: How to Save and How to Spend* (Indianapolis, In.: Bobbs-Merrill, 1915), p. 20.

69. Marden, *Pushing to the Front*, p. 762.

70. Beecher, *Lectures to Young Men*, pp. 35–36.

71. William Cobbett, *Advice to Young Men* (New York: John Doyle, 1831), pp. 55–58.

72. Jacob Abbott, *Willie and the Mortgage* (New York: Harper & Bros., 1854), p. 95; Freeman Hunt, *Worth and Wealth* (New York: Stringer and Townsend, 1856), p. 363; Calvin Colton [Junius], *The Crisis of the Country* (Philadelphia: T. K. and P. G. Collins, 1840), pp. 4, 6, 12.

73. Thayer, *The Ethics of Success*, p. 284; Wilson, *Wealth*, p. 149; Beecher, *Lectures to Young Men*, p. 35; John Whipple, "The Usury Laws" (1855), in *Pamphlets on Economic Theory and Economic Conditions*, vol. 64 (Chicago: John Crerar Library), p. 26; Wise, *The Young Man's Counsellor*, p. 140; Barnum, *Dollars and Sense* p. 49.

74. Samuel Smiles, *Thrift* (New York: A. L. Burt, n.d.), p. 261.

75. "The middle class hell" is a term used by William Carleton [Frederic Orin Bartlett] in his allegedly autobiographical memoir *One*

Way Out: A Salary-Drawing New Englander Emigrates to America (New York: Grosset & Dunlap, 1911), p. 47. The terror of economic failure as reflected in English novels of bankruptcy is explored by Barbara Weiss in *The Hell of the English: Bankruptcy and the Victorian Novel* (Cranbury, N.J.: Associated University Presses, 1986).

76. Howells, *The Rise of Silas Lapham*, p. 863.

77. Cotton Mather, *The Diary of Cotton Mather*, 2 vols. (New York: Frederick Ungar, n.d.), 1:136.

78. Cotton Mather, *Fair Dealing between Debtor and Creditor, A Very Brief Essay upon the Caution to Be Used about Coming In to Debt and Getting Out of It"* (Boston: B. Green, 1716).

79. Francis E. Clark, *Our Business Boys (What 83 Businessmen Say)* (Boston: D. Lothrop, 1884), p. 56.

80. The historiography on republicanism in the United States is voluminous, but one might start with two scholars who argue that republicanism and Protestantism were discourses that often merged in the thinking of nineteenth-century Americans: Isaac Kranmick, *Republicanism and Bourgeois Radicalism: Political Ideology in Late Eighteenth Century England and America* (Ithaca, N.Y.: Cornell, 1990), pp. 163–199; and Christopher Lasch, *The True and Only Heaven: Progress and Its Critics* (New York: W. W. Norton, 1991), pp. 170–202. The point made by both Kramnick and Lasch is worth making here: American republicans were not centered solely in the tradition of civic humanism, as made out by the revisionism of Pocock-Bailyn-Wood, but were heavily influenced by the ideas of both John Locke and by "work-ethic protestantism." The best recent overview of republicanism can be found in Daniel Rogers, "Republicanism: The Career of a Concept," *Journal of American History* 79 (June 1992): 11–38. For earlier views stressing the influence of republican ideas, see J.G.A. Pocock, *The Machiavellian Moment: Florentine Political Thought and the Atlantic Republican Tradition* (Princeton, N.J.: Princeton University Press, 1975); Bernard Bailyn, *The Ideological Origins of the American Revolution* (Cambridge, Mass.: Harvard University Press, 1967); Gordon Wood, *The Creation of the American Republic* (Chapel Hill: University of North Carolina Press, 1969); Robert E. Shalhope, "Toward a Republican Synthesis: The Emergence of an Understanding of Republicanism in American Historiography," *William and Mary Quarterly*, 3rd ser., 29 (January 1972): 49–80; and John F. Kasson, *Civilizing the Machine: Technology and Republican Values in America, 1776–1900* (New York: Viking Press, 1976), pp. 4–11, 14–17, 192–234.

81. Franklin, "Poor Richard Improved, 1758," pp. 1300–1302. All other quotations by Franklin come from this version of "The Way to Wealth." The most quoted Franklinism in the nineteenth century was probably "Tis hard for an empty bag to stand upright." Significantly, it has not survived into the twentieth.

82. John Todd, *The Young Man* (Northampton, Mass.: J. H. Butler, 1845), p. 63.

83. I. H. Mayer, *Domestic Economy, or How to Make Hard Times Good and Good Times Better* (Lancaster, Pa.: published by the author, 1893), p. 74.

84. Epigram quoted in Clarence Wassam, *The Salary Loan Business in New York City* (New York: Charities Publication Committee, 1908), p. 11; Browne [Artemus Ward], *Artemus Ward in London*, p. 71; Mark Twain and Charles Dudley Warner, *The Gilded Age: A Tale of Today* (1873; New York: New American Library, Meridian Classic, 1985), p. 193; Butler quoted in the *Nation*, 15 September 1887, p. 205; Beecher quoted in Barnum, *Dollars and Sense*, pp. 49–50.

85. William Van Doren, *Mercantile Morals* (New York: C. Scribner's Sons, 1852), p. 89.

86. Rieff's functionalist interpretation of culture is put forward in *The Triumph of the Therapeutic: Uses of Faith after Freud* (Chicago: University of Chicago Press, 1987), pp. 232–233.

87. See Mather's "A Christian at His Calling," in *The American Gospel of Success: Individualism and Beyond*, ed., Moses Rischin (Chicago: Quadrangle Books, 1965), pp. 27–28.

88. Adam Smith, *The Wealth of Nations* (New York: Collier, 1909), p. 291. The same idea is expressed in J. S. Mill, *Principles of Political Economy*, book III, ch. 11, number 2.

89. W. Cunningham, *The Use and Abuse of Money* (New York: C. Scribner's Sons, 1891), pp. 175–176.

90. Thomas Nixon Carver, "How to Use Farm Credit," quoted in Arthur W. Dunn, *Community Civics for City Schools* (Boston: D. C. Heath, 1921), p. 316.

91. "The Credit System," *Banker's Magazine* 42 (May 1888): 833.

92. George K. Holmes, "Private and Public Debt in the United States," *Bulletin of the Department of Labor* 1 (1895): 53–54.

93. Allan G. Bogue, *Money at Interest: The Farm Mortgage on the Middle Border* (Ithaca, N.Y.: Cornell University Press, 1955), pp. 1–4, 268–269, 271–272.

94. Cobbett, *Advice to a Young Man*, pp. 55–56.

95. Colton, *The Crisis of the Country*, p. 4.

96. H. L. Reade, *Money, and How to Make It* (New York: John P. Jewett, 1872), p. 565.

97. "A Charity Pawnshop," *Christian Union* 45, 23 April 1892, p. 791.

98. Robert P. Porter, "Public and Private Debts," *North American Review* 153 (November 1891): 619.

99. On speculation, see Cobbett, *Advice to a Young Man*, pp. 60–61; Francis Wayland, *The Moral Law of Accumulation*, 2nd ed. (Boston: Gould, Kendall & Lincoln, 1837), pp. 8–16; and Henry Clay, *Economics: An Introduction for the General Reader* (New York: Macmillan, 1918), pp. 67–88.

100. Reade, *Money, and How to Make It*, p. 559.

101. Barton Cheney, "Buying a House without Cash," *Ladies Home Journal* 15 (April 1898): 28; Erastus Wiman, "The Hope of a Home," *North American Review* 156 (February 1893): 231–233.

102. Reade, *Money, and How to Make It*, pp. 570–576.

103. Jonathon Gilmer Speed, "Pawnbrokers and the Poor," *Harper's Weekly* 36, 3 September 1892, 862.

104. Ernest Walter Lyman, *Financial Independence* (Chicago: Perry, 1907), p. 120.

105. Ibid.

106. See Atherton, *The Frontier Merchant in Mid-America*, pp. 142–153.

107. Barnum, *Dollars and Sense*, p. 50.

108. Fletcher, *The Diary of Calvin Fletcher*, 1:4–6.

109. Ibid., 1:238.

110. Ibid., 1:296–297, 300–301, 308.

111. Ibid., 1:320.

112. Ibid., 1:431.

113. Ibid., 2:49, 132.

114. Ibid., 2:464, n. 1.

115. Ibid., 2:208–209.

116. Ibid., 8:295–297

117. Ibid., 2:132.

118. Ibid., 2:187.

119. Ibid., 6:546, 569; 7:111.

120. Ibid., 7:35.

121. Ibid., 4:400.

122. Colin Campbell, *The Romantic Ethic and the Spirit of Modern Consumerism* (Oxford: Basil Blackwell, 1987), pp. 69, 95. Campbell is not the first to make this point. See Mark Twain, "The $30,000 Bequest," in *The $30,000 Bequest, and Other Stories* (New York: Harper & Bros., 1906), pp. 1–47.

CHAPTER 3
SMALL-LOAN LENDING AND THE RISE OF THE
PERSONAL FINANCE COMPANY

1. "National Debate Questions," *Rostrum*, no. 5 (January 1981): 10.

2. Exodus 22:25; Deuteronomy 23:19ff; Leviticus. 25:35ff. The Code in Deuteronomy allows that foreigners may be charged interest.

3. Aristotle *Politics* 1.10.1258^b.

4. John T. Noonan Jr., *The Scholastic Analysis of Usury* (Cambridge, Mass.: Harvard University Press, 1957), p. 2.

5. Quotations in this paragraph from Calvin's letter on usury are in Fernand Braudel, *Civilization and Capitalism, 15th–18th Century*, vol. 2: *The Wheels of Commerce*, trans, Sian Reynolds (New York: Harper & Row, 1982), p. 568; and Jeremy Bentham, *Usury Laws: Their Nature, Expediency, and Influence*, Economic Tracts No. IV (New York: Society for Political Education, 1881), p. 35.

6. For overviews of the history of usury see Benjamin N. Nelson, *The Idea of Usury: From Tribal Brotherhood to Universal Otherhood* (Princeton, N.J.: Princeton University Press, 1949), pp. xv–xvii, 1–4; and Braudel, *The Wheels of Commerce*, pp. 559–562.

7. Braudel, *The Wheels of Commerce*, p. 566.

8. Following the example of Great Britain in 1854, usury laws were repealed in Denmark in 1855, in Spain in 1856, in Sardinia, Holland, Norway, and Geneva in 1857, in Saxony and Sweden in 1864, in Belgium in 1865, and in Prussia and the North German Confederation in 1867.

9. A late nineteenth-century survey of usury laws in the United States can be found in David A. Wells, "Present Status of Usury Laws," in *Usury Laws: Their Nature, Expediency, and Influence*, pp. 61–66. The best historical survey of usury laws in the United States is still Louis N. Robinson and Rolf Nugent, *Regulation of the Small Loan Business* (New York: Russell Sage Foundation, 1935). See especially pp. 28–31, 65–66.

10. Blackstone quoted in Arthur H. Ham, *The Campaign against the*

Loan Shark (New York: Russell Sage Foundation, 1914), p. 3. Bentham's *Letters in Defense of Usury* (1787) appeared in many editions in the United States in the early nineteenth century.

11. Rolf Nugent, *Consumer Credit and Economic Stability* (New York: Russell Sage Foundation, 1939), pp. 59–61; Robinson and Nugent, *Regulation of the Small Loan Business*, pp. 30–31.

12. Their petition is reprinted in Franklin W. Ryan, *Usury and the Usury Laws* (Boston: Houghton Mifflin, 1924), pp. 197–200.

13. Robinson and Nugent, *Regulation of the Small Loan Business*, p. 37.

14. Ibid., p. 43.

15. Ibid., pp. 38–47.

16. Ibid., p. 38.

17. *A History of Household Finance Corporation* (Chicago: Household Finance, 1965), p. 7; Clarence Wassam, *The Salary Loan Business in New York City* (New York: Charities Publication Committee, 1908), p. 42; Robinson and Nugent, *Regulation of the Small Loan Business*, p. 47.

18. Susan Strasser, *Satisfaction Guaranteed: The Making of the American Mass Market* (New York: Pantheon Books, 1989), pp. 222. According to Strasser, Cincinnati's Great Western Tea Company (Later the Kroger Grocery and Baking Company) operated 36 stores in 1902, while Frank R. Woolworth had 59 five-cent stores in 1900. That same year, McCrory had 20 stores, Kress 11, and S. S. Kresge still only 1.

19. Arthur H. Ham, "Remedial Loans as Factors in Family Rehabilitation," *Proceedings of the National Conference of Charities and Correction* (New York: Russell Sage Foundation, Department of Remedial Loans, 1911), p. 11.

20. Clipping, Box 39:2, Russell Sage Foundation files, Rockefeller Archive Center, North Tarrytown, N.Y.

21. Case reported in Rudolph Blankenburg, *Report of the Operations of the Citizen's Permanent Relief Committee of Philadelphia in Relieving Distress in the City during the Winter of 1893–1894* (Philadelphia: Loag Printing House, 1894), pp. 52–53.

22. Robinson and Nugent, *Regulation of the Small Loan Business*, p. 57; Blankenburg, *Report of the City's Permanent Relief Committee*, pp. 31–55; Victor K. Meador, *Loan Sharks in Georgia* (n.p.: Junior Bar Conference, American Bar Association, 1949), pp. 1–5.

23. Robinson and Nugent, *Regulation of the Small Loan Business*, pp. 76–79.

24. *The Provident Loan Society of New York: Fifty Years of Remedial Lending* (New York: the Society, 1944), pp. 1–5, 30; Rolf Nugent, *The Provident Loan Society of New York: An Account of the Largest Remedial Loan Society* (New York: Russell Sage Foundation, 1932), pp. 8–17, 51.

25. David J. Gallert, Walter S. Hilborn, and Geoffrey May, *Small Loan Legislation: A History of the Regulation of the Business of Lending Small Sums* (New York: Russell Sage Foundation, 1932), pp. 13–14, 18–52; Robinson and Nugent, *Regulation of the Small Loan Business*, pp. 65–66.

26. See Gallert et. al., *Small Loan Legislation*, p. 18; John M. Glenn, Lilian Brandt, and F. Emerson Andrews, *Russell Sage Foundation, 1907–1946*, 2 vols. (New York: Russell Sage Foundation, 1947), 1:144; Irving S. Michelman, *Consumer Finance: A Case History in American Business* (New York: Frederick Fell, 1966), p. 139.

27. Robinson and Nugent, *Regulation of the Small Loan Business*, p. 29.

28. U.S. Congress, House, Representative Fiorella La Guardia speaking against national legislation to amend the state usury laws, 72nd Cong., 2nd sess., 10 December 1932, *Congressional Record* 76: 291.

29. Quoted in Michelman, *Consumer Finance*, p. 17.

30. In La Guardia, *Congressional Record*, p. 291.

31. Glenn al., *Russell Sage Foundation*, 1:3–11.

32. W. Frank Persons, "Personal Finance in the Credit Field," *Personal Finance News* 17 (September 1932): 4; Glenn, et al., *Russell Sage Foundation*, 1:19, 136.

33. For biographical information on Ham, see Michelman, *Consumer Finance*, pp. 45–52, 68–71, 82–85.

34. Arthur H. Ham, *The Chattel Loan Business* (New York: Russell Sage Foundation, 1909), p. 2.

35. See Louis R. Harrison, "The Usurer's Grip," *Moving Picture World*, 5 October 1912, pp. 22–25.

36. Michelman, *Consumer Finance*, p. 127.

37. Ham's activities in the first year of his appointment are covered in Glenn et al., *Russell Sage Foundation*, pp. 139–141.

38. Herbert Corey, "Franklin Brooks," *System* (February 1913): 23, 164–168.

39. Charles F. Bigelow, *Proceedings of the National Federation of Remedial Loan Societies* (n.p., 1909), pp. 42–43.

40. Ham, "Remedial Loans as a Factor in Family Rehabilitation," pp. 3–4, 8.

41. Ham, *The Chattel Loan Business*, pp. 36–37.

42. Glenn et al., *Russell Sage Foundation*, pp. 137–138.

43. Ibid., p. 142.

44. Ibid., pp. 138–139; Robinson and Nugent, *Regulation of the Small Loan Business*, pp. 97–99.

45. Robinson and Nugent, *Regulation of the Small Loan Business*, pp. 97, 133. By their tally, from 1904 to 1933 the number of bills affecting small loans numbered 1,078.

46. Ibid., pp. 97–98.

47. Arthur H. Ham, "Report of the Year's Progress," *Bulletin of the National Federation of Remedial Loan Societies* 1 (1912): 17; H. A. Cone, "Situation in Detroit," ibid. p. 20.

48. Michelman, *Financing the Consumer*, pp. 130–133.

49. Glenn et al., *Russell Sage Foundation*, p. 141.

50. Robinson and Nugent, *Regulation of the Small Loan Business*, pp. 103–104.

51. The last paper to decline revenues from the loan sharks was Joseph Pulitzer's *New York World*.

52. Glenn et al., *Russell Sage Foundation*, p. 141.

53. Ibid., p. 145.

54. Robinson and Nugent, *Regulation of the Small Loan Business*, pp. 113–115.

55. The complete draft of the Uniform Small Loan Law can be found in Gallert et al., *Small Loan Legislation*, pp. 90–94.

56. The progress of the Uniform Small Loan Law is given in detail in ibid., pp. 99–107; and Robinson and Nugent, *Regulation of the Small Loan Business*, pp. 118–134.

57. H. A. Cone, *Proceedings of the National Federation of Remedial Loan Societies* (1909), p. 36.

58. Robinson and Nugent, *Regulation of the Small Loan Business*, p. 113.

59. Michelman, *Consumer Finance*, p. 117.

60. *Loan Gazette* 1 (July 1916): 1.

61. On the history of professionalization, see Robert H. Wiebe, *The Search for Order* (New York: Hill & Wang, 1967), pp. 111–163; Nathan O. Hatch, ed., *The Professions in America* (South Bend, Ind.: University of Notre Dame Press, 1988); Samuel Haber, *The Quest for Authority and*

Honor in the American Professions, 1750–1900 (Chicago: University of Chicago Press, 1991); and Bruce A. Kimball, *The Professionalization of America: The Emergence of the True Professional Ideal* (Cambridge, Mass.: Basil Blackwell, 1992).

62. M. R. Neifeld, *Personal Finance Comes of Age* (New York: Harper & Bros., 1939), p. 76.

63. From the statement of purpose, which is reprinted in Robinson and Nugent, *Regulation of the Small Loan Business*, p. 113.

64. *Loan Gazette* 1 (September 1916): 2.

65. Ibid., p. 1.

66. Robinson and Nugent, *Regulation of the Small Loan Business*, pp. 139–140.

67. Clarence Hodson, *Financing the Workingman* (New York: Legal Reform Bureau to Eliminate the Loan Shark Evil, 1922), p. 7.

68. *Industrial Lenders News* 5 (August 1920): 7–8. A list of reformed practices is given in Clarence Hodson, "What the American Association Has Accomplished," *Loan Gazette* 2 (July 1917): 1–2.

69. Ibid., pp. 1–2.

70. *Industrial Lenders News* 10 (April 1926): 5.

71. Evans Clark, *Financing the Consumer* (New York: Harper & Bros., 1930), p. 30. Clark estimated, based on figures from Leon Henderson, Ham's replacement at the Division of Remedial Loans, that illegal lenders advanced $750 million in 1929, compared with the personal finance companies' $500 million. Illegal lenders were estimated to serve three million borrowers, compared with the licensed lenders' two million.

72. The tactics of salary-buying are described in Gallert et al., *Small Loan Legislation*, pp. 218–233; and in Robinson and Nugent, *Regulation of the Small Loan Business*, pp. 157–161.

73. *Loan Gazette* 1 (September 1916): 2.

74. Hodson, *Financing the Workingman*, p. 9.

75. Clarence Hodson, *Anti-Loan Shark License Laws and Economics of the Small Loan Business* (New York: Legal Reform Bureau to Eliminate the Loan Shark Evil, n.d.), p. 5.

76. Rolf Nugent, "The Loan Shark Problem," *Law and Contemporary Problems*, Duke University School of Law, 8 (Winter 1941): 7.

77. Glenn, et al., *Russell Sage Foundation*, p. 342.

78. Ibid., p. 344; *Better Business Bureau Bulletin*, Kansas City, Mo., 6 June 1928, p. 1.

79. Michelman, *Consumer Finance*, pp. 239–241.

80. By 1932, the Uniform Small Loan Law was on the books of all the

industrial states, and in many of the partially industrial states. According to Robinson and Nugent, the states that did not possess adequate regulatory loan laws were dominated by "agricultural communities, who have little conception of the small loan problem and who oppose any relaxation of the general statutes restricting interest rates." See *Regulation of the Small Loan Business*, p. 137.

81. Daniel T. Rodgers, "In Search of Progressivism," *Reviews in American History* 10 (December 1982): 124–126.

82. Reprinted in *Industrial Lenders News* 3 (November 1918): 3.

83. Ham, "Remedial Loans as Factors in Family Rehabilitation," p. 4.

84. *Chicago Commerce*, 6 June 1925.

85. *Industrial Lenders News* 5 (November 1920): 4–5.

86. *Industrial Lenders News* 11 (April 1927): 9.

87. Samuel Spring, "Is There Enough Banking?" *Industrial Lenders News* 5 (June 1921): 7.

88. Robert Kreps, "What the Loan Office Needs in the Way of Advertising," *Industrial Lenders News* 9 (May 1925): 6.

89. Clarence Hodson, *Money-Lenders, License Laws, and the Business of Making Small Loans* (New York: Legal Reform Bureau to Eliminate the Loan Shark Evil, 1919), p. 53.

90. Benjamin Blumburg, "The Industrial Borrower and Legislation," *Industrial Lenders News* 5 (July 1920): 2.

91. Ibid.

92. Ibid.

93. Ibid.

94. Edgar F. Fowler, "The Licensed Lender," *Annals of the American Academy of Political and Social Science* 196 (March 1938): 133–134.

95. *Personal Finance News* 16 (November 1931): 8.

96. Charles W. Wild, "Mobilizing an Advanced Guard," *Personal Finance News* 20 (November 1935): 17.

97. Clark, *Financing the Consumer*, p. 45.

98. Neifeld, *Personal Finance Comes of Age*, p. 14; Clark, *Financing the Consumer*, p. 30.

99. M. R. Neifeld, *The Personal Finance Business* (New York: Harper & Bros., 1933), p. 138.

100. Neifeld, *The Personal Finance Business*, p. 138; Nugent, *Consumer Credit and Economic Stability*, p. 99.

101. Neifeld, *The Personal Finance Business*, p. 139.

102. Clark, *Financing the Consumer*, pp. 48–60; Robinson and Nugent, *Regulation of the Small Loan Business*, pp. 142–143.

103. Glenn et al., *Russell Sage Foundation*, p. 345; Michelman, *Consumer Finance*, pp. 189–190.

104. Solomon Kuznets, after examining the evidence drawn from lenders' files, pronounced it "scarcely worth considering." Studies built on such data, in his words, "do not encourage optimism" for ever coming up with reliable statistical information about who borrowed, and why. Solomon Kuznets, "Statistics of Consumer Credit" (Washington, D.C., 1934, mimeograph).

105. Attempting to make generalizations based on loan company records, I examined all of the following sources, which are offered here as a partial list of available loan records and investigative studies: (1) fifteen thousand applicants to the Provident Loan Society, Milwaukee, 1905–1911, in J. H. Rubin, *Proceedings of the National Federation of Remedial Loan Societies* (Boston, 1911), pp. 27–28; (2) Atlanta Loan & Saving Co., 1914, in Hodson, *Money-Lenders*, pp. 53–56; (3) five Chicago loan offices, 1916 [?], in Hodson, *Money-Lenders*, pp. 59–76; (4) one hundred loan offices, 1922–1923, Louis N. Robinson and Maude E. Stearns, *Ten Thousand Small Loans* (New York: Russell Sage Foundation, 1930); (5) 2,444 borrowers from a "typical" office, *Industrial Lenders News* 9 (August 1924): 8; (6) Willford Isbell King, *The Small Loan Situation in New Jersey in 1929* (Trenton, N.J.: New Jersey Industrial Lenders Association, 1929); (7) 23,478 borrowers from a "typical" large company in 1928–1929, in Neifeld, *The Personal Finance Business*, pp. 162–212; (8) report to Wisconsin legislature, 1929, in *Personal Finance News* 14 (January 1930): 13; (9) interview with L. C. Harbison, president of Household Finance Corp., 100,810 borrowers in 1930, in *Personal Finance News* 14 (March 1930): 11–13; (10) 335,000 borrowers in 1934, *Bulletin of the Household Finance Corporation* (Chicago, 1934), p. 14; (11) various studies, 1930–1936, in Neifeld, *Personal Finance Comes of Age*, pp. 126–135; (12) Ralph A. Young and associates, *Personal Finance Companies and Their Credit Practices*, Studies in Consumer Instalment Financing, no. 1 (New York: National Bureau of Economic Research, 1940).

106. Charles F. Bigelow, "The New Borrower," *Proceedings of the National Federation of Remedial Loan Societies* (Newark, N.J.: 1920), pp. 12–16.

107. Ibid., p. 16.

108. *Proceedings of the National Federation of Remedial Loan Societies* (n.p., 1924), p. 2.

109. See the studies listed in note 105.

110. Franklin W. Ryan, "The Fundamental Rightfulness of the Family Finance Business," *Industrial Lenders News* 14 (November 1929): 1–4; Franklin W. Ryan, "Financing the American Family during 1930 and 1931," *Personal Finance News* 16 (May 1932): 10–12.

111. Neifeld, *The Personal Finance Business*, pp. 174.

112. Franklin W. Ryan, "The Future of the Small Loan Business," *Industrial Lenders News* 12 (April 1928): 3.

113. Mary Ross, "The Family Welfare Aspects of the Small Loan Business," *Personal Finance News* 14 (January 1930): 13. An interesting report on Household Finance Corporation's educational booth at the 1939 New York World's Fair appeared in *Personal Finance News* 24 (June 1940): 17.

114. Walter Schafer, "Fair Dealing in Earning Public Confidence," *Personal Finance News* 20 (December 1935): 6.

115. Burr Blackburn, "Financial Consultation Services," *Personal Finance News* 16 (January 1932): 22.

116. *Industrial Lenders News* 12 (April 1928): 3; "The Financial Doctor," *Personal Finance News* 18 (February 1934): 17; *Personal Finance News* 24 (June 1940): 17; Frank Parker, "Rationalization of Consumer Credit," *Personal Finance News* 16 (August 1931): 6.

CHAPTER 4
HARD PAYMENTS: THE RISE OF INSTALLMENT SELLING

1. Popular accounts of the history of installment credit usually say it was invented by Crassus, the Roman statesman of legendary wealth. The story appears to have originated with E.R.A. Seligman, who told of how Crassus used the installment plan to gain control of half of Rome through speculative real-estate ventures. Seligman cited Plutarch, but Plutarch makes no mention of Crassus's credit terms. Seligman also reports that houses and land were sold on installments in ancient Egypt and the great cities of classical antiquity. Whether this is true or not is hard to tell, given that his sources are obscure documents not easily checked. See Edwin R. A. Seligman, *The Economics of Instalment Selling: A Study in Consumers' Credit*, 2 vols. (New York: Harper & Bros., 1927), 1:10–11.

2. *Oxford English Dictionary*, 2nd ed., *s.v.* "instalment," "stalment," and "e'stall." The Pilgrims' credit history figures prominently in William Bradford's *Of Plymouth Plantation, 1620–1647* (New York: Modern Library, 1967), pp. 36–46, 93–96, 184–188, 194–200, 213–215, 399–403.

3. For examples, see Ralph Harris, Margot Naylor, and Arthur Selden, *Hire Purchase in a Free Society* (London: Institute of Economic Affairs, 1961), p. 20; and Rolf Nugent, *Consumer Credit and Economic Stability* (New York: Russell Sage Foundation, 1939), p. 54.

4. Harris et al., *Hire Purchase in a Free Society*, pp. 20–21. In popular histories of the installment plan, the countess of Blessington is sometimes credited, erroneously, with bringing the installment plan to America. See Christine Frederick, *Selling Mrs. Consumer* (New York: Business Bourse, 1929), p. 380.

5. Seligman, *Economics of Instalment Selling*, 1:14–15; Julian Goldman, *Prosperity and Consumer Credit* (New York: Harper & Bros., 1930), pp. 6–9.

6. Richard Y. Giles, *Credit for the Millions: The Story of Credit Unions* (New York: Harper & Bros., 1951), pp. 61–63; Carl W. Drepperd, *American Clocks and Clockmakers* (Garden City, N.Y.: Doubleday, 1947), pp. 77, 79, 90–91.

7. Rolf Nugent, *Consumer Credit and Economic Stability* (New York: Russell Sage Foundation, 1939), p. 56.

8. "Land Act of 1800," *Annals of America* (Chicago: Encyclopaedia Britannica, 1976), 4:129. Statistics are from Samuel Eliot Morison, *The Oxford History of the American People* (New York: Oxford University Press, 1965), p. 404.

9. Noah Webster, *A Dictionary of the English Language* (1828), *s.v.* "installment."

10. Ad is in Margaret G. Myers, *A Financial History of the United States* (New York: Columbia University Press, 1970), p. 105; Webster, *A Dictionary of the English Language, s.v.* "installment."

11. On the mechanization of agriculture, see Allan G. Bogue, *From Prairie to Corn Belt: Farming on the Illinois and Iowa Prairies in the Nineteenth Century* (Chicago: University of Chicago Press, 1963), pp. 148–168: Graeme R. Quick and Wesley F. Buchele, *The Grain Harvesters* (St. Joseph, Mich.: American Society of Agricultural Engineers, 1978), pp. 1–112; John T. Schlebecker, *Whereby We Thrive: A History of American Farming, 1607–1972* (Ames: Iowa State University Press, 1975), pp. 113–120; Joseph Schafer, *The Social History of American Agriculture* (New York: Macmillan, 1936), pp. 83–89.

12. Price lists of machinery and estimates of income can be found in Bogue, *From Prairie to Corn Belt*, pp. 167–168, 250–258; and Quick and Buchele, *The Grain Harvesters*, p. 32.

13. Stewart H. Holbrook, *Machines of Plenty: Pioneering in American Agriculture* (New York: Macmillan, 1955), p. 34.

14. Cyrus McCormick, *The Century of the Reaper* (New York: Houghton, Mifflin, 1931), pp. 50–51; Robert A. Lynn, "Installment Credit before 1870," *Business History Review* 31 (Winter 1957): 415–417. Advertisements for reapers often listed credit terms. For examples, see *The Prairie Farmer* 13 (May 1853): 211; *Emory's Journal of Agriculture* 2, 23 December 1858, p. 411.

15. William T. Hutchinson, *Cyrus Hall McCormick: Seed-Time, 1809–1856* (New York: Century, 1930), pp. 362–363; William T. Hutchinson, *Cyrus Hall McCormick: Harvest, 1856–1884* (New York: Century, 1935), pp. 71–75, 469–471; McCormick, *Century of the Reaper*, pp. 51–52.

16. Quoted in Holbrook, *Machines of Plenty*, p. 36.

17. Charles Barnard, "A Hundred Thousand Homes: How They Were Paid For," *Scribner's Monthly* 11 (February 1876): 487; H. Morton Bodfish, *History of Building and Loan in the United States* (Chicago: U.S. Building and Loan League, 1931), p. 134; Horace Russell, *Savings and Loan Associations* (New York: Matthew Bender, 1956), p. 26.

18. Nugent, *Consumer Credit and Economic Stability*, pp. 55, 66; Illinois Bureau of Labor Statistics, "Statistics of Mortgages," *Fifth Biennial Report* (1888), pp. lxxxiv, xcvi; Lynn, "Installment Credit before 1870," pp. 420–422.

19. Frederick G. Bourne, "American Sewing Machines," in *One Hundred Years of American Commerce*, ed. Chauncey M. Depew, 2 vols. (New York: D. O. Haynes, 1895), 2:525–539; Ruth Brandon, *Singer and the Sewing Machine: A Capitalist Romance* (London: Barrie & Jenkins, 1977), pp. 34–99; Andrew B. Jack, "The Channels of Distribution for an Innovation: The Sewing-Machine Industry in America, 1860–1865," *Explorations in Entrepreneurial History* 9 (February 1957): 114–118.

20. *Scientific American* 3, 22 September 1860, p. 195.

21. Sarah Hale, "Value of a Sewing Machine," *Godey's Lady's Book and Magazine* 74 (January 1867): 192.

22. *Scientific American* 7, 17 July 1852, p. 349. For the social repercussions of the sewing machine, see James Parton, "The History of the Sewing Machine," *Atlantic Monthly* 19 (May 1867): 541; Susan Strasser, *Never Done: A History of American Housework* (New York: Pantheon Books, 1982), pp. 131–137.

23. Robert Bruce Davies, *Peacefully Working to Conquer the World: Singer Sewing Machines in Foreign Markets, 1854–1920* (New York: Arno Press, 1976), pp. 20–22.

24. Parton, "The History of the Sewing Machine," p. 540.

25. Brandon, *Singer and the Sewing Machine*, pp. 101, 116; Davies, *Peacefully Working to Conquer the World*, p. 56.

26. For a typical advertisement emphasizing the beauty of a sewing machine, see the Singer ad in *Emory's Journal of Agriculture* 2, 23 December 1858, p. 411.

27. Sales resistance, design, and innovative marketing techniques are covered in Jack, "The Channels of Distribution for an Innovation: The Sewing-Machine Industry in America, 1860–1865," pp. 122–132; and Brandon, *Singer and the Sewing Machine*, pp. 115–128.

28. In addition to installment selling, Clark developed several marketing innovations that became widely copied. These included the franchise system of distribution (in Singer's case, each employed a salesman, a mechanic, and a female demonstrator), the old-model "trade-in" for new models, and the practice of "loss leading," in which Singer sold machines at a deep discount to public opinion leaders such as newspaper editors and the wives of clergymen. See Jack, "The Channels of Distribution for an Innovation: The Sewing-Machine Industry in America, 1860–1865," pp. 122–132; Brandon, *Singer and the Sewing Machine*, pp. 117–133.

29. Quoted in Brandon, *Singer and the Sewing Machine*, p. 117.

30. This coincidence is noted in Lynn, "Installment Credit before 1870," p. 423.

31. Davies, *Peacefully Working to Conquer the World*, p. 20; Brandon, *Singer and the Sewing Machine*, p. 117.

32. Bourne, "American Sewing Machines," p. 530.

33. Davies, *Peacefully Working to Conquer the World*, pp. 56–61; Brandon, *Singer and the Sewing Machine*, pp. 112–113, 118.

34. Craig H. Roell, *The Piano in America, 1890–1940* (Chapel Hill: University of North Carolina Press, 1989), pp. 99–101.

35. R. M. Goode, *Hire-Purchase Law and Practice* (London: Butterworths, 1962), pp. 1–3; E. Campbell-Salmon, *Hire-Purchase and Credit Sales: Law and Practice* (London: Sir Isaac Pitman and Sons, 1962), pp. 1–2; and Roy E. Maskell, *The Hire-Purchase and Instalment Habit: Trends in Australia, New Zealand, Great Britain, and the USA* (Melbourne: Law Book Company of Australasia, 1964), pp. 14–16.

36. Willis A. Estrich, *The Law of Installment Sales of Goods* (Rochester, N.Y.: Lawyers' Co-operative Publishing, 1926), pp. 3, 77–

78, 105–143; Roger Sherman Hoar, *Conditional Sales: Law and Local Practices* (New York: Ronald Press, 1929), pp. v, 3; National Commission on Consumer Finance, *Consumer Credit in the United States* (Washington, D.C.: Government Printing Office, 1972), pp. 27–30.

37. These references are given in Mitford M. Mathews, ed., *A Dictionary of Americanisms on Historical Principles* (1951), *s.v.* "instalment."

38. Charles Macomb Flandrau, *Harvard Episodes* (Boston: Copeland and Day, 1897), p. 91; Charles Fort, *The Outcast Manufacturers* (New York: B. W. Dodge, 1909), p. 317.

39. Dorothy S. Brady, "Relative Prices in the Nineteenth Century," *Journal of Economic History* 24 (June 1964): 175–176; Harold G. Vatter, "Has There Been a Twentieth-Century Consumer Durable Revolution?" *Journal of Economic History* 27 (March 1967): 9–10.

40. William Howard Shaw, *Value of Commodity Output since 1869* (New York: National Bureau of Economic Research, 1947), pp. 8–9, 17, 28. Martha Olney provides a full breakdown of these figures in *Buy Now, Pay Later: Advertising, Credit, and Consumer Durables in the 1920s* (Chapel Hill: University of North Carolina Press, 1991), pp. 6–56.

41. Melvyn Dubofsky summarizes the relevant literature on wages in the period, and makes the necessary qualifications, in *Industrialism and the American Worker, 1865–1920* (Arlington Heights, Ill.: AHM Publishing, 1975), pp. 13–19.

42. Nugent, *Consumer Credit and Economic Stability*, p. 67.

43. Massachusetts Bureau of Statistics of Labor, *Thirtieth Annual Report, March, 1900*, p. 5.

44. Ibid., pp. 51–56. Quotation is from p. 54.

45. Ibid., pp. 49–51. Quotation is from p. 50.

46. On the new mass retailing, see William R. Leach, *Land of Desire: Merchants, Power, and the Rise of a New American Culture* (New York: Vintage Books, 1994); Susan Strasser, *Satisfaction Guaranteed: The Making of the American Mass Market* (New York: Pantheon Books, 1989), pp. 203–251; Neil Harris, "Museums, Merchandising, and Popular Taste: The Struggle for Influence," in *Cultural Excursions: Marketing Appetites and Cultural Tastes in Modern America* (Chicago: University of Chicago Press, 1990), pp. 63–66; Susan Porter Benson, *Counter Cultures: Saleswomen, Managers, and Customers in American Department Stores* (Urbana: University of Illinois Press, 1986); and Boris Emmet and John E. Jeuck, *Catalogues and Counters: A History of Sears, Roebuck, and Company* (Chicago: University of Chicago Press, 1950).

47. Massachusetts Bureau of Statistics of Labor, *Thirtieth Annual Report*, pp. 40–41, 45, 48–58. Quotation is from p. 45.

48. Ibid., p. 50.

49. Elizabeth Beardsley Butler, *Women and the Trades: Pittsburgh, 1907–1908* (Pittsburgh: University of Pittsburgh Press, 1984), p. 347.

50. Louise Odencrantz, *Italian Women in Industry* (New York: Russell Sage Foundation, 1919), p. 233.

51. William Dean Howells, *The Minister's Charge* (Boston: Houghton Mifflin, 1886), p. 206.

52. Massachusetts Bureau of Statistics of Labor, *Thirtieth Annual Report*, p. 49.

53. Upton Sinclair, *The Jungle* (1906; New York: Bantam Books, 1981), pp. 1–29.

54. The most prominent installment houses were the Siegel-Cooper Store, the May, Stern and Company, and the Boston Store. See Orange A. Smalley and Frederick D. Sturdivant, *The Credit Merchants: A History of Spiegel, Inc.* (Carbondale: University of Southern Illinois Press, 1973), pp. 25–26.

55. Sinclair, *The Jungle*, pp. 53–55.

56. Smalley and Sturdivant, *The Credit Merchants*, pp. 23–33.

57. Ibid., pp. 43–50.

58. Ibid., pp. 50, 81–82, 98.

59. According to Louise Bolard More, installment buying was "almost universal" among the families she visited. See her *Wage-Earners' Budgets: A Study of Standards and Cost of Living in New York City* (New York: Henry Holt, 1907), p. 145. A similar finding was reported by Louise Odencratz in *Italian Women in Industry*, pp. 232–233. For other cities, see Margaret F. Byington, *Homestead: The Households of a Mill Town* (New York: Charities Publication Committee, 1910), p. 85; U.S. Bureau of Labor, "Conditions of Living among the Poor," *Bulletin of the Bureau of Labor* 12 (1906): 633; Kansas Bureau of Labor, "Chattel Mortgages," *Second Annual Report of the Bureau of Labor* 2 (1887): 101. Impressionistic testimony on the popularity of installment buying among the lower classes can be found in William Harmon, "Capital and Labor Unified: An Essay on the Application of the Instalment System to Investments," *Proceedings of the Academy of Political Science in the City of New York* 2 (October 1911): 9; and Marion Foster Washburne, "A Trap for the Newly Married," *Ladies' Home Journal* 26 (April 1909): 14.

60. Henry R. Mussey, *The Fake Instalment Business* (New York: Uni-

versity Settlement Society, 1904; reprint, New York: Russell Sage Foundation, 1936), p. 14.

61. Ibid., p. 10.

62. Ibid., pp. 11–14.

63. Ibid., pp. 15, 42–43. Quotation is on p. 42.

64. Ibid., pp. 43–44; Herbert Tetenbaum, "The Survival of the Installment Peddlar," *Journal of Retailing* 16 (February 1940): 11–13; Elizabeth Ewen, *Immigrant Women in the Land of Dollars* (New York: Monthly Review Press, 1985), p. 170.

65. Samuel Chotzinoff, *A Lost Paradise: Early Reminiscences* (New York: A. A. Knopf, 1955), pp. 113, 122–124.

66. Marie Jastrow, *A Time to Remember: Growing Up in New York before the Great War* (New York: W. W. Norton, 1979), pp. 147–155.

67. Andrew Heinze, *Adapting to Abundance: Jewish Immigrants, Mass Consumption, and the Search for American Identity* (New York: Columbia University Press, 1990), pp. 47–48.

68. Mussey, *The Fake Instalment Business*, pp. 18–33.

69. Ibid.

70. Ibid., p. 32.

71. *The Century Dictionary: An Encyclopedic Lexicon of the English Language* (1899), *s.v.* "instalment plan."

72. Milan Ayres, "Forecasting the Future of Financing," an address before the eighth annual meeting of the National Association of Personal Finance Companies, Chicago, 17 November 1931, Library of Congress, Washington, D.C.

73. Ibid.

74. C. W. Tabor, *The Business of the Household* (Philadelphia: J. B. Lippincott, 1918), p. 90. The same claim is made in Margaret Sangster's editorial column, "Bankrupt Wage-Earners and Wives," *Harper's Bazar* 33 (December 1900): 2210.

75. Wilbur Plummer, "Social and Economic Consequences of Buying on the Instalment Plan," *Annals of the American Academy of Political and Social Science* 129, suppl. (January 1927): 50.

76. *Scientific American* 51, 9 August 1884, p. 80; 4 October 1884, p. 217.

77. Corra Harris, "On the Instalment Plan," *Harper's Monthly Magazine* 127 (August 1913): 342–343.

78. Ibid., pp. 342–353.

79. Quoted in Goldman, *Prosperity and Consumer Credit*, pp. 30–31.

80. Frank Parker, "The Pay-as-You-Use-Idea," *Annals of the American Academy of Political and Social Science* 196 (March 1938): 59.

81. Evans Clark, *Financing the Consumer* (New York: Harper & Bros., 1930), p. 20.

82. Furniture was second, accounting for less than one-fourth of retail credit sales. See Seligman, *Economics of Instalment Selling*, 1:98–119; Olney, *Buy Now, Pay Later*, pp. 93, 96.

83. *Chicago Tribune*, 6 June, 1909, sec. 9, p. 17; 5 June 1910, sec. 10, p. 19; 4 June 1911, sec. 10, p. 19. I surveyed the classified ads in the *Tribune* from 1900 to 1925, using for my sample the first Sunday in June.

84. Quoted in Richard S. Tedlow, *New and Improved: The Story of Mass Marketing in America* (New York: Basic Books, 1990), pp. 118–119.

85. John B. Rae, *The American Automobile: A Brief History* (Chicago: University of Chicago Press, 1965), p. 200; Tedlow, *New and Improved*, p. 118.

86. In his biography of General Motors, Sloan divided the history of the automobile into three periods: the "class" era (to 1908), the "mass" era (1908–1925), and the "mass-class" era (1925 on). See *My Years with General Motors* (Garden City, NY: Doubleday, 1964), p. 150.

87. Model T prices are in John Bell Rae, *The American Automobile* (Boston, Mass.: Twayne Publishers, 1984), p. 61. Salary figures from U.S. Bureau of the Census, *Historical Statistics of the United States, Colonial Times to 1970* (Washington, D.C.: Government Printing Office, 1975), 1:167–168.

88. "Terms to City Buyers" offered by the Cole Motor Co., in the *Chicago Tribune*, 2 June 1912, sec. 8, p. 8.

89. William A. Grimes, *Financing Automobile Sales by the Time-Payment Plan* (Chicago: A. W. Shaw, 1926), pp. 11, 33.

90. For the history and theory of the sales finance company, see Seligman, *Economics of Instalment Selling*, 1:33–43; William A. Grimes, *The Story of Commercial Credit Company* (Baltimore, 1946), pp. 1–5; Grimes, *Financing Automobile Sales by the Time-Payment Plan*, pp. 13, 17–18; Carl A. Dauten, *Financing the American Consumer*, Consumer Credit Monograph, no. 1 (St. Louis: American Investment Company of Illinois, 1956), p. 52. Martha Olney also provides valuable information on the genesis of sales finance companies. Olney argues that manufacturers set up sales finance companies almost entirely as a production-smoothing device. It is true that manufacturers wanted to help out their dealers, but, as my evidence shows, the needs of customers were equally

high on their minds. In other words, both manufacturing and marketing imperatives were important in setting up the first sales finance companies. See *Buy Now, Pay Later*, pp. 118–130.

91. *Saturday Evening Post*, 8 April 1916, pp. 28–29.

92. In 1916, the National Automobile Chamber of Commerce passed a resolution warning that the advertising of deferred payments was likely to hurt the business and was "not in keeping with the standards of the business." This was reported in *Automobile Trade Journal* 29, 1 December 1924, p. 57.

93. Grimes, *The Story of Commercial Credit*, p. 26.

94. Edward A. Rumely to Edsel Ford, 16 April 1916, Acc. 6, Box 253, Ford Motor Company archives, Dearborn, Michigan. The memo was originally written to Gaston Plaintiff, FMC's New York branch manager. But Rumely sent the memo on to Detroit, noting in a cover letter that "developments here in New York in the 'Credit' situation are rapid." He also passed along a copy of Guarantee's ad in the *Saturday Evening Post*.

95. For more on this problem, see J. A. Estey, "Financing the Sale of Automobiles," *Annals of the American Academy of Social and Political Science* 116 (November 1924): 44.

96. Edward A. Rumely to Edsel Ford, 16 April 1916, Acc. 6, Box 253, Ford Motor Company archives, Dearborn, Michigan.

97. Undated clipping (but with price figures for 1914) in Acc. 6, Box 253, Ford Motor Company archives, Dearborn, Michigan. Earlier, in 1909, Ford had explained his hard line to the dealers. "We cannot finance the business of 2,000 Ford Dealers," Ford told them. The reason: If the company accepted notes on delivery, it would drive automobile unit costs up and sales would decrease. Therefore, Ford advised dealers to "borrow to the limit" from their own sources. Showing little sympathy for the dealers' position, Ford warned them to stop their grousing: "The dealer who expects to do all his business on . . . the factory's money is not a satisfactory man for the factory to hook up with." See "What Constitutes a Satisfactory Automobile Dealer?" *Ford Times* 3, 1 December 1909, p. 5.

98. Edsel Ford to Clarence H. Booth, quoted in Allan Nevins and Frank Ernest Hill, *Ford, Expansion and Challenge, 1915–1933* (New York: C. Scribner's Sons, 1957), p. 148.

99. Rae, *The American Automobile*, pp. 62, 66–67; Arthur J. Kuhn, *GM Passes Ford, 1918–1938* (University Park: Pennsylvania State University Press, 1986), pp. 275, 280, 312–313.

100. Sloan, *My Years with General Motors*, pp. 150–151, 163, 302–303.

101. Seligman, *Economics of Instalment Selling*, 1:46, 48–51; Clyde William Phelps, *The Role of Sales Finance Companies in the American Economy* (Baltimore: Commercial Credit Company, 1952), pp. 57–58.

102. Estey, "Financing the Sale of Automobiles," p. 46.

103. Harry Emerson Wright, *The Financing of Automobile Sales* (Chicago: A. W. Shaw Company, 1927), pp. 30–31; E. W. Imberman, "Time Is Money: History of Motor Car Securities Corporation" (M.A. thesis, University of Chicago, 1965), pp. 18–20; H. Bertram Lewis, "Installment Facts Refute Installment Fancies," *Banker's Magazine* 113 (February 1926): 193.

104. Seligman, *Economics of Instalment Selling*, p. 50; Imberman, "Time Is Money: History of Motor Car Securities Corporation," pp. 29–53.

105. General Motors figures show that in 1919, 74.8 percent of their lowest-priced cars were sold on installments, while only 8.3 percent of their high-priced cars were sold on time. For 1925, the comparable figures were 68.6 percent and 28.7 percent respectively. See Seligman, *Economics of Instalment Selling*, 2:426–427.

106. Nevins and Hill, *Ford: Expansion and Challenge*, p. 264.

107. Ibid.

108. Kuhn, *GM Passes Ford, 1918–1938*, pp. 279–281; Seligman, *Economics of Instalment Selling*, 2:455; Tedlow, *New and Improved*, pp. 158–160.

109. "The Ford Plan," Acc. 6, Box 296, Ford Motor Company archives, Dearborn, Michigan; Nevins and Hill, *Ford: Expansion and Challenge*, pp. 268–269.

110. "The Ford Plan," Acc. 6, Box 296, Ford Motor Company archives, Dearborn, Michigan.

111. Reported in the *Denver Colorado News*, 8 April 1923, found in clipping file of Acc. 3, Box 1, Ford Motor Company archives, Dearborn, Michigan.

112. Quoted in Nevins and Hill, *Ford: Expansion and Challenge*, pp. 268–269.

113. *New York American*, 10 April 1923, in the clipping file of Acc. 3, Box 1, Ford Motor Company archives, Dearborn, Michigan.

114. *New York Times*, 30 May 1923, p. 21.

115. "Universal Credit Corporation Educational Manual" and "Con-

fidential Report of the Universal Credit Company," Acc. 33, Box 95, Ford Motor Company archives, Dearborn, Michigan; Kuhn, *GM Passes Ford*, pp. 312–313.

116. Quoted in David L. Cohn, *The Good Old Days: A History of American Manners and Morals as Seen through the Sears, Roebuck Catalogs 1905 to the Present* (New York: Simon and Schuster, 1940), p. 523.

117. *New York Times*, 3 June 1939, p. 22.

118. Arthur H. Hert, "Charge Accounts of Retail Merchants," *Annals of the American Academy of Political and Social Science* 196 (March 1938): 114.

119. Emmet and Jeuck, *Catalogues and Counters*, pp. 264–275.

120. Ibid., pp. 267–268.

121. Sales figures do not reflect this development, but then in the recession of 1920–1921 installment credit was adopted not so much to increase sales as to keep them from declining further. The consensus of many observers was that the postwar recession gave a giant boost to installment selling. See Goldman, *Prosperity and Consumer Credit*, pp. 16–17; and Cohn, *The Good Old Days*, pp. 525–526.

122. Arthur H. Hert, "Charge Accounts of Retail Merchants," *Annals of the American Academy of Political and Social Science* 196 (March 1938): 111–114.

123. Emmet and Jeuck, *Catalogues and Counters*, p. 506; James E. Brice, "Consumer Demand or Credit Accommodation Today," *Journal of Retailing* 12 (April 1936): 1.

124. James True, "The Rising Tide of Time Payments," *Printer's Ink* 126, 28 February 1924, p. 3.

125. John W. Stiers, "Will Installment Buying Affect Our Credit Structure," *Credit World* (August 1936): 31. See also George F. Johnson in J. M. Head, "Is the Installment Plan an Artificial Stimulus to Prosperity?" *Magazine of Wall Street*, 19 June 1926, p. 360; *Philadelphia Retail Ledger*, April 1926, p. 10; March 1926, p. 1.

126. J. Johnson in Wilbur C. Plummer, "Social and Economic Consequences of Buying on the Instalment Plan," p. 8; Robert S. Lynd and Helen Merrell Lynd, *Middletown: A Study in American Culture* (New York: Harcourt, Brace, 1929), pp. 255–256; Olney, *Buy Now, Pay Later*, pp. 56–85.

127. Clark, *Financing the Consumer*, pp. 13, 191; Robert S. Lynd, "The People as Consumers," in *Recent Social Trends in the United States* (New York: McGraw-Hill, 1933), p. 862.

128. Ray B. Westerfield, "Effect of Consumer Credit on the Business Cycle," *Annals of the American Academy of Political and Social Science* 196 (March 1938): 100–101.

129. Estimates based on figures from Seligman, *Economics of Instalment Selling*, pp. 112–114; *Encyclopaedia of the Social Sciences* (1933), *s.v.* "instalment selling," by Wilbur C. Plummer; and Lynd, "The People as Consumers," p. 862.

130. "Debtor's Cowardice," *Saturday Evening Post*, 11 February 1922, p. 23. The article may very well have been written by a banker in order to promote savings accounts. Other articles and stories in the 1920s also assumed that installment buyers were middle-class people. See "Please Remit," *Saturday Evening Post* 11 November 1922, p. 22; Clara Belle Thompson, "Charge It, Please," *Saturday Evening Post* 26 July 1924, p. 14; and William Ellis Jones, "Charge It!" *American Magazine* 99 (January 1925): 29.

131. On the percentage of households buying on the installment plan, Robert S. Lynd summarized the results of budget studies for federal employees in five cities (1928), Ford Motor Co. employees in Detroit (1930), and apartment dwellers in New York City (1930), in *The People as Consumers"*, p. 862. The findings in these studies correspond with a 1926 survey of consumers in New York City, Newark, New Jersey, and Chicago, which found that 41 percent had bought something with installment credit. See "What Is the Public's Opinion of Installment Selling," *Philadelphia Retail Ledger*, 1 May 1926, p. 10.

132. Plummer, "Social and Economic Consequences of Buying on the Instalment Plan," p. 11.

133. *Encyclopaedia of the Social Sciences, s.v.* "Instalment Selling."

134. From Plummer, "Social and Economic Consequences of Buying on the Instalment Plan," p. 12. Based on a synopsis of three large-scale credit investigations.

135. Frank Stricker, "Affluence for Whom? Another Look at Prosperity and the Working Classes in the 1920s," *Labor History* 24 (Winter 1983): 30–32; Jessica B. Peixotto, *Getting and Spending at the Professional Standard of Living: A Study of the Cost of Living an Academic Life* (New York: Macmillan, 1927), p. 269.

136. Goldman, *Prosperity and Consumer Credit*, pp. 103, 169–172. For more on Goldman and the marketing of installment credit, see Chapter 6.

137. Lizabeth Cohen, *Making a New Deal: Industrial Workers in*

Chicago, 1919–1939 (Cambridge: Cambridge University Press, 1990), p. 104.

138. Blanche Bernstein, *The Pattern of Consumer Debt, 1935–36*, Financial Research Program, Studies in Consumer Instalment Financing, no. 6 (New York: National Bureau of Economic Research, 1940), pp. 19–40. The sample in this study covered sixty thousand nonrelief families.

139. The economic significance of installment credit has received much study. Beginning with E.R.A. Seligman, installment credit's first historian, economists have maintained that installment credit was to the second industrial revolution what commercial credit was to the first industrial revolution: the crucial financial mechanism sparking economic growth. Economists have debated whether increases in the credit supply caused a "consumer durables revolution" in the 1920s, or, vice versa, whether overproduction of consumer durables caused the credit supply to increase. The answer, apparently, is yes: installment credit was both cause and consequence of a "consumer durables revolution." In addition, economists have studied installment credit's collateral effects, such as the rapid expansion of the economy's financial sector, the rising importance of credit as a source for retail profits, the stabilization of factory production, and the government's increasing reliance on consumer credit as a tool for speeding up and slowing down the nation's economic growth. On these subjects, see Seligman, *Economics of Instalment Selling*, 2:249–337; Thorsten Sellin, gen. ed., *Annals of the American Academy of Political and Social Science* 196 (March 1938); *Consumer Credit*, ed. Paul F. Douglass, pp. 52–204; Nugent, *Consumer Credit and Economic Stability*, pp. 147–244; Reavis Cox, *The Economics of Instalment Buying* (New York: Ronald Press, 1948), pp. 3–74, 369–429; Gottfried Haberler, *Consumer Installment Credit and Economic Fluctuations* (New York: National Bureau of Economic Research, 1942); National Commission on Consumer Finance, *Consumer Credit in the United States* (Washington, D.C.: Government Printing Office, 1972), pp. 45–53, 109–147, 201–216; Board of Governors of the Federal Reserve System, *Consumer Instalment Credit*, 3 vols. (Washington D.C.: Board of Governors, 1957). The best guide, though, is Olney, *Buy Now, Pay Later*, pp. 57–85, 118–130.

140. Maxwell Droke, *Credit: The Magic Coin of Commerce* (Indianapolis, Ind.: Business Letter Institute, 1930), pp. 50–51.

141. Massachusetts Bureau of Statistics of Labor, *Thirtieth Annual Report, March, 1900*, p. 50.

142. As of June 1930, delinquent accounts (past due over thirty days) for the nation's four largest automobile finance companies amounted to only 0.5 percent, and this was up considerably from earlier in the decade due to the Great Depression. See notes 12 and 13 in chapter 6.

CHAPTER 5

FROM CONSUMPTIVE CREDIT TO CONSUMER CREDIT

1. For an illuminating contemporary account of the change in women's function from producer to consumer, see Belle Squire, "Women and Money Spending," *Harper's Bazar* 39 (December 1905): 1142–1143. Squire's ideas about a "new age" of consumption anticipate a similar and better-known thesis laid out by Simon Patten a few years later in his *The New Basis of Civilization* (New York: Macmillan, 1907). More conscious than Patten of the way gender affected historical experience, Squire argued that the new era of abundance impacted women more directly than men, because it changed their role in the family economy, replacing the role of producer with the new role of buyer and spender. The home economics movement attempted to address this development. We still await a contemporary book-length treatment of the home economics movement. In its absence, see Susan Strasser, *Never Done: A History of American Housework* (New York: Pantheon Books, 1982), pp. 202–223.

2. Edith Elmer Wood, "The Ideal and Practical Organization of a Home," *Cosmopolitan* 26 (April 1899): 661.

3. Marion Foster Washburne, "A Trap for the Newly-Married," *Ladies' Home Journal* 26 (April 1909): 14.

4. For examples, see Mary Eleanor Wilkins Freeman's novel *Debtor*, serialized in *Harper's Bazar* beginning 38 (December 1904): 1165; W. B. MacHarg, "The Debts of Antoine," *McClure's* 28 (December 1906): 188–197; M. S. Briscoe, "Debt of Honor," *Everybody's Magazine* 16 (January 1907): 80–86; Edith L. Wharton, "Debt," *Scribner's Monthly* 46 (August 1909): 165–172; John Kenneth Turner, "Debt," *Everybody's Magazine* 25 (August 1911): 198–208; Perceval Gibson, "Debt," *McClure's* 39 (May 1912): 27–35; Corra Harris, "On the Instalment Plan," *Harper's Monthly Magazine* 127 (August 1913): 342–353.

5. Irving Bacheller, *Keeping Up with Lizzie* (New York: Harper & Bros., 1911); *"Charge It!" or, Keeping Up with Harry* (New York: Harper & Bros., 1912).

6. A. J. Hanna, "A Bibliography of the Writings of Irving Bacheller," *Rollins College Bulletin* 35 (September 1939): 24; Charles E. Funk, *Heavens to Betsy! and Other Curious Sayings* (New York: Harper & Bros., 1955), pp. 141–142; Richard M. Huber, *The American Idea of Success* (New York: McGraw-Hill, 1971), pp. 187–189.

7. Bacheller, "*Charge It!*," pp. 116–117.

8. "What Every Grocer Knows: Fifteen Years' Observation of the American Housekeeper by a Grocery Clerk," *McClure's* 41 (September 1913): 125–129.

9. G. W. Steevens, *The Land of the Dollar* (New York: Dodd, Mead, 1897), p. 24 (emphasis added).

10. Squire, "Women and Money Spending," p. 1143.

11. W. H. Kniffen Jr., "The Theory and Practice of Credit," *Banker's Magazine* 89 (December 1914): 664.

12. Margaret Sangster, "Bankrupt Wage-Earners and Wives," *Harper's Bazar* 33 (December 1900): 2211.

13. Squire, "Women and Money Spending," pp. 1143, 1144.

14. W. de Wagstaffe, "Cost of Living in New York," *Harper's Weekly* 52, 23 May 1908, p. 17.

15. Sangster, "Bankrupt Wage-Earners and Wives," p. 2210.

16. Squire, "Women and Money Spending," pp. 1142, 1143.

17. Ibid., p. 1142; Wagstaffe, "Cost of Living in New York," p. 17; Walter Rauschenbusch, *Christianity and the Social Crisis* (New York: Macmillan, 1907), p. 265.

18. Julian Goldman, *Prosperity and Consumer Credit* (New York: Harper & Bros., 1930), pp. 16–17.

19. Charles Connard Hanch, "The Case for Instalment Buying," *Forum* 77 (May 1927): 660.

20. On the "domino theory" of consumer credit expansion, see "Living and Dying on Installments," *World's Work* 50 (October 1925): 576.

21. Quoted in "The Epidemic of 'Easy Little Payments,'" *Literary Digest* 89, 1 May 1926, p. 14.

22. James E. Moffatt, "Is Instalment Selling a Boon or a Menace?" *Banker's Magazine* 112 (February 1926): 221–229; O. R. Johnson, "Wage Earner's Debts and the Savings Margin," *Banker's Magazine* 111 (July 1925): 9–14.

23. S. W. Straus, *History of the Thrift Movement in America* (Philadelphia: J. B. Lippincott, 1920), p. 36; George Zook, "Thrift in the

United States," *Annals of the American Academy of Political and Social Science* 87 (January 1920): 208.

24. On Straus and the War Savings Movement, see David M. Tucker, *The Decline of Thrift in America* (New York: Praeger, 1991), pp. 68–69, 83–98.

25. Ibid., pp. 96–97.

26. "What Do Bankers Think of Installment Selling?" *Philadelphia Retail Ledger*, 1 July 1926, p. 7.

27. Alex Dunbar, "Instalment Buying," *Banker's Magazine* 113 (July 1926): 79.

28. Quoted in Arthur Pound, "The Land of Dignified Credit," *Atlantic Monthly* 137 (February 1926): 258.

29. George E. MacIlwain, "Mortgaging To-Morrow Puts 'Pep' into Today," *Forbes* 17, 1 March 1926, p. 13; letter in *Forbes* 17, 1 May 1926, p. 42; J. George Frederick, "Dollar-Down Serfdom," *Independent* 117, 11 September 1926, p. 299.

30. *Philadelphia Retail Ledger*, 2 February 1926, p. 3.

31. Johnson quoted in J. M. Head, "Is the Installment Plan an Artificial Stimulus to Prosperity?" *Magazine of Wall Street*, 19 June 1926, p. 360.

32. Pound, "The Land of Dignified Credit," p. 258; *Philadelphia Retail Ledger*, 1 March 1926, p. 1; 2 April 1926, p. 10.

33. B. J. Duncan, "Installment Buying—Should it Cause Alarm?" *Forbes* 17, 1 April 1926, p. 15.

34. Houston *Chronicle*, 6 May 1926, 24 June 1926, 13 May 1926. The series of ads ran from 6 May to 5 August. Reproductions of some of the Zindler advertisements accompany an article on the company's anti-debt campaign in the *Philadelphia Retail Ledger*, 1 July 1926, p. 4.

35. James Couzens, "The Instalment Buyer Worries Me," *Nation's Business* 14 (December 1926): 36; C. Reinold Noyes, "Financing Prosperity on Next Year's Income," *Yale Review* 16 (January 1927): 228, 242; J. R. Sprague, "Sales Resistance Stiffens," *American Mercury* 4 (February 1925): 218. For others mentioned, see Thomas Nixon Carver, *The Economy of Human Energy* (New York: Macmillan, 1924), p. 231; Mary Hinman Abel, *Successful Family Life on the Moderate Income* (Philadelphia: J. B. Lippincott, 1921), pp. 35–36; Hoover quoted in *Ladies Home Journal* 37 (August 1920): 100.

36. E.R.A. Seligman calculated that in 1925 the ratio of cash sales to credit sales was $38 billion to $4.5 billion. See Edwin R. A. Seligman, *The*

Economics of Instalment Selling: A Studying in Consumer's Credit, 2 vols. (New York: Harper & Bros., 1927), 1:118.

37. Savings bank deposits in 1920 totaled $6.5 billion, in 1925 $9.1 billion. See Seligman, *Economics of Instalment Selling,* 1:272.

38. George Horace Lorimer, "Installment Buying," *Saturday Evening Post,* 29 May 1926, 26.

39. Thomas Nixon Carver, "Consumer Credit and Economic Instability," *Annals of the American Academy of Political and Social Science* 196 (March 1938): 98; Couzens, "The Installment Buyer Worries Me," p. 36; Economic Policy Commission, "A Word of Caution on Installment Selling," *American Bankers Association Journal* 19 (November 1926): 280.

40. Frederick, "Dollar-Down Serfdom," p. 300 (emphasis added).

41. James Couzens, "Installment Buying and Its Costs," *Forum* 77 (May 1927): 657.

42. Letter to the editor, H. C. Currier to *Forbes* 18, 1 May 1926, p. 42.

43. Frederick, "Dollar-Down Serfdom," p. 300.

44. For a lucid discussion of the concepts of "public culture" and "culture war," see James Davison Hunter, *Culture Wars: The Struggle to Define America* (New York: Basic Books, 1991), pp. 53–57. On the cultural struggles of the 1910s and 1920s, see Henry May, *The End of American Innocence* (New York: Oxford University Press, 1959).

45. Martha Olney, *Buy Now, Pay Later: Advertising, Credit, and Consumer Durables in the 1920s* (Chapel Hill: University of North Carolina Press, 1991), pp. 88–89, 96.

46. Evans Clark, "Are 'Easy Payments' the Hardest?" *New York Times Book Review* 15 January 1928, p. 18.

47. "What Is the Public's Opinion of Instalment-Selling?" *Philadelphia Retail Ledger,* 1 May 1926.

48. "University of Oregon Investigation Throws Light on Public's Reaction to Instalment Sales," *Philadelphia Retail Ledger,* 2 February 1926, p. 1.

49. The University of Oregon survey allowed people to write in their own words what they thought about the installment plan. Many of their remarks are published in *Philadelphia Retail Ledger,* 2 February 1926, p. 2.

50. On this point see Colin Campbell, "Understanding Traditional and Modern Patterns of Consumption in Eighteenth-Century England: A

Character-Action Approach," in *Consumption and the World of Goods*, ed. John Brewer and Roy Porter (London: Routledge, 1993), pp. 43–45.

51. E. A. Hungerford, "Installments—From a Consumer's Viewpoint," *Forbes* 18, 1 May 1926, p. 23.

52. American Bankers Association, Economic Policy Commission, "A Word of Caution on Installment Selling," *American Bankers Association Journal* 19 (November 1926): 280; "A. F. of L. Research Report: Instalment Buying," *American Federationist* 34 (April 1927): 482–483.

53. "Installment Buying," *Saturday Evening Post*, 29 May 1926, p. 26.

54. *American Magazine* 101 (February 1926): 204; 101 (March 1926): 220; 102 (July 1926): 178–179.

55. The Associated Press story is reprinted, with commentary, in *Industrial Lenders News* 10 (February 1926): 12.

56. Seligman has no biographer. For more information on his life, see the memorials and material collected in *Edwin Robert Anderson Seligman, 1861–1939* (Stamford, Conn.: Overbrook Press, 1942); Ross L. Muir and Carl J. White, *Over the Long Term: The Story of J & W Seligman and Company* (New York: J & W Seligman, 1964), p. 79; Geoffrey T. Hellman, "Sorting Out the Seligmans," *New Yorker*, 30 October 1954, pp. 34–65.

57. *American Economic Review* 29 (December 1939): 911–912.

58. One exception was Wilbur C. Plummer of the University of Pennsylvania, who became interested in installment credit about the same time as Seligman. See "Social and Economic Consequences of Buying on the Instalment Plan," *Annals of the American Academy of Political and Social Science* 129 (January 1927): iii–V, 1–57.

59. Seligman, *Economics of Instalment Selling*, 1:v.

60. Clark, "Are 'Easy Payments' the Hardest?" p. 11.

61. For more on the budding relationships between academia and corporate business in the 1920s, see William Leach, *Land of Desire: Merchants, Power, and the Rise of a New American Culture* (New York: Vintage Books, 1993), pp. 285–292.

62. Thomas Bender, *Intellect and Public Life: Essays on the Social History of Academic Intellectuals in the United States* (Baltimore: Johns Hopkins University Press, 1993), p. 58.

63. Seligman, *Economics of Instalment Selling*, 1: v.

64. The five studies were published as the second volume of *Economics of Instalment Selling*.

65. Seligman, *Economics of Instalment Selling*, 1:123.

66. Ibid., 1:221, 162.

67. Ibid., 1:337.

68. Ibid., 1:144–153.

69. Ibid., 1:153.

70. Ibid., 1:176.

71. Ibid., 1:117.

72. Ibid., 1:153.

73. Ibid., 1:140–141.

74. Ibid., 1:141. Did Seligman coin these terms? The first use of the term "consumers' credit" that I know of appeared in William G. Shepherd, "They Turn Your Promise into Cash," *Collier's Weekly* 79, 19 February 1927, p. 8. This article was published while Seligman's book was going to press. Since the article was based on an interview with John J. Raskob, it is likely that the new term came from him. Perhaps Raskob heard the term in conversations with Seligman.

75. Thomas Nixon Carver, *This Economic World, and How It May Be Improved* (Chicago: A. W. Shaw, 1928), pp. 94–95. The classical theory of credit can also be found in Carver, *The Economy of Human Energy*, p. 231; W. H. Kniffen Jr., "The Theory and Practice of Credit," *Bankers Magazine* 89 (December 1914): 666–668; Farmers' Loan and Trust Company, *Installment Buying* (New York, 1926), pp. 22–23; and Noyes, "Financing Prosperity on Next Year's Income," p. 231.

76. Seligman, *Economics of Instalment Selling*, 1:168–169.

77. Ibid., 1:157–171.

78. Ibid., 1:160, 164–165.

79. Ibid., 1:165–167.

80. Ibid., 1:171–172.

81. Seligman's fourfold scheme of utilization was not treated well by critics. See N. R. Danielian, "The Theory of Consumers' Credit," *American Economic Review* 19 (September 1929): 394.

82. *Annals of the Academy of Political and Social Science* 137 (May 1928): 269; *World's Work* 55 (January 1928): 242; *New York Times Book Review*, 15 January 1928, p. 11.

83. See Frank Parker, "Rationalization of Consumer Credit," *Personal Finance News* 16 (August 1931): 5–7.

84. Alfred P. Sloan Jr., *My Years with General Motors* (Garden City, N.Y.: Doubleday, 1964), p. 306.

85. Esra Christian Buehler, *A Debate Handbook on the Instalment Buying of Personal Property* (Knoxville: University of Tennessee Press, 1929), p. 1.

86. The ideas of Seligman show up in obvious ways in the following books: Ray Osgood Hughes, *Economic Citizenship* (Boston: Allyn & Bacon, 1933); Harvey A. Blodgett, *Making the Most of Your Income* (New York: Macmillan, 1933); Sidonie Matsner Gruenberg and Benjamin C. Gruenberg, *Parents, Children, and Money: Learning to Spend, Save, and Earn* (New York: Viking, 1933); Benjamin R. Andrews, *Economics of the Household* (New York: Macmillan, 1935); David F. Owens, *Controlling Your Personal Finances* (New York: McGraw-Hill, 1937). Of course, some financial advisors continued to decry installment buying, but theirs was increasingly a minority view after 1927.

87. Seligman, *Economics of Instalment Selling*, 1:256.

88. Ibid., 1:272–274.

89. Ibid., 1:277.

90. This was a popular belief as revealed by the University of Oregon public opinion survey. See the survey results in *Philadelphia Retail Ledger*, 1 March 1926, p. 2. The belief also cut across education levels; see the remarks made by Walter E. Frew, chairman of the Corn Exchange Bank, in "Is the Installment Plan an Artificial Stimulus to Prosperity?" *Magazine of Wall Street*, 19 June 1926, p. 317.

91. Seligman, *Economics of Instalment Selling*, 1:222–225.

92. *Harvard Business Review* 6 (April 1928): 368.

93. Danielian, "The Theory of Consumers' Credit," p. 393.

94. Reginald Heber Smith, "Performance Beats Propaganda," *Personal Finance News* 15 (October 1930): 12. For "wise borrowing" and "foolish borrowing" as the terms of choice in the money management advice books of the 1930s, see note 83.

95. Seligman, *Economics of Instalment Selling*, 1: 260.

96. Ibid., 1:239–241.

97. Michel De Certeau, *The Practice of Everyday Life*, trans. Steven Rendall (Berkeley: University of California Press, 1984), p. xx.

98. Seligman, *Economics of Instalment Selling*, 1:258.

99. Franklin W. Ryan, "The Future of the Small Loan Business," *Industrial Lenders News* 12 (April 1928): 11.

100. See Henry G. Hodges, "Financing the Automobile," *Annals of the American Academy of Political and Social Science* 116 (November 1924): 51.

101. M. R. Neifeld, speech in *Personal Finance News* 22 (October 1937): 18.

CHAPTER 6
CONSUMER CREDIT IN THE GREAT DEPRESSION

1. Edward M. Steimle, "Is Installment Selling Being Overdone," *Industrial Lenders News* 11 (December 1926): 11.

2. On margin trading and the crash of 1929, see Michael E. Parrish, *Anxious Decades: America in Prosperity and the Great Depression* (New York: W. W. Norton, 1992), pp. 217–232. Parrish can also be consulted for an annotated bibliography on the voluminous literature relating to the crash, its causes, and the immediate aftermath.

3. *New York Times*, 10 December 1929, p. 29.

4. *New York Times*, 7 December 1929, p. 22. In some circles, installment credit continued to be a villain for a long time. Five years after the crash, a banker in Muncie, Indiana, told Robert and Helen Lynd that the cause of the depression was "speculation, overproduction, and the wide use of installment-plan buying." See Robert S. Lynd and Helen Merrell Lynd, *Middletown in Transition: A Study in Cultural Conflicts* (New York: Harcourt, Brace, 1937), p. 18.

5. See Alfred P. Sloan Jr., "I Believe in Time Payments—Why?" *Nation's Business* 14 (April 1926): 18; Edwin R. A. Seligman, *Economics of Instalment Selling: A Study in Consumers' Credit*, 2 vols. (New York: Harper & Bros., 1927), 1:329–330.

6. *Business Week*, 28 May 1930, p. 33; ibid., 4 December 1929, p. 35.

7. U.S. Department of Commerce, Bureau of the Census, *Historical Statistics of the United States, Colonial Times to 1970* (Washington, D.C.: Government Printing Office, 1975); Roger Biles, *A New Deal for the American People* (Dekalb: Northern Illinois University Press, 1991), p. 11; Irving Bernstein, *The Lean Years: A History of the American Worker, 1920–1933* (Boston: Houghton Mifflin, 1960), pp. 316–321.

8. Martha Olney, *Buy Now, Pay Later: Advertising, Credit, and Consumer Durables in the 1920s* (Chapel Hill: University of North Carolina Press, 1991), p. 89.

9. Ibid., p. 93; Rolf Nugent, *Consumer Credit and Economic Stability* (New York: Russell Sage Foundation, 1939), p. 103.

10. Lynd and Lynd, *Middletown in Transition*, pp. 10–11, 475. A group of businessmen told the Lynds, "[Workingmen] seem to have learned *this* much: they're not rushing to buy houses and tie themselves down with debts, because they have a darned lively sense now of how easily a plant can be moved in and out of a town."

11. Commercial Credit Company report, in *Literary Digest* 111, 17 October 1931, p. 40.

12. National City Bank report, in *Literary Digest* 106, 30 August 1930, p. 40.

13. *Fortune* 7, 1 January 1933, p. 68; Ray B. Westerfield, "Effect of Consumer Credit on the Business Cycle," *Annals of the American Academy of Political and Social Science* 196 (March 1938): 109.

14. Lynd and Lynd, *Middletown in Transition*, p. 265.

15. Reported in Stuart Chase, *A New Deal* (New York: Macmillan, 1934), pp. 111–112.

16. *Business Week*, 11 February 1931, p. 14.

17. M. R. Neifeld, *Personal Finance Comes of Age* (New York: Harper & Bros., 1939), pp. 257, 260.

18. Roger Daniels, *The Bonus March: An Episode of the Great Depression* (Westport, Conn.: Greenwood, 1971), pp. 44–46; Donald J. Lisio, *The President and Protest: Hoover, Conspiracy, and the Bonus Riot* (Columbia: University of Missouri Press, 1974), pp. 38–40; and Walter J. Waters, *B. E. F.: The Whole Story of the Bonus Army* (New York: AMS Press, 1970), pp. 11–12.

19. *Business Week*, 13 April 1932, p. 25.

20. M. R. Neifeld, *The Personal Finance Business* (New York: Harper & Bros., 1933), p. 312.

21. *Business Week*, 20 January 1932, p. 13; Isador Lubin, "The Problem of Consumer Credit," *New Republic* 67, 29 July 1931, p. 289.

22. *Business Week*, 20 January 1932, p. 13.

23. Ralph A. Young, *Personal Finance Companies and Their Credit Practices* (New York: National Bureau of Economic Research, 1940), p. 64.

24. Studs Terkel, *Hard Times: An Oral History of the Great Depression* (New York: Pocket Books, 1970), p. 99.

25. Neifeld, *The Personal Finance Business*, p. 155.

26. Young, et al. *Personal Finance Companies*, p. 79.

27. *Business Week*, 11 February 1931, p. 14.

28. U.S. Bureau of the Census, *Sixteenth Census: 1940 . . . Retail Trade: 1939, Part I* (Washington, D.C.: Government Printing Office, 1941), p. 798.

29. Report of the Commercial Credit Company, in *Literary Digest* 111, 17 October 1931, p. 40.

30. Quoted in Roland Marchand, *Advertising the American Dream:*

Making Way for Modernity, 1920–1940 (Berkeley: University of California Press, 1985), p. 300.

31. Jesse Rainsford Sprague, "Panics and Time Payments," *Harpers Monthly* 162 (April 1931): 612.

32. William Trufant Foster and Waddill Catchings, *Business without a Buyer* (Boston: Houghton Mifflin, 1927), pp. 57–76; "Where Instalment Buying Breaks," *New Republic* 46, 7 April 1926, pp. 186–187.

33. Isador Lubin, "What Delays Revival," *New Republic* 67, 10 June 1931, pp. 92–93.

34. N. R. Danielian, "Theory of Consumers' Credit," *American Economic Review* 19 (September 1929): 411. During the Depression, American economists echoed Danielian, sometimes blaming consumer credit as a contributory factor in the Depression and sometimes dismissing it as irrelevant. See William E. Stoneman, *A History of the Economic Analysis of the Great Depression in America* (New York: Garland Publishing, 1979), pp. 65–99. Individual economists went back and forth over the question, sometime within the pages of a single book, as in John Maurice Clark's influential *Strategic Factors in Business Cycles* (New York: National Bureau of Economic Research, 1935), pp. 45–46, 88, 120–121. Amazingly, Danielian's original hesitancy still appears to be the state of the question among economists today. See the debate on the impact of consumer credit on the post–World War II era in J. Bradford Delong and Lawrence H. Summers, "The Changing Cyclical Variability of Economic Activity in the United States," in *The American Business Cycle: Continuity and Change*, ed. Robert J. Gordon (Chicago: University of Chicago Press, 1986), pp. 679–734.

35. Olney, *Buy Now, Pay Later*, p. 89.

36. Milan Ayres, "The Instalment Debt and Business Revival," *New Republic* 67, 29 July 1931, pp. 288–89. Ayres worked feverishly to put out fires lit by credit critics; excerpts from his rebuttal articles appear in *Literary Digest* 111, 17 October 1931, p. 40.

37. Olney, *Buy Now, Pay Later*, pp. 93–94.

38. Nugent, *Consumer Credit and Economic Stability*, p. 108.

39. *Business Week*, 7 May 1930, p. 16.

40. Figures from the Board of Governors of the Federal Reserve System, *Consumer Installment Credit* (1957), in Olney, *Buy Now, Pay Later*, pp. 93–94. A fuller description of the credit expansion is given by Nugent, *Consumer Credit and Economic Stability*, pp. 105–109.

41. Nugent, *Consumer Credit and Economic Stability*, p. 110.

42. *Business Week*, 16 July 1930, p. 8; 28 January 1931, p. 9; 9 March 1932, p. 25; 4 May 1935, p. 35; *Women's Wear*, 22 September 1938; Nugent, *Consumer Credit and Economic Stability*, p. 109.

43. *Business Week*, 30 July 1930, pp. 11–12.

44. Ralph Merle Hower, *History of Macy's of New York, 1858–1919* (Cambridge, Mass.: Harvard University Press, 1943), p. 49; and Margaret Case Harriman, *And the Price Is Right* (Cleveland, Ohio: World Publishing, 1958), pp. 23, 162.

45. *New York Times*, 8 October 1939, pp. 22–23, 52.

46. *New York World Telegram*, 2 October 1939, p. 7; *Business Week*, 7 October 1939, pp. 29–30.

47. *New York Times*, 8 October 1939, sec. L, p. 11; Jack I. Straus, *Macy's Annual Report: 1940* (New York, 1940), p. 2.

48. James Grant, *Money of the Mind: Borrowing and Lending in America from the Civil War to Michael Milken* (New York: Farrar Straus Giroux, 1992), pp. 219–220; Jordan A. Schwarz, *The Interregnum of Despair: Hoover, Congress, and the Depression* (Urbana: University of Illinois Press, 1970), p. 93; Joan Hoff Wilson, *Herbert Hoover: Forgotten Progressive* (Boston: Little, Brown, 1975), pp. 146, 156–157.

49. Kenneth T. Jackson, *Crabgrass Frontier: The Suburbanization of the United States* (New York: Oxford University Press, 1985), p. 194.

50. M. R. Neifeld, "Competitive Consumer Credit Developments," *Personal Finance News* 20 (October 1935): 18.

51. Ibid., p. 20; Philip J. Funigiello, *Toward a National Power Policy: The New Deal and the Electric Utility Industry, 1933–1941* (Pittsburgh: University of Pittsburgh Press, 1973), pp. 132, 158–159; Thomas K. McCraw, *TVA and the Power Fight, 1933–1939* (Philadelphia: J. B. Lippincott, 1971), pp. 61–62, 124.

52. Franklin D. Roosevelt, *The Public Papers and Addresses of Franklin D. Roosevelt*, ed. Samuel I. Rosenman, vol. 4: *The Court Disapproves* (New York: Random House, 1938), p. 311.

53. C. Lowell Harriss, *History and Policies of the Home Owners' Loan Corporation* (New York: National Bureau of Economic Research, 1951), pp. 2, 11; Jackson, *Crabgrass Frontier*, pp. 196–203.

54. Jackson, *Crabgrass Frontier*, p. 196.

55. J. Carroll Moody and Gilbert C. Fite, *The Credit Union Movement: Origins and Development, 1850–1970* (Lincoln: University of Nebraska Press, 1971), pp. 149–168.

56. Franklin D. Roosevelt, *The Public Papers and Addresses of Frank-

lin D. Roosevelt, ed. Samuel I. Rosenman, vol. 3: *The Advance of Recovery and Reform* (New York: Random House, 1934), p. 232.

57. Jackson, *Crabgrass Frontier*, p. 205.

58. Neifeld, "Competitive Consumer Credit Developments," p. 19.

59. Quoted in A. L. Roe, "Bankers and Thrift in the Age of Affluence," *American Quarterly* 17 (Winter 1965): 619.

60. Evans Clark, *Financing the Consumer* (New York: Harper & Bros., 1930), pp. 75–76.

61. Raymond Goldsmith, *A Study of Saving in the United States* (Princeton, N.J.: Princeton University Press, 1955), p. 699; Nugent, *Consumer Credit and Economic Stability*, p. 343.

62. "Our Biggest Bank to Serve Small Borrowers," *Literary Digest* 97, 19 May 1928, p. 76.

63. Charles G. Muller, "The National City Bank Plan of Small Loans," *Industrial Lenders News* 13 (August 1928): 17.

64. Donaldson B. Thorburn, "Bank Credit Goes on a Retail Business," *Burroughs Clearing House* 21 (October 1936): 9.

65. Nugent, *Consumer Credit and Economic Stability*, p. 343.

66. Paul B. Trescott, *Financing American Enterprise: The Story of Commercial Banking* (New York: Harper & Row, 1963), p. 186.

67. But retail merchants extend more credit in the form of credit for goods. See W. David Robbins, *Consumer Instalment Loans: An Analysis of Loans by Principal Types of Lending Institutions and by Types of Borrowers* (Columbus, Ohio: Bureau of Business Research, Ohio State University Press, 1955), pp. 17, 19; *Federal Reserve Bulletin* 77 (December 1991): A37.

68. Muller, "The National City Bank Plan of Small Loans," p. 18.

69. Neifeld, *Personal Finance Comes of Age*, pp. 131–136, especially tables 54–55, 59; David H. Rogers, *Consumer Banking in New York* (New York: Trustees of Columbia University, 1974), pp. 35–37.

70. For a description of the massive merchandising campaign for Bank of America's 1936 "TimePlan" credit program, see Donaldson B. Thorburn, "Bank Credit Goes on a Retail Basis," pp. 8–11. The only lenders really to lose out when commercial banks entered the field were the Morris Plan "industrial" bankers. Since commercial banks competed directly for Morris Plan clients, and could draw on much cheaper money, industrial banks either went out of business or converted themselves into regulated commercial banks. See Trescott, *Financing American Enterprise*, p. 181; Rogers, *Consumer Banking in New York*, pp. 37–38; Neifeld, "Competitive Consumer Credit Developments," p. 19.

71. Nugent, *Consumer Credit and Economic Stability*, p. 22.

72. *Business Week*, 25 November 1933, p. 12. Similar rumors are collated and reported in *Literary Digest* 117, 14 April 1934, p. 45.

73. The Social Credit Party controlled the Alberta Assembly from 1935 to 1971, and was active in other provinces as well, but the Party abandoned the social credit theories of C. H. Douglas in the late 1930s. See C. H. Douglas, *Social Credit* (London: Eyre & Spottiswoode, 1924); J. R. Mallory, *Social Credit and the Federal Power in Canada* (Toronto: University of Toronto Press, 1954), pp. 57–90; C. B. MacPherson, *Democracy in Alberta: Social Credit and the Party System* (Toronto: University of Toronto Press, 1953), pp. 142–168; John A. Irving, *The Social Credit Movement in Alberta* (Toronto: University of Toronto Press, 1959), pp. 1–7.

74. Edgar L. Heermance, "The Community Credit Plan" (n.p., 1933, mimeograph). Correspondence with representatives of the National Retail Credit Association is included in an appendix to this prospectus.

75. Nugent, *Consumer Credit and Economic Stability*, p. 23.

76. Lynd and Lynd, *Middletown in Transition*, p. 478.

EPILOGUE

1. Edwin R. A. Seligman, *The Economics of Instalment Selling: A Study in Consumers' Credit*, 2 vols. (New York: Harper & Bros., 1927), 1:198. Twenty-five years later, a butcher in Syracuse, N.Y., advertised "Would you like to buy a steak?—$1 down and $1 a week." See Penn Kimball, "Cradle to Grave on Easy Terms," *New York Times Magazine*, 1 June 1952, p. 15.

2. Quoted in Nancy Shepherdson, "Credit Card America," *American Heritage* (November 1991): 131.

3. On this point, see Sheffield Boardman, "Our Sixth Freedom—The Pursuit of Freedom," *Vital Speeches*, 1 December 1960, pp. 113–114.

4. *Federal Reserve Bulletin* 45 (February 1959): 188; *New York Times*, 9 September 1998, p. C2.

5. For more on the recent history of consumer credit, see Richard Worsnop, "Consumer Debt," *Congressional Quarterly Researcher* 6 (15 November 1996): 1019–1031; Lewis Mandell, *The Credit Card Industry: A History* (Boston: Twaine Publishers, 1990); Nancy Shepherdson, "Credit Card America," *American Heritage* 42 (November 1991): 125–132.

6. Robert S. Lynd and Helen Merrell Lynd, *Middletown: A Study in*

American Culture (New York: Harcourt, Brace, 1929), pp. 28–29. I want to thank Otis Pease for directing my attention to this story.

7. Robert Brigham, "How To Spend $542 a Month on an Income of Only $511," *Life* 52 (6 April 1962): 42–43, 46.

8. Ibid., pp. 43–44, 46.

9. Ibid., p. 42.

10. William H. Whyte Jr., "Budgetism: Opiate of the Middle Class," *Fortune* 53 (May 1956): 172.

11. Ibid., p. 133.

12. Ibid., p. 137.

13. Ibid.

14. Ibid., p. 136.

15. Ibid., p. 133.

16. Daniel Bell, *The Cultural Contradictions of Capitalism* (New York: Basic Books, 1976), pp. 3–30, 54–84. The quoted question is from p. 84.

17. A sociologist, Bell is not primarily concerned with making an historical examination of the role asceticism played in the development of capitalism, or determining precisely when asceticism yielded to hedonism, or examining whether hedonism itself has a history and has shown development over time. In fact, in a new preface written for the twentieth-anniversary edition of *The Cultural Contradictions of Capitalism*, Bell admits that the transformation he describes from ascetic producers to hedonistic consumers may be historically "misleading"; it is "ideal types" he has in mind. The fundamental question raised in Bell's book then— Can liberalism survive its contradictions by coming up with a viable public philosophy that will buy society enough time to await the construction of an entirely new cultural order to replace the broken down "Puritan" order, a process that cannot be engineered and that will require the work of centuries?—receives a sociological analysis, not a historical one.

18. On this last question, see Michael Barton, "The Victorian Jeremiad: Critics of Accumulation and Display," in *Consuming Visions: Accumulation and Display of Goods in America, 1880–1920*, ed., Simon J. Bronner (New York: Norton, 1989), pp. 62–67; T. H. Breen, " 'Baubles of Britain': The American and Consumer Revolutions of the Eighteenth Century," *Past and Present* 119 (May 1988): 73–104; and Daniel Shi, *The Simple Life: Plain Living and High Thinking in American Culture* (New York: Oxford, 1985).

19. See Witold Rybczynski, *Waiting for the Weekend* (New York: Viking, 1991).

20. This subject is touched on in many books and articles written about consumer culture, but the best introduction to the subject is Victoria de Grazia and Ellen Furlough, eds., *The Sex of Things: Gender and Consumption in Historical Perspective* (Berkeley: University of California Press, 1996).

21. Elaine Tyler May, *Homeward Bound: American Families in the Cold War Era* (New York: Basic Books, 1988), p. 166.

22. Quotation from Whyte, "Budgetism: Opiate of the Middle Class," p. 134.

23. Mary Fields, "The Drama of Wages," *American Magazine* 74 (November 1912): 76.

24. See David Caplovitz, *Consumers in Trouble: A Study of Debtors in Default* (New York: Free Press, 1974).

25. The most recent statistics can be found in U.S. Congress, House, Committee on Banking and Financial Services, *Consumer Debt: Hearing before the Committee on Banking and Financial Services*. 104th Cong., 2nd sess., 1996, pp. 142, 148–149. For contrasting interpretations of the indebtedness of consumers in the 1990s, see Robert Pollin, *Deeper in Debt: The Changing Financial Conditions of U.S. Households* (Washington, D.C.: Economic Policy Institute, 1990); and C. Alan Garner, "Can Measures of the Consumer Debt Burden Reliably Predict an Economic Slowdown?" *Economic Review*, Federal Reserve Bank of Kansas City, 81, no. 4 (1996): 63–76.

* *Index* *

Abbott, Jacob, 93
Abbott, Lyman, 72
Abel, Mary Hinman, 230
Acres of Diamonds (Conwell), 64
Adams, James Truslow, 4
Adams, William Taylor, 62
advertising, 13, 29–30; of installment
    credit, 162, 172, 173, 189, 200,
    201, 203, 220, 222, 254–257, 275;
    of small loans, 52–53, 117, 138,
    142, 143, 145
Advice to Young Men (Cobbett), 92
The Affluent Society (Galbraith), 25
African-Americans, 176, 292, 324–
    325n43
agricultural credit, 116, 123, 160,
    168, 213, 284
Alajalov, Constantin, 305n3
Alberta, 288
Alger, Horatio, Jr., 238
American Association of Personal Fi-
    nance Companies, 148, 260
American Association of Small Loan
    Brokers (AASLB), 133, 134–137
American Association of University
    Professors, 240
American Bankers Association, 231,
    236
American Bar Association, 242
American dream, 3–5, 111–112, 155,
    262, 290, 294, 299
American Economic Association, 71,
    239
American Federation of Labor, 236,
    242
The American Frugal Housewife
    (Child), 90
American Grocer, 71
American Industrial Licensed Lenders
    Association, 137, 144, 146, 148
The American Magazine, 193, 196,
    236–237
American Mercury, 230

American Society for Thrift, 223
amortization, 67–68, 281
Aquinas, Thomas, 80
Aristotle, 80, 113
"Ask Marilyn," 3
Atherton, Lewis, 70
Austin, J. M., 87
automobile: cost of, 185–186; desir-
    ability of, 201, 207; significance
    for installment credit of, 19, 184;
    socioeconomic status of owners of,
    203
automobile dealers, 186–195, 242
automobile financing: auto manufac-
    turers and, 186, 189–190; diffu-
    sion and extent of, 19, 184, 201,
    203–204, 219–220, 234, 274–
    275; finance companies and, 186–
    195, 199, 266–267; Ford Motor
    Co. and, 189–191, 194–199; Gen-
    eral Motors and, 191–192, 199; re-
    medial loan societies and, 150;
    work disciplines required by, 252
Ayres, Milan V., 180–181, 265, 273–
    274

Babson, Roger, 264
Babson Statistical Association, 264
Bacheller, Irving, 21, 213–217, 218,
    223, 237
Baldwin, D. H., and Company, 165
Baldwin, Dwight H., 165
Bank of the United States, 146
Banker's Magazine, 99, 223
Bankers Trust Company, 240
bankruptcy, 219, 231, 276, 294,
    302
banks. *See* commercial banks; indus-
    trial banks; Morris Plan banks; na-
    tional banks; savings banks
Barnum, P. T., 83, 91, 93, 94, 103
barter, 76–77
Baudrillard, Jean, 7

The Bawlerout (Halsey), 315n44
"bawlerouts," 54
Becker, Carl, 22
Beecher, Catherine, 89, 90
Beecher, Henry Ward, 87, 92, 97
Bell, Daniel, 12, 25, 30, 299–300, 363n17
Bell's Easy Payment Store, 57
Beneficial Corporation, 19, 133, 138, 144, 148, 268–270
Beneficial Management Corporation, 152
Bentham, Jeremy, 116, 122
Bergengren, Roy F., 281
Bible, 10, 107, 113
Bigelow, Charles F., 150
Blackburn, Burr, 153
Blackstone, William, 116, 122
Blumberg, Benjamin, 146
Bogue, Allan, 100
Bonus March, 268
book credit, 59–60, 103–104, 156, 166, 213, 237
books, 60, 79, 167, 176, 180, 187, 200, 222, 241
Boorstin, Daniel, 10, 11
"borax" stores, 56–57, 60, 72, 173–175, 254
borrowers: disciplines required of, 28–32, 54–55, 206–208, 294–303; of pawnbrokers, 43–44, 46–48; of small-loan lenders, 51–52, 149–151
Boston, 46, 49, 56, 58, 65–66, 84, 94, 116, 117, 120, 158, 168–171, 207
Braudel, Fernand, 114
Breen, T. H., 61
Brookings Institution, 272
Brooks, Franklin, 128
Browne, Charles Farrar (Artemus Ward), 37
budgeting, 90, 207, 297
budgetism, 297–299
building and loan associations, 66–68, 86, 161, 278
Business Week, 265, 288
Butler, Benjamin Franklin, 97

Cahn, B. J., 226
Calkins, Ernest Elmo, 13
Calvin, John, 113–114
Campbell, Colin, 107
capitalism, 8, 77, 89, 98, 114, 288, 299–300
Carey, H. C., 75, 78
Carnegie, Andrew, 88
Carnegie Foundation, 125
Carver, Thomas Nixon, 230, 231, 246
Case, J. I., 160–161
Case Threshing Machine Company, 160
cash buying, 69–72, 181, 206, 230
cash credit. *See* illegal lenders; pawnbroking; personal finance companies; small-loan lending
Catchings, Waddill, 272
Census Bureau, 270
census of 1890, 15, 39–40, 68, 73, 100, 241, 287
The Century Dictionary, 180
Century Magazine, 183
Chapin, Robert, 43
character, 87, 258
charge accounts, 71–72, 200, 254, 276
Charge It (Garson), 21
Charge It! Or, Keeping Up with Harry (Bacheller), 214
Charity Organization Society (NYC), 121, 125
The Chattel Loan Business (Ham), 127
Chattel Loan Society of New York, 130–131, 135
chattel mortgage lenders, 133, 136
chattel mortgages, 51, 53, 55, 117, 126, 148, 192, 270
Chevalier, Michael, 75
Chevrolet, 195, 198
Chicago, 45, 46, 47, 51, 52, 57, 117, 168; installment selling in, 171–175, 185, 186
Chicago Tribune, 84
Child, Lydia, 90–91

Chotzinoff, Samuel, 178, 182
Christian tradition: consumer culture and, 8–9; usury and, 113–114. *See also* Protestantism
The Christian Union, 100
Christmas Club plans, 197
Clark, Edward, 164
Clark, Evans, 16, 20, 138, 147, 234, 249, 287
Clavier, Etienne, 76
clothing, 57, 169–171, 177, 200, 226, 241, 266, 276
Cobbett, William, 70, 92
Cohen, Lizabeth, 204
Coin's Financial School (Harvey), 81
Collateral Loan Company, 120
collections, 54, 139, 161, 165, 270
Collier's Weekly, 208
Colton, Calvin, 93, 100
Columbia University, 126, 175, 238
commercial banks, 66, 68, 146, 271, 278, 283, 292; lending principles of, 187, 283–284; personal loan departments of, 19, 283–286
commercial credit, 271, 284, 285–286
Commercial Credit Company, 192
Commercial Investment Trust Corporation, 192
Community Credit Plan, 289–290
conditional sales, 166, 192
Cone, H. A., 134
Connecticut Association of Personal Finance Companies, 153
Consumer Advisory Board, 287, 289
consumer credit: American dream and, 5, 294, 291, 299; attitudes toward, 20, 23–26, 73, 234–235, 260–261; consumer culture and, 11–12, 30–32, 206–208, 294–303; controversy in 1920s over, 13–14, 20–22; critics and criticisms of, 24, 32, 211–235, 250, 258, 271–273, 292–294; defenders and defenses of, 230–231, 235–261, 273–274, 286; definition of, 5; disciplines demanded by, 28–32, 54–55, 206–208, 294–303; econo-

mists of 1920s and, 239; emergence of, 16–22, 24, 27; gender roles and, 181–183, 218–220, 231–234, 258; Great Depression and, 18, 25, 32, ch. 6, 359n34; historians and, 10–11, 12–15, 243; institutional foundations of, 17–18; legitimization of, 20, 101, 141–147, 206, 235–261, 262, 290, 300–303; postwar developments in, 291–294; significance of, 5, 11–12, 13–14, 206, 291; U.S. government support for, 278–283, 285; volume of, 9–10, 18–19, 25, 73, 234, 244, 263, 265, 291
Consumer Credit and Economic Stability (Nugent), 290
consumer culture, 28, 33, 112, 156, 183, 212, 298, 300; as American culture, 8–9, 257–258; commodification of time in, 208; competing cultural traditions and, 8–9; definition of, 6–8; expansion of, 8; the "good life" in, 7; hedonism and, 9, 16, 28–31, 33, 294–303; ideal man and woman of, 8; legitimization of, 257–259, 303; male identity in, 231–233, 258; moral status of consumer in, 231–234, 250–251, 258; "regulated abundance" of, 207–208; tensions within, 29–31, 33, 207, 299–303; vocabulary of, 20, 23, 355n74
consumer debt, amount of, 9–10, 18–19, 25; in 1858, 39; in 1888, 39; in 1890, 40, 73; 1900–1920, 18, 73; in the 1920s, 18–19, 234, 263; in the 1930s, 265, 273–274, 287, 289; since 1940, 291, 293
consumer durable goods: financing of, 19, 151, 158, 199, 201, 203, 207–208, 274–275; mass production of, 107, 162, 167–168
consumer finance companies. *See* personal finance companies; small-loan lending
consumer society, 11–12, 299

consumption: definition of, 7; as disease, 103, 233; as hard work, 28–29; as production, 255–260, 302–303; Seligman's theory of, 244–249

consumptive debt/credit, 107, 111; deconstruction of concept of, 244–245, 250–251, 259–260; definition of, 98–99, 103–104, 237–238; opposition to, 155, 211–213, 216, 231–233; usury laws' discouragement of, 112, 122, 123

Conwell, Russell, 64

Coolidge, Calvin, 237

Coughlin, Father Charles E., 289

Couzens, James, 230, 231, 232–233

Cowen, B. R., 89

Cowperthwaite and Sons, 158, 176

credit: character and, 87–88; language of, 211–212, 234–235, 237–238, 244–245, 250–251, 257, 292; necessity of, 93, 100, 291

credit cards, 16, 17, 72, 220, 292, 293

credit investigation, 54

credit revolution, 18–22, 24, 27, 111, 156, 211, 290, 291

credit system: seventeenth century, 39; eighteenth century, 61–62; early nineteenth century, 76; Gilded Age, ch. 1; Progressive Era, 124; since 1940, 291–292

Credit: The Magic Coin of Commerce (Droke), 206

Credit Union National Extension Bureau, 281

credit unions, 19, 263, 281–282

Cross, Gary, 302

Crump, Thomas, 80, 322n23

The Cultural Contradictions of Capitalism (Bell), 25; 299–300

culture: controls and releases of, 29, 97; definition of, 6

Cunard Steamship Lines, 275

Cunningham, W., 99

Currier & Ives, 71

Cutting, Bronson, 289

Dailey, John, 144

Danielian, N. R., 253–254, 273

Dawley, Alan, 42

debt: approbation of, 97–98, 103, 107; attitudes toward, 73, 74, 107, 140–141, 147, 260–261, 269; before the credit revolution, ch. 1; as a commodity, 140–141; "consumptive" versus "productive" debt, 98–104, 142–143, 231–232; discouragement of, 10, 91–98, 107, 112, 123, 202, 212–217, 227–230; moral nature of, 74, 93–96, 202, 211; speculative debt, 101. See also consumer debt

De Certeau, Michel, 259

The Decline of Thrift in America (Tucker), 25

default, 60, 207, 220, 266–267, 269–270, 302

delay of gratification, 107, 197

delinquency, 54, 176, 207, 242, 266–267, 270, 302

Department of Commerce, 201

department stores, 71–72, 170, 199–200, 217, 226, 275–277

Dictionary of the English Language (Webster), 158

Domestic Economy (Mayer), 96

Douglas, C. H., 288

Douglass, Paul, 20

Douglas, William O., 287

Droke, Maxwell, 206

Dubofsky, Melvyn, 42

Dunbar, Alex, 224

Durant, William, 184

Eben Holden (Bacheller), 214

Eclectic Magazine, 88

The Economics of Installment Selling (Seligman), 238, 242–244, 249–250, 253–256, 259, 260

economic virtues, 84

economy, 89, 90–91

Edgeworth, Maria, 92

Egan Act (N.J., 1914), 132

Electric Home and Farm Authority (EHFA), 279
Elson, Ruth Miller, 88
Emergency Relief and Construction Act (1932), 279
Emergency Relief Bureau (NYC), 267
Emerson, Ralph Waldo, 82, 90
Encyclopaedia of the Social Sciences, 239
Endicott Johnson Corporation, 226
England, 114, 123
Everett, Edward, 39
Everett, George B., 275

The Fair Store (Chicago), 275
Farm Credit Administration (FCA), 280
farmers, 100, 159–161, 190, 206, 216, 280
farm implements, 157, 159–161, 166, 186, 190, 200, 203, 222
Father Abraham, 87, 96, 294
Federal Credit Union Act (1934), 281–282
Federal Deposit Insurance Corporation (FDIC), 283, 285
Federal Home Loan Bank System, 278, 280
Federal Housing Administration (FHA), 282–283, 285, 290
Federal Reserve, 9, 75, 206, 224, 278
Filene, Edward A., 281
financial advice literature, 63, 70, 84–86, 87, 92, 250
financial discipline: consumer credit and, 28–29, 30–31, 54–55, 156–157, 206–208, 295–303; industrial wages and, 168; monetarization and, 84; mortgage debt and, 68–69
Flam, Helena, 10
Flandrau, Charles M., 167
Fletcher, Calvin, 78, 104–107
Fletcher, Jr., Calvin, 106
Forbes, 225, 233, 235
Ford, Edsel, 189, 191, 197, 207
Ford, Henry, 13, 184, 185, 186, 263, 277; opposition to installment selling, 191, 195–199, 226, 227, 230
Ford, Janet, 19
Ford Motor Company, 189–199, 226, 292, 298
Ford Times, 191
Ford Weekly Purchase Plan, 195–199, 207, 276, 298
de Forest, Robert W., 121, 125
Fort, Charles, 167
Foster, William Trufant, 272
France, 146
Franklin, Benjamin, 32, 84–85, 87, 89, 95–96, 98, 107, 233, 301
Frederick, J. George, 231
friends and family, credit from, 38, 40, 60–64, 66, 267, 268, 316n57
frugality, 89, 90–91
furniture, 56, 60, 161–162, 169, 176, 180, 201, 203, 204, 241, 266, 276

Galbraith, John Kenneth, 11, 25
Gallatin, Albert, 76
Ganz, Maria, 43, 56
garment trade. See clothing
Garson, Harry, 21
gender: consumer credit and, 181–183, 218–220, 231–233; consumption and, 181–182, 218–219, 258
General Education Board, 125
General Finance Corporation, 154
General Motors Acceptance Corporation, 192–193, 195, 198, 208, 240–242
General Motors Corporation, 191–192, 195, 199, 239–241, 250, 292
Germany, 146
The Gilded Age (Twain and Warner), 23, 214
Gimbel's, 132, 277
Gladden, Washington, 82
Glorious Revolution (1688), 27
Goldman, Julian, 204, 205, 222, 250, 254–257
Goldman's Department Stores, 205, 222, 255–256
Goldsmith, Raymond, 18, 73

Great Atlantic and Pacific Tea Company, 118

Great Depression, 18, 25, 32, 147, 262, 265; consumer debt in, 265–271, 273; consumer credit tested by, 262–271; installment credit in, 265–267, 269, 273; installment plan blamed for, 263–265, 271–274, 359n34; personal finance companies in, 268–271

The Green-Back Peril (Ham), 128

Greenwood, A. E., and Company, 51

grocers, 201, 226

Grover and Baker Sewing Machine Company, 162

Guarantee Securities Company, 187–190, 192

Guinness Book of World Records, 3

Hall, Baynard Rush, 76

Halsey, Forrest, 315n44

Ham, Arthur, 52, 125–135, 143

Hare and Chase, 192

Harper's Bazaar, 219

Harper's Monthly, 182

Harper's Weekly, 103

Harris, Cora, 182

Harvard Business Review, 253

Harvard Episodes (Flandrau), 167

Harvard University, 253, 273

Harvey, William, 81

Hebrew Free Loan Society, 120

hedonism, 16; consumer credit's restraints on, 28–31, 294–303; consumer culture and, 9, 33

Heermance, Edgar L., 289

Heinze, Andrew, 178

Henderson, Leon, 287

Henry VIII, 114

Heuzinga, Johann, 14

Hilborn, Walter S., 132

Hill, James J., 89

hire purchase, 158, 164, 165–166

Hodson, Clarence, 133, 137, 138, 139, 145

Holmes, George, 100

home economists, 212–213, 230

home mortgages, 38, 59, 64–69, 101, 161, 172, 213, 280–283, 285

Home Owners' Loan Corporation, 280–281

Home Owners' Refinancing Act (1933), 280

Hoover, Herbert, 230, 271, 278–279, 280

household finance, 14, 41–42, 48, 212–213, 267

Household Finance Company, 118, 135, 137, 148, 153, 268, 270

Houston Chronicle, 227–229

Houston Trunk Factory, 201

Howe, Elias, 162

Howells, William Dean, 63, 81, 94, 171

Hubachek and Hubachek, 139

Hume, David, 253

Hunt, Freeman, 62–63, 93

Hunt's Merchant's Magazine, 62

illegal lenders: advertising of, 129, 132; campaigns against, 118–119, 125–135; licensed lenders and, 133–134, 138–140; opposition to small-loan laws from, 131–133; regulatory reform and, 139–140, 153; usury laws and, 114–119, 122. See *also* loan sharks; small-loan lending

Illinois Association of Industrial Lenders, 143

immigrants, 63, 68, 86, 166, 167, 171–173, 177–179, 218

Indiana Association of Industrial Lenders, 142

The Industrial Acceptance Corporation, 192

industrial banks, 19, 263, 283

industrialization, 167–168

industrial lenders. See small-loan lending; personal finance companies

Industrial Lenders News, 137, 138, 145, 151, 249, 259, 286

Ingraham, Lloyd, 21

installment buying, 111; farmers and, 159–161; immigrants and, 178;

middle class and, 56, 157, 169, 180–181, 202–206, 291; motivations for, 57–58, 165, 171, 298–299; social conditions behind, 167–168; spread of, 60, 157, 166; stigma of, 171, 180, 183; women and, 181–183; workers and, 169–173, 175

installment credit, 17, 55, 105, 144, 149, 151–152, ch. 4; advertising of, 162, 172, 173, 189, 200, 201, 203, 220, 222, 254–257, 275; attitudes toward, 180–181, 206, 234–235, 260; before 1920, 157–183; building and loan associations and, 161; collections of, 161, 176; commercial banks and, 285–286; commodification of time and, 208; contracts for, 60, 267; critics and criticisms of, 200–201, 211–235, 271–273; defenders and defenses of, 235–261, 263, 273–274; definition of, 156–157, 180; delinquency and defaults, 60, 176, 200; department stores and, 72; disciplines required by, 28–29, 30–31, 54–55, 156–157, 206–208, 294–303; economic significance of, 349n139; expansion of, 166–201, 234, 275–280; Great Depression's effect on, 265–268; law regarding, 165–166, 267, 276; legacies of, 206–208, 302; legitimization of, 183–184, 206, ch. 5; reasons for growth of, 167–168, 184; small-loan lending and, 151–152; socioeconomic status of users of, 158, 166, 169, 176, 202–206; stigmatization of, 166–183, 206; terms of, 161, 164, 165, 169, 176, 177, 185, 191, 192, 194; volume of, 201, 244, 266

installment peddlers, 55–56, 176–178

installment plan: adoption by retailers of, 200–201; automobiles and, 185; credit revolution and, 156; introduction of, 60, 159, 161, 164, 167; legacies of, 206–208, 294–303; "pay as you use" and, 199; small-loan lending and, 151. *See also* installment buying; installment credit; installment selling

installment selling: and appliance stores, 200; of automobiles, 184–199, 201, 203, 204, 241, 274–275; department stores and, 200, 226, 276–277; "fake" installment business and, 176, 179–180; of farm implements, 157, 159–161, 166, 200, 203, 222; of furniture, 60, 157–158, 161–162, 166, 169, 176, 180, 201, 203, 204, 241, 276; of garments, 169–171, 177, 200, 203, 222, 226, 241, 276; hardware stores and, 200, 226, 241; "high-grade" trade of, 59–60, 169, 176; of jewelry, 200, 201, 203, 241, 276; of land, 158; losses in, 161, 200, 266–267; "low-grade" trade of, 176–179; mail-order retailing and, 173, 175, 275; motivations for, 57, 170; peddling and, 55–56, 177–179; of pianos, 60, 162, 164, 165, 176, 180, 200, 203, 222, 241; public utility companies and, 275; of radios, 201, 203, 204; of sewing machines, 60, 162–165, 166, 176, 180, 203, 222; of stocks, 158

interest rates: of commercial banks, 146, 286; determining "fairness" of, 130–134; of Gilded Age pawnbrokers, 48–49; of Gilded Age small-loan lenders, 50; of remedial loan societies, 130; of wage assignment loans, 133. *See also* Uniform Small Loan Law; usury laws

International Congress for Thrift, 223

International Shoe Company, 201

International Typographical Union, 224–225

Italians, 63, 80, 179

Italy, 146

Jackson, Andrew, 146

Jackson, Kenneth, 281

Jacobs, Dave and Betty, 295–297
Jarrell, Randall, 6, 8, 11
Jastrow, Marie, 178
Jefferson, Thomas, 26
jewelry, 179, 200, 201, 203, 241, 266, 276
Jews, 178
Johnson, George F., 226
Johnson, Samuel, 24
Jones, Jesse, 279–280
Journal of Home Economics, 230
The Jungle (Sinclair), 171–173

Kantzer, Kenneth, 197
Kasson, John, 319n1
Keeping Up with the Joneses, 214
Keeping Up with Lizzie (Bacheller), 214–217, 218
Keeping Up with Lizzie (Ingraham), 21
Kehr, George W., 137
B. Kuppenheimer and Company, 226

labor unions, 224–225
Ladies Home Journal, 66, 68, 101, 222
La Guardia, Fiorella, 124
Land Act of 1800, 158
Lasch, Christopher, 25, 30
Leach, William, 8, 72
Lears, Jackson, 29–30, 31
Lewis, C. S., 31
Life, 295
Lilienthal, David E., 279
Lindsley, Philip, 83
Lit Brothers (Philadelphia), 71
Literary Digest, 198
The Loan Gazette, 135, 137
loan sharks: campaign against, 125–135; chicanery of, 119–120, 139; clients of, 52, 55; credit reformers and, 111, 121; in Depression, 268; in 1920s, 263; opposition to usury law reforms, 122, 138–139; secrecy of, 14, 19, 41; stigma attached to, 20, 51, 140, 144. *See also* illegal lenders; small-loan lending

Loevy, Raymond, 13
Long, Clarence, 70
Lorimer, George Horace, 23, 231, 236
Lubin, Isador, 272–273
luxury, 150, 252–254, 301
Lynd, Helen and Robert, 11, 201, 266–267, 290, 294–295

McClure's, 216
McCormick, Cyrus, 160
Mackenzie, John, 82–83
Mackey, Frank J., 118, 148
Macy's, 71, 200, 226–227, 276–277
mail-order retailers, 71, 173, 175, 182, 199–200, 275
Mammon, 83, 94
A Manual of Ethics (Mackenzie), 82–83
Marden, Orison Swett, 87, 89, 92
margin trading, 263
Married Women's Property Acts, 86
Marx, Karl, 80, 81, 245
Massachusetts Bureau of Statistics of Labor, 64, 168–171
Mather, Cotton, 94–96, 98
May, Elaine Tyler, 301
Mayer, I .H., 96
Means, Gardiner C., 287
Medill, Joseph, 84
men, credit buying and, 231–233
Mencken, H. L., 230, 283
The Merchants and Manufacturers Securities Corporation, 192
Merchants National Bank (St. Paul), 230
Merseles, Theodore F., 226
Michelman, Irving, 10
middle class, 94, 254; attitudes toward installment credit, 180–181; cash buying and identity of, 181, 206; as debtor class, 11, 20, 64, 72, 202–206, 294; debts of, 58–68, 202–206; household finances of, 58–60; small-loan business and, 150, 286

Middletown (Lynd and Lynd), 11, 201, 266, 290, 294–295
Mill, John Stuart, 81, 98
Mills, A. L., 223
The Minister's Charge (Howells), 171
Miss Saigon, 5
Missouri, 139–140
Mitchell, Charles E., 284
Mitchell, Wesley, 239
monetarization, 74–80, 84, 95, 107–108, 218
money: advice literature about, 84–86; Americans' passion for, 75, 79–80; baffling nature of, 77–79, 324n39; diffusion of, 74–80, 95, 107–108; importance of management of, 77, 80, 84; in late-nineteenth century literature, 81, 323n27; and the "money question," 80–81; moralization of, 82–84, 87, 94; popular thinking about, 80, 82; private nature of, 14; qualitative changes in, 77–78, 107–108; quantitative changes in, 77; symbolic uses of, 79–80; variety of forms of, 78–79
Money and How to Make It (Reade), 63
money management ethic. *See* Victorian money management ethic
Montgomery Ward, 71, 173, 200, 226, 275, 296
monts-de-piete, 49, 114, 121, 146
More, Louise, 43, 48
Morgan, J. Pierpont, 238, 258
Morris Plan banks, 263, 361n70
mortgage lending. *See* home mortgages
Mulholland, John, 118
Mussey, Henry, 175–180
mutual benefit societies, 63
myth of lost economic virtue, 22–31, 33, 220–221

Napier, Charles, 117, 140
National Association of Finance Companies, 194, 265, 273

national banks, 68, 78
National Bond and Investment Company, 192
National Bureau of Economic Research, 204, 269
National City Bank (NY), 284, 286
National Conference of Charities and Correction, 125, 129
National Federation of Remedial Loan Associations (NRFLA), 121, 127, 129, 130, 132, 133, 134, 149, 150–151
National Forensic League, 111
National Grocers Association, 226
National Hardware Association, 226
National Recovery Administration, 280, 287
National Retail Credit Association, 289
National Thrift Week, 224, 235
Neifeld, M. R., 24, 147, 152, 260–261, 268, 270, 279
New Deal, 273, 274, 279–283, 289–290
New Republic, 272
New York City, 41, 66, 68, 158, 164, 218, 267; credit reformers in, 120–121, 128, 132; installment trade in, 72, 175–180, 226; pawnbroking in, 43, 44, 46; small-loan lending in, 49, 52, 117
New York Evening Post, 78, 158
New York Legal Aid Society, 128, 175
New York Post, 124
New York School of Philanthropy, 126
New York Times, 24, 249, 264
New Yorker Volks-Zeitung, 41
1920s, and nostalgia for golden age of thrift, 23–26
non-importation resolutions, 26
Norris, George W., 224
North American Review, 79
Noyes, C. Reinold, 230
Nugent, Rolf, 117, 123, 284, 287, 290

Ohio Finance Company, 146
Olds, Ransom, 185
Olney, Martha, 10, 12, 18–19, 201, 222, 344–345n90
Optic, Oliver, 62, 65
organs, 182
Our Beacon Light (Cowen), 89
Our Business Boys, 95
The Outcast Manufacturers (Fort), 167
Outlook, 72

Pacific Finance Company, 192
Panic of 1837, 104
Panic of 1857, 3
Park, Robert, 63
Patten, Simon, 242, 246, 253
Paul, St., 92, 96
pawnbroking, 14, 19, 20, 38, 40, 120–121, 292; in the Gilded Age, 42–49; in the 1920s, 153–154, 156, 263; in the 1930s, 268
Pawner's Bank of Boston, 49
Peavey, Leroy D., 264
peddling, 55–56, 177–179
Peirce, Charles Sanders, 80
Peixotto, Jessica, 203
Penney's, J. C., 71
The People's Outfitting Company (Chicago), 174
perishable goods, 226, 231
personal finance, private nature of, 14
The Personal Finance Business (Neifeld), 260
personal finance companies, 14, 224; growth of, 147–148, 263, 268–271; loan market of, 149–151, 286; public image of, 135–141; struggle for public esteem of, 141–147, 257. *See also* small-loan lending
Persons, W. Frank, 125
Philadelphia, 46, 67, 71, 76, 119, 120, 148, 161
Philadelphia Retail Ledger, 226, 227
physicians, 201
pianos, 101, 105, 164, 165, 166, 167,

176, 180, 186, 187, 200, 203, 222, 241
Pilgrims, 26, 157
Plummer, Wilbur R., 180–181, 202–203, 249, 354n58
Poe, Edgar Allen, 81
Political Science Quarterly, 239
Poor Richard, 32, 84, 87, 89, 96, 294, 301
Poor Richard's Almanac, 84, 94
Populism, 26, 81, 123
Porter, Robert, 15, 40, 73, 100
Post, Walter and Lillie, 58–59, 60–61
Pound, Ezra, 288
Price, J. A., 39
Princeton, 185
producerism, 8–9, 29, 32, 246–247, 250, 257
production, 244–249
productive debt/credit: deconstruction of concept of, 244–245; definition of, 98–101, 106–107, 237–238; small-loan lenders' appeal to, 142–145, 259–260; Victorians' approval of, 99–100, 106–107, 216, 232
Progressive Era, 141, 146
progressives, 111, 120–122, 123, 124–125, 130, 134, 155, 239
Prosperity and Consumer Credit (Goldman), 250
Prosser, Seward, 240
Protestantism, 8–9, 82, 92, 94–96
Provident Loan Society (Detroit), 134
Provident Loan Society (New York), 49, 120–121, 125, 127
public utility companies, 275, 279
Pujo Committee, 258

The Quality of Mercy (Howells), 81

radios, 201, 203, 204, 266
Ramsey, Anna, 269–270
Raskob, John J., 191, 208, 240
Rauschenbusch, Walter, 221
Reade, H. L., 63, 101, 102

reapers, 101

Reconstruction Finance Corporation, 279

remedial loan societies, 19, 120–122, 123, 125–127, 129–130, 135, 143, 150, 263

repossession, 176, 270, 276

republicanism, 8–9, 94, 95–96, 143, 327n80

retail credit, 38; before the Civil War, 76; in the Gilded Age, 19, 55–60; in the Great Depression, 266, 274–277; women and, 220. *See also* installment credit; installment plan; installment selling

retailers, and the credit revolution, 111

revolving credit, 281, 292, 296

Rhode Island Aquidneck Coal Mine, 158

Ricardo, David, 81, 98

Rieff, Philip, 29, 97

Riesman, David, 4, 11

The Rise of Silas Lapham (Howells), 81

Ritzer, George, 12

Robinson, Louis, 117, 123

Rockefeller Foundation, 125

Rockefeller, John D., 125

Rockefeller, Percy, 121

Rodgers, Daniel T., 141

Rogers, Will, 214

Roosevelt, Franklin Delano, 274, 279–283, 289

Rumely, Edward, 189–191, 207

Ruml, Beardsley, 277

Russell Sage Foundation, 124–128, 130–133, 135, 287

Ryan, Franklin W., 22, 151–153, 259–260

Ryan, William, 197

Sagan, Carl, 10

Sage, Margaret, 124–125

Sage, Russell, 124

St. Bartholomew's Loan Association, 130, 150

The Salary Loan Business in New York City (Wassam), 127

salary loan buying, 139–140

sales finance companies, 19, 187–190, 192–194, 224, 240, 266, 274–275, 283

San Francisco, 46

Sangster, Margaret, 219, 220

The Saturday Evening Post, 3, 23, 167, 189, 201, 231, 236

saving, 65, 89–90, 197, 244, 251–252, 290

savings banks, 65, 86, 223–224, 230, 251, 278

Scientific American, 162, 163, 181

scientific management, 28, 225

Sears, Roebuck and Company, 71, 173, 200, 275, 292, 296

Seligman, Edwin R. A., 238–260, 272, 291, 302

Seligman, Joseph, 238

sewing machines, 60, 101, 162–165, 168, 176, 180, 181–182, 186, 200, 203, 222, 258

Shakespeare, William, 10

Shays's Rebellion, 26

Shergold, Peter, 42, 44, 52, 315n40

Simmel, Georg, 80, 81

Sinclair, Upton, 171–173

Singer, I. M., 164

Singer & Company's Gazette, 164

Singer Sewing Machine Company, 162–165

Sloan, Alfred P., Jr., 185–186, 192, 250

Slosson, Preston William, 24

small-loan lending, ch. 3; advertising for, 117, 138, 142, 143, 145; "brokering" and, 137; chain offices and, 118, 148; chattel mortgages and, 51, 53, 55, 117; economics of, 115–116, 140; in the Gilded Age, 49–55, 117–122; growth in the 1920s of, 147–148, 151–152; growth in the 1930s of, 263, 268–271; image of, 135, 140–141; justifications for, 141–147, 257;

small-loan lending (*cont.*)
legal foundation for, 124–135;
lenders' intentions for, 111–112,
129–130, 142, 144–145, 152–153;
loan market of, 52, 149–151, 286;
professionalization of, 136–140;
state regulation of, 122, 131–134,
136, 139–140, 147; Uniform Small
Loan Law, 134–136; usury laws
and, 115; volume of, 147, 268;
wage assignments and, 53, 54, 55,
117. *See also* commercial banks; illegal lenders; loan sharks; remedial
loan societies
small loans, reasons for wanting,
151–152, 269
Smiles, Samuel, 93
Smith, Adam, 8, 80, 81, 98–99, 245
social class: Gilded Age credit system
and, 41–69; installment buyers
and, 169, 202–206; small-loan borrowers and, 149–151
social credit, 288–289
Social Darwinism, 141
speculation, 101, 105, 107
Speyer, James, 121
Spiegel House Furnishings Company,
171, 173–175
Spiegel, Modie, 173
Spurgeon, Charles, 92
Squire, Belle, 218, 220, 221, 350n1
The Star Loan Bank, 45
Steward, Ira, 59
Stewart's, A. T. (New York), 71
Stiers, John, 201
stoves, 182
Strasser, Susan, 72
Straus, Simon W., 223
Stricker, Frank, 203
Susman, Warren, 8–9

Tabor, C. W., 180
Tawney, R. H., 39
Taylor, Frederick W., 28, 225
Taylor, Henry, 88
Tennessee Valley Authority, 279
Ten Thousand a Year (Warren), 81

Terkel, Studs, 269
Terry, Eli, 158
Thayer, William Makepeace, 79
Thernstrom, Stephan, 68
thrift, 24, 25, 89–91, 94, 112, 130,
145, 153, 197, 207, 223–224, 232,
244, 246, 301
Thrift, 223
time payments. *See* installment credit;
installment plan
De Tocqueville, Alexis, 79
Todd, John, 96
Tolman, Daniel H., 50, 118, 132
Tucker, David, 25, 30, 224
Twain, Mark, 23, 24, 37, 38, 94, 214
Twentieth Century Fund, 287

Uniform Small Loan Law, 134–136,
137, 139, 140, 147, 221, 263
Universal Credit Corporation, 199,
275
The Use and Abuse of Money (Cunningham), 99
The Usurer's Grip, 128
usury, 128, 132, 141
usury laws: in the U.S., 112, 114–116,
122–123, 130, 286; in Europe,
113–114, 122

Vanderbilt, Cornelius, 121
Victorian culture, 82, 216, 246,
319n1
Victorian money management ethic,
74, 77, 123, 156, 197; budgeting
and, 90–91; cash ideal in, 69–70;
"character" in, 87–88; cultural as-
cendancy of, 84–87; debt and, 31–
32, 91–104; decline of, 107–108,
250, 251, 290; economy and, 89,
91; literature of, 84; moralization
of money in, 82–84; small-loan
lenders' appeal to, 141, 142, 145,
self-discipline in, 207; thrift and,
89–91
Voice to Youth (Austin), 87
Voltaire, 253
vos Savant, Marilyn, 3, 4

wage assignment lenders, 117, 133
wage assignment loans, 53, 54, 55, 126, 127, 132, 139–140
Walras, 80
Wanamaker, John, 13
Wanamaker's (Philadelphia), 72, 275
Ward, Artemus, 37, 38, 97, 214
Warner, Charles Dudley, 23
Warner, Sam Bass, 65
Warren, Samuel, 81
War Savings Division, 224
de Warville, Brissot, 76
Washburne, Marion Foster, 213
Washington, George, 26
Wassam, Clarence, 52, 126
Waters, Walter, 268
The Way to Wealth (Franklin), 84, 87, 324n40
Weaver, L. F., 187
Weber, Max, 29
Webster, Noah, 158
Weed, Clive, 208
Weston, George, 77
Wheeler and Wilson Manufacturing Company, 162, 164
Whipple, John, 93
Whitman, Walt, 64
Wholesale and Retail Credit Men's Association, 262
Whyte, William H., 25, 297–299
Wiebe, Robert, 76
Wiggam, Albert E., 146
Wild, Charles W., 146–147
Williams, William Carlos, 288

Willys-Overland Company, 189, 191
Wilson, Franklin, 89
Wilson, Woodrow, 185
Wise, Daniel, 87, 93
women: as consumers, 181–182, 212, 218; credit and, 166, 181–183, 218; as loan office agents, 53; money and, 86, 218; myth of the female credit abuser, 181–183, 217–220; pawnbroking and, 46–48, sewing machines and, 163–164
Wood, Edith Elmer, 213
Wood, W. G., 139
working class: debts of, 42–58, 63, 118; household finances of, 41–42, 116–117, 172; installment buying among, 169, 172, 202–204; lenders to, 42–58, 63, 117–118; wages of, 70, 168
Workingmen's Loan Association, 120
Workingmen's Movement, 26
World's Work, 21, 249
World War I, 224
World War II, 18, 290, 291

Yale Law School, 287
The Young Man (Todd), 96
The Young Man's Counsellor (Wise), 87
Young Men's Christian Association, 223

Zindler, Benjamin, 227
Zindler's Clothing Store, 227–230, 232, 256